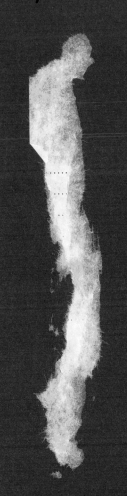

The Encyclopaedia of
BADMINTON

The Encyclopaedia of
BADMINTON

by
PAT DAVIS

796.34'5 0321

ROBERT HALE · LONDON

Robert Hale Limited
Clerkenwell House
Clerkenwell Green
London EC1R 0HT

British Library Cataloguing in Publication Data

Davis, Pat
   The encyclopaedia of badminton.
   1. Badminton (Game)—Dictionaries
   I. Title
   796.34'5'0321   GV1007

   ISBN 0-7090-2796-6

Photoset in North Wales by
Derek Doyle & Associates, Mold, Clwyd
Printed in Great Britain by
St Edmundsbury Press, Bury St Edmunds, Suffolk
Bound by Hunter and Foulis Ltd.

Contents

Foreword

I am delighted to have been asked to write a Foreword to Pat Davis's eighth book on badminton. I started playing badminton when I was only 8 years old, but even after innumerable tournaments and many titles won all over the world I can still find much useful information and amusing anecdote in Pat Davis's invaluable new book. It is unique in that it covers every conceivable aspect of the game – from 'Air Shot' to 'Zip Area' – with scores of potted biographies of all the great players and administrators, succinct but comprehensive descriptions of tactics and techniques, and expert coverage of the game abroad from America to Thailand. I am particularly grateful for the thorough lists of records and results from major events worldwide over many years.

'Encyclopaedia' may sound a bit stuffy but Pat Davis has a lively pen, a sense of humour and infectious enthusiasm. And who better to write one than a former BA of E National Coach, a Welsh international and a record-breaking All-England Veterans' Men's Doubles Champion who edited the *Badminton Gazette* for ten years and who still coaches and watches the game as eagerly as ever.

I found this book both entertaining and a mine of information; whether you are a Club Secretary, an experienced player or a novice I am sure you will too.

Morten Frost, 1986

List of Illustrations

Picture Credits

The following photographs have been reproduced by kind permission of: Mervyn Rees: 9, 14, 30, 34; Peter Richardson: 4, 5, 13, 17, 19, 28, 42; Louis Ross: 6, 12, 15, 16, 29, 38, 39, 40, 41, 46. A few illustrations of unknown source are believed to be free of copyright, but the author, c/o the publishers, would be pleased to hear from any unacknowledged photographer.

Introduction

Badminton has always received a mere tithe of the Press coverage of lawn tennis. Even today the 'popular' dailies can spare only half-a-dozen lines for the game's biggest events. And until comparatively recently in its history the *Badminton Gazette* was the only source of results. Worldwide coverage was virtually unknown until *World Badminton* was first published in 1972.

Even then, Asian badminton countries often failed to report major events or to include full scores. Unhappily such reticence continues today. Despite repeated letters (since this book's late 1984 genesis) to governing bodies and leading players, and the efforts of the IBF itself, it has been impossible to obtain championship records from such great badminton countries as China, Indonesia, Japan, and Malaysia.

Whilst every care has been taken to check and re-check facts, omissions or inaccuracies may have crept in among the vast list of dates, scores, venues, events, initials and names – particularly the latter, for Asian players have a confusing habit of changing their names in mid-career, whilst the spelling thereof often varies from programme to programme. Even Europe's Svend Pri started life as Andersen! And marriage, of course, may change a famous name to an unknown one overnight. The author will, therefore, be grateful for any suggested amendments for future editions. (60 St Martin's Hill, Canterbury, Kent.)

The text was written between December 1984 and 1985 and major events added up to June 1986.

Grateful thanks are tendered to both the BAE and IBF for their permission to quote from *Badminton Gazette* and *Badminton Now* and *World Badminton* as well as their respective handbooks.

So many people have helped me in the compilation of this book that it would be invidious to single out individuals. Except one – my wife. She has uncomplainingly striven to decipher scrawled script, to distinguish 'a' from 'o', undotted 'i' from loopless 'e'; unravelled ambiguities; cut through bewildering verbiage; mastered the baffling intricacies of foreign names; typed, retyped and typed again some 80,000 words with unfailing accuracy – and extraordinary good humour. Thank you, Pat!

Abbreviations

In order to save space and avoid annoying repetition, the following well-known abbreviations have been used:

ABC	Asian Badminton Confederation
AEC	All-England Championships
AQ	Alba Quartz World Cup
BAE	Badminton Association of England
BC(BK)	Badminton Club
CG	Commonwealth Games
EBU	European Badminton Union
ESBA	English Schools Badminton Association
IBF	International Badminton Federation
ICC	Inter County Championship
LD(GD)	Ladies' (Girls') Doubles
LS(GS)	Ladies' (Girls') Singles
MD(BD)	Men's (Boys') Doubles
MS(BS)	Men's (Boys') Singles
Mxd D	Mixed Doubles
q.v.	refer to
quarters	quarter-finals
semis	semi-finals
TC	Thomas Cup
U.15 etc	Under 15 etc
UC	Uber Cup
WC	World Championships

Note: Players' ages, recorded where dates of birth are unavailable, are as at March 1986.

A

ACE
Term for a point: a word now little used though it may still be seen on some score sheets.

AFFILIATION FEE
Fee paid by an individual, or by a club on behalf of its members, to a governing body of the game. Every sport needs such a body to promote the game generally and to unify laws and regulations.

In England this fee is generally paid by a club to its county association. The latter deduct their own agreed affiliation fee and then pass on the remainder to the BAE. At present (1986) the latter's fee is £1.20 for each playing member, with a minimum of £19.20 for each club. The county fee varies from county to county but is in the region of 30-50p per player.

There are now over 5,000 affiliated clubs in England alone. It is estimated there are, in addition to casual players in sports centres, double that number of clubs who have not affiliated because, playing at a low standard, they mistakenly feel that the facilities offered are of little interest to them.

These include (1) provision of county and international matches at both senior and junior level; (2) organization of tournaments; (3) provision of coaching, handbooks and the Association's monthly publication *Badminton Now* (q.v.); (4) reduced AEC prices. Recently the BAE have added personal accident and public liability insurance, badges and clothing at cheap rates.

AFRICAN BADMINTON FEDERATION
ABF was formed in 1977 at the suggestion of the Nigerian BA. Its founder members were Ghana, Mauritius, Mozambique, Kenya, Nigeria and Tanzania. ABF team and individual championships are hosted in turn by each member state biennially.

AIR-SHOT
A stroke in which the air – not the shuttle – is hit. It is usually caused by the player taking his eye off the shuttle just before impact or by very poor hand-eye co-ordination.

ALBA QUARTZ WORLD CUP
Brainchild of Craig Reedie and IBF; sponsored by Alba Quartz (US$118,000 US prize money). Organized by BA of Malaysia with the backing of IMG, this Far Eastern prestige event was first played (singles only) in Kuala Lumpur, 1981. Doubles were added in 1983.

Venue
1981	Kuala Lumpur
1982	Kuala Lumpur
1983	Kuala Lumpur
1984	Jakarta
1985	Jakarta

Men's Singles
1981	Prakash Padukone
1982	Liem Swie King
1983	Han Jian
1984	Han Jian
1985	I. Sugiarto

Ladies' Singles
1981	Chen Ruizhen
1982	Lene Køppen
1983	Han Aiping
1984	Li Lingwei
1985	Li Lingwei

Men's Doubles
1981 —
1982 —
1983 Joo Bong Park/Moon Soo Kim
1984 Liem Swie King/Kartono
1985 Liem Swie King/Kartono

Ladies' Doubles
1981 —
1982 —
1983 Han Aiping/Li Lingwei
1984 Wu Dixi/Lin Ying
1985 Lin Ying/Wu Dixi

Mixed Doubles
1981 —
1982 —
1983 M. Dew/G. Gilks
1984 T. Kihlström/N. Perry
1985 C. Hadinata/I. Lie

ALBERT HALL, London

Fittingly, this huge, domed concert hall was the venue for two of badminton's greatest events.

In September 1979 the first English Friends' Provident Masters (also in 1980 and 1981) and in 1982 the Thomas Cup finals were played here. The former was the first ever international open tournament; the latter, played in front of the Queen and Prince Philip, was the first time that prestigious event had been played in England for thirty-three years. It culminated in a remarkable last-ditch victory for recently IBF-accepted China.

In both cases, a single, green Hova court was laid in the centre of the encircling rows of red plush seats and tier upon tier of gilded boxes. Surely the world's most glamorous badminton venue!

ALEXANDER, Dr John, B.

When 'Tiny' Lucas (q.v.) was unable to act as Linesman Controller for the first 'Masters' event in 1979, the BAE recruited Salford University biology professor and Lancashire BA Committee man (1978) John Alexander to do the job — and also for the much more onerous seven-court AEC (1982). He, his court stewards and computer ensure the orderly deployment of 140+ linesmen to cover 235 matches spread over five days. He is also responsible for transmitting results to the Press Room. Three months' planning lies behind the slick organization.

ALL-ENGLAND CHAMPIONSHIPS

The first major national championships ever held. They were, until official World Championships were held in 1977, recognized as such and were regarded as the Wimbledon of badminton.

In 1898 the little Guildford BC staged the first-ever tournament. It was so successful that the Badminton Association followed suit in 1899 with a one-day event. This was played in the drill hall of the London Scottish Rifles at Buckingham Gate, London, on 4 April. Lines were marked in chalk; some voluminously dressed ladies wore large 'fruit'-laden hats, and one even turned up with an old-fashioned battledore.

In 1900, singles for men and women were added to the three doubles events. Women, then, played fifteen up, not today's eleven. Courts No. 1 and 4 were partially overhung by galleries, which resulted in numerous 'lets' (q.v.).

In 1902, so popular had the event become, it was moved to the wider spaces of the central transept of the Crystal Palace. There six courts were kept occupied for three days. It was further dignified by changing its title from 'The Badminton Association Tournament' to 'The All-England Badminton Championships', to be in line with other major sporting events – and to show it was open to players throughout England.

1903 saw yet another change. The London Rifle Brigade's HQ in Bunhill Row was preferred to the less central Crystal Palace, which had a 'drift' (q.v.) to equal that of today's Wembley Arena. Although conditions were cramped and both snow on the roof and fog inside were on occasion too much for the gas-burners, it remained the AEC venue until 1910.

In 1910 the Championships were held in the Horticultural Hall, Vincent Square, Westminster, centrally situated just behind the Army & Navy Stores. Although they were to remain there for nearly thirty years, there were teething problems, with a slippery floor and difficult overhead natural lighting, so often the bugbear of badminton's early days. Neither liberal application of resin nor the laying of a canvas drugget (which under pressure of fast-moving players often creased or broke from its fastenings) solved the problem. At length the gallery court was boarded over (and another court taken over for the erection of stands). So successful was this that the remaining courts were similarly treated. All Championship events were played by daylight.

In the early years, handicap as well as open events were played. So popular did they become that they were divided into A, B and C classes according to entrants' abilities. Even leading players often entered these events. This was partly because little top-class competitive play was available and partly because, with no seeding, 'life expectancy' in open events could be short. Seeding (q.v.) was successfully initiated in 1932 but the names of the seeds were delicately withheld in order not to give offence to the unseeded.

International matches were instituted prior to World War I and played on the Friday evening. Finals, on Saturday, were played on a court surrounded by low green screening before a crowd of 600-700 enthusiasts who wore their overcoats to counter the chill.

The Horticultural Hall days were the halcyon ones of British badminton. There, were seen the greats of the between-Wars era: Sir George Thomas, J.F. Devlin, G.S.B. Mack, D.C. Hume and R.C.F. Nichols; Margaret Tragett, Kitty McKane, Marjorie Barrett, the Kingsbury sisters and Betty Uber.

Great though they were, they did not know international competition until 1931, when Jack Purcell, the Canadian champion, was the first foreign entrant. The first large contingent did not arrive until 1938, when thirteen Danes tackled a rough North Sea and England's best − and R.C.F. Nichols staving off the challenge received a winner's voucher for 2 guineas. England just held off the invaders but in 1939 the writing was clearly on the wall: Tage Madsen (Denmark) and Dorothy Walton (Canada) won the singles and Tonny Olsen and Ruth Dalsgaard (Denmark) the ladies' doubles, the latter trio the first ever non-English players to win these titles.

With the fillip of a high-class international entry, the BAE boldly decided a bigger venue was needed for 1940 − no less than the 12,000-seater Harringay Arena, where seven courts could be laid. It was to be the death-knell of concurrent Handicap and Veterans events. The war,

however, put paid to such plans.

The Championships were revived in 1947 − at Harringay. Gale-swept snow blew through ventilators, and only six matches could be played on a skating-rink floor on the first day. Time was made up but England's best, denied play during the war years, lost all titles to Danish or Danish-born players, who had been able to play and were vastly improved.

1949, with entries from Malayan, American and Danish Thomas Cup teams as well as Swedes and Indians, saw the first fully international entry.

Harringay had been over-ambitious. From 1950-56 Empress Hall, Earl's Court, became badminton's Mecca. In 1957 building repairs forced a move to Wembley Arena (then Wembley Pool) on whose seven excellent courts the Championships have gone from strength to strength, and the international entry has risen from fewer than a dozen countries to over twenty. Today some 8,000 enthusiasts pack the arena to see the semi-finals. These are more popular even than the finals, for several reasons: there are more games; games in which English players are more likely to be competing; games often more fiercely and more lengthily contested.

Until 1980 semi-finals were played on Friday evening on three courts, and finals on Saturday. This was then altered to quarter-finals on Friday on three courts; semi-finals on Saturday on two courts, and finals on Sunday on a single court. This had the advantages of more gate-money; hopefully, extra TV coverage and fee; and semi-final enthusiasts being spared the difficult choice of which of three matches to follow. (In 1979 Drug Testing had been initiated in accordance with Olympic practice.)

In 1977, for the first time, the All-England received financial support, from John Player. This valuable assistance continued until 1984, when similar help was received from the big Japanese racket- and shuttle-manufacturing firm Yonex. In the same period the number of trade exhibitor stalls increased considerably.

In 1985 650 entries from twenty-nine nations were received for consideration.

Previous Winners

Men's Singles
1899 *No Competition*
1900 S.H. Smith
1901 Capt. H.W. Davies
1902 Ralph Watling
1903 Ralph Watling
1904 Dr H.N. Marrett
1905 Dr H.N. Marrett
1906 N. Wood
1907 N. Wood
1908 Dr H.N. Marrett
1909 F. Chesterton
1910 F. Chesterton
1911 G.A. Sautter
1912 F. Chesterton
1913 G.A. Sautter
1914 G.A. Sautter
1915 to 1919 *No Competition*
1920 Sir G.A. Thomas, Bart.
1921 Sir G.A. Thomas, Bart.
1922 Sir G.A. Thomas, Bart.*
1923 Sir G.A. Thomas, Bart.*
1924 G.S.B. Mack (Ireland)
1925 J.F. Devlin (Ireland)
1926 J.F. Devlin (Ireland)
1927 J.F. Devlin (Ireland)*
1928 J.F. Devlin (Ireland)
1929 J.F. Devlin (Ireland)
1930 D.C. Hume
1931 J.F. Devlin (Ireland)
1932 R.C.F. Nichols
1933 R.M. White
1934 R.C.F. Nichols
1935 R.M. White
1936 R.C.F. Nichols
1937 R.C.F. Nichols
1938 R.C.F. Nichols*
1939 Tage Madsen (Denmark)
1940 to 1946 *No Competition**
1947 Conny Jepsen (Sweden)
1948 Jorn Skaarup (Denmark)
1949 D.G. Freeman (USA)
1950 Wong Peng Soon (Malaya)
1951 Wong Peng Soon (Malaya)
1952 Wong Peng Soon (Malaya)*
1953 E.B. Choong (Malaya)
1954 E.B. Choong (Malaya)
1955 Wong Peng Soon (Malaya)
1956 E.B. Choong (Malaya)
1957 E.B. Choong (Malaya)*
1958 Erland Kops (Denmark)
1959 Tan Joe Hok (Indonesia)
1960 Erland Kops (Denmark)
1961 Erland Kops (Denmark)
1962 Erland Kops (Denmark)*
1963 Erland Kops (Denmark)
1964 K.A. Nielsen (Denmark)
1965 Erland Kops (Denmark)
1966 Tan Aik Huang (Malaysia)
1967 Erland Kops (Denmark)
1968 R. Hartono (Indonesia)
1969 R. Hartono (Indonesia)
1970 R. Hartono (Indonesia)*
1971 R. Hartono (Indonesia)

1972 R. Hartono (Indonesia)
1973 R. Hartono (Indonesia)*
1974 R. Hartono (Indonesia)
1975 S. Pri([37]) (Denmark)
1976 R. Hartono (Indonesia)
1977 F. Delfs (Denmark)
1978 Liem Swie King (Indonesia)
1979 Liem Swie King (Indonesia)
1980 P. Padukone (India)
1981 Liem Swie King (Indonesia)
1982 M. Frost (Denmark)
1983 Luan Jin (P.R. of China)
1984 M. Frost (Denmark)
1985 Zhao Jianhua (P.R. of China)
1986 M. Frost (Denmark)
* Trophy won outright.

Ladies' Singles
1899 *No Competition*
1900 Miss E. Thomson([1])
1901 Miss E. Thomson([1])
1902 Miss M. Lucas([21])
1903 Miss E. Thomson([1])
1904 Miss E. Thomson([1])*
1905 Miss M. Lucas([21])
1906 Miss E. Thomson([1])
1907 Miss M. Lucas([21])
1908 Miss M. Lucas([21])
1909 Miss M. Lucas([21])*
1910 Miss M. Lucas([21])
1911 Miss M. Larminie([2])
1912 Mrs R.C. Tragett
1913 Miss L.C. Radeglia
1914 Miss L.C. Radeglia
1915 to 1919 *No Competition*
1920 Miss K. McKane([3])
1921 Miss K. McKane([3])
1922 Miss K. McKane([3])*
1923 Miss L.C. Radeglia
1924 Miss K. McKane([3])
1925 Mrs A.D. Stocks
1926 Mrs F.G. Barrett
1927 Mrs F.G. Barrett
1928 Mrs R.C. Tragett
1929 Mrs F.G. Barrett
1930 Mrs F.G. Barrett*
1931 Mrs F.G. Barrett
1932 Miss L.M. Kingsbury([4])
1933 Miss A. Woodroffe([5])
1934 Miss L.M. Kingsbury([4])
1935 Mrs H.S. Uber
1936 Miss T. Kingsbury([16])
1937 Miss T. Kingsbury([16])
1938 Miss D.M.C. Young([17])
1939 Mrs W.R. Walton, Jr. (Canada)
1940 to 1946 *No Competition*
1947 Miss Marie Ussing([25]) (Denmark)
1948 Miss Kirsten Thorndahl([24]) (Denmark)
1949 Miss A. Schiott Jacobsen (Denmark)
1950 Mrs Tonny Ahm (Denmark)
1951 Miss A. Schiott Jacobsen (Denmark)
1952 Mrs. Tonny Ahm (Denmark)
1953 Miss Marie Ussing([25]) (Denmark)
1954 Miss J. Devlin([27]) (USA)
1955 Miss M. Varner([33]) (USA)
1956 Miss M. Varner([33]) (USA)

1957	Miss J. Devlin[27] (USA)
1958	Miss J. Devlin[27] (USA)
1959	Miss H.M. Ward[28] (USA)
1960	Miss J. Devlin[27] (USA)
1961	Mrs G.C.K. Hashman (USA)
1962	Mrs G.C.K. Hashman (USA)
1963	Mrs G.C.K. Hashman (USA)*
1964	Mrs G.C.K. Hashman (USA)
1965	Miss U.H. Smith[34]
1966	Mrs G.C.K. Hashman (USA)
1967	Mrs G.C.K. Hashman (USA)
1968	Mrs E. Twedberg[39] (Sweden)
1969	Miss H. Yuki (Japan)
1970	Miss E. Takenaka[43] (Japan)
1971	Mrs E. Twedberg[39] (Sweden)
1972	Mrs N. Nakayama (Japan)
1973	Miss M. Beck[42]
1974	Miss H. Yuki (Japan)
1975	Miss H. Yuki (Japan)
1976	Mrs M.A. Gilks
1977	Miss H. Yuki (Japan)*
1978	Mrs M.A. Gilks
1979	Miss L. Køppen (Denmark)
1980	Miss L. Køppen (Denmark)
1981	Miss Sun Ai Hwang (Korea)
1982	Miss Zhang Ailing (P.R. of China)
1983	Miss Zhang Ailing (P.R. of China)
1984	Miss Li Lingwei (P.R. of China)
1985	Miss Han Aiping (P.R. of China)
1986	Miss Yun Ja Kim (Korea)

Men's Doubles

1899	D. Oakes/S.M. Massey
1900	H.L. Mellersh/F.S. Collier
1901	H.L. Mellersh/F.S. Collier
1902	H.L. Mellersh/F.S. Collier*
1903	S.M. Massey/E.L. Huson
1904	A.D. Prebble/Dr H.N. Marrett
1905	C.T.J. Barnes/S.M. Massey
1906	Dr H.N. Mattett/G.A. Thomas
1907	A.D. Prebble/N. Wood
1908	Dr H.N. Marrett/G.A. Thomas
1909	F. Chesterton/A.D. Prebble
1910	P.D. Fitton/E. Hawthorn
1911	Dr H.N. Marrett/G.A. Thomas
1912	Dr H.N. Marrett/G.A. Thomas*
1913	F. Chesterton/G.A. Thomas
1914	F. Chesterton/G.A. Thomas
1915 to 1919	*No Competition*
1920	A.F. Engelbach/R. du Roveray
1921	Sir G.A. Thomas, Bt.,/F. Hodge
1922	J.F. Devlin (Ireland)/G.A. Sautter
1923	J.F. Devlin/G.S.B. Mack (Ireland)
1924	Sir G.A. Thomas, Bt.,/F. Hodge
1925	H.S. Uber/A.K. Jones
1926	J.F. Devlin/G.S.B. Mack (Ireland)
1927	J.F. Devlin/G.S.B. Mack (Ireland)
1928	Sir G.A. Thomas, Bt.,/F. Hodge
1929	J.F. Devlin/G.S.B. Mack (Ireland)
1930	J.F. Devlin/G.S.B. Mack (Ireland)
1931	J.F. Devlin/G.S.B. Mack (Ireland)
1932	D.C. Hume/R.M. White
1933	D.C. Hume/R.M. White
1934	D.C. Hume/R.M. White*
1935	D.C. Hume/R.M. White
1936	L. Nichols/R.C.F. Nichols
1937	L. Nichols/R.C.F. Nichols
1938	L. Nichols/R.C.F. Nichols*
1939	T.H. Boyle/J.L. Rankin (Ireland)
1940 to 1946	*No Competition*
1947	Tage Madsen/Poul Holm (Denmark)
1948	Preben Dabelsteen/Borge Frederiksen (Denmark)
1949	Ooi Teik Hock/Teoh Seng Khoon (Malaya)
1950	Preben Dabelsteen/Jorn Skaarup (Denmark)
1951	E.L. Choong/E.B. Choong (Malaya)
1952	E.L. Choong/E.B. Choong (Malaya)
1953	E.L. Choong/E.B. Choong (Malaya)*
1954	Ooi Teik Hock/Ong Poh Lim (Malaya)
1955	Finn Kobbero/J. Hammergaard Hansen (Denmark)
1956	Finn Kobbero/J. Hammergaard Hansen (Denmark)
1957	J.C. Alston (USA)/H.A. Heah (Malaya)
1958	E. Kops/P.E. Nielsen (Denmark)
1959	Lim Say Hup/Teh Kew San (Malaya)
1960	Finn Kobbero/P.E. Nielsen (Denmark)
1961	Finn Kobbero/J. Hammergaard Hansen (Denmark)
1962	Finn Kobbero/J. Hammergaard Hansen (Denmark)
1963	Finn Kobbero/J. Hammergaard Hansen (Denmark)
1964	Finn Kobbero/J. Hammergaard Hansen (Denmark)
1965	Ng Boon Bee/Tan Yee Khan (Malaysia)
1966	Ng Boon Bee/Tan Yee Khan (Malaysia)
1967	E. Kops/H. Borch (Denmark)
1968	E. Kops/H. Borch (Denmark)
1969	E. Kops/H. Borch (Denmark)*
1970	T. Bacher/P. Petersen (Denmark)
1971	Ng Boon Bee/P. Gunalan (Malaysia)
1972	Christian Hadinata/Ade Chandra (Indonesia)
1973	Christian Hadinata/Ade Chandra (Indonesia)
1974	Tjun Tjun/J. Wahjudi (Indonesia)
1975	Tjun Tjun/J. Wahjudi (Indonesia)
1976	B. Froman/T. Kihlström (Sweden)
1977	Tjun Tjun/J. Wahjudi (Indonesia)
1978	Tjun Tjun/J. Wahjudi (Indonesia)*
1979	Tjun Tjun/J. Wahjudi (Indonesia)
1980	Tjun Tjun/J. Wahjudi (Indonesia)
1981	R. Heryanto/H. Kartono (Indonesia)
1982	Razif Sidek/Jalani Sidek (Malaysia)
1983	T. Kihlström/S. Karlsson (Sweden)
1984	R. Heryanto/H. Kartono (Indonesia)
1985	Kim Moon Soo/Park Joo Bong (Korea)
1986	Kim Moon Soo/Park Joo Bong (Korea)

* Trophies won outright.

Ladies' Doubles
1899 Miss M. Lucas[21]/Miss Graeme
1900 Miss M. Lucas[21]/Miss Graeme
1901 Miss St. John/Miss E.M. Moseley[8]
1902 Miss M. Lucas[21]/Miss E. Thomson[1]
1903 Miss M.C. Hardy[7]/Miss D.K. Douglas[8]
1904 Miss M. Lucas[21]/Miss E. Thomson[1]
1905 Miss M. Lucas[21]/Miss E. Thomson[1]
1906 Miss M. Lucas[21]/Miss E. Thomson[1]*
1907 Miss M. Lucas[21]/Miss G.L. Murray
1908 Miss M. Lucas[21]/Miss G.L. Murray
1909 Miss M. Lucas[21]/Miss G.L. Murray*
1910 Miss M. Lucas[21]/Miss M.K. Bateman[14]
1911 Miss A. Gowenlock/Miss D. Cundall[9]
1912 Miss A. Gowenlock/Miss D. Cundall[9]
1913 Miss H. Hogarth/Miss M.K. Bateman[14]
1914 Mrs R.C. Tragett/Mrs E.G. Peterson
1915 to 1919 *No Competition*
1920 Miss L.C. Radeglia/Miss V. Elton
1921 Miss K. McKane[3]/Miss M. McKane[10]
1922 Mrs R.C. Tragett/Miss H. Hogarth
1923 Mrs R.C. Tragett/Miss H. Hogarth
1924 Mrs A.D. Stocks/Miss K. McKane[3]
1925 Mrs R.C. Tragett/Miss H. Hogarth
1926 Mrs A.M. Head/Miss V. Elton
1927 Mrs R.C. Tragett/Miss H. Hogarth
1928 Mrs F.G. Barrett/Miss V. Elton
1929 Mrs F.G. Barrett/Miss V. Elton
1930 Mrs F.G. Barrett/Miss V. Elton*
1931 Mrs H.S. Uber/Mrs R.J. Horsley
1932 Mrs F.G. Barrett/Miss L.M. Kingsbury[4]
1933 Miss T. Kingsbury[16]/Miss M. Bell[11]
1934 Miss T. Kingsbury[16]/Mrs M. Henderson
1935 Miss T. Kingsbury[16]/Mrs M. Henderson*
1936 Miss T. Kingsbury[16]/Mrs M. Henderson
1937 Mrs H.S. Uber/Miss D. Doveton
1938 Mrs H.S. Uber/Miss D. Doveton
1939 Mrs R. Dalsgard/Miss T. Olsen[19] (Denmark)
1940 to 1946 *No Competition*
1947 Miss K. Thorndahl[24]/Miss T. Olsen[19] (Denmark)
1948 Miss K. Thorndahl[24]/Mrs G. Ahm (Denmark)
1949 Mrs H.S. Uber/Miss Q.M. Allen[20]
1950 Miss K. Thorndahl[24]/Mrs G. Ahm (Denmark)
1951 Miss K. Thorndahl[24]/Mrs G. Ahm (Denmark)*
1952 Miss A. Jacobsen/Mrs G. Ahm (Denmark)
1953 Miss I.L. Cooley[23]/Miss J.R. White[22]
1954 Miss S. Devlin[26]/Miss J. Devlin[27] (USA)

1955 Miss I.L. Cooley[23]/Miss J.R. White[22]
1956 Miss S. Devlin[26]/Miss J. Devlin[27] (USA)
1957 Mrs A. Hammergaard Hansen/Mrs K. Granlund (Denmark)
1958 Miss M. Varner[33] (USA)/Miss H.M. Ward[28]
1959 Mrs W.C.E. Rogers/Mrs E.I. Timperley
1960 Miss S. Devlin[26]/Miss J. Devlin[27] (USA)
1961 Mrs F.W. Peard (Ireland)/Mrs G.C.K. Hashman (USA)*
1962 Mrs T. Holst-Christensen (Denmark)/Mrs G.C.K. Hashman (USA)
1963 Mrs F.W. Peard (Ireland)/Mrs G.C.K. Hashman (USA)
1964 Mrs K. Jorgensen/Miss U. Rasmussen [29] (Denmark)
1965 Mrs K. Jorgensen/Mrs U. Strand (Denmark)
1966 Mrs F.W. Peard (Ireland)/Mrs G.C.K. Hashman (USA)
1967 Miss I. Rietveld[30] (Netherlands)/Mrs U. Strand (Denmark)
1968 Miss Minarni[40]/Miss R. Koestijah (Indonesia)
1969 Miss M.B. Boxall[41]/Mrs P.E. Whetnall
1970 Miss M.B. Boxall[41]/Mrs P.E. Whetnall
1971 Miss N. Takagi[38]/Miss H. Yuki (Japan)
1972 Miss M. Aizawa/Miss E. Takenaka[41] (Japan)
1973 Miss M. Aizawa/Miss E. Takenaka[41] (Japan)
1974 Miss M. Beck[42]/Mrs M.A. Gilks
1975 Miss M. Aizawa/Miss E. Takenaka[41] (Japan)
1976 Mrs M.A. Gilks/Mrs P.E. Whetnall
1977 Miss E. Ueno/Mrs E. Toganoo (Japan)
1978 Miss A. Tokuda/Miss M. Takada (Japan)
1979 Miss Verawaty[45]/Miss I. Wigoeno (Indonesia)
1980 Mrs G.M. Gilks/Mrs J.P. Perry
1981 Mrs J.P. Perry/Miss J.A. Webster[46]
1982 Miss Lin Ying/Miss Wu Dixi (P.R. of China)
1983 Miss Xu Rong/Miss Wu Jianqiu (P.R. of China)
1984 Miss Lin Ying/Miss Wu Dixi (P.R. of China)
1985 Miss Li Lingwei/Miss Han Aiping (P.R. of China)
1986 Miss Myung Hee Chung/Miss Hye Young Hwang (Korea)
* Trophies won outright.

Mixed Doubles
1899 D. Oakes/Miss St. John
1900 D. Oakes/Miss St. John
1901 F.S. Collier/Miss E.M. Stawell-

Brown([32])
1902 L.U. Ransford/Miss E.M. Moseley([6])
1903 G.A. Thomas/Miss E. Thomson([1])
1904 Dr H.N. Marrett/Miss D.K.
Douglass([8])
1905 Dr H.N. Marrett/Miss H. Hogarth
1906 G.A. Thomas/Miss E. Thomson([1])
1907 G.A. Thomas/Miss G.L. Murray
1908 Norman Wood/Miss M. Lucas([21])
1909 A.D. Prebble/Miss D. Boothby([13])
1910 G.A. Sautter/Miss D. Cundall([9])
1911 G.A. Thomas/Miss M. Larminie([2])
1912 E. Hawthorn/Miss H. Hogarth
1913 G.A. Sautter/Miss M.E. Mayston([15])
1914 G.A. Thomas/Miss H. Hogarth
1915 to 1919 *No Competition*
1920 Sir G.A. Thomas, Bt.,/Miss H.
Hogarth
1921 Sir G.A. Thomas, Bt.,/Miss H.
Hogarth*
1922 Sir G.A. Thomas, Bt.,/Miss H.
Hogarth
1923 G.S.B. Mack (Ireland)/Mrs R.C.
Tragett
1924 J.F. Devlin (Ireland)/Miss K.
McKane([3])
1925 J.F. Devlin (Ireland)/Miss K.
McKane([3])
1926 J.F. Devlin (Ireland)/Miss E.G.
Peterson
1927 J.F. Devlin (Ireland)/Miss E.G.
Peterson
1928 A.E. Harbot/Mrs R.C. Tragett
1929 J.F. Devlin (Ireland)/Mrs R.J. Horsley
1930 H.S. Uber/Mrs H.S. Uber
1931 H.S. Uber/Mrs H.S. Uber
1932 H.S. Uber/Mrs H.S. Uber*
1933 D.C. Hume/Mrs H.S. Uber
1934 D.C. Hume/Mrs H.S. Uber
1935 D.C. Hume/Mrs H.S. Uber*
1936 D.C. Hume/Mrs H.S. Uber
1937 I. Maconachie (Ireland)/Miss T.
Kingsbury([16])
1938 R.M. White/Mrs H.S. Uber
1939 R.C.F. Nichols/Miss B.M. Staples([18])
1940 to 1946 *No Competition*
1947 P. Holm/Miss T. Olsen([19]) (Denmark)
1948 J. Skaarup/Miss K. Thorndahl([24])
(Denmark)
1949 Clinton Stephens/Mrs Stephens (USA)

1950 P. Holm/Mrs G. Ahm (Denmark)
1951 P. Holm/Mrs G. Ahm (Denmark)
1952 P. Holm/Mrs G. Ahm (Denmark)*
1953 E.L. Choong (Malaya)/Miss J.R.
White([22])
1954 J.R. Best/Miss I.L. Cooley([23])
1955 F. Kobberø/Miss K. Thorndahl([24])
(Denmark)
1956 A.D. Jordan/Mrs E.J. Timperley
1957 F. Kobberø/Mrs K. Granlund
(Denmark)
1958 A.D. Jordan/Mrs E.J. Timperley
1959 P.E. Nielsen/Mrs I.B. Hansen
(Denmark)
1960 F. Kobberø/Miss K. Thorndahl([24])
(Denmark)
1961 F. Kobberø/Miss K. Thorndahl([24])
(Denmark)*
1962 F. Kobberø/Miss U. Rasmussen([29])
(Denmark)
1963 F. Kobberø/Miss U. Rasmussen([29])
(Denmark)
1964 A.D. Jordan/Miss H.J. Pritchard([31])
1965 F. Kobberø/Mrs U. Strand (Denmark)
1966 F. Kobberø/Mrs U. Strand (Denmark)
1967 S. Andersen/Mrs U. Strand
(Denmark)
1968 A.D. Jordan/Miss S.D. Pound([32])
1969 R.J. Mills/Miss G.M. Perrin([36])
1970 P. Walsoe/Miss Molgaard Hansen([35])
1971 S. Pri([37])/Mrs U. Strand (Denmark)
1972 S. Pri([37])/Mrs U. Strand (Denmark)
1973 D. Talbot/Mrs M.A. Gilks
1974 J.D. Eddy/Mrs P.E. Whetnall
1975 E.C. Stuart/Miss N.C. Gardner([44])
1976 D. Talbot/Mrs M.A. Gilks
1977 D. Talbot/Mrs M.A. Gilks
1978 M.G. Tredgett/Mrs J.P. Perry
1979 Christian/Miss I. Wigoeno (Indonesia)
1980 M.G. Tredgett/Mrs J.P. Perry
1981 M.G. Tredgett/Mrs J.P. Perry
1982 M.C. Dew/Mrs G.M. Gilks
1983 T. Kihlström (Sweden)/Mrs G.M.
Gilks
1984 M.C. Dew/Mrs G.M. Gilks
1985 W.A. Gilliland (Scotland)/Mrs J.P.
Perry
1986 Park Joo Bong/Miss Myung Hee
Chung (Korea)
* Trophies won outright

([1]) Later Mrs D.R. Larcombe
([2]) Later Mrs R.C. Tragett
([3]) Later Mrs L.A. Godfree
([4]) Later Mrs H. Middlemost
([5]) Later Mrs R.J. Teague
([6]) Later Mrs Allen
([7]) Later Mrs Lionel Smith
([8]) Later Mrs Lambert Chambers
([9]) Later Mrs B.L. Bisgood
([10]) Later Mrs A.D. Stocks
([11]) Later Mrs M. Henderson
([12]) Later Mrs Hemsted
([13]) Later Mrs A.C. Geen
([14]) Later Mrs Flaxman
([15]) Later Mrs Walker
([16]) Later Mrs C.W. Welcome

([17]) Later Mrs J. Warrington
([18]) Later Mrs J.B. Shearlaw
([19]) Later Mrs G. Ahm
([20]) Later Mrs F.G. Webber
([21]) Later Mrs King Adams
([22]) Later Mrs E.J. Timperley
([23]) Later Mrs W.C.E. Rogers
([24]) Later Mrs P. Granlund
([25]) Later Mrs A. Nylen
([26]) Later Mrs F.W. Peard
([27]) Later Mrs G.C.K. Hashman
([28]) Later Mrs E.B. Nielsen
([29]) Later Mrs U. Strand
([30]) Later Mrs K.A. Nielsen
([31]) Later Mrs H.J. Horton
([32]) Later Mrs P.E. Whetnall

([33]) Later Mrs W.G. Bloss
([34]) Later Mrs L. Oakley
([35]) Later Mrs K. Kaagaard
([36]) Later Mrs M.A. Gilks
([37]) Formerly S. Andersen
([38]) Later Mrs N. Nakayama
([39]) Later Mrs E.C. Stuart
([40]) Later Mrs Soedaryanti
([41]) Later Mrs E.J. Allen
([42]) Later Mrs R.J. Lockwood
([43]) Later Mrs E. Toganoo
([44]) Later Mrs J.P. Perry
([45]) Later Mrs V. Fajrin
([46]) Later Mrs P. Sutton

ALL-ENGLAND CLUB

A club, formed in 1963, meeting only during the AEC, with its own suite of rooms at Wembley Arena. Its very select membership is limited to internationals, All-England title-winners, All-England Committee members and Councillors, and invited guests.

ALL-ENGLAND VETERANS' CHAMPIONSHIPS

Started in 1905 (1985 was the 70th Championship), this event has recently had a new lease of life.

Until 1959, when ladies' doubles were introduced (45+), it was a 'men only' preserve (50+). Mixed doubles followed in 1960.

Until the former year it was a handicap event with a quarter point given for each year over fifty. It was long played concurrently with the All-England proper. When the latter grew too big to accommodate it, it was played at Wimbledon with the qualifying rounds for the All-England, though some finalists were allowed to revive old memories by 'playing off' alongside the AEC proper.

In 1960, for the first time, it became a self-contained event 'without those interloping "qualifiers"'. It was played through at Epsom BC: a friendly club setting for a friendly event.

Among former international winners are E. Hawthorn, A. Titherley, H.J. Wingfield, J.D. McColl, W. Shute, C.T. Beacom, P.R. Davis (Wales), I. Hume (Scotland), E. Kops (Denmark), N.M. Natekar (India), E. Choong (Malaysia); Mrs K.M. Henderson, Miss D.B. Grace, Mrs W.C. Rogers, Mrs J.R. Timperley, Mrs Heather Nielsen, Miss B. Carpenter, Mrs H.J. Horton, Mrs G.C.K. Hashman, Mrs F.W. Peard (Ireland), Mrs T. Holst-Christensen (Denmark). Of those, the most capped pairings were McColl (31) and Shute (39), and Rogers (52) and Timperley (44).

The most wins undoubtedly go to Sylvia Ripley and Margaret Bayley, with eleven successive wins (1964-74). Among the men, P.R. Davis has won the title seven times, with Cyril Denton on six occasions.

Recently there has been a growing number of entries from distinguished foreign players: Kops, Choong, Natekar, the Holst-Cristensens and the foreign-born former Devlin sisters.

AMATEUR STATUS

In general terms, an amateur player may not earn his main source of income by playing badminton. He is, however, allowed to take employment as a PE/sports teacher giving elementary instruction. Also to accept (1) expense grants administered through the BAE while training for or playing in the Olympic Games or international sports competitions; (2) single-event prize money up to 1,000 Swiss francs (about £300); (3) compensation for loss of earnings; (4) fees for coaching from civic or education authorities; or from government or nationally recognized sports authorities, and private individuals (part-time) provided he is at least a BAE Advanced Coach. He may *not* normally be involved in advertising or wear extra advertising material in major competitions. Badminton's acceptance for Olympic Games status may necessitate some re-drafting of the above.

Individual countries may make their own amateur regulations stricter than those laid down by the IBF.

ANDREW, Prince

In August 1984, on the death of the Duke of Beaufort, the Prince became the BAE's new Patron, the game's highest office.

Although at Gordounstoun he had played a wide variety of games, his only contact with badminton had been when he saw England take 'gold' in the team event during the 1978 Edmonton Commonwealth Games. Nevertheless, it was felt that his 'youthful vigour and vitality' echoed the game's own image and would further youth recruitment to it.

The prince now plays badminton with one of his detectives, but cannot yet beat his father, Prince Philip (q.v.). In 1986 he presented the prizes at the AEC finals, and officially opened the BAE's National Badminton Centre (q.v.) at Milton Keynes.

ANGLE OF RETURN

Angle formed by possible returns to each sideline. The greatest angle is from the back corners of the court; the narrowest from the centre of the court. The greater the angle, the further the receiver may have to run. It is therefore good tactics to hit, if out of position or off balance, to the centre to narrow the angle. The receiver should take up his stance on the line bisecting the angle, unless anticipating the more common straight return.

ASIAN BADMINTON CONFEDERATION

ABC was formed on the initiative of the Malayan BA after a meeting called by Prime Minister Tunku Abdul Rahman Putra, Al Haj, in Kuala Lumpur in 1959. Its founder members, Burma, Ceylon, India, Indonesia, Malaya, Taiwan and Thailand, formulated its constitution and the rules and regulations for the first individual and team championships, which were held in 1962 in the newly built Stadium Negara in Kuala Lumpur.

The first Hon. Secretary was Teh Gin Sooi (Malaya); today the Hon. Secretary General is Dr Lee Kin Tat (Singapore) (q.v.) with Ms Lu Shengrong (PRC) as joint SG. The first President was naturally Tunku Abdul Rahman (q.v.) and today is Zhu Ze (PRC) (q.v.).

There are seventeen affiliated countries: Burma, Ceylon, India, Indonesia, Hong Kong, Japan, Khmer (now Kampuchea), Korea, Laos, Malaysia, Nepal, Pakistan, Philippines, PR of China, Singapore, Thailand, Vietnam.

Men's Singles
1962	Teh Kew San
1965	Dinesh Khana
1969	Muljadi
1971	Tan Aik Mong
1976	Hou Chia Chang
1983	Chen Changjie
1985	Zhao Jianhua

Ladies' Singles
1962	Minarni
1965	A.M. Bairstow
1969	Pan Yuet Mui
1971	Utami Dewi
1976	Liang Chiu Hsia
1983	Yoo Sang Hee
1985	Zheng Yuli

Men's Doubles
1962	Tan Yee Khan/Bill Ng
1965	N. Porchima/C. Chumkum
1969	Ng Boon Bee/P. Gunalan
1971	Nara Sudiana/Indra Gunawan
1976	Tjun Tjun/Ade Chandra
1983	Jian Guoliang/He Shang Quan
1985	Joo Bong Park/Moon Soo Kim

Ladies' Doubles
1962	Jap Happy/C. Kawilarang
1965	A.M. Bairstow/U.H. Smith
1969	Lee Young Soon/Kang Young Sing
1971	Retno Koestijah/Intan
1976	T. Widiastuti/R. Masli
1983	G. Weizhen/Fan-Ming
1985	Kim Jun Ya/Sang Hee Yoo

ASIAN GAMES

These quadrennial games, with 'Ever Onward' as their motto, were inaugurated in 1949 by Afghanistan, Burma, India, Pakistan and the Philippines. Planned in detail at the 1948 London Olympics, they were backed by Pandit Nehru.

The first meeting was held in 1951, but badminton was not included until 1962. In 1966 team events and a mixed doubles event was added. In 1962 and 1966, once a clear result had been obtained, the *winning* team conceded the unplayed games outstanding.

4th Games	1962
5th Games	1966
6th Games	1970
7th Games	1974
9th Games	1982

Men's Singles
1962	Tan Joe Hok
1966	Muhjadi
1970	P. Gunalan
1974	Hou Chia Chang
1982	Han Jian

Ladies' Singles
1962	Minarni
1966	N. Takagi
1970	H. Yuki
1974	Chen Yu Niang
1982	Zhang Ailing

Men's Doubles
1962	Tan Yee Khan/Ng Boon Bee
1966	Tan Yee Khan/Ng Boon Bee
1970	P. Gunalan/Ng Boon Bee
1974	Tjun Tjun/J. Wahjudi
1982	I. Sugiarto/C. Hadinata

Ladies' Doubles
1962	Minarni/R. Koestijah
1966	Minarni/R. Koestijah
1970	M. Aizawa/E. Takenaka
1974	Liang Chi-hsia/Cheng Hui Ming
1982	Sun Ai Hwang/Heung Seuk Kang

Mixed Doubles
1962	—
1966	Teh Kew San/R.S. Ang
1970	Ng Boon Bee/S. Ng
1974	C. Hadinata/R. Masli
1982	C. Hadinata/Ivana Lie

ASIAN YOUTH TRAINING CAMP

Proposed by the ABC and supported by the IBF, the camp was first held in 1984. The second camp, 1985, in Hong Kong, saw 106 players and officials participating from China, India, Sri Lanka, Japan, Philippines, Singapore, Thailand, Indonesia, Korea and Hong Kong.

Choi Il-hym (Korea), Willy K. Budhiman (Indonesia) and S.T. Lin (China) were in charge of a programme that included theory, physical fitness, sports psychology, sports injuries, pre-match preparation, game analysis, skills training and friendly competition.

AUSTRALIA BA

Badminton was first played at Freemantle in 1900, when a Mr Moore returned from a holiday in Britain with eight rackets. Badminton 'evangelist' the Reverend Mr Bryant took not only the Gospel but also the game to every parish he visited. Its popularity spread across the continent to Victoria, where R. Clendinnen and H. Wray, a fine tennis-player, helped form a National Association which today boasts some 13,000 players.

Even Australia's vast distances do not deter competition. The eight Associate States meet for a week-long carnival for national honours and the Clendinnen Shield (as do juniors for the Maddern Trophy). The Melbourne Silver Bowl attracts home and foreign players, and New Zealand is opposed on a biennial basis for the Whyte Trophy.

Names of the past are W.R. Hindson, player and administrator for forty years; H.R. Brady, Secretary of the ABA for twenty years. No great players have yet emerged but P. Kong, Miss M. Evans, M. Scandolera, brother and sister Darren and Julie Macdonald are fast improving, having been to an Indonesian training camp. Sze Yu (q.v.), a Hong Kong immigrant, reached world class by beating Morten Frost in the 1985 Pro-Kennex semis. M. Scandolera and A. Tuckey won the CG mixed doubles in 1986.

AUSTRALIAN CARNIVAL

A fortnight's solid badminton! The first week is devoted to inter-State matches for the Ede-Clendinnen Shield; the second to the Australian Championships (including junior events).

AVIA AWARD

A junior award sponsored by the Louis Newmark Group. Unique in that it is awarded for service to the game rather than playing ability, and for good *academic* results achieved whilst continuing such active participation. The two awards each consist of a miniature trophy, an Avia watch, and a £300 voucher for playing- or coaching-equipment.

Winners

1981-2
    Tracy Andrews   Russell Walters

1982-3
    Gillian Dalton   Neil Milner

1983-4
    Clare Gregory   Michael Lawrence

1984-5
    Caroline Williams Tim Vickers

AXFORD, Graham D.

Hardworking BAE administrator who currently holds the important post of Chairman of the Council (1984-). Hailing from Warwickshire, his first love was umpiring (BUAE committee member for many years). Has been a member of the Finance and Events Committee and the Committee of Management for the AEC, as well as of the West Midlands Sports Council.

B

BB & O

The initials of the three counties, Bucks, Berks and Oxon, who, when weak, played as one county. Today, stronger, each fields its own team.

BACHER, Tom (Denmark)
Born 16 November 1941

He has done it *all* – with infectious enthusiasm! In 1967 Bacher was Danish National Singles runner-up and 'capped' for Denmark in the first of his three TC series. In 1970 he won the AEC doubles with Poul Petersen.

As leading international umpire, he was 'in the chair' in 1967 when play had to be abandoned in the unhappy Malaysia v. Indonesia Thomas Cup *débâcle* (q.v.).

A skilled coach at the Greve BC, he moved on to administration for the DBF and later for the IBF as energetic Chairman of its Open Badminton Committee.

BACK AND FRONT

Basic formation adopted almost throughout in mixed doubles, and alternatively, in men's doubles.

In mixed, the stronger, faster man covers the court from base-line to short service line. The woman, to protect her from attack by the stronger opposing man, covers the court from short service line to the net where her attributes of neatness of movement and deft touch are more effectively employed.

Although the woman is thus responsible for less than half the area covered by the man, her role is just as difficult. Because of her proximity to the net, she is cramped and has roughly only half the time to intercept a shuttle often travelling nearly twice as fast. Until recently this formation was strictly maintained but now, with greater athleticism, the woman frequently drops back to 'sides' (q.v.) in defence or even takes over briefly at the back if the man is out of position.

This formation is also adopted in men's and ladies' doubles by the *attacking* pair. It is effective in that the opponents' weak returns near the net are much more likely to be intercepted above tape-height by a player *in situ* than if the rear-court striker had had to run in to deal with them. The front player's very presence at the net often forces the desired 'lift' to the 'back' player.

BACKHAND

The left side of the body for a right-hander; the right side for a left-hander. So called because the back of the hand, not the palm, is facing the net at impact. At lower levels of play this side is generally vulnerable to attack, partly because the backhand is not a natural throwing action but largely because club players do not practise backhand strokes (q.v.) sufficiently.

BACKHAND STROKES

Exactly the same range of strokes may be played backhanded as forehanded. The action employed is not, however, a natural throwing action, in which the body as well as arm can play its full part. At club level therefore, power is often lacking. At advanced level skilled players, even quite young girls, can clear the length of the court by employing a strong wrist, good technique and perfect timing.

Nevertheless, except in comparatively rare players such as Wolfgang Bochow (West Germany) and Flemming Delfs (Denmark), the backhand smash is inevitably weaker than the forehand one. On the other hand, the backhand low serve (see *Serves*) is simpler and possibly more effective than the forehand one.

The basic technique for all backhand strokes is, briefly, as follows. The forehand grip may be used but most players change, quickly and automatically, to a special backhand grip. For this, the grip is slightly relaxed and the racket is rolled some thirty degrees to the right so that the thumb lies flat roughly along the back bevel. In overhead strokes it lies more towards the narrower bevel; in defence, care should be taken to turn the wrist back, to angle the racket slightly upwards and 'open' the face.

In *preparation*, the right foot is pointed at the flightpath of the shuttle while the racket is fully drawn back (arm bent; wrist cocked) by bringing the right hand near the left shoulder. *Execution* is by a strong flinging (*not* pushing) action in which the arm is snapped straight, the wrist uncocked and the shoulder turned into the stroke. The *follow-through* is natural and in line with the target area, except in the clear (virtually nil) and the smash (limited) which are 'snap' or 'bounce' strokes.

In the lob, at top level, the backswing is minimal and the forward swing little more than a strong wrist flick, as less power needs to be used from the forecourt. If in the latter stroke the shuttle is met very close to the net, a sweeping follow-through is employed, as the shuttle must be hit upwards, steeply, to avoid being hit into the net, and high, to gain as much length as possible.

Agile and expert players prefer to play shuttles high on their backhand with a 'round-the-head' action (q.v.) rather than a backhand action. This give forehand power and generally leaves them better placed for quick recovery.

BADDELEY, Steve (England)
Born 28 March 1961, Hove

Six foot, red-haired, left-handed, Baddeley was wooed from swimming to badminton and soon played for his county, Sussex. He won the national U.18 men's doubles with D. Burden in 1978-9 and the senior National singles, 1981/2. Since then has won eighty-two caps, and the No.1 ranking position.

Despite prolific tournament entries, which put him third round the Pro-Kennex circuit, he has yet to win the 'Big One'. Nevertheless, he has beaten Sugiarto, Arbi and Misbun Sidek (the latter twice in key Thomas Cup games). During the 1984 Korea and China tours he was unbeaten in the former, and twice took Zhao Jianhua (later AEC winner) to three games.

In 1985 he reached the Hong Kong Open and Taipei Masters semis.

Deservedly seeded in the AEC singles, he attained the quarters despite an ankle injury. Baddeley showed himself also a world-class doubles player when, with Dew, he beat second seeds Hadinata and Hadibowo (15-4, 12-15, 15-9) and lost only narrowly in a $1\frac{1}{2}$ hour semi to Christiansen and Kjeldsen (18-15, 14-18, 13-18). He won the English National singles title again before running Sugiarto very close in the World Championships. His best haul: in the 1985 Indira Gandhi Indian Open when he won singles and men's doubles and was runner-up in the mixed – before falling to dysentery.

Baddeley holds a biology degree; and with journalistic aspirations, he reports regularly for *World Badminton* and has blossomed into TV commentator abroad. He played a major part in launching the Badminton Players Federation.

BADMINTON ASSOCIATION

The forerunner of today's Badminton Association of England. It was formed on 12 September 1893, when fourteen clubs, realizing the need for uniformity (courts at that time might differ by ten feet (three metres) in length), banded together in this the first-ever association. Its formation was largely the work of Colonel S.S.C. Dolby, who was elected not only President (1892-8) for his efforts but also Hon. Treasurer and Hon. Secretary (1893-9).

Numbers grew slowly. Ireland and Scotland formed their own unions but affiliated to the BA, as did also a handful of overseas clubs. By 1903-4, Middlesex led the way with twenty-one affiliated clubs, followed by Surrey with nineteen, whilst Dublin could boast thirteen. In 1914 there were 467 clubs; in 1923 550, and by 1934 the thousand mark was well in sight. In that year the BA handed over its administration of badminton world-wide to the IBF (q.v.). The Badminton Association, as one of the nine founding member countries, then changed its title to the Badminton Association of England.

Presidents
1893-8   Col. S.S.C. Dolby
1898-1907 P. Buckley
1907-13   C. Agnew Turner
1913-19   W. Baddeley
1919-27   Vacant
1927-34   Col. A. Hill

Honorary Treasurers
1893-9   Col. S.S.C. Dolby
1899-1906 G.W. Vidal
1906-10   C. Dudfield Willis
1910-27   Col. A. Hill
1927-34   F.W. Hickson

Honorary Secretaries
1893-9   Col. S.S.C. Dolby
1899-1906 G.W. Vidal
1906-10   C. Dudfield Willis
1910-27   Col. A. Hill

Secretary
1927-34   F.W. Hickson

BADMINTON ASSOCIATION OF ENGLAND

The governing body of the game in England: founded in 1934 when the Badminton Association (q.v.) handed over world-wide control to the International Badminton Federation (q.v.). Its offices, for many years in Bromley, Kent, were made more central in 1980 at Bradwell Road, Loughton Lodge, Milton Keynes, MK8 9LA (0908 568822).

The Association has an elected Patron (q.v.) and, currently, eight elected Hon. Vice-Presidents who have no votes.

Its Council consists of a President, up to five Vice-Presidents, an Hon. Treasurer (elected annually), two nominees of the English Schools BA and one of the Badminton Umpires' Association

of England and, currently fifty-six nominees of the forty-one County Associations on the basis of one for each for each 150 clubs or 3,000 playing members. In addition there are eleven co-opted members, generally experienced administrators and/or leading players, past or present. A quorum is twenty; it must represent at least ten different County Associations.

In addition there are eight full-time, salaried, professional administrators who have no vote: Chief Executive (Air Vice-Marshal G.C. Lamb (q.v.)); Administrative Secretary (J.E. Gowers); England Team and Coaching Manager (Jake Downey); Accountant (J.D. Betley); Coaching Administrator (B. Wadsworth); Promotions Manager (T.E. Marrs); Staff Coach (L.D. Wright); Press and Publicity Officer (C. Searle).

Its work of unifying and promoting the game, the organization of major events at international level, and co-operation with the counties is carried out by six standing committees: Emergency; Executive; Finance; Events; Coaching and Technical; Development and Planning.

Over 5,300 clubs representing some 100,000 players and non-playing enthusiasts are affiliated to the BAE. This is only the tip of the playing iceberg as, unfortunately, many more individuals and clubs feel no obligation to support their national body. As a result only about one-third of the BAE's annual revenue is obtained from this source; the remainder comes from Sports Council grants and sponsorship, gate receipts and TV fees.

BADMINTON GAZETTE

'The official organ of the BAE.' First published in November 1907, it then consisted of only twelve pages (increased that year to twenty) and cost 2d. per issue. In its pages, shuttles were advertised at 5s. 6d. per dozen, and rackets (Indian-made) at 5s. 9d. It was largely the brainchild of C. Dudfield Willis and A.D. Prebble who were no longer prepared to support the indignity of badminton's being very much the junior partner in *Lawn Tennis and Croquet*.

In its early days, its amateur editors were also distinguished players. S.M. Massey was followed by G.A. Thomas,

Miss L.C. Radeglia, Mrs R.C. Tragett and J.F. Devlin (q.v.): all internationals.

Unquestionably the greatest editor was Herbert Scheele (q.v.), Secretary of the BAE, who with his wife Betty (writing under the pseudonym 'Velma'), gave yeoman service for twenty-five years.

Action photographs, despite appalling lighting conditions, were pioneered in the 1930s by R.W. Butler, John Newland and Pat M. Turner. Graham Habbin and Louis Ross (q.v.) in the 1970s, with much better equipment, gave unstinted and generous help. Syd Robinson's caricatures encapsulated the quirks of the 1960s greats. Much was owed to 'backroom boys', K.L. Livingstone and Dorothy Lodge, both of RSL (q.v.), who acted as business managers.

Despite everyone's efforts, the *Gazette*, largely because the club copy was passed from hand to hand, never found its rightful place on newsagents' shelves alongside the seemingly legion magazines on tennis, golf, squash etc.

Upon the advent of Open Badminton in 1979, with the *Gazette* now seventy-two years old, the BAE opted for a bigger, glossier, professional publication. The *Gazette* was retired. *Badminton*, under Fleet Street editorship of Ron Willis, was a bright and comprehensive publication but, due to lack of club-level support, was seldom sold on bookstalls as had been envisaged. In 1982 Marsh Publications went bankrupt and, after a short hiatus, *Badminton* was replaced, under BAE auspices, by *Badminton Now* (q.v.), its new 'official journal'.

Badminton Gazette Editors

1907	S.M. Massey
1907-12	G.A. Thomas
1912-13	S.M. Massey and Miss L.C. Radeglia
1913-15	G.A. Thomas and Miss L.C. Radeglia
1921-2	Mrs R.C. Tragett
1922-6	Miss H.E.D. Pocock
1926-7	Mrs R.C. Tragett
1927-30	Miss L.C. Radeglia
1930-31	J.F. Devlin
1931-9	D.L.H. Mercer
1946-70	H.A.E. Scheele
1970-79	P.R. Davis

BADMINTON, History of

Battledore-and-shuttlecock (q.v.) has been played for many centuries. But it is hard to say precisely when it was first changed into something like the game we know today.

The late Duke of Beaufort was firmly of the opinion that the daughters of the Seventh Duke first played it in the hall of Badminton House (*c.* 1840-50). S.M. Massey, in the first-ever book on badminton gave the credit to John Loraine Baldwin. As the latter was a frequent visitor and delighted in rule-making, the credit may well be shared for the first game played there by family and guests one rainy day.

If the germ of the game sprang from Badminton House, some credit for its evolution must seemingly go to India. Army officers, guests at Badminton, surely took the game there rather than the reverse. Photos are extant of the game being played there in 1867. It was definitely played at Poona in the 1870s, where the first rules were formed in 1877 by a (then) Lieutenant Selby. Either there or in Karachi, barrack doors opening *inwards* were responsible for the hour glass court, which was not abolished until 1901. The Poona rules, revised in 1887 and 1890, were the basis for the first official Badminton Association rules.

BADMINTON HOUSE

Stately home in Gloucestershire of the Dukes of Beaufort from which the game derives its name. Reputedly the game was first played as such in the spacious entrance hall (*c.* 1850). The 'net' was probably a string from door-handle to marble fireplace. The former opened inward and *may* have been responsible for the original hourglass-shaped court. Early battledores and shuttlecocks are still preserved there.

In 1979 leading players in period costume re-enacted there badminton's early days for the BBC's *Better Badminton* TV series.

BADMINTON NOW

With the advent of Open Badminton, the BAE had visions of a glossier professional official magazine to replace the long-established, amateur (in the best sense of the word) *Badminton Gazette* (q.v.). Publication was accordingly handed over to Marsh Publications who, under the guidance of experienced Fleet Street journalist Ron Willis as editor and former

Gazette editor Pat Davis as consultant editor, produced an excellent monthly, *Badminton*. Unfortunately, club players were parochially uninterested, so shops naturally refused to add it to the plethora of magazines on every other conceivable hobby and sport on their long ranging shelves.

For other reasons Marsh Publications went bankrupt. The BAE at first felt unable to take on the financial burden of its own publication but, unheralded, in October 1982, *Badminton Now* suddenly appeared with a growing wealth of new advertising and under the enthusiastic editorship of Promotions Manager Tommy Marrs. Since then it has increased its circulation but has yet to achieve W.H. Smith bookshop status.

In 1985 Caroline Searle, the BAE's newly appointed publicity officer, subject to a previously appointed editorial board, took over the editorship.

BADMINTON PLAYERS' FEDERATION

Brainchild of English international Derek Talbot, ahead of his time in 1976 in seeing the inevitability of Open Badminton. More recently piloted by Billy Gilliland (Scotland), Steve Baddeley (England) and, currently, Steen Fladberg (Denmark). It has well over a hundred members, mainly European.

It seeks to work with – not against – the IBF. It now has a member on the latter's working group and hopes, more positively, for a seat on the Council. Naturally interested in bigger prize money, it also endeavours to (1) standardize tournament conditions; (2) suggest any necessary alterations of the Laws; (3) lay down a code of game ethics; (4) increase off-court sociability; (5) decide the pros and cons of fifteen-up ladies' singles; (6) inaugurate an insurance scheme against injury. (If players are side-lined for over three months, their endorsement contracts may be cancelled.)

Baddeley, in Calgary, complained it was 'scandalous that an Open World Championships *with prize money* was not on the IBF agenda'. Frost supported him: 'The IBF is making a lot of money from this event on the backs of the players.' IBF President P.E. Nielsen offered little hope of immediate help as the IBF was building up reserves for Olympic travelling expenses for developing countries.

BADMINTON UMPIRES' ASSOCIATION OF ENGLAND

BUAE was born in the heart of London in the comfort of the Charing Cross Hotel, London, on 19 November 1952. Its aims: in co-operation with the BAE, to improve the standard of umpiring and to provide umpires and service-judges when requested.

The first request for such services was at an international trial a month later. In that season six events were umpired by the thirty members; in 1984-5 no fewer than 350 events were serviced by the 250 member-umpires. Initially the BAE kept a firm finger on the pulse, with its chairman officiating and five out of nine members nominated by it.

Today the ratio is reduced to one in nine, and regional secretaries (North, South, Midlands, East, South-West, Guernsey and Jersey) are also included in the twenty-two-strong team of officers and committee. The latter is divided into sub-committees dealing with selection, training, grading and technical matters. Regional committees organize all events in their locality except those promoted by IBF or BAE.

The original draft 'Recommendations to Umpire' were issued in 1953 – and an updated version formed those adopted by the IBF in 1960. The grading of umpires was first mooted in 1954 – and instituted twenty years later. In 1964 the BUAE Committee was minuted as 'deploring the decline in players' behaviour and manners on court'. In 1983 the BUAE drafted for the IBF a new law to cater for 'players' misconduct'.

Early pioneers to whom the BUAE owed much were Peter Birtwistle, 'Tiny' Lucas and Eric Hinchcliff. Today Michael Gilks shoulders the secretarial burden. The BUAE as umpiring innovators have had requests for their help and services from worldwide. Its handbook gives, amongst other details, a great deal of worthwhile advice on the art of umpiring and implementation of the laws. They are of interest not only to aspiring umpires but also to players who too often do not appreciate the scope or difficulties of the umpire's task, which is done on a purely voluntary basis.

BADMINTON WRITERS' ASSOCIATION

Formed by badminton writers, Fleet Street and freelance, under the secretaryship of *Exchange Telegraph*'s Eric Brown and chairmanship of *The Times*' Richard Streeton, to 'further the interests of badminton, those involved in its media coverage, and any other associated matters'.

Their first award, to the player who had done most for the game, went to Ray Stevens; the second to his partner, Mike Tredgett; and the third to England Team Manager, Ciro Ciniglio.

BALDWIN, John Loraine

The man who changed battledore-and-shuttlecock into badminton? S.M. Massey (who made six appearances for England between 1903 and 1914) firmly stated in his book *Badminton* that it was Baldwin who started the game.

If circumstantial evidence is also needed, we know he frequently visited Badminton House, only twenty miles from his home near Tintern Abbey. He was a keen if inactive sportsman, having had a hand in founding the select 'I Zingari' cricket team and the cricketing-actors, the 'Old Stagers', who have performed for over a hundred years at Canterbury Cricket Week.

Moreover, he was well known as a rule-maker: *Rules of Short Whist* and those for the *Four in Hand Club* bear his name. It seems quite possible that, seeing the Duke of Beaufort's daughters or guests indulging in a random pastime, he regularized it into a game.

BALL BADMINTON

A distant cousin of badminton, played out of doors in India and South-east Asia. The court measures 40 by 80 feet (12 by 24 metres) – roughly four badminton courts; the net is six feet (1.8 metres); rackets are generally all wood; the missile, a ball of yellow wool. It is usually played by five players on a full court; four on a half court, and two on a quarter court. Scoring is up to 29 (best of three games), with three consecutive points needed at 27 to clinch the game.

BARCLAYS BANK NATIONAL SCHOOLS CHAMPIONSHIP

Formerly the ESBA Top Schools Competition. Embracing some 1,200 players annually, it is played at U.16 level in three categories, Boys' and girls' singles and mixed doubles, on a regional basis before Northern and Southern Finals, and then National Finals are played off. Barclays Bank now sponsor inter-regional travel and general expenses.

1972	*Mixed*	: Glenburn School, Lancashire
1973	*Boys'*	: Hurlfield School, Yorkshire
	Girls'	: Whitehaven School, Cumberland
	Mixed	: Gordano School, Somerset
1974	*Boys'*	: Chase Cross School, Essex
	Girls'	: Wallington High School, Surrey
	Mixed	: Henry Cavendish School, Derby
1975	*Boys'*	: Henry Cavendish School, Derby
	Girls'	: Regents Park School, Southampton
	Mixed	: Smithills School, Bolton
1976	*Boys'*	: Henry Cavendish School, Derby
	Girls'	: Upton Hall, Liverpool
	Mixed	: Henry Cavendish School, Derby
1977	*Boys'*	: William Edwards School, Essex
	Girls'	: Upton Hall, Liverpool
	Mixed	: Henry Cavendish School, Derby
1978	*Boys'*	: Beauchamps School, Essex
	Girls'	: Upton Hall, Liverpool
	Mixed	: Henry Cavendish School, Derby
1979	*Boys'*	: Hull Grammar School
	Girls'	: Maidstone Grammar School
	Mixed	: St Mary's High and Hull Grammar School
1980	*Boys'*	: William Edwards School, Essex
	Girls'	: Torells School, Essex
	Mixed	: Torells School, Essex
1981	*Boys'*	: Torells School, Essex
	Girls'	: Torells School, Essex
	Mixed	: Torells School, Essex
1982	*Boys'*	: St George's School, Avon
	Girls'	: Greenbank High School, Merseyside
	Mixed	: Torells School, Essex
1983	*Boys'*	: Torells School, Essex
	Girls'	: Torells School, Essex
	Mixed	: Torells School, Essex

Retitled Barclays Bank National Schools Badminton Championships

1984	*Boys'*	: Torells School, Essex
	Girls'	: Torells School, Essex

	Mixed	: Torells School, Essex
1985	Boys'	: Campion School, Northants
	Girls'	: Torells School, Essex
	Mixed	: Tomlinslete School, Surrey
1986	Boys'	: Wildern School, Southampton
	Girls'	: Purley School, Surrey
	Mixed	: Collingwood School, Camberley

BARGE, Dr Heinz

As President of the FR Germany BA, he saw membership trebled and a seven-court training centre built in Mulheim. EBU President, 1982-4, he was also awarded the prestigious Federal Service Cross for service to medicine and surgery in 1984.

BATTLEDORE

The earliest type of racket used: largely for domestic recreation before badminton became an established sport. In the seventeenth, eighteenth and nineteenth centuries they were frequently depicted in portraits of young children. Possibly the only known sculpture showing battledores is in Chilham Church near Canterbury: a memorial to two brothers who died young.

The first battledores were little more than very roughly shaped pieces of wood. Gradually they evolved into racket-shape. The heads varied in size; $7\frac{1}{2}$ inches long by 4 inches at its widest was perhaps typical. So too did shafts, from 6-8 inches (12-18 centimetres). The $\frac{3}{4}$ inch light wood frame was generally covered with velvet, which also encircled the shaft. The latter tapered slightly but was seldom shaped even into the semblance of a handle.

They were generally double faced with vellum and appropriately known as 'drum-bats'. One type (about 1877) was strung with gut on one side and vellum on the other – later solely with gut. The larger battledores with wider, almost circular heads and 15"-18" shafts may be seen at Badminton House; the smaller ones employed in the elegant and lackadaisical *jeu de volant* are seldom seen except in eighteenth- and nineteenth-century illustrations.

BATTLEDORE-AND-SHUTTLECOCK

The precursor of badminton, this game dates back well over two thousand years, when it was a child's game played in ancient Greece, Sumeria and Far Eastern civilizations such as Japan, India and China. In the latter country, feet rather than battledores were often used. That it was popular in medieval times is proved in woodcuts showing crude all-wooden bats in use.

The game was also more succinctly called 'shuttlecock'. James VI and I's son, Prince Henry, is recorded as 'playing shuttlecock', and in 1609 in *Two Maides of Moreclacks* one character states, 'To play shuttlecock methinks is the game now.' Somewhat later Pepys records playing at 'shittlecock'. On the Continent, played by the nobility as well as by children, indoors as well as outdoors, it was known as *jeu de volant*.

The object was to hit the shuttlecock not away from but to one's partner, to see how long or for how many hits it could be kept in flight. On one of the battledores at Badminton House (q.v.) used by the seventh Duke of Beaufort's children is written: 'The Lady Henrietta Somerset in February 1845 kept up with Beth Mitchell 2018' and on another: 'Kept up with Geraldine Somerset on Saturday 12th January 1830, to 2117. Henrietta Somerset.' Not very active perhaps but incredible concentration for two young girls using small-headed battledores and crude, heavy shuttles!

BAULK, to

To obstruct, prevent or put off an opponent from playing a stroke – often, at the net, by waving a racket in front of him as he essays a kill. To do so is a fault, contravening Laws 14 (d) and (j). A player may, however, play a single stroke in reasonable anticipation of his opponent's, or protect his face.

BEAUFORT, Tenth Duke of, KG, PC, GCVO, JP

As many authorities believe that badminton as such was first played at the Duke's ancestral home, Badminton House, Gloucestershire, (more famous for horse trials and eventing), it was natural that he should be invited to become the BAE's Patron (1960).

As landowner, Master of the Queen's Horse and a hunting fanatic who felt a day not in the saddle was a day wasted, he had little spare time for other activities. Nevertheless, he asked for half-yearly reports and made perceptive comments on them.

On occasions he attended the All-England Championships and other major functions with bluff good humour. And he was always a willing host to touring teams whose itinerary inevitably included a trip to the cradle of the game.

On the Duke's death, in 1984, Prince Andrew became Patron.

BEE, NG BOON (Malaysia)

Only 5 feet 3 inches in height (1.59 metres) and barrel-chested, Bee was almost as often diving to retrieve drop-shots as jumping high to smash. He was a player of concentration, zest and power who, coming to the game from Association Football, won his last major title at thirty-five and played his last international at thirty-seven.

He and Tan Yee Khan were worthy All-England successors to the great Danes Kobbero (q.v.) and Hansen, winning the AEC title in 1965 and 1966. It was his again in 1971 with Punch Gunalan after winning the 1969 Asian title with him.

A much less happy occasion was in the 1967 Thomas Cup final when he and Khan led 15-2, 10-2 in a match that would have won the cup for Malaysia. But under intense barracking by Indonesian supporters, 10-2 slid to 13-18 before the referee Herbert Scheele abandoned the tie. Nevertheless Bee, with Gunalan, was back in action again in the 1970 series, winning one long three-setter and losing the other to Hartono and Gunawan.

Bee was chosen Malaysian Sportsman of the Year in 1968.

BELL'S SCOTCH WHISKY CHAMPIONSHIPS OF THE HIGHLANDS

A friendly, early season Scottish Open tournament established in 1975 and played in the fine (though not always waterproof) Bell's Centre in Perth. Prize money has risen from £250 to £3,600. A favourite of Nora Perry who in its first seven years won sixteen out of a possible seventeen titles.

Motto? 'Will ye no have another wee dram afore ye go?'

BENGTSSON, Maria (Sweden)
Born 5 March 1964, Malmö

Petite, blonde and charming, she first made her mark in 1978 by winning the Swedish U18 GD for the first of four victories. Improved on that in the Swedish Nationals by winning the doubles five times with Magnusson and the singles (1981) once. Runner-up in the 1985 Scottish Open LD – with established partner Magnusson.

Emerged as a quicksilver mixed doubles player with sturdy defence by winning the Swedish Open with Kihlstrom in 1984, and with Karlsson in 1985. Reached high-water mark with the latter when they were runners-up in the 1985 World Championships.

BERG, Torsten
Born 7 April 1948

Hon. Secretary of the Denmark BF and a talented coach, he has lectured at major international seminars and coached widely overseas from France to Mozambique. One of the 'Big Three' of the IBF's Development Committee, he is in charge of the European Area.

BIRD

Colloquial term for a shuttlecock, derived, of course, from the shuttle's flight and the fact it is made largely of feathers.

BIRTWISTLE, W.G.P.
(Lancashire & England)

A Council member of the BAE since 1952 and a Vice-President since 1963. As Chairman of the Events Committee, for eighteen years he organized many international events and was manager of the England team that visited China in 1974. For these services he was awarded the Herbert Scheele Memorial Award (q.v.) in 1985.

He was a long-serving member of the Lancashire BA team and represented England five times between 1948 and 1952. A POW for much of the war, he nevertheless somehow managed to run highly popular badminton leagues and tournaments in various Stalags despite tremendous difficulties.

His wife Sheila organized the AEC Dinner for some years with equal efficiency.

BLAZER, All-England,

A blazer that can be worn only by All-England title-winners. Made of green cloth, it had narrow red, white and blue stripes. On the breast pocket: the white rose and the letters AEBC.

The blazer awarded to England players had narrow green, white and blue stripes on a red background. On the breast pocket: the red rose and BAE.

With the advent of the more suitable tracksuit, they are no longer awarded – and therefore not seen as in the past on ceremonial occasions.

BLOOMER, David L. (Scotland)
Born 1 September 1912,
Glasgow

Bloomer has done badminton great service over a long span of years. Inclined to *embonpoint*, he nevertheless played for Scotland, gaining eight caps largely due to pertinacity, strong backhand defence and a rooted Scots dislike of *giving* away points.

In 1949 the insurance broker turned impresario when he and John McCarry were entrusted with the staging of the first Thomas Cup semi-final in Glasgow's Kelvin Hall. So successful was it that in the following years he staged, in weeks proximate to the AEC, some fifteen World Invitation Tournaments that brought the world's top players to Scotland (including Ken Davidson's hilarious 'Gladminton' act).

On the IBF Council (1953-5); Chairman (1962-9); Vice-President (1955-65); President (1965-9). One of the most knowledgeable *Gazette* contributors and almost certainly its most delightfully witty stylist, he was also a masterly after-AEC Dinner speaker.

'Addicted with lurid asides to a game loosely called golf.'

BOARD SYSTEM

System of play adopted in many clubs in the UK.

Players' names are placed on a board in order of their arrival. The first player may then make up a four from the next seven (or agreed number) of players. The new top players of those remaining similarly makes up a four. Players' names are taken off the board as they go on court and returned to the bottom on completion of their game.

The advantages are: (1) that club members are forced to mix; (2) each gets roughly the same number of games; and (3) it is generally stipulated that the same four players cannot play successive games together.

Its disadvantages are: (1) a player may not be able to make up a four entirely of his own choice all night: (2) fours may be ill-balanced in strength or sex of players; (3) team pairs are unlikely to get practise together and against suitably strong opposition.

Such a system may maintain the sociability of a club but does little to improve playing standards unless team practices are instituted, a colour coding system is employed or a certain amount of 'free choice' is allowed.

BOCHOW, Wolfgang (FR of
Germany)
Born 26 May 1944

One of West Germany's finest players. His backhand power was unequalled until the arrival of Flemming Delfs, his courage unsurpassed as he fought – and beat – cancer.

Over a period of fourteen years (1962-75) he won his National singles title eight times, the men's doubles twice, and the mixed five times. He also won three National Open titles.

He won the European singles title in 1972 after having been runner-up in 1968 and was a semi-finalist also in 1970 and 1976. Bochow was awarded the Silver Laurel wreath – FRG's highest sporting honour.

BOOKS

British Badminton has not been blessed with a large literature, and most of those books written have been on technique and tactics rather than on the game in general.

The first book, *Badminton*, by international S.M. Massey (1911), was a mixed bag of 'how to play' and badminton history. Other great players, as ever, also turned author: Sir George Thomas with *The Art of Badminton*, Margaret Tragett *Badminton for Beginners* and J.F. Devlin *Badminton for All*.

First of the post-war books (1949) was *That Badminton Racket* by Better Uber, an interesting personal review of play and players world-wide. Ken Davidson's *Winning Badminton* set a new standard in coaching presentation and comprehensiveness.

Other coaches followed, including one-time BAE Chief Coach Roger Mills, *Modern Badminton* and *Badminton*, but most prolific of all undoubtedly were National Coaches Jake Downey, who made a big hit with *Better Badminton for All* and *Winning Doubles* amongst others, and Pat Davis, with seven books to his name, including the still popular *Badminton Complete* and *Badminton: A Complete Practical Guide*.

Post-war AEC champions Judy Hashman, Derek Talbot and Sue Whetnall all followed Sir George Thomas's example.

Recent books with a difference are *The Guinness Book of Badminton*, Pat Davis again: Bernard Adam's *Badminton Story*, a history of the game for the BBC; *Gillian Gilks*, the only study of a player, by David Hunn; and numerous 'picture books' of the champions by ace photographer Louis Ross.

BOSTOFTE, Christina

Fourteen-year-old Danish 'dark-filly'. In 1985, in her first ever senior tournament, unseeded, she beat top seed Charlotte Hattens and National Champion Lisbet Stuer-Lauridsen to win the coveted Carlsberg Cup. She also reached the Danish open semis, losing narrowly to a very worried Kirsten Larsen.

Her mother – and practice chopping-block – is Lonny Bostofte, herself a National Champion as recently as 1976-7.

BOX

Colloquial term for the deep, corner rectangles ($2\frac{1}{2}$ feet by $1\frac{1}{2}$, 0.76 metre by 0.45) formed by the meeting of the two sidelines and the two long service lines.

A shot accurately placed into such an area, especially on the backhand, is regarded as a skilful one, forcing the opponent deep back in court, thereby blunting his attack, driving him away from the central base, and leaving him in possible doubt as to whether or not the shuttle is falling 'in' or 'out' of court.

BOYCOTT

In 1975, dissatisfied with the IBF's third refusal to expel Taiwan BA and so make it politically possible for the People's Republic of China to apply for admission, and also with the loss of a 'one Association, one vote' proposal, the Asian Badminton Confederation ordered its members to boycott all tournaments organized by the BAE. (Possibly also because the impartial IBF chairman was English, and Asians and Africans thought it unfair that Ireland, Wales and Scotland should each receive votes as separate countries. They did not appreciate that in all sports – and in badminton virtually since inception – they have been autonomous.

BRITISH TROUT ASSOCIATION INTER-CLUB COMPETITION

Originally known as Foster's Draught National Inter-Club Championships in 1984, it was taken over by BTA in 1985. Early rounds are regionalized; the last sixteen play off over a weekend on a knock-out basis. Each tie consists of one men's singles, one ladies' singles, two men's doubles, two ladies' doubles and three mixed doubles.

Winners are nominated by the BAE to play in the Europe Cup.

1983/4 Middlesbrough BC 6 – Markland Hill BC (Bolton) 3

1984/5 Markland Hill BC (Bolton) 8 – Middlesbrough 1

1985/6 Markland Hill. (A new format with three group leaders, Markland, Headingly and Southport, playing each other in a final group.)

BRUSH STROKE

One of the surprisingly wide variety of strokes by which shuttles are returned from close to the net. It is used when the shuttle is too tight to the net to be hit down without danger of striking the net (a fault). The racket-head is brushed across the shuttle with a circular motion that moves forward only fractionally: it should be tilted slightly upwards if the shuttle is a few inches below the tape. It is a doubly effective stroke as the circular motion tends to deceive the opponent as to direction and length of shot.

BRYAN, née O'Sullivan, Mary, and
KELLY, Yvonne (Ireland)

Ireland's two greatest lady players cannot be split off court any more than on. Mary Bryan annexed fifty-three caps between 1955 and 1975 and twenty-three National and ten Open titles; Yvonne Kelly from 1955 to 1976 gained fifty-seven caps and twenty-four National and ten Open titles. Together they won nine National and five Open titles. Between them they monopolized the National singles title sixteen times out of seventeen from 1955/6 to 1971/2.

BUTLER, Steve P. (England)
Born 27 September 1963

Coming from a badminton-oriented family, 'Butters' won a string of National and ESBA titles from U.14 to U.21. He made the first of his twenty-eight appearances for England in 1982, and a major impact when in the TV Poco Homes Challenge he beat Indonesia's Danny Sartika. In the Far Eastern heat, he reached the quarters of 1984 Malaysian and Thailand Championships, taking Frost to thirteen in the former; he beat former World Champion Sugiarto in the Thomas Cup and won seven of his nine singles during 1984 tours of England by Korean and Chinese teams.

Best ever: runner-up in the 1985 English Masters when he ran Frost to three close games over seventy-eight minutes. 22, 6-feet 2-inches (1.87 metres) tall, super-fit, England's No. 3, he trains with Coventry City FC 'Sky Blues' and, for on-court activity, is nicknamed 'Turbo'. Thirty-seven caps.

BYE

A position in a tournament draw in which the player or pair so drawn are exempt from play until the second round. This is necessary to reduce the number of entries to a power of 2 (2, 4, 8, 16, 32, 64) unless that already pertains.

The number of byes in a round shall be the difference between the number of entries and the next highest power of two (i.e. if entries are 19, the next highest power of 2 is 32: the difference, 32-19, is 13, the number of byes). If the number of byes is even, they are divided equally and placed at the top and bottom of the draw. If odd, the greater number are placed at the bottom.

Below is an illustration of placing byes in an event with eleven entrants. Next highest power of 2 is 16. Difference is 16-11 = 5. So two byes at the top and 3 at the bottom.

Men's All-Time Singles

1st Round	2nd Round	Semi-Final	Final	Winner
1 Bye	Frank Devlin			
2 Bye	Luan Jin	Luan Jin		
3 Dave Freeman	Freeman		Frost	
4 Erland Kops				
5 Morten Frost	Frost	Frost		Frost
6 Liem Swie King				
7 Ralph Nichols	Choong			
8 Eddy Choong		Han Jian		
9 Bye	Han Jian		Soon	
10 Bye	Bill White	Soon		
11 Bye	Wong Peng Soon			

C

CALENDAR, INTERNATIONAL

Owing to the rapid proliferation of major tournaments throughout the world, the IBF publishes an annual calendar to prevent unfortunate clashes.

CALENDAR OF BADMINTON EVENTS, INTERNATIONAL

January	*Hong Kong Open
	*Chinese-Taipei Open
	*Japan Open
	Finlandia Cup
February	Inter City Championships
	Reserved for National Championships
	Dutch Open
	Nigerian International
	Irish International
	THOMAS/UBER CUP QUALIFYING ROUNDS
March	*German Open
	*Scandinavian Open
	Reykjavik International
	*All-England Open
	French International
April	European Championships
	Israel International
	Austrian Open
May	**THOMAS/UBER CUP FINALS (22 APRIL-4 MAY)
	Bermuda International
	Malta International
	Plume D'Or
	*China Open
	Slovenian International
June	Portuguese International
	Auckland International
	Mozambique International
	Silver Bowl International
July	*Thailand Open
	*Malaysian Open
	*Indonesian Open
	Commonwealth Games
September	New Zealand International
	Australian International
	Asian Games
October	Bells Open
	Czechoslovakian International
	*Victor Cup
	*English Masters
	Europe Cup
	*Danish Open
	USSR International
November	*Canadian Open
	Hungarian International
	**WORLD CUP VI
	Norwegian International
	*Indian Open
	US Open
	Nordic Championships
	*Scottish Open
	Mexican International
	Polish International
December	Welsh Open
	**GRAND PRIX FINALS

* Grand Prix Tournaments
** IBF events

CALLING

A means of helping one's partner decide whether to play or leave a shuttle falling near boundary lines.

The striker, eyes on shuttle, may be so totally absorbed in making a return that he has no time to think of or to gauge whether it will drop in or out if left.

His partner, not so urgently occupied, can and should observe the shuttle's flight. He should call early and incisively 'No' or 'Yes' or 'Watch'. (The latter means that the caller himself is doubtful, so the decision is up to the striker.)

Accurate calling can be cultivated and save many points.

CAMPBELL, Allan

He has done much to raise Scottish morale and status. Appointed SBU

Director of Coaching in November 1980, after being a Scottish Group Coach for several years, he was also director of a project for encouraging badminton in 'Areas of Special Need'. Peripatetic but based at SBU's six-court Cockburn Centre, Glasgow.

CANADIAN BADMINTON ASSOCIATION

Foundation membership of the IBF and 100% participation in Uber and Thomas Cups since inception show Canadian enthusiasm. So do powerful English touring teams (led by Sir George Thomas) in 1924 and 1929; many purpose-built halls; employment of star players from J.F. Devlin and G.S.B. Mack to Ratana-Saeng-Suang and Paul Whetnall as coaches; indifference to Canada's vast distances; thriving magazines, and 50,000 members.

Canada's famous players range from Jack Purcell and Don Smythe, Yves Paré and Jamie Paulsen, Marjorie Shedd and Dorothy Tinline to today's Bob Mac-Dougall and Mark Butler, Wendy Carter, Denyse Julien and Johanne Falardeau.

CARLSEN, Torben (Denmark) Born 17 April 1962

Part of Denmark's recently found strength in depth. Has matched his fitness and consistency with those of Nick Yates, losing to him in the 1985 German Open but beating him (seeded) in the World Championships to take an unexpected quarter-finals place, and again in the strong 1986 Japanese Open when he reached the quarters only to lose to the winner, Danish scourge, Yang Yang. Subsequently AEC 5/8 seeded, he suffered a shock first day, first round, two-game defeat against his compatriot – National champion, Høyer-Larsen.

CARLTON EUROPEAN U14 BADMINTON CHALLENGE

This popular junior event started in 1977 with four teams, became the Six Nations in 1979, Seven Nations (1984), and Eight Nations (1985) when the event was sponsored by Carlton.

Division A	Division B (Started 1979)
1977 England	–
1978 FR of Germany	–
1979 England	Austria
1980 England	Austria
1981 England	Austria
1982 England	Austria
1983 England	Austria
1984 England	Austria
1985 England	Austria

Division A (1985)
1. England 2. Netherlands 3. FR of Germany 4. Scotland
Division B (1985)
1. Austria   2. Wales   3. Belgium
4. Switzerland

CARLTON SPORTS COMPANY

Now a household name in badminton circles, the company owes its inception to Bill Carlton, production engineer and badminton player, who in 1949 decided man-made plastic shuttles could better Nature's feathered ones. Accordingly a small factory was set up in Hornchurch, Essex, with one one-shot injection moulding machine and facilities for precision light engineering. Demand for shuttles increased and light engineering flourished.

A new, larger factory was built at Saffron Walden in 1960. Plastic products as diverse as separators for crated beer and milk bottles, egg-trays and tyre-savers were developed. So also, in 1966, in time for the Jamaican Commonwealth Games, was the first Carlton metal-framed and shafted racket (the 3.9). It was heralded: 'Badminton began in the courtyards of princes; today's democratic prices are due entirely to research by Carlton.'

Two years later, Carlton Sports became part of Dunlop International Sports Company though operating as a separate organization. Today, with forty-one moulding machines, Carlton produces wide ranges of shuttles, and rackets in huge numbers for the home and export markets, as well as selling sports clothing and badminton accessories.

Carlton helps to stimulate interest in badminton by projects such as the ESBA Carlton Badminton Awards and the Carlton Challenge (q.v.).

Retirement to Malta did not stifle Bill Carlton's inventive genius: the

Wimbledon 'electronic eye' is his brainchild.

CENTRAL AMERICAN PEACE GAMES

Five nations (Costa Rica, El Salvador, Honduras, Guatemala and Nicaragua), participated in 25 different sporting events at the third Games in Guatemala City, which included badminton for the first time (1986).

Play between Costa Rica, Guatemala and Honduras was on three courts in an open-air theatre specially covered and converted. Organizers were Guatemalan-based Dane Stellan Erichsen, his wife Elizabeth, and Edgar Sandoval, 1985 EBU Summer School student. All three nations are applying for IBF membership, full or associate.

Winners

MS	R Mendez (G)
LS	R Vasquez (G)
MD	R Mendez and F Samayoa (G)
LD	A R Palarea and P Samayoa (G)
Mxd D	F Samayoa and S Palarea (G)

CHADHA, Ram

His badminton battle honours are legion. He won the Madhya Pradesh State Championship for over five years and was captain and coach of the 1960 Indian Thomas Cap team and captain of the Asian team (v. Europe) in Edinburgh in 1974. After eleven years committee work for the Badminton Association of India, he was Secretary from 1962-76, Secretary of the Asian BC for ten years and elected in 1975 a Vice-President of the IBF.

Chadha is a busy hotelier who relaxes by playing badminton and bridge.

CHANGING ENDS

In some halls, one end of a court may be more difficult to play on than the other, because of poor or glaring lighting, shiny or light-coloured background opposite, drift, obstruction, slippery or rough floor. To ensure that players share these difficulties equally, ends are changed after each game. And, if a third is played, again when a score of 8 (6 in ladies' singles of 11 up) is first reached by one player or pair. In games of 21-up, ends are changed at 11.

In handicap games, these figures have to be adjusted *pro rata*, so that ends are changed when a player reaches half his new total of possible points: e.g. if, in 15 up, A is +9 and B -5, A's maximum possible scored points are $15-9 = 6$, B's are $5+15 = 20$. Therefore ends are changed when half these numbers have been scored, i.e. when A reaches 12 $(9+3)$ or B, 5 $(-5+10)$. The BAE Handbook contains specially worked-out tables for 11, 15 and 21 up.

CHAPMAN, Lisa (Derbyshire)
Born 4 June 1966

'Consistently cheerful, happy and helpful' are characteristics that do not always lead to top badminton honours. But add to them a victory at the age of fifteen (with Cheryl Morgan) over Gillian Gilks and Paula Kilvington, and a 1983 AEC 'three-setter' against Japan's Tokuda and Yonekura, and you surely have the makings of a full international.

Lisa Chapman highlighted them in the 1982/3 European Junior Championships with a double 'Gold', team event and ladies' doubles (with June Shipman). In 1983/4 she won the ENJC girls' doubles and mixed doubles. All this from badminton-remote Buxton.

She trained with the Uber Cup Squad and toured Indonesia and China while still in her teens, won the 1983/4 National U.21 ladies (J. Shipman) and mixed (A. Wood) titles – despite a severely cut hand, and has five U.23 'caps' (1983/4). After glandular fever, and despite Sports Management studies at Sheffield Polytechnic, is working hard for a first full cap.

CODE OF CONDUCT

Badminton has long had a very high reputation for sporting behaviour. County matches until recently were played without umpires or linesmen; even championship tournaments, without linesmen. Players called their own lines remarkably fairly as well as calling, sometimes quixotically, their own 'doubles', 'woods', 'slings' or 'touches'. Laws were breached but generally through ignorance or unawareness rather than deliberately. The ESBA rightly taught its youngsters from the outset 'A Code of Game Ethics' as firmly as the technique of the smash.

In 1984, however, after five years of 'Open' play in widely separated countries, sometimes with different interpretation of the Laws, the Badminton Players' Federation (q.v.) felt a need to put its own house in order. It therefore asked the International Badminton Umpires Organization to instruct its officials to observe more closely and, where necessary, penalize:

1. Serving, at impact, with the whole of racket-head not *discernibly* below the holding hand.
2. Receiver moving before service impact.
3. Attempted 'intimidation' of court officials.
4. Player's failure to admit shuttle touching hair, clothing or racket before it was hit by partner.
5. Covert interference with the speed of the shuttle.

CHEN, CHANGJIE (China)
Born 4 January 1959

Sheer power of smash won him the 1981 World Games title, beating both Padukone and Frost, but lack of all-round skills saw him lose to the former in the AQ and, in the quarter-final 'battle of the smashers' at the 1982 AEC to Swie King. The latter beat him again in the 1982 TC (where Chen won five or six matches) and disastrously in the 1983 World Championships. Intensive training, however, saw him beat Padukone to give his inexperienced team the 1983 ABC team event; and Kurniawan to win the individual MS.

Engaged to China's No. 1 lady Zhang Ailing, he declared: 'Give me eighteen months to become World No. 1, then we marry.' On that score the wedding tea-ceremony seems far off as Chen, born 'when the sun came shining through in summer', was not selected for the 1985 AEC or WC and played only once in the all-conquering 1984 China Thomas Cup team.

A shooting star?

CHEN, Ruizhen (China)
Born 10 September 1960

Trained at the Fujian Sports Institute. Singles were her forte: 1980 All-China National, 1981 Alba Quartz WC and 1983 English Masters. She was not among the so-powerful Chinese Uber Cup winners in 1984.

CHILTON, Humphrey Farwell

A BAE Vice-President (Chairman of the Council 1970-75) who did sterling work for the BAE in that capacity from 1959 until 1983 when, on retirement, he was elected Hon. Vice-President. He was also Vice-President of the IBF from 1959-69, President, 1969-71.

Played first at the In & Out Club at Eton (so called because of its proximity to a public house), then for BB & O (q.v.) for whom he also held virtually all administrative positions. A serious eye injury sustained while playing cricket against his old school, King's, Canterbury, fortunately in no way hindered his penchant for deception or his nimbleness of foot, which had caught the Queen's eye when she watched an exhibition match at the opening of Slough Community Centre.

He is currently engaged in writing the history of the BAE at his Gnomes' Cottage home, Penn, Buckinghamshire.

CHINA – BADMINTON ASSOCIATION OF THE PEOPLE'S REPUBLIC OF CHINA (BAPRC)

Formed only in 1954, the stripling has, with some 100,000 affiliated members, and vastly more unaffiliated, quickly become the giant of the badminton world. Its men, first entry winners of the Thomas Cup in 1982, rank second only to Indonesia, to whom they lost narrowly in 1984. Its women are, in depth and class, unbeatable. They did not drop a single match, and only five games out of fifty-five, in winning the 1984 UC on their first appearance.

There are sixteen regional associations which come together for annual National classification events for teams and individuals, junior, senior and élite.

Its early players – such as Hou Chia-chang and Tang Hsien-hu (q.v.) who took England by storm in 1972/3 – were held to have learnt the game in Indonesia. Its present dedicated champions are definitely home raised and include a wealth of famous names ranging from Zhang Ailing to Yao

Ximing and Chen Changjie to Wu Dixi.

China affiliated to the IBF only in 1981, owing to political differences. She always maintains (though her players sweep up trophies worldwide): 'Victory is transitory; friendship everlasting.' Her representatives have finely upheld that tenet by sportsmanship and courtesy on court and off.

Won both Thomas and Uber Cups in 1986 by defeating Indonesia 3-2 on both occasions.

CHOICE OF ENDS

The player winning the toss at the beginning of a game may, if he wishes, choose at which end he will start.

Some players choose the best end first. They hope thus to win the first game, so boosting their morale and undermining their opponents' and perhaps laying the foundation of a straight two-game win.

Others choose the worst end first, so that if the match does go to three games, they will have the advantage of the best end for the last vital points.

CHOONG, David and Eddy (Malaysia)

Brothers who, as students in London in the 1950s, revitalized England's war-weary badminton.

David, the elder, a master tactician, excelled in mixed, winning the AEC title in 1953 with June White (later Timperley) in the brilliant era of John Best, Tony Jordan (q.v.) and Finn Kobbero (q.v.).

Eddy, extrovert and acrobatic, who leapt high in attack and dived low in defence, won the AEC singles in 1953, 1954, 1956 and 1957. He and fellow Malayan Wong Peng Soon (q.v.) mono-polized that title from 1950 to 1957.

On retirement, living very hospitably in Penang, Eddy bred Doberman Pinschers, raced fast cars – and crashed them – and coached the Malaysian team. He returns to Britain welcomely and frequently and in 1984 won yet another AEC Men's Doubles – the Veterans' with N.M. Natekar – thirty-three years after his first.

Together, E.L. (David) and E.B. (Eddy) won the AEC men's doubles titles (1951-3) and so the trophy outright. They brought skill, thought, training and joy to the game, as well as 'speed and sportsmanship, fun and fireworks'.

CHRISTIANSEN, Mark Thomas (Denmark)
Born 21 October 1963, Aalborg

At 6 feet 4 inches (1.93 metres) and 13 stones 2 lb (83 kg), he is in the Skovgaard-Delfs mould. Probably he has a heavier smash and an even longer reach, which helps rank him No. 1 in Danish Mixed Doubles.

First playing in 1973, he won the 1981 European Junior with regular partner Kjeldsen and was runner-up, with Dorte Kjaer, in the mixed. He made his mark in 1984 as Danish National Mixed and Men's Champion, and runner-up (MD) in the Scandinavian Cup.

Christiansen set the seal on this in the 1985 AEC by beating, with Kjedelsen, the Sideks, Kihlstrom and Karlsson, Baddeley and Dew, before taking Park and Kim to three games in the final. He reached the World Cup semis but lost to runners-up Yongbo and Bingyi 16-18, 18-14, 3-15.

Left-handed, the Gentofte BC player is a menacing receiver of serve and powerful in the rear-court.

CINIGLIO, Ciro
Born 17 April 1933, Nuneaton

Peripatetic, he played for no fewer than five counties (Warwickshire, Middlesex, Wiltshire, BB & O and Oxfordshire) and by winning various open tournaments must have been considered for an England cap. However, he did not become well known until 1979 when he was appointed England Team and Coaching Manager – England surprising-ly lost 3-6 to Sweden in the Thomas Cup!

But under his guidance in Copenhagen, in 1980/1, England achieved their first victory (4-3) for thirty-seven years against a mixed Danish team. They beat a Chinese team (1984) and won Team Championship gold medals at the 1982 Brisbane Commonwealth Games, the European Games Team Championship 1982 and 1984, gold, silver and bronze medals in the 1983 World Cham-pionships in Indonesia, and in 1984 the bronze medal in the Thomas Cup and the silver medal in the Uber Cup at Kuala Lumpur.

Ciniglio's success sprang from his ability to motivate, from his careful selection, preparation and, above all, willingness to experiment, and from a confidence in youth that made him give them early and vital Far East baptism. He made himself popular with his teams by his attention to detail and his ever-ready helpfulness, affection and encouragement – even though in moments of crisis he sometimes could not bear to watch them play critical points and used *Il Trovatore* to soothe his jangled nerves.

In December 1984 he resigned to take up the post of IBF marketing manager. His departure was unhappily headlined by Fleet Street 'England Boss in Quit Stunner' and 'Badminton's Ice-cream Man Ciniglio is Flavour of the Month.' He resigned within a year to join the Walker International Sports Management team.

Succeeded by Jake Downey (q.v.).

CLARK, Gillian (England)
Born 2 September 1961, Baghdad

A robust and lively character, Gillian Clark made her mark in the late 1970s, winning the EJNC Girls' U.18 Doubles no fewer than three times, as well as the 1979 European Junior title with Sally Leadbeater (later Podger). 1980 saw the first of her eleven U.23 caps and thirty-five England caps.

In 1982/3 she won the National Mixed with Mike Tredgett and the 1982 European Senior title with Gillian Gilks. A severe knee injury in the 1983 English Masters might have ended her career but for the skill of BAE Hon. Surgeon William Taor and her own determined fitness training (which included a one-meal-a-day diet).

In 1984 she again joyously won 'Gold' at the European Championships (with Karen Chapman), got a team 'Gold', and a mixed 'Bronze' with Nigel Tier, but lost, with Nora Perry, 5+1, to Lin Ying and Wu Dixi at the Masters.

1985 was a highlight! A scratch pairing with Thomas Kihlström saw her lose only narrowly in the AEC final to Gilliland and Kihlström's former partner, Nora Perry, 10-15, 12-15. She won the National ladies' doubles with Gillian Gowers. Bitterly disappointed at not being chosen for World Championship ladies' doubles, she hinted at severance of

relations with the BAE.

In 1986 won her third European LD title but, as in 1984, failed to complete her first Uber Cup game – struck in the eye by a shuttle hit by her partner! Forty-seven caps.

CLASSIFICATION

System of play employed in some European countries. All players are classified according to ability and play within that category in their clubs and in tournaments only against similarly classified players. Players may apply for reclassification as they improve.

CLEAR

A basic overhead power stroke used mainly in singles. It is played generally from between the two long service lines to the same area at the other end.

The *defensive* clear is hit as high and deep as possible to gain time for the striker's recovery to mid-court base, to blunt the opponent's attack and to give the shuttle a high, vertically falling trajectory which makes it rather more difficult to time and hit cleanly.

The *attacking* clear is hit much flatter, but just high enough to prevent early interception. It is used to hurry and tire an opponent, to force a weak return or to snatch a point in the rear-court when the opponent is momentarily off-balance or too far advanced mid-court.

Both are played for deception with the same throwing action as for smash and drop but, where the point of impact for the *defensive* clear is roughly over the right shoulder, that for the *attacking* one is just forward of the head.

CLOSED RACKET-FACE

A racket face that is tilted downwards at impact thereby giving the shuttle a downward trajectory.

CLOTHING

Women
In tune with the times, badminton clothing has changed a great deal since the early days of this century. As a result, women today have unhampered mobility.

In the 1880s little of the female body was exposed to air or male eye. White blouses had leg-of-mutton sleeves and were kept fastened at the wrist as well as the throat, where short or bow ties were worn. Waists were doubtless tightly corseted, and round them a fairly wide buckled belt helped to keep full black or blue skirts just above the feet. Though invisible, stockings were worn. In the very early days, play was simply in ordinary, everyday clothes – the whole ensemble often topped by a large hat, generally, and generously fruit- or flower-adorned.

As late as the 1914 AEC, women were still very similarly clad though now all in white and hatless.

War-time emancipation changed all that for the better. Blouses were worn open-necked, and skirts were no more than calf-length. Bandeaux and V-necked sweaters often completed the outfit. By the 1930s divided knee-length skirts were the fashion, and although as late as 1938 Bervic Patent Corset Garters were advertised, knee-length white socks were often worn. Shirts were short-sleeved and of an aertex material. By the 1950s, shorts were popular, as were flared or pleated skirts which were often worn with pastel-hued sweaters and cardigans. Blazers, at international level, added colour and distinction.

With skirts becoming ever shorter for the sake of both fashion and mobility, panties were frilled and more decorative. Specially designed bras too became useful as women played ever more athletically.

Today, women's dress is eminently practical for quick and simple laundering and unrestricted movement of leg and arm. The old 'all-white' dictum is discreetly broken by splashes of colour in inverted pleats and panels. 'Predominantly white' is the new watchword. But the wearing of even all-one-colour (blue) shorts and/or shirts is left to the discretion of the tournament committee. At major events they are officially accepted if *both* players wear clothing in their national colours (Swedish players, for example, sometimes wear blue shorts and yellow shirts).

Men

The pendulum of men's fashions has not swung as widely as that of women's. Early times saw the game played in everyday clothing, but a uniform of white shirt, with sleeves rolled up and a coloured tie at the throat, rather tight trousers and a broad belt, gradually evolved. Black socks and brown sandshoes did little for the ensemble.

Long-sleeved sweater, V-necked and with colour there and at the cuff and waist, soon became popular – Sir George Thomas, as befitted his style of play, preferred the elegance of a cardigan. Until the 1960s, the peacock finery of striped blazers brought colour to the courts. Today the tracksuits, for women as well as men, matches blazer brightness if not elegance and provides quick pre- and after-match warmth necessary to prevent stiffness and pulled muscles (At club level an unfortunate and sloppy tendency to *play* in them has developed.)

In the 1930s English international Bill White was the innovator of the then daring shorts now customary for men. As they grew ever tighter, an anguished cry was heard in the *Gazette*: '… ludicrous, should never be worn at a greater tension than 10 lb to the square inch'.

Today clothing is often unisex, colourful and convenient.

COACHING

Ralph Nichols, England's pre-War No. 1, averred, 'Coaching is definitely detrimental to playing ability.' Today few would agree with him. Skilled coaches stand behind great athletes and players of all sport worldwide. They offer the distilled essence of experience, fitness know-how and an observant awareness of a player's own unobserved faults in technique and tactics and of an opponent's weaknesses and strengths.

Before World War I there seems to have been no official coaching – and only one instructional book. After it, private lessons were advertised in the *Badminton Gazette* by Colonel C. de V. Duff CBE, Captain H.C. Evans, Miss I. Plomer-Walker and even Miss L.C. Radeglia (AEC Singles champion 1913, 1914 and 1923). In the 1930s, talented players such as J.F. Devlin and G.S.B. Mack (Ireland), B.P. Cook (England), W. Basil Jones (Wales) and James Barr (Scotland) turned coach – but only in wealthy Canadian clubs.

After World War II, with UK badminton in the doldrums, the first group coaching was undertaken in Dublin and by Lancs and Cheshire BA. The BAE ran courses at Littlehampton and Lilleshall with Rhona Barlow, Ken Gregory, H.L.K. Brock and Ian Palmer much to the fore, and published an instructional booklet for the coaches being trained. Nancy Horner (q.v.), followed by Olive Johnson, Ollie Cussen and Barbara Wadsworth, was the first BAE Coaching Secretary. 'Focus on Badminton' demonstrations were arranged by the Central Council of Physical Recreation and, in Ireland, by Morton's Male Circus, which included hairy-legged, blue-jowelled colleens of Junoesque proportions.

1968 saw the appointment of the BAE's first full-time professional coach, Ken Crossley, quickly followed by ex-international Roger Mills (q.v.). Following the latter's dismissal, for breach of contract, and subsequent legal dispute before the Industrial Tribunal, Les Wright was appointed Staff Coach, whilst England teams received sporadic coaching from recently retired internationals, and an England Youth Squad was placed in the care of Nev MacFarlane (q.v.) aided by Ian Graham and Alon Horrocks.

Today, the former score of top-grade national coaches who gave so much voluntary service having been culled; there are now only three of the newly created senior coaches, all professionals: Paul Whetnall (q.v.), i/c U.14, U.16, U.18, U.23 Squads, Roger Mills and Les Wright, with Jake Downey as England Coaching Manager. In addition there are some seventy county coaches.

Registered assessors (140) run and assess country-wide coaching courses that have produced great numbers of elementary, intermediate and advanced coaches who work in clubs and at evening classes.

Each county has its own Coaching Secretary, and these co-operate with their own regional co-ordinators (eight in all). The English Schools BA have their own basically similar system pitched at a lower level.

As a result of this broad-based, highly organized set-up, and very early blooding of promising youngsters in European and Far Eastern tournaments, England, with strength in depth, has now ousted Denmark as Europe's No. 1 and is at last producing world-class players not only in doubles but also in singles.

COCKING THE WRIST

The wrist, rather like the universal joint in a motor-vehicle, can virtually rotate through 360° degrees. With the hand held up, the wrist and hand can be bent back, or *cocked*. Opposedly from that same position, it can be bent sharply downwards or *uncocked*.

If, using this action, an imaginary overhead stroke is 'shadowed' (q.v.), a distinct whistle will be heard. This is caused by extra, last-second, wrist-generated racket-head speed which, added to arm-speed, gives that vital snap to all power strokes. It is used similarly in side-arm and under-arm strokes.

This action can also be used for last-second deception (see *Holding*). And, simultaneously, the wrist can be turned left or right for a late change of shuttle direction to backhand or forehand; or to impart 'cut' (q.v.).

Over-use of the wrist by beginners can lead to mis-hitting and hitting into the net – or even down at the feet; lack of use, to flat and weak smashing.

COMMONWEALTH GAMES

This multi-sport, quadrennial event started life at Hamilton, Ontario, Canada, in 1930 as the British Empire and Commonwealth Games. Before the war it was held in London and Sydney; after (in 1950) at Auckland, then in Vancouver, Cardiff and Perth.

Badminton was accepted as one of the nine sports included in the 8th Games held at Kingston, Jamaica, in August 1966, when temperatures soared above 100°F. England has won fourteen of the twenty-five gold medals: all the mixed but never the men's singles until 1986.

Other venues have been: 1970 Edinburgh, Scotland; 1974 Christchurch, New Zealand; 1978 Edmonton, Canada; 1982 Brisbane, Australia; 1986 Edinburgh, Scotland.

Date/Venue
1966   Jamaica
1970   Edinburgh
1974   Christchurch
1978   Edmonton
1982   Brisbane
1986   Edinburgh

Men's Singles
1966   Tan Aik huang
1970   J. Paulson

1974 P. Gunalan
1978 P. Padukone
1982 S. Modi
1986 S. Baddeley

Ladies' Singles
1966 A. Bairstow
1970 M. Beck
1974 G. Gilks
1978 S. Ng
1982 H. Troke
1986 H. Troke

Men's Doubles
1966 Tan Aik Huang/Yew Cheng Hoe
1970 Ng Boon Bee/P. Gunalan
1974 D. Talbot/E. Stuart
1978 R. Stevens/M. Tredgett
1982 R. Sidek/B. Ong
1986 W. Gilliland/D. Travers

Ladies' Doubles
1966 J. Horton/V. Smith
1970 M. Boxall/S. Whetnall
1974 M. Beck/G. Gilks
1978 N. Perry/A. Statt
1982 C. Backhouse/J. Falardeau
1986 G. Clark/G. Gowers

Mixed Doubles
1966 R. Mills/A. Bairstow
1970 D. Talbot/M. Boxall
1974 D. Talbot/G. Gilks
1978 M. Tredgett/N. Perry
1982 M. Dew/K. Chapman
1986 M. Scandolera/A. Tuckey

CONTINUOUS PLAY

Law 23 states that play must be *continuous* from first service to last except that; 1. in international competitive events; 2. in countries where climatic conditions make it desirable; 3. in circumstances not within the players' control, a break of five minutes is allowed between the second and third games in (1) and (2), at the umpire's discretion in (3).

Without breaching this rule, players may move off court to change rackets or *very quickly* 'towel down', provided opponents are not kept waiting. In the 1985 World Championships Wu Jianqui was penalized at championship point for this offence.

The umpire has to use his/her discretion to see that this is not done too frequently or too long; that rally intervals are not prolonged; that time is not taken to regain wind or strength, or receive advice; that shuttles are not changed or tested too frequently.

Equal care has to be taken that the five-minute interval, when taken, is not exceeded. To this end the umpire announces clearly after three minutes: 'Court No. –, two minutes remaining, two minutes remaining.' If the players have not returned, he repeats an amended warning a minute later and immediately notifies the referee.

Such a situation arose at the 1979 AEC, when Tjun Tjun and Wahjudi were actually disqualified and opponents Iino and Tsuchida awarded the match – only for the umpire's decision to be reversed by the referee for reasons never disclosed. Similarly in the 1977 World Championships, Delfs was disqualified but reinstated on appeal by Ray Stevens – his very sporting opponent.

Injury creates a problem. The umpire has to use his discretion in granting minimal respite yet not putting opponents at a disadvantage through getting cold or stiff or losing concentration. An example was evidenced in the 1985 AEC semi-final when at a critical point against Gillian Gilks and Nora Perry, Wu Dixi fell and a full two minutes delay ensued. When play resumed, Gilks flicked Wu, who leapt back with her usual mobility to win the point – and later the match.

COURT DIMENSIONS

The diagrams below are self-explanatory. The much greater distance a cross-court shot has to travel is sometimes not fully appreciated.

Court areas are reduced for disabled players (q.v.).

(Singles & Doubles Diags from BAE H'bk)

See pages 32-33.

COURTSIDE BAG

As play must be continuous, the wise player provides for all emergencies by carrying a special sports bag to the courtside. At major events, in order not to offend the TV eye, they and their contents are placed inside unobtrusive containers. In order to avoid any waste of time, they should be moved with the player at change of ends.

They will contain some or all of the following: spare rackets and shoes; laces; hand resin or talc; bandeau; spectacles demister; spare shirt, glucose/salt drink; safety pins; copy of the Laws (if no umpire); small towel.

CROSS-COURT, to

To hit the shuttle from one side of the court to the other in order to hurry an opponent into error or to gain a direct winner in an open space. A telling shot provided it is (1) disguised; (2) played when opponent has first been moved from the centre to the side-lines (3) hit flat or downwards the *full* width of the court. It loses surprise and effect if over-used.

CRYSTAL PALACE

Huge prefabricated iron-and-glass building originally erected in Hyde Park, London, for the 1851 Great Exhibition. Later it was re-erected in the suburbs at Sydenham, and its central transept was the venue for the 1902 AEC. It became the home of London's most prestigious club, Crystal Palace BC.

In 1922 the club moved to the nearby Canada Building where the thirteen courts included the secluded 'Shy Ladies' court where Betty Uber (q.v.) perfected her metronome low serve. Fire destroyed the main building in 1936 and the escaping rats were, slanderously, alleged to have found refuge in the adjacent club.

CUMPSTEY CUP

Trophy subscribed for by friends on the early death of Charles Cumpstey. Although playing in tiny, remote Westmorland (and handicapped by poor eyesight), by enthusiasm and dedication Cumpstey reached near-international playing standard, umpired AEC finals and became an innovative National Coach. He also played cricket, tennis and later golf to high local standards.

The trophy was given to the ESBA for their Top Schools Competition (now the Barclays Bank National Schools Championship).

CUT OFF, to

To intercept a shuttle, especially at the net, before it reaches its intended target area.

CUT STROKES

These are deceptive strokes in which the shuttle is not hit squarely with the full face of the racket. Instead, by a turning of the wrist, the racket face cuts across the side of both feathers (or skirt) and base of the shuttle. This diminishes the power transmitted to the shuttle but is effective because racket speed still appears deceptively fast to an opponent, although the shuttle speed is slowed and the shuttle travels less far than anticipated.

'Cut' cannot be imparted to a shuttle quite as effectively and as variously as to a tennis ball, but its use has been recognized by experimenters in the last fifteen years or so. It is employed as above in smash and drop-shot and, more particularly, in net-shots (q.v.). Its highly effective use in the low serve has been made illegal.

CZECHOSLOVAKIA – Ceskoslovensky Badmintonovy Svaz

Originally (1957) with only two clubs, both in Prague, the Association now has 150+ clubs, (4,100 affiliated players). An increase due perhaps partly to the inspiration of holding the European Junior Championships in 1971 at Gottwaldov, and to generous Press and TV coverage.

An efficient coaching system has produced Michael Maly, who was awarded the first EBU Coaching Scholarship in 1981.

Ironically, further expansion in the country that provided British badminton with millions of feathers is said to be prevented by shuttle scarcity!

Czechoslovakia hosted the 1969 Helvetia Cup and won it in 1973.

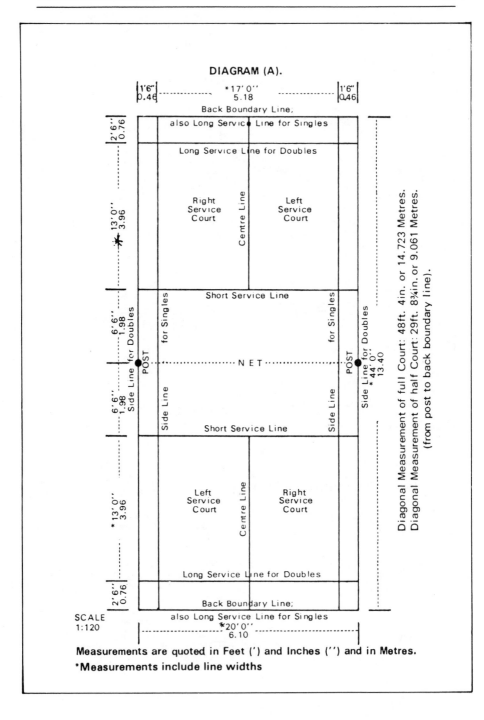

DIAGRAM (A).

Measurements are quoted in Feet (') and Inches ('') and in Metres.
*Measurements include line widths

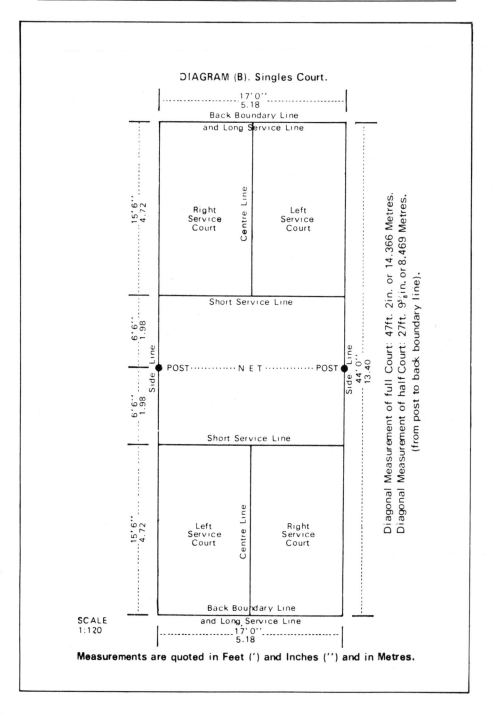

DIAGRAM (B). Singles Court.

SCALE
1:120

Measurements are quoted in Feet (') and Inches ('') and in Metres.

D

DAB

A crisp downward stroke with minimal backswing and follow-through played in the forecourt (by the net player) often to gain an outright winner to the lower body or a gap.

It is executed by extending a bent forearm and uncocking the wrist firmly. If the latter action is omitted, the shuttle will be hit flat and – with only some twenty-three feet from striker to baseline – out. It is also effectively used in a 'rush' or attacking return of serve (q.v.).

DANISH WIPE

A hybrid backhand stroke, a cross between a lob and a drive, used to loft a shuttle from one end of the court to the other.

The racket is swept down, then up and under the shuttle (which has been allowed to drop to knee height) to finish with a strong follow-through. So called because it was used by petite Danish girls and demanded *strong* arm and body action.

It is a useful stand-by for women with weak wrists until they can hit a good length with an overhead backhand stroke (q.v.). The latter is much more effective because, with the shuttle taken earlier and higher, it (1) gives the opponent less time; (2) can hit the shuttle *down*: (3) offers a wider variety of stroke.

DAVIDSON (Ken) MEMORIAL AWARD (USA)

An annual award, both senior and junior, to the player 'whose sportsmanship, attitude and achievement best exemplify the spirit of badminton held in such high esteem by Ken Davidson himself'. Adult winners since 1955 include Eddy Choong, Sue Devlin, Ethel Marshall, Judy Devlin, Bea Massman, Wynn Rogers and Stanton Hales (also as a junior).

DAVIDSON, Kenneth R. (Yorkshire and Scotland) Born 24 December 1905, Calverley

Cricket's loss; badminton's gain. In his first full season with Yorkshire he scored over a thousand runs at No. 4, but it was at badminton that he made his name as player, coach, author – and comedian.

He first joined Headingley Wesleyans, but his many mixed and men's championship victories soon saw him playing for Yorkshire (1927-35) and Scotland (1932-5), thus becoming Yorkshire's first-ever international. No lesser expert than Sir George Thomas described him as 'an artist with a beautiful wrist and a sure and delicate touch', while John McCarry labelled him 'a virtuoso with incredible fantasticisms all his own'.

This skill he used when he emigrated to America (1935). There he put on a performance of trick shots and humour seven times a day six days a week on the Roxy Circuit. He played also at Radio City, and the London Coliseum – in Royal Command performances. He also spread the badminton gospel in America, captained and coached its Thomas Cup team to semi-final and challenge round appearances, and wrote *Winning Badminton*.

A strict non-smoker, non-drinker, he was nevertheless the life and soul of any party, especially with his 'drunk' act.

Davidson died tragically in an air crash

at Prestwick on Christmas morning 1955 when returning home to New York from a Malayan/Indian tour, the day after celebrating his 49th birthday in Yorkshire.

DAVIS, Patrick R. (Kent and Wales)

Kent county player and Welsh international (with a record span of twenty-one years for his six appearances). With Charles Cumpstey and then Cyril Denton he won the AE Veterans' men's doubles title a record seven times and reached the final nine times in eleven years (1962-72).

He was a BUAE umpire. As a National coach he was invited to USA, Canada, Jamaica, France and Malta as well as coaching at major centres in the UK. He was appointed referee for the European Junior Championships at Edinburgh in 1981.

As editor of the *Badminton Gazette* for ten years, assistant editor of *Badminton* and author of seven books, he is, after Herbert Scheele, the most prolific writer on the game. His most successful books were *Badminton Complete, Badminton Coach, Badminton: A Complete Practical Guide*, the *Guinness Book of Badminton* and *Badminton is Fun* — which was translated into Japanese.

DEAF, Badminton for the

The Federation of London Deaf Clubs started a London Badminton League and Championship in 1932. The British Deaf Sports Council started a National Tournament in 1965. In 1985 seventy-five men and forty-five women from all over UK entered. An inter-club tournament is also now run.

In 1985 badminton was included in the World Games for the Deaf held at Los Angeles. Rodney Fletcher (ten times UK Singles Champion) beat Martin Bogard (six times runner-up) in the men's singles final; Fiona Wilson (seven times UK Champion) won the mixed doubles with Fletcher; and Fletcher and Bogard together won the men's doubles.

Players travelled to London every two months for eighteen months for weekend training under Middlesex Coach-Assessor Ray Learney, and themselves paid £300 of their £1000 expenses.

DELFS, Flemming (Denmark)

Mr Backhand! A blonde, elegant and seemingly casual Adonis, with whip-lash backhand power strokes but, as a critic once bitingly observed: 'no more than a powder-puff smash'. What he lacked in power he made up for in technique and chess-board tactics: his tape-tight cut net-shots earned him points as surely as the 'big bang' of other players. A 'natural', he disliked training; that and doubtless his own metabolism, made him a shadow of himself in such steamy locations as Indonesia's Senayan Stadium.

Among his many victories the best undoubtedly were the 1977 AEC final, when he wore down Liem Swie King 15-17, 15-11, 15-8, and the first World Championships, when he beat compatriot Svend Pri 15-6, 15-5. He won the Nordic Championships once only (1976) but took the European singles title three times (1976, 1978 and 1980), the Danish National singles twice, and men's doubles three times.

With peaks scaled and prize-money still derisory, he had little incentive for the rigorous training he disliked. He retired from serious competitive play after being unseeded in the 1981 AEC (despite reaching the AEC semis in 1980 with victories over Sidek and Pongoh) and being drawn in the first round against second seed Rudy Hartono.

DENMARK

Denmark's meteoric rise to European domination — in a little over a decade, 1925-39, its players grew from complete novices to AEC champions — is owed a little to chance. A Copenhagen sports club, Skovshoved Idraets Forenig, found their gymnasium unsuitable for indoor tennis, and it so happened that a sports-dealer member had some outdoor badminton rackets in for repair. Their owners, — names now to conjure with — Henning Hansen, F. Nexoe-Larsen, P. Schrader and S. Olsen, agreed to give members an indoor demonstration. Just six members turned up to watch!

Discouraged, the evening demonstration would have been cancelled had not two of the spectators, the brothers Hans and Aksel Hansen volunteered to undertake it. Drop-shots were considered 'cissy', shuttles were played with to the last feather, and matches were best of five games – 21 up in each! Aksel became an international; Hans, the badminton professor, pioneered the game in Norway and Sweden.

SIF was quickly followed by the now world-famous Københavns BK and Gentofte BK. The game's rapid growth from 10,000 players in 1939 to 171,049 in 1985 made it Denmark's top participant sport, and badminton's second biggest membership.

This resulted from numerous factors: the building of halls throughout Denmark exclusively for badminton; visits from Irish, English and Welsh teams; permission to play throughout the war; early administrators of the calibre of A.C.J. van Vossen and W.P. Kristensen; a systematic coaching system, at all levels from U.10, inaugurated by Richard Heilbo and carried on by Ole Mertz and Torsten Berg; and the creation of a high-prestige National Team Championship which puts 20,000 trained and competitive players on court annually.

On this foundations has been built Denmark's skyscraper list of 'greats', from Tage Madsen, Poul Holm and Jorn Skaarup, through Finn Kobbero and Hammergaard Hansen, Erland Kops and Henning Borch, and on to today's Flemming Delfs, Morten Frost, Mark Christiansen and Michael Kjeldsen. Small wonder that Denmark relentlessly defeated even England from 1947 to 1980 and won all thirteen of the Thomas Cup European zone finals though climatic conditions have probably been a major factor in their failure to win the trophy.

Denmark has produced equally talented women: Marie Ussing, Kirsten Thorndahl, Tonny Ahm, the Rasmussen sisters, Kirsten Larsen, Dorte Kjaer, Nettie Nielsen and, queen of them all, Lene Koppen. Denmark lost to the USA in the first two Uber Cup finals and has since reached the inter-zone finals twice. In the preliminary European zone she has beaten her only real rival, England, four times and lost four.

Denmark hosted the 3rd World Championships in Copenhagen in 1983 and has given staunch support to the IBF through officers such as Ole Mertz and Tom Bacher and current President Poul-Erik Nielsen.

DANISH OPEN CHAMPIONSHIPS

Men's Singles

1935-6	Poul Vang Nielsen
1936-7	M.W. Field
1937-8	H.S. Ong
1938-9	Tage Madsen
1939-45	Ikke afviklet
1945-6	Conny Jepsen
1946-7	Poul Holm
1947-8	Jørn Skaarup
1948-9	D.G. Freeman
1949-50	Nils Jonson
1950-1	Wong Peng Soon
1951-2	Jørn Skaarup
1952-3	Ikke afviklet
1953-4	Eddy B. Choong
1954-5	Ikke afviklet
1955-6	Finn Kobberø
1956-65	Ikke afviklet
1965-6	Svend Pri
1966-7	Tan Aik Huang
1967-8	Erland Kops
1968-9	Svend Pri
1969-70	Ippei Kojima
1970-1	Rudy Hartono
1971-2	Svend Pri
1972-3	Rudy Hartono
1973-4	Svend Pri
1974-5	Rudy Hartono
1975-6	Svend Pri
1976-7	Flemming Delfs
1977-8	Liem Swie King
1978-9	Flemming Delfs
1979-80	Prakash Padukone
1980-1	Morten Frost
1981-2	Morten Frost
1982-3	Morten Frost
1983-4	Morten Frost
1984-5	Morten Frost
1985-6	Morten Frost

Ladies' Singles

1935-6	Ruth Frederiksen[1]
1936-7	Tonny Olsen[2]
1937-8	D.M.C. Young[3]
1938-9	Tonny Olsen[2]
1939-45	Ikke afviklet
1945-6	Tonny Olsen[2]
1946-7	Tonny Ahm
1947-8	Tonny Ahm
1948-9	Tonny Ahm
1949-50	Tonny Ahm
1950-1	Tonny Ahm
1951-2	Aase Schiøtt Jacobsen
1952-3	Ikke afviklet

1953-4	Aase Schiøtt Jacobsen
1954-5	Ikke afviklet
1955-6	Aase Schiøtt Jacobsen
1956-65	Ikke afviklet
1965-6	Lizbeth von Barnekow([13])
1966-7	Noriko Takagi([15])
1967-8	Eva Twedberg
1968-9	Hiroe Yuki
1969-70	Eva Twedberg
1970-1	Noriko Takagi([15])
1971-2	Eva Twedberg
1972-3	Hiroe Yuki
1973-4	Hiroe Yuki
1974-5	Lene Køppen
1975-6	Lene Køppen
1976-7	Hiroe Yuki
1977-8	Lene Køppen
1978-9	Lene Køppen
1979-80	Yoshiko Yonekura
1980-1	Lene Køppen
1981-2	Wu Jianqiu
1982-3	Qian Ping
1983-4	Kirsten Larsen
1984-5	Han Aiping
1985-6	Yun Ja Kim

Men's Doubles

1935-6	AkselHansen/Sven Strømann
1936-7	T.H. Boyle/K. Wood
1937-8	Tage Madsen/Carl Frøhike
1938-9	R.C.F. Nichols/R.M. White
1939-45	Ikke afviklet
1945-6	Jørn Skaarup/Preben Dabelsteen
1946-7	Jørn Skaarup/Preben Dabelsteen
1947-8	Tage Madsen/Børge Frederiksen
1948-9	Ooi Teik Hock/Teoh Seng Khoon
1949-50	Avre Lossmann/John Nygaard
1950-1	Ong Poh Lim/Ismail bin Marjan
1951-2	Ib Olesen/John Nygaard
1952-3	Ikke afviklet
1953-4	E.L. Choong/Eddy B. Choong
1954-5	Ikke afviklet
1955-6	Finn Kobberø/Jørgen Hammergaard Hansen
1956-65	Ikke afviklet
1965-6	Ng Boon Bee/Tan Yee Khan
1966-7	Ng Boon Bee/Tan Yee Khan
1967-8	Ippei Kojima/I. Nishino
1968-9	Ippei Kojima/Bjarne Andersen
1969-70	Erland Kops/Henning Borch
1970-1	Ng Boon Bee/Per Gunalan
1971-2	Ng Boon Bee/Per Gunalan
1972-3	Tjun Tjun/Johs. Wahjudi
1973-4	Tjun Tjun/Johs. Wahjudi
1974-5	Tjun Tjun/Johs. Wahjudi
1975-6	David Eddy/Eddie Sutton
1976-7	Bengt Fröman/Thomas Kihlström
1977-8	Flemming Delfs/Steen Skovgaard
1978-9	Masao Tsuchida/Yochitaka Iino
1979-80	Flemming Delfs/Steen Skovgaard
1980-1	Christian Hadinata/Ade Chandra
1981-2	Joo Bang Park/Eun Ku Lee
1982-3	Thomas Kihlström/Stefan Karlsson
1983-4	Joo Bang Park/Moon Soo Kim
1984-5	Zhang Qiang/Zhou Jincan
1985-6	S. Fladberg/J. Helledie

Ladies' Doubles

1935-6	Tonny Olsen([2])/Bodil Rise([4])
1936-7	Ruth Dalsgaard/D. Graham
1937-8	Tonny Olsen([2])/Bodil Rise([4])
1938-9	Ruth Dalsgaard/Q.M. Allen([7])
1939-45	Ikke afviklet
1945-6	Tonny Olsen([2])/Kirsten Thorndahl
1946-7	Aase Schiøtt Jacobsen/Marie Ussing([11])
1947-8	Tonny Ahm/Kirsten Thorndahl
1948-9	Tonny Ahm/Kirsten Thorndahl
1949-50	Tonny Ahm/Kirsten Thorndahl
1950-1	Tonny Ahm/Kirsten Thorndahl
1951-2	Tonny Ahm/Kirsten Thorndahl
1952-3	Ikke afviklet
1953-4	Iris L. Cooley([8])/June R. White([9])
1954-5	Ikke afviklet
1955-6	Anni Jørgensen([10])/Kirsten Thorndahl
1956-65	Ikke afviklet
1965-6	Karin Jørgensen/Ulla Strand
1966-7	Noriko Takagi([15])/H. Amano
1967-8	Noriko Takagi([15])/H. Amano
1968-9	Noriko Takagi([15])/Hiroe Yuki
1969-70	Etsuko Takenaka/Machiko Aizawa
1970-1	Noriko Takagi([15])/Hiroe Yuki
1971-2	Noriko Nakayama/Hiroe Yuki
1972-3	Joke van Beusekom/Marjan Luesken([17])
1973-4	Etsuko Takenaka/Machiko Aizawa
1974-5	Imelda Wiguno/Theresia Widiastuty
1975-6	Joke van Beusekom/Marjan Luesken([17])
1976-7	Barbara Giles([18])/Jane Webster
1977-8	Wiharjo Verawaty/Imelda Wiguno
1978-9	Mikiko Takada/Atsuko Tokuda
1979-80	Gillian Gilks/Nora Perry
1980-1	Nora Perry/Jane Webster
1981-2	Lin Ying/Wu Dixi
1982-3	Nora Perry/Jane Webster
1983-4	Yun Ja Kim/Sang Hee Yoo
1984-5	Lin Ying/Wu Dixi
1985-6	Yun Ja Kim/Sang Hee Yoo

Mixed Doubles

1935-6	Poul Vang Nielsen/Ruth Frederiksen([1])
1936-7	T.H. Boyle/O. Wilson
1937-8	H.S. Ong/F.M. Green([5])
1939-9	R.C.F. Nichols/B.M. Staples([6])
1939-45	Ikke afviklet
1945-6	Tage Madsen/Kirsten Thorndahl
1946-7	Tage Madsen/Kirsten Thorndahl
1947-8	Tage Madsen/Kirsten Thorndahl
1948-9	Chan Kon Leong/Tonny Ahm
1949-50	Børge Frederiksen/Tonny Ahm
1950-1	Arve Lossmann/Kirsten Thorndahl
1951-2	E.L. Choong/Tonny Ahm
1952-3	Ikke afviklet
1953-4	Eddy B. Choong/Agnete Friis([12])
1954-5	Ikke afviklet
1955-6	Jørn Skaarup/Anni Jørgensen([10])
1956-65	Ikke afviklet
1965-6	Finn Kobberø/Ulla Strand
1966-7	Svend Pri/Ulla Strand
1967-8	Per Walsøe/Pernille Mølgaard

Hansen[14]

1968-9	Henning Borch/Imre Rietveld Nielsen
1969-70	Klaus Kaagaard/Ulla Strand
1970-1	Svend Pri/Ulla Strand
1971-2	Wolfgang Bochow/Marie Louise Wackerow[16]
1972-3	Elo Hansen/Ulla Strand
1973-4	Elo Hansen/Ulla Strand
1974-5	Tjun Tjun/Regina Masli
1975-6	Steen Skovgaard/Lene Køppen
1976-7	Steen Skovgaard/Lene Køppen
1977-8	Steen Skovgaard/Lene Køppen
1978-9	Ray Stevens/Nora C. Perry
1979-80	Mike Tredgett/Nora C. Perry
1980-1	Mike Tredgett/Nora C. Perry
1981-2	Thomas Kihlström/Nora Perry
1982-3	Thomas Kihlström/Nora Perry
1983-4	Martin Dew/Gillian Gilks
1984-5	Martin Dew/Gillian Gilks
1985-6	Nigel Tier/Gillian Gowers

[1] Mrs R. Dalsgaard
[2] Mrs G. Ahm
[3] Mrs J. Warrington
[4] Mrs B. Duus
[5] Mrs Henderson
[6] Mrs J.B. Shearlaw
[7] Mrs F.G. Webber
[8] Mrs W.C.E. Rogers
[9] Mrs E.J. Timperley
[10] Mrs J. Hammergaard Hansen
[11] Mrs A. Nylen
[12] Mrs O. Varn
[13] Mrs L. Yvind
[14] Mrs P. Kaagaard
[15] Mrs M. Nakayama
[16] Mrs M.L. Zizmann
[17] Mrs M. Ridder
[18] Mrs B. Sutton
[19] Mrs I. Kurniawan

DEVELOPMENT SUB-COMMITTEE

An IBF committee – Torsten Berg, Emile ter Metz and Charoen Wattanasin (q.v.) – set up in 1985 to supplement the Ferry Sonneville Coaching Fund (q.v.).

Steps taken to help inexperienced badminton countries will be (1) provision of equipment and coaches; (2) production of videos showing highlights, VIPS and large crowds to convince reluctant authorities that badminton deserves support; (3) instructional videos; (4) a detailed coaching handbook in English for translation into a country's own language; (5) more contact with top-class badminton; (6) invitation to European coaching schools and setting up of similar schools in each continent.

The IBF envisages ploughing back a large proportion of its growing income into fostering the game world-wide.

DEVLIN CUP

An annual competition between mixed teams from the USA and Canada inaugurated by J.F. Devlin in 1966.

DEVLIN, J. Frank (Ireland)

One of the 'Golden Greats' of the 1920s. Determined and aggressive, he was 'a colossus who strode the courts breathing fire'.

Devlin won eighteen AEC titles (six men's singles, five in succession; seven men's doubles (six with G.S.B. Mack) and five mixed doubles). He also sired two daughters of almost equal distinction: Judy Hashman, ten times winner of AEC singles title, and Sue Peard who, with Judy, won the doubles title six times.

He had a supple wrist (and an elbow reputedly double-jointed), an aggressive return of service, deceptive drop-shots, a consistently accurate smash and 'the most remarkable retrieving powers ever seen'. He was the first player to use and perfect the overhead backhand clear. In full flow, he 'steamed like mother's copper', to use the words of John Vincent.

He edited the *Badminton Gazette* for a short time and wrote *Badminton for All*.

At his peak Devlin moved to N. America, to coach in Winnipeg and Baltimore. Now, aged eighty-four, he is still coaching – in a village hall near Dublin. Awarded IBF's DS Award.

DEW, Martin (Middlesex and England)
Born 16 August 1958

Believing in 'seizing my chance', he did so in the 1981 English Masters when, comparatively unknown and deputizing at the last moment for an injured Ray Stevens, he was paired with fellow left-hander Mike Tredgett – to gain a fairy-story victory over favourites Kihlstrom and Karlsson (15-9, 2-15, 15-10) and £750.

Since then he has achieved world class. With Tredgett he reached the 1983 World Championship and the 1984 AEC finals – only to lose both. The latter was compensated for by the European Championships title. Now partnering another left-hander, Steve Baddeley, he reached the semis of both the Japanese Open and the 1985 AEC, losing only narrowly 18-15, 14-18, 13-18 in the latter to Kjeldsen and Christiansen.

Gillian Gilks and he became virtually unassailable in mixed. Between 1982 and 1984 they won the AEC (twice), Alba Quartz, European Championship (twice), Scandinavian Cup (twice), English Masters and Danish, Japanese and Indonesian Opens – yet surprisingly lost in the 1985 AEC SF to the scratch pair Kihlstrom and Clark, and in the World Championships to ultimate winners un-seeded Koreans Park and Yoo 6-15, 15-0, 10-15 in the quarters.

Moving fast round the court, jumping for the early take, he is powerful in smash and drive on both wings, and an aggressive receiver. A shrewd tactician, his dead-pan coolness on court seems almost arrogant.

Still working to complete a PhD, he was not a full-time player. In 1985 he acquired his doctorate, a Danish girl-friend and, sadly for England, a plum job with NKT near Copenhagen.

A fine cricketer, Dew might have been capped for Middlesex but has been capped eighty-one times for badminton (England).

DISABLED, Amended Rules for

The Laws have been amended for *semi-ambulant* (those using stick(s) crutch(es), zimmer, leg-brace(s) for erect perambulation or artificial leg(s)); *non-ambulant* (those needing support in sedentary posture by chair, stool or wheelchair). Amended court diagrams are shown overleaf.

In doubles, players serve from and receive throughout within the same service courts as those adopted at the beginning of a game. When points are won, the serve passes alternately from one partner to the other, so rendering unnecessary physical movement to the other service court.

In singles, players serve and play from court areas directly opposite each other.

Service Law 14a is not applicable to non-ambulant players. In 14c, 'mechan-ical aid' or 'support' must be within the court boundary; 14(i) is extended so that if 'mechanical aid' or 'support' is hit by the shuttle, it is a fault. Law 16, 'mechanical aid' and 'supports' in contact with the floor must also be, within court boundaries, stationary, until the service is delivered.

Shuttles of regulation speed, tested by an ambulant or able-bodied player of average strength on a standard court, are used.

All other Laws are unchanged.

See pages 40-41.

DIVORCE AREA

Narrow rectangle 8-11 feet (2.4-3.3 metres) from the net, between rear-court and fore-court players, and between the side-lines.

It is so called in relation to mixed play when irate husbands have been known to berate over-enthusiastic wives when they have clashed rackets in this area normally regarded as sacrosanct to the male. Worse still, the male, when playing with the club 'dolly-bird', tends to be apologetic – not aggressive.

In all seriousness, it *is* a vulnerable target area. If a push shot played with deception is hit fast enough to beat the net player but not fast enough to put it on the man's racket at tape-height, one of several benefits may result. These are: (1) a clash of rackets; (2) a strokeless 'leave' by both players; (3) misunderstanding; (4) a lifted return by the man; (5) a weak, uncontrolled shot by the woman; (6) remainder of court left open.

DOBSON, Chris (Worcestershire and England) Born 25 December 1963, Barnsley

One of England's most promising men's doubles players, Dobson won the 1981-2 English National U.18 with Dipak Tailor as well as the Six Nations Junior and the National 1982 U.21 titles. On the strength of the latter, he gained valuable experience when selected for the 1982 China Tour.

In a 1983 return fixture at Leicester he dislocated his shoulder and was side-lined for nine months but was back in time to play in the 1984 Thomas Cup and against a visiting Chinese team. He owes a powerful smash and consistency (especially in serving) to former national coach (and Glamorgan cricketer) Maur-ice Robinson.

1984 Victor Cup MD with D. Tailor (achieved by beating three Indonesian

SEMI-AMBULANT   NON-AMBULANT

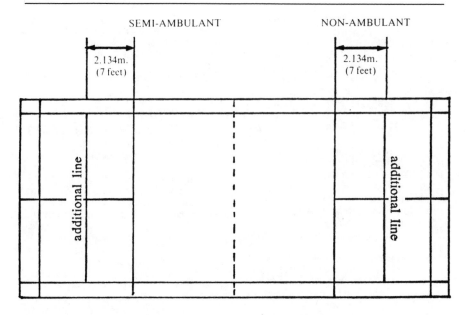

pairs) is his best win to date. Fifteen caps. Ranked No. 10. Now living in Halesowen.

DOLBY, Colonel S.S.C.

The godfather of badminton? It was due to his initiative that fourteen clubs were called together to found the first-ever Badminton Association in 1893.

It was his hard work and inspiration, not merely as President (1893-98) but also as Hon. Secretary and Hon. Treasurer (1893-99) before sterner duties called him to the Boer War, that led to its continued success. He was also a member of the Services Club at Southsea, Hon. Secretary until 1920 of Ealing BC and, in 1912, winner of the AEC Veterans Men's Doubles.

DOUBLE-HIT

A seemingly single stroke, in which the player, generally involuntarily, hits the shuttle with two almost simultaneous strokes. This is a fault and should be so called by the striker himself where there is no umpire (Law 14(h)). Without this Law it would be possible for a player to hit a shuttle up to himself and then 'kill' it.

It is also a fault if one player just tips the shuttle before his partner hits it over the net.

DOWNEY, Jake
Born 5 July 1936, Manchester

A Middlesex and potential England player, his active career was ended in Germany when after an all-night journey on his 125 Vespa he dozed off, crashed and sustained serious leg and knee injuries.

Out of evil came good. As a National Coach, he worked individually with such leading players as Gillian Gilks and Ray Stevens, as well as coaching the 1972 and 1975 Uber Cup teams. Today he is one of the BAE's four senior coaches.

Seven detailed coaching books, including *Get Fit for Badminton, Better Badminton for All* and *Winning Doubles*, carry his name as author.

In 1985 he was appointed England Team Manager in succession to Ciro Ciniglio, with the added brief to reorganize and improve the whole standard of coaching.

Top players petitioned for his removal when he dropped Dew and Nora Perry from Thomas and Uber Cup teams when they pleaded inability to travel *with* the rest of the team for early acclimatization. He was backed by the BAE but they nevertheless sent Paul Whetnall and Heather Nielsen with him as necessary aides.

(Doubles Play) shaded area indicates extent of court

Left service court   side line

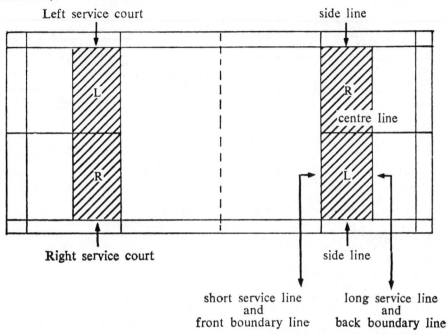

centre line

Right service court   side line

short service line
and
front boundary line

long service line
and
back boundary line

Singles Play   shaded area indicates extent of court

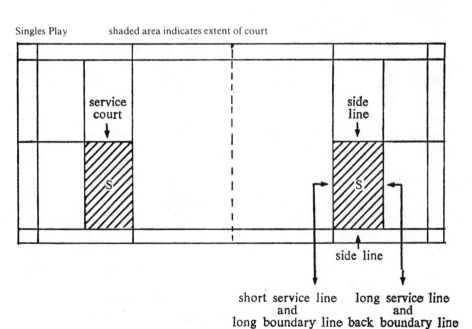

service
court

side
line

side line

short service line   long service line
and   and
long boundary line back boundary line

DOYLE, J.P. 'Chick' (Ireland), 1930-85

Encouraged by his father, coached by Frank Peard and Geoff Trapnell and putting in six hours' practice a day, Doyle won four caps before he was twenty-one. Then he emigrated to Victoria, Australia, in furtherance of his career – as a chicken-sexer. He might have been winner rather than runner-up in the Australian Championship Singles (his forte) had he not played hard (he knew no other way) every night of the preceding fortnight.

He is reputed to have written to Irish title-holder Frank Peard, 'Don't get beaten till I come back.' In fact, after his return he won the National singles eight times in succession (1953/4-1960/1). Fine footwork (he was also a champion Irish step-dancer), a wide range of strokes, and deception helped him to win thirty-five caps (1953-65).

On retirement, he worked wholeheartedly for Leinster (becoming President) and is proud of having won the father/child tournament there with each of his children, all four of whom have gained various junior provincial honours.

Humorist and enthusiast, life-long teetotaller and non-smoker, he was a queasy traveller reputed to have taken a for once un-used Aer Lingus 'bag' onto London buses – just in case!

DRAW

The chance arrangement of tournament entrants in a particular event which determines a player's immediate and possible opponents in subsequent rounds up to the final.

Seeds (q.v.) have first to be allotted their correct 'slots' or positions. Only then are the other entrants drawn into those remaining. By incredible and unique coincidence, Heather Guntrip, wife of a bookmaker, beat millions-to-one against odds by being drawn No. 2 in all three AEC events – thus each time meeting the top seeds, who included the Devlin sisters, Margaret Varner and P.E. Nielsen!

There are, of course, no seeds in a handicap event as players or pairs are *ipso facto* deemed, after handicapping, of equal ability.

In tournaments with an international entry, to prevent an early ludicrous meeting between players from the same country, possibly the same club, who have travelled thousands of miles to play, other regulations apply: (a) any 2 seeded entries from the same country will be drawn in separate halves; any three or four in separate quarters; (b) two unseeded entries will be placed in separate halves; four best entries in separate quarters, and the next best entries, up to four, in separate eighths.

DRIFT

Strong air current, down or cross-court, often present in large halls not specially built for badminton. Even top players find it difficult to adjust to or to retain concentration in these conditions.

Lene Köppen in her own Bronby Hallen consistently hit 'out' with the drift, and 'short' into it in the World Championships. In a Wembley Arena mixed final, 1954, Finn Kobbero frequently left side-line shots apparently falling 12-18 inches out, only to see them drift 'in' – and was demoralized! At the same venue, joker Svend Pri, suffering the same fate, begged spectators: 'Please, shut the door!'

DRIVE

A hard-hit attacking stroke played generally from the side-lines, mid-court, when the shuttle, just above tape-height, is not high enough to be smashed downwards.

It may be used in men's or ladies' doubles though against a well-placed defending pair its very speed may rebound against an off-balance attacker. It is therefore much more used in mixed doubles where, with the man generally having to defend the whole width of the court, the side-lines are vulnerable.

It is a side-arm stroke played with the right foot across and a shoulder-high throwing action somewhat akin to that used from cover-point in cricket, or in skimming a stone or throwing a frisbee. Struck just in front of the body with full arm and wrist action, the shuttle travels fast, flat and straight. Taken 12 to 18 inches (30 to 45 centimetres) further forward, or by accentuating the use of the wrist, it can be hit cross-court.

The latter, tending to be the more natural action, tends to be over-used by beginners and so loses surprise. It is most effectively used when *both* opponents have first been lured from central bases to the side-line and the shuttle can be hit flat, or downwards, across the full width of the court without undue fear of interception.

It may also be used in singles, flat or lofted, when an attacking lob or clear, is falling behind the player.

DROP-SHOT

The third of the three basic overhead strokes. Unlike the other two, clear and smash (q.v.), it is a delicate stroke, relying on touch and deception, not power, for its success. There are two types, the slow and the fast, and both may be played conventionally or sliced.

Slow drop-shot
The aim is to hit the shuttle gently downwards so that it drops as close to the net as possible – ideally within 2 feet (0.6 metres). If very deceptively and accurately played it may be an outright winner. More often, however, it is used from the baseline as an alternative to the clear, maintaining the attack and forcing, hopefully, a short lob that can be smashed.

It is used frequently in singles where, by alternating it with the attacking clear, it is part and parcel of the general strategy of moving the opponent up and down the length of the court. It is also used in men's and ladies' doubles to maintain the attack when a smash is impracticable.

It is played for the sake of deception, with a strong throwing action identical to that for the clear or smash. At the last possible split second, arm and wrist are slowed down and the shuttle is hit downwards with gentle but firm follow-through. Further deception is added when, with a slight turn of the wrist, the shuttle is deflected to the corner. This is done mainly in singles; in doubles the shuttle is generally hit to the centre to cause possible confusion as to the taker and to narrow the angle of return, or nearer the slower or weaker player.

Fast drop-shot
With the woman permanently at the net in mixed doubles, a slow drop-shot to that area would receive short shrift. The fast drop-shot is then employed to hit the shuttle to the 'divorce area' (q.v.) between man and woman. It is just fast enough to pass the woman but slow enough to force the man to move in and to lift.

DRUG-TESTING

This was introduced at the AEC in 1979 in accordance with Olympic Committee recommendation. The man in charge was Peter Mascarenhas.

The tests are for amphetamines etc and anabolic steroids which can artificially augment a player's performance mentally or physically. Six event positions are randomly selected before the draw is made, so chance alone decides the players to be tested. These give a urine sample immediately after the match but results cannot be formulated until thirty-six hours later. If a positive result is found, it can be challenged and another test made by different analysts from the remaining half of the sample.

E

EARLY BADMINTON

E.C. St John recounted how his father (R.F. St Andrew St John, a professor of Hindustani) founded a club in a West Ealing drill hall in 1890. Play was on a court 60 by 30 feet, with a net 6 feet high at the posts. Players generally numbered three or four a-side, five if women played, as they never ran.

Rackets were either Sealkot rackets or squash or tennis 'bats'. Woollen balls were superseded by rubber-based, heavy 'cauliflower' shuttles which often broke the Sealkot rackets. The game was familiarly known as 'hit and scream' because women did just that when in danger of being hit.

By 1892, courts (in Ealing Swimming Baths) had been reduced to the standard 44 × 20 feet and 5-foot-high net – but narrowed to a 16-foot waist at the net. Drive strokes outside the posts were invalid. (In 1901 the 'waist' was abolished.) Matches – 15 points up – were arranged and Ealing, with such famous early names as S.M. Massey, A.D. Prebble, J.H.E. Hart and G.W. Vidal, were unbeaten for seven years.

It was R.W. St A. St John who organized the first Badminton Association tournament (three events in one day) in 1899.

EBU HANDBOOK

A brave attempt by Nada Benesova of Prague to keep alive at least the European records section of the IBF Handbook which was forced to cease publication by financial difficulties.

It involved researching scattered data in 500 issues of twelve magazines in seven different languages. Its 181 one-sided pages were typed, duplicated and bound.

Unhappily it was a project that could not be sustained.

EBU PLAYING SCHOLARSHIP

Instituted in 1981 this is an award to 'a promising and dedicated player of an exemplary on-court and off-court behaviour' of one of the 'emergent' European countries. It grants free attendance at the EBU Summer School (q.v.).

Winners
1982 Michael Maly (Czechoslovakia)
1983 Mark Richards (Wales)
1984 Pontus Jantli (Finland)
1985 Hans Sperre (Norway)
1986 Christine Jacobs (Belgium)

EFFECTIVE AREA OF RESPONSE

That part of a racket's stringing where it is at its most positive. It radiates from roughly the centre of the racket outwards until the frame causes 'rigiding'.

It has been established that this area is some eighty per cent of the whole of a fine gut strung racket but only about twenty per cent of one with a poor-quality synthetic gut. This small centre area is struck perhaps only twice in ten strokes by lower-class players.

ELLIOTT, Fiona (Surrey and England)
Born 13 November 1963, Farnborough

England's No. 4 who was National Singles Champion in 1983/4 and 1984/5 – though with Helen Troke absent. She was keen enough to pay her own fare to go on Far East tour. U.21 ladies' singles and mixed doubles in 1983. Twenty-one U.23 caps and sixteen 'full' caps.

Awarded £1000 bonus by the sponsors of Prudential Lancashire Open to cover expenses to 1986 Japanese Open in which she reached the Mixed 'quarters'.

ENDORSEMENT

The use, for advertising purposes, of a famous player's name to recommend the use of one specific firm's rackets, shuttles, shoes or clothing. The player concerned is paid a fee and contracted to use only that firm's equipment.

ENGLISH MASTERS

Foreseeing the IBF sanctioning of Open badminton in June 1979, the BAE beat the world to it by presenting the first (already planned) Masters event – in September – and in the prestigious Albert Hall, London, at that. The first venture was generously sponsored by Friends' Provident Life Office. So were the 1980 and 1981 Masters. The 1982 event was cancelled because BBC viewing figures were so low that it was not considered viable; the sponsors not surprisingly withdrew support. In 1983 it was revived with Famous Grouse sponsorship at Warrington, and in 1984 and 1985, backed by British Airways, at Portsmouth and Bournemouth respectively. 1986 back at the Albert Hall.

Men's Singles
1979 P. Padukone
1980 Liem Swie King
1981 Luan Jin
1983 J.P. Nierhoff
1984 M. Frost
1985 M. Frost

Ladies' Singles
1979 L. Køppen
1980 L. Køppen
1981 Zhang Ailing
1983 Chen Ruizhen
1984 K. Larsen
1985 K. Karsen

Men's Doubles
1979 T. Kihlström/B. Froman
1980 C. Hadinata/A. Chandra
1981 M.C. Dew/M.G. Tredgett
1983 T. Kihlström/S. Karlsson
1984 C. Hadinata/S. Hadibowo
1985 N. Tier/A. Goode

Ladies' Doubles
1979 N. Perry/J. Webster
1980 Y. Yonekura/A. Tokuda
1981 Liu Xia/Zhang Ailing
1983 Chen Ruizhen/Zheng Jian
1984 Lin Ying/Wu Dixi
1985 K. Beckman/S. Halsall

Mixed Doubles
1979 —
1980 C. Hadinata/I. Wigoeno
1981 M.G. Tredgett/N. Perry
1983 M.C. Dew/G. Gilks
1984 M.C. Dew/G. Gilks
1985 W. Gilliland/G. Gowers

ENGLISH NATIONAL CHAMPIONSHIPS

The winners of the English Invitation Tournament, started in 1953/4, were long regarded as English champions. As the invitees were limited in number, it was felt, in 1963/4, that in fairness every player desirous of competing should be given the opportunity to do so. Accordingly the English National Championships were instituted that year at Wimbledon. The entry was so big that two evenings had to be allocated to qualifying rounds.

Unfortunately the event has recently lost some status as top players do not always enter because of the paucity of the prize-money or their overseas commitments.

Additionally, in 1971/2, in order to improve English singles play vis à vis Asian players, the English Invitation Singles Tournament was instituted.

An attempt to rectify this was made in 1986 with qualifying rounds at Altrincham and finals – to accommodate top players returning from Japan – two days later at Woking.

Men's Singles
1963-4 W.F. Havers
1964-5 R.J. Mills
1965-6 R.J. Mills
1966-7 R.J. Mills
1967-8 R.J. Sharp
1968-9 R.J. Sharp
1969-70 P.E. Whetnall
1970-1 D. Talbot
1971-2 D. Talbot
1972-3 R.P. Stevens
1973-4 D. Talbot
1974-5 P.E. Whetnall
1975-6 P.E. Whetnall
1976-7 R.P. Stevens
1977-8 D. Talbot
1978-9 R.P. Stevens
1979-80 R.P. Stevens

1980-1	R.P. Stevens
1981-2	S.J. Baddeley
1982-3	K.R. Jolly
1983-4	A.B. Goode
1984-5	S.J. Baddeley
1985-6	D. Hall

Ladies' Singles

1963-4	Miss U.H. Smith([5])
1964-5	Miss A.M. Bairstow([4])
1965-6	Miss U.H. Smith([5])
1966-7	Miss U.H. Smith([5])
1967-8	Miss A.M. Bairstow([4])
1968-9	Miss G.M. Perrin([6])
1969-70	Miss G.M. Perrin([6])
1970-1	Mrs M.A. Gilks
1971-2	Miss M. Beck([8])
1972-3	Miss M. Beck([8])
1973-4	Miss M. Beck([8])
1974-5	Miss M. Beck([8])
1975-6	Mrs. M.A. Gilks
1976-7	Mrs R.J. Lockwood
1977-8	Mrs M.A. Gilks
1978-9	Mrs G.M. Gilks
1979-80	Mrs G.M. Gilks
1980-1	Mrs G.M. Gilks
1981-2	Miss J.A. Webster([14])
1982-3	Mrs K.S. Beckman
1983-4	Miss F. Elliott
1984-5	Miss F. Elliott
1985-6	Miss H. Troke

Men's Doubles

1963-4	C.T. Coates/A.D. Jordan
1964-5	J.N. Havers/W.F. Havers
1965-6	C.J. Beacom/A.D. Jordan
1966-7	R.J. Mills/D.O. Horton
1967-8	C.J. Beacom/A.D. Jordan
1968-9	J.D. Eddy/R.A. Powell
1969-70	R.J. Mills/A.D. Jordan
1970-1	E.C. Stuart/D. Talbot
1971-2	E.C. Stuart/D. Talbot
1972-3	R.P. Stevens/M.G. Tredgett
1973-4	E.C. Stuart/D. Talbot
1974-5	J.D. Eddy/E.H. Sutton
1975-6	R.P. Stevens/M.G. Tredgett
1976-7	R.P. Stevens/M.G. Tredgett
1977-8	R.P. Stevens/M.G. Tredgett
1978-9	R.P. Stevens/M.G. Tredgett
1979-80	R.P. Stevens/M.G. Tredgett
1980-1	R.P. Stevens/M.G. Tredgett
1981-2	M.C. Dew/D.P. Bridge
1982-3	M.C. Dew/M.G. Tredgett
1983-4	M.C. Dew/M.G. Tredgett
1984-5	S.J. Baddeley/M.G. Tredgett
1985-6	N. Tier/A. Goode

Ladies' Doubles

1963-4	Miss U.H. Smith([5])/Miss H.J. Pritchard([1])

1964-5	Miss U.H. Smith([5])/Miss H.J. Pritchard([1])
1965-6	Miss A.M. Bairstow([4])/Mrs G.W. Barrand
1966-7	Miss S.D. Pound([2])/Miss M.B. Boxall([7])
1967-8	Miss S.D. Pound([2])/Miss M.B. Boxall([7])
1968-9	Mrs P.E. Whetnall/Miss M.B. Boxall([7])
1969-70	Mrs P.E. Whetnall/Miss M.B. Boxall([7])
1970-1	Miss M. Beck([8])/Mrs W.R. Rickard
1971-2	Mrs G.C.K. Hashman/Mrs M.A. Gilks
1972-3	Mrs G.C.K. Hashman/Mrs M.A. Gilks
1973-4	Miss N.C. Gardner([9])/Mrs M.A. Gilks
1974-5	Mrs P.E. Whetnall/Miss M.B. Boxall([7])
1975-6	Mrs P.E. Whetnall/Mrs M.A. Gilks
1976-7	Miss B. Giles([10])/Mrs M.A. Gilks
1977-8	Mrs J.P. Perry/Mrs A.E. Statt
1978-9	Mrs G.M. Gilks/Miss J.A. Webster([14])
1979-80	Mrs J.P. Perry/Miss K.T. Puttick([12])
1980-1	Miss K. Bridge/Mrs B. Sutton
1981-2	Mrs J.P. Perry/Miss J.A. Webster([14])
1982-3	Mrs J.P. Perry/Miss J.A. Webster([14])
1983-4	Mrs G.M. Gilks/Miss P.M. Kilvington
1984-5	Miss G.M. Clark/Miss G.C. Gowers
1985-6	Miss G.C. Gowers/Miss H. Troke

Mixed Doubles

1963-4	C.J. Beacom/Miss H.J. Pritchard([1])
1964-5	R.J. Mills/Mrs G.W. Barrand
1965-6	A.D. Jordan/Miss J.E. Charles([3])
1966-7	D.O. Horton/Mrs D.O. Horton
1967-8	R.J. Mills/Miss G.M. Perrin([6])
1968-9	R.J. Mills/Miss G.M. Perrin([6])
1969-70	P.E. Whetnall/Miss M.B. Boxall([7])
1970-1	R.J. Mills/Mrs M.A. Gilks
1971-2	D. Talbot/Mrs M.A. Gilks
1972-3	D.R. Hunt/Mrs M.A. Gilks
1973-4	D. Talbot/Mrs M.A. Gilks
1974-5	D. Talbot/Mrs M.A. Gilks
1975-6	D. Talbot/Mrs M.A. Gilks
1976-7	M.G. Tredgett/Miss N.C. Gardner([9])
1977-8	M.G. Tredgett/Mrs J.P. Perry
1978-9	M.G. Tredgett/Mrs J.P. Perry
1979-80	M.G. Tredgett/Mrs J.P. Perry
1980-1	M.G. Tredgett/Mrs J.P. Perry
1981-2	M.C. Dew/Mrs J.P. Perry
1982-3	M.G. Tredgett/Miss G.M. Clark
1983-4	M.C. Dew/Mrs G.M. Gilks
1984-5	D:P. Tailor/Mrs G.M. Gilks
1985-6	N. Tier/Miss G.C. Gowers

([1]) Later Mrs D.O. Horton
([2]) Later Mrs P.E. Whetnall
([3]) Later Mrs W.R. Rickard
([4]) Later Mrs H.I. Palmer
([5]) Later Mrs L. Oakley
([6]) Later Mrs M.A. Gilks
([7]) Later Mrs E.J. Allen
([8]) Later Mrs R.J. Lockwood
([9]) Later Mrs J.P. Perry
([10]) Later Mrs E.H. Sutton
([11]) Later Mrs A.E. Skovgaard
([12]) Later Mrs K. Chapman
([13]) Later Mrs K.S. Beckman
([14]) Later Mrs P. Sutton

ENGLISH NATIONAL UNDER 21 CHAMPIONSHIPS

Men's Singles
1978   A.R. Goode
1979   K.R. Jolly
1980   S.J. Baddeley
1981   S.J. Baddeley
1982   S.P. Butler
1983   D.J. Hall
1984   D.J. Hall

Ladies' Singles
1978   Miss K.S. Bridge[1]
1979   Miss K.S. Bridge[1]
1980   Miss H.S. Troke
1981   Miss H.S. Troke
1982   Miss W.J. Massam
1983   Miss F. Elliott
1984   Miss A.D. Fisher

Men's Doubles
1980   N.W. Goode/N.G. Tier
1981   G.S. Asquith/A.B. Goode
1982   D.P. Tailor/C.C. Dobson
1983   R.J. Outterside/G.J. Milton
1984   D.J. Hall/A. Wood

Ladies' Doubles
1980   Miss D. Simpson/Miss L.M. Whitaker
1981   Miss M.A. Leeves/Miss S.J. Leeves
1982   Miss G.M. Clark/Miss J.M. Pringle[2]
1983   Miss G.C. Gowers/Miss W.J. Massam
1984   Miss L.J. Chapman/Miss J.A. Shipman

Mixed Doubles
1980   S.H. Wootton/Miss J.M. Pringle
1981   R.J. Outterside/Miss Jill Benson
1982   M.J. Cattermole/Miss N.R. Bewley
1983   S.P. Butler/Miss F. Elliot
1984   A. Wood/Miss L.J. Chapman

[1] Later Mrs K.S. Beckman
[2] Later Mrs B. Wallwork

ENGLISH INVITATION TOURNAMENT

(*Discontinued after 1963*)

Men's Singles
1953-4   F.J. Shaw
1954-5   A.D. Jordan
1955-6   J.D. McColl
1956-7   A.D. Jordan
1957-8   P.J. Waddell
1958-9   A.D. Jordan
1959-60 C.T. Coates
1960-1   P.J. Waddell
1961-2   P.J. Waddell
1962-3   C.J. Beacom

Ladies' Singles
1953-4   Miss I.L. Cooley[2]
1954-5   Miss A.J. Stone[7]
1955-6   Miss I.L. Cooley[2]
1956-7   Miss H.M. Ward[4]
1957-8   Miss H.M. Ward[4]
1958-9   Miss H.M. Ward[4]
1959-60 Miss B. Bird
1960-1   Miss U.H. Smith[6]
1961-2   Miss U.H. Smith[6]
1962-3   Miss U.H. Smith[6]

Men's Doubles
1953-4   J.D. McColl/A.D. Jordan
1954-5   W. Shute/J.R. Best
1955-6   J.D. McColl/A.D. Jordan
1956-7   F.J. Shaw/R. Quiddington
1957-8   F.J. Shaw/J.D. McColl
1958-9   J.R. Best/A.D. Jordan
1959-60 P.J. Waddell/A.D. Jordan
1960-1   H.T. Findlay/R.J. Lockwood
1961-2   P.J. Waddell/A.D. Jordan
1962-3   P.J. Waddell/A.D. Jordan

Ladies' Doubles
1953-4   Miss I.L. Cooley[2]/Miss J.R. White[1]
1954-5   Miss A.J. Stone[7]/Mrs R.C.F. Nichols
1955-6   Miss I.L. Cooley[2]/Mrs E.J. Timperley
1956-7   Mrs W.C.E. Rogers/Mrs E.J. Timperley
1957-8   Mrs W.C.E. Rogers/Mrs E.J. Timperley
1958-9   Miss H.M. Ward[4]/Miss B.J. Carpenter
1959-60 Miss A.M.J. Marshall[3]/Miss U.H. Smith[6]
1960-1   Mrs C.F.R. Wilson/Miss U.H. Smith[6]
1961-2   Miss J.E. Charles[8]/Miss U.H. Smith[6]
1962-3   Mrs G.W. Barrand/Miss U.H. Smith[6]

Mixed Doubles
1953-4   A.D. Jordan/Miss J.R. White[1]
1954-5   J.R. Best/Miss A.J. Stone[7]
1955-6   J.R. Best/Miss I.L. Cooley[2]
1956-7   J.R. Best/Mrs W.C.E. Rogers
1957-8   A.D. Jordan/Mrs E.J. Timperley
1958-9   A.D. Jordan/Mrs E.J. Timperley
1959-60 R.J. Lockwood/Miss A.M.J. Marshall[3]
1960-1   W.E. Havers/Miss H.J. Pritchard[5]
1961-2   K.R. Derrick/Mrs G.W. Barrand
1962-3   A.D. Jordan/Mrs E.J. Timperley

[1] Later Mrs E.J. Timperley
[2] Later Mrs W.C.E. Rogers
[3] Later Mrs C.F.R. Wilson
[4] Later Mrs E.B. Nielsen
[5] Later Mrs H.J. Horton
[6] Later Mrs L. Oakley
[7] Later Mrs K. Dance
[8] Later Mrs W.R. Rickard

ENGLISH INVITATION SINGLES TOURNAMENT

Men's
1971-2	R.P. Stevens
1972-3	R.P. Stevens
1973-4	P.E. Whetnall
1974-5	R.P. Stevens
1975-6	P.E. Whetnall
1976-7	No Competition
1977-8	R.P. Stevens
1978-9	K.R. Jolly
1979-80	R.P. Stevens

Ladies'
1971-2	Miss M. Beck([1])
1972-3	Miss M. Beck([1])
1973-4	Miss M. Beck([1])
1974-5	Miss M. Beck([1])
1975-6	Mrs M.A. Gilks
1976-7	No Competition
1977-8	Miss P.M. Kilvington
1978-9	Miss J.A. Webster
1979-80	Miss K.S. Bridge

Now discontinued
([1]) Later Mrs R.J. Lockwood

ENGLISH NATIONAL JUNIOR CHAMPIONSHIPS

In 1950 the first All-England Junior Championships (U.18) were held at Wimbledon S & BC – and, because of an unexpectedly large entry, at Ebbisham BC as well. Cups had been donated by such great players as Sir George Thomas (BS), Mrs P.D. McFarlane (GS), D.C. Hume and R.C.F. Nichols (BD), Margaret Tragett and Betty Uber (GD) and E. Hawthorn and Judge A.F. Engelbach (Mxd D). F.J. Shaw (Notts) was a Triple Champion (and again in 1951); and fifteen-year-old Tony Jordan (later to earn a hundred English caps) was noted as 'outstanding'.

An U.15 Championship was instituted in 1962/3 for singles only. The girls' singles was won by G.M. Perrin (aged twelve and under six stone!) later to be the only Englishwoman to gain a hundred caps. Boys' and girls' doubles followed in 1969/70 and mixed in 1975/6.

In 1979/80 the AEJC became known as the English National Junior Championships to bring it in line with the senior event; in 1982/3 the old-fashioned U.15 became U.16, and by 1984/5 U.14 and U.12 events had logically been added.

The AEJC was played at the famous Wimbledon S & BC until 1978; then, because of increasing size, it was moved to Woking SC, and again to Watford SC.

(Restricted to competitors under 18 at midnight on the preceding 31st August/1st September and currently eligible to play for England. Up to 1979-80 known as All-England Junior Championships)

Boys' Singles
1949-50	F.J. Shaw
1950-1	F.J. Shaw
1951-2	A.D. Jordan
1952-3	G.H. King
1953-4	D. Jones
1954-5	A.P. Billingham
1955-6	P.J. Waddell
1956-7	Oon Chong Jin
1957-8	R.J. Mills
1958-9	R.J. Mills
1959-60	R.J. Mills
1960-1	Oon Chong Hau
1961-2	R.J. Westmorland
1962-3	Oon Chong Hau
1963-4	Oon Chong Hau
1964-5	Oon Chong Hau
1965-6	C.J. Kirk
1966-7	C.J. Kirk
1967-8	C.J. Kirk
1968-9	R.P. Stevens
1969-70	K.P. Arthur
1970-1	P.J. Gardner
1971-2	J.C. Stretch
1972-3	P.H. Wood
1973-4	P.H. Wood
1974-5	G.J. Scott
1975-6	G.J. Scott
1976-7	K.R. Jolly
1977-8	A.B. Goode
1978-9	N. Yates
1979-80	S.D. Wassell
1980-1	D.P. Tailor
1981-2	S.P. Butler
1982-3	D.J. Hall
1983-4	D.J. Hall
1984-5	M.A. Smith
1985-6	P. Bush

Girls' Singles
1949-50	Miss M.W. Glassborow
1950-1	Miss U.H. Smith([11])
1951-2	Miss U.H. Smith([11])
1952-3	Miss M. Semple([3])
1953-4	Miss H.M. Ward([4])
1954-5	Miss H.M. Ward([4])
1955-6	Miss H.M. Ward([4])
1956-7	Miss H.M. Ward([4])
1957-8	Miss A.M. Bairstow([12])
1958-9	Miss A.M. Bairstow([12])
1959-60	Miss A.M. Bairstow([12])
1960-1	Miss A.C. Price([7])
1961-2	Miss A.J. Swinstead([15])
1962-3	Miss M.B. Boxall([22])
1963-4	Miss S. Jones (Essex)
1964-5	Miss G.M. Perrin([18])
1965-6	Miss G.M. Perrin([18])
1966-7	Miss G.M. Perrin([18])
1967-8	Miss G.M. Perrin([18])
1968-9	Miss M. Beck([23])

1969-70 Miss M. Beck[23]
1970-1 Miss N.C. Gardner[25]
1971-2 Miss N.C. Gardner[25]
1972-3 Miss A.E. Forrest[21]
1973-4 Miss J.A. Webster[36]
1974-5 Miss P.M. Kilvington
1975-6 Miss K.S. Bridge[35]
1976-7 Miss K.S. Bridge[35]
1977-8 Miss K.S. Bridge[35]
1978-9 Miss S.J. Leadbeater[34]
1979-80 Miss S.J. Leadbeater[34]
1980-1 Miss M.A. Leeves
1981-2 Miss H.S. Troke
1982-3 Miss B.V. Blair
1983-4 Miss D. Hore
1984-5 Miss S.L. Halsall
1985-6 Miss S. Hore

Boys' Doubles
1949-50 F.J. Shaw/B.T. Grozier
1950-1 F.J. Shaw/B.T. Grozier
1951-2 A.D. Jordan/H.T. Findlay
1952-3 G.H. King/B.E. Fletcher
1953-4 D. Jones/E.J.R. Stanford
1954-5 G. Bell/L. Ellwood
1955-6 P.J. Waddell/A.E. Flashman
1956-7 P.J. Waddell/D. Winthrop
1957-8 D. Curtis/K. Paul
1958-9 R.J. Mills/D.J. Minton
1959-60 R.J. Mills/D.J. Minton
1960-1 J. Gisborne/D.J. Smith
1961-2 P.A. Seaman/P.R. Falle
1962-3 Oon Chong Hau/M.J. Boutle
1963-4 Oon Chong Hau/B.E. Jones
1964-5 Oon Chong Hau/B.E. Jones
1965-6 C.J. Kirk/P. Wing
1966-7 M. Beck/G.A. Connor
1967-8 C.J. Kirk/I.P. Clark
1968-9 T.A. Goode/J.F. Walter
1969-70 D.E. Hounslow/D.R.M. Pither
1970-1 J.C. Stretch/J.K.H. Woodgate
1971-2 J.C. Stretch/J.K.H. Woodgate
1972-3 R.A. Rofe/D.S. Whitfield
1973-4 R.A. Rofe/D.S. Whitfield
1974-5 D.P.B. Bridge/S.R. Stranks
1975-6 G.J. Scott/S.R. Stranks
1976-7 K.R. Jolly/N.G. Tier
1977-8 C.J. Fetherston/D.L. Roebuck
1978-9 S.J. Baddeley/D. Burden
1979-80 R.J. Outterside/N.S. Sargent
1980-1 D.P. Tailor/A.R. Wood
1981-2 C.C. Dobson/D.P. Tailor
1982-3 D.J. Hall/S.A. Spurling
1983-4 R.W. Baddeley/D.J. Hall
1984-5 A. Casey/P. Holden
1985-6 M. Bennett/R. Harmsworth

Girls' Doubles
1949-50 Miss J.R. White[1]/Miss L.M. Cash
1950-1 Miss I.A. Kenningham[2]/Miss U.H. Smith[11]
1951-2 Miss I.A. Kenningham[2]/Miss U.H. Smith[11]
1952-3 Miss M. Semple[3]/Miss K. Parr[5]
1953-4 Miss M. Semple[3]/Miss K. Parr[5]
1954-5 Miss H.M. Ward[4]/Miss S.A. Hole

1955-6 Miss H.M. Ward[4]/Miss H.J. Pritchard[6]
1956-7 Miss H.M. Ward[4]/Miss M.A. Bonney
1957-8 Miss G.H. Lawrence/Miss P.S. Wheating[9]
1958-9 Miss A.M. Bairstow[12]/Miss P.S. Wheating[9]
1959-60 Miss A.M. Bairstow[12]/Miss C.E. Lindsay
1960-1 Miss A.C. Price[7]/Miss S.D. Pound[10]
1961-2 Miss S. Jones/Miss A.J. Swinstead[15]
1962-3 Miss S. Jones/Miss M.B. Boxall[22]
1963-4 Miss M. Bridge[19]/Miss L.M. Veasey[28]
1964-5 Miss P. Protheroe/Miss L.M. Veasey[28]
1965-6 Miss W.J. Wilson/Miss L.M. Veasey[28]
1966-7 Miss G.M. Perrin[18]/Miss J.S. Colman[17]
1967-8 Miss M. Beck[23]/Miss C.M. Wightman
1968-9 Miss M. Beck[23]/Miss C.M. Wightman
1969-70 Miss B. Giles[29]/Miss S.B. Ringshall
1970-1 Miss B. Giles[29]/N.C. Gardner[25]
1971-2 Miss M.J.A. Brewer[24]/Miss N.C. Gardner[25]
1972-3 Miss A.E. Forrest[21]/Miss K. Redhead
1973-4 Miss A. Gardner/Miss K. Redhead
1974-5 Miss K.T. Puttick[30]/Miss A.G. Tuckett[26]
1975-6 Miss K.S. Bridge[35]/Miss R. Heywood[32]
1976-7 Miss K.S. Bridge[35]/Miss K.T. Puttick[30]
1977-8 Miss K.S. Bridge[35]/Miss G.M. Clark
1978-9 Miss G.M. Clark/Miss S.J. Leadbeater[34]
1979-80 Miss S.J. Leadbeater[34]/Miss G.M. Clark
1980-1 Miss M.A. Leeves/Miss S.J. Leeves
1981-2 Miss J.A. Edwards/Miss G.C. Gowers
1982-3 Miss L.J. Chapman/Miss J.A. Shipman
1983-4 Miss L.J. Chapman/Miss C.E. Palmer
1984-5 Miss C.E. Palmer/Miss C. Johnson
1985-6 Miss T. Dineen/Miss J. Munday

Mixed Doubles
1949-50 F.J. Shaw/Miss L.M. Cash
1950-1 F.J. Shaw/Miss D. Pratt
1951-2 A.D. Jordan/Miss I.A. Kenningham[2]
1952-3 G.H. King/Miss G.A. Smith[33]
1953-4 D. Jones/Miss J. Quilliam
1954-5 A.P. Billingham/Miss H.M. Ward[4]
1955-6 A.E. Flashman/Miss H.M. Ward[4]
1956-7 P.J. Waddell/Miss H.M. Ward[4]

1957-8	R.J. Mills/Miss M.K. Bishop[14]
1958-9	R.J. Mills/Miss A.M. Bairstow[12]
1959-60	R.J. Mills/Miss A.M. Bairstow[12]
1960-1	L. Brown/Miss C.E. Lindsay
1961-2	R.J. Westmorland/Miss J. McDonald[8]
1962-3	Oon Chong Hau/Miss J. McDonald[8]
1963-4	Oon Chong Hau/C.F. Bird[16]
1964-5	P.E. Whetnall/Miss L.M. Veasey[28]
1965-6	A.I. Morton/Miss G.M. Perrin[18]
1966-7	I.P. Clark/Miss G.M. Perrin[18]
1967-8	I.P. Clark/Miss G.M. Perrin[18]
1968-9	P. Bullivant/Miss C. Barron
1969-70	D.R.M. Pither/Miss B. Giles[29]
1970-1	P.J. Gardner/Miss B. Giles[29]
1971-2	J.C. Stretch/Miss N.C. Gardner[25]
1972-3	R.A. Rofe/Miss D.J. Kirby
1973-4	R.A. Rofe/Miss D.J. Kirby
1974-5	T.B. Stokes/Miss K.T. Puttick[30]
1975-6	G.J. Scott/Miss K.T. Puttick[30]
1976-7	K.R. Jolly/Miss K.S. Bridge[35]
1977-8	A.B. Goode/Miss K.S. Bridge[35]
1978-9	C.V. Back/Miss G.M. Clark
1979-80	D.P. Tailor/Miss M.A. Leeves
1980-1	D.P. Tailor/Miss M.A. Leeves
1981-2	D.P. Tailor/Miss G.C. Gowers
1982-3	M.D. Lawrence/Miss N.S. Roope
1983-4	D.J. Hall/Miss L.J. Chapman
1984-5	A. Casey/Miss C. Johnson
1985-6	M. Pallant/Miss F. Gallup

ENGLISH NATIONAL JUNIOR UNDER 15 CHAMPIONSHIPS

(Restricted to competitors under 15 at midnight on the preceding 31st August/1st September and currently eligible to play for England. Up to 1979/80 known as All-England Junior under 15 Championships. Discontinued in 1982-3)

Boys' Singles

1962-3	J.P. Farmer
1963-4	S. Aylmer
1964-5	C.J. Kirk
1965-6	J.F. Walter
1966-7	K.P. Arthur
1967-8	P.J. Gardner
1968-9	J.C. Stretch
1969-70	R.D. Wallace
1970-1	P.G. Kidger
1971-2	G.J. Scott
1972-3	S.R. Stranks
1973-4	K.R. Jolly
1974-5	A.B. Goode
1975-6	C.V. Back
1976-7	S.D. Wassell
1977-8	C.R. Wood
1978-9	S.P. Butler
1979-80	N.J. Fraser
1980-1	D.J. Hall
1981-2	M.A. Smith

Girls' Singles

1962-3	Miss G.M. Perrin[18]
1963-4	Miss G.M. Perrin[18]
1964-5	Miss G.M. Perrin[18]
1965-6	Miss M. Beck[23]
1966-7	Miss M. Beck[23]
1967-8	Miss B. Giles[29]
1968-9	Miss S. Storey[20]
1969-70	Miss K. Whiting
1970-1	Miss K. Redhead
1971-2	Miss S.E. Coates[27]
1972-3	Miss K.S. Bridge[35]
1973-4	Miss K.S. Bridge[35]
1974-5	Miss K.S. Bridge[35]
1975-6	Miss S.J. Leadbeater[34]
1976-7	Miss G.M. Clark
1977-8	Miss W.J. Poulton
1978-9	Miss W.J. Poulton
1979-80	Miss H.S. Troke
1980-1	Miss S. Louis
1981-2	Miss D. Hore

Boys' Doubles

1969-70	A.P. Fish/I. Loten
1970-1	G.L. Scott/P.H. Wood
1971-2	S.R. Stranks/J. Virdee
1972-3	S.R. Stranks/D.P.B. Bridge
1973-4	G.M. Reeves/N.G. Tier
1974-5	A.B. Goode/S.J. Perry
1975-6	C.V. Back/N. Yates
1976-7	M.J. Cattermole/A.G. Plater
1977-8	M.P. Methven/P.J. Scott
1978-9	M.D. Parker/D.P. Tailor
1979-80	P.N. Goddard/P.J. Walden
1980-1	A.J. Downes/D.J. Hall
1981-2	A. Nielsen/M.A. Smith

Girls' Doubles

1969-70	Miss S.A. Martin/Miss K. Whiting[31]
1970-1	Miss S. Parker/Miss K. Redhead
1971-2	Miss S.E. Coates[27]/Miss A.B. Maine[33]
1972-3	Miss K.S. Bridge[35]/Miss K.T. Puttick[30]
1973-4	Miss K.S. Bridge[35]/Miss K.T. Puttick[30]
1974-5	Miss K.S. Bridge[35]/Miss L.P. Bunday
1975-6	Miss N.A. Rollason/Miss R. Wardle
1976-7	Miss S.J. Leadbeater[34]/Miss S.R. Tardif
1977-8	Miss W.J. Poulton/Miss C.T. Sanders
1978-9	Miss W.J. Poulton/Miss R.M. Rollason
1979-80	Miss D. Simpson/Miss H.S. Troke
1980-1	Miss A.D. Fisher/Miss N.S. Roope
1981-2	Miss D. Hore/Miss C. Johnson

Mixed Doubles

1975-6	A.J. Pryce/Miss N.A. Rollaston
1976-7	M.J. Cattermole/Miss S.J. Leadbeater[34]
1977-8	C.R. Wood/Miss S.J. Leeves
1978-9	D.P. Tailor/Miss G.C. Gowers

1979-80 P.J. Walden/Miss D. Simpson
1980-1 D.J. Hall/Miss A.D. Fisher
1981-2 P. Edevane/Miss C.E. Palmer

(1) Later Mrs E.J. Timperley
(2) Later Mrs J.A. Turner
(3) Later Mrs G.W. Barrand
(4) Later Mrs E.B. Nielsen
(5) Later Mrs W.L. Hunter
(6) Later Mrs H.J. Horton
(7) Later Mrs F. Darlington
(8) Later Mrs P. Stephens
(9) Later Mrs Downs
(10) Later Mrs P.E. Whetnall
(11) Later Mrs L. Oakley
(12) Later Mrs H.I. Palmer
(13) Later Mrs Primett
(14) Later Mrs J. Soldan
(15) Later Mrs T. Gower
(16) Later Mrs Cook
(17) Later Mrs M.J. Boutle
(18) Later Mrs M.A. Gilks
(19) Later Mrs J.D. Eddy
(20) Later Mrs M. Beck
(21) Later Mrs A.E. Skovgaard
(22) Later Mrs E.J. Allen
(23) Later Mrs R.J. Lockwood
(24) Later Mrs S. Ellison
(25) Later Mrs J.P. Perry
(26) Later Mrs J.C. Stretch
(27) Later Mrs C. Martin
(28) Later Mrs L. Bird
(29) Later Mrs E.H. Sutton
(30) Later Mrs K. Chapman
(31) Later Mrs M.G. Tredgett
(32) Later Mrs R. Durman
(33) Later Mrs S.C. Jordan
(34) Later Mrs S. Podger
(35) Later Mrs K.S. Beckman
(36) Later Mrs P. Sutton)

ENGLISH JUNIOR RANKINGS 1985-6

Boys' Singles
1 Peter Bush
2 Richard Harmsworth
3 Martin Pallant
4 Steve Adams
5 Gary Brocklesby
6 Trevor Darlington
7 Andrew Fairhurst
   Simon Whale
9 Clive Palmer
10 Chris Hunt
    Peter Knowles

Girls' Singles
1 Sara Halsall
2 Sarah Hore
   Joanne Muggeridge
4 Tracy Salmon
5 Felicity Gallup
6 Tracy Allwright
7 Julie Munday
8 Lorna Midgelow
9 Tracy Dineen
10 Nicola Greenwood
    Tanya Groves

ENGLISH SCHOOLS' BADMINTON ASSOCIATION

This essential base of England's badminton structure was founded in 1965 due largely to the efforts of Len Wright, a Cumbrian schoolmaster, far from badminton's main centres. In 1973, having built up a thriving organization, he retired. The work has since been carried on by a closely knit group of enthusiastic volunteers under the chairmanship of Nev McFarlane (q.v.). Today virtually every county in England participates.

Badminton is encouraged in nearly every school in the country – with the accent on *enjoyment*. A host of events are organized throughout the season: the Carlton Teaching and Pupils Award Scheme (q.v.), U.12, U.14, U.16 national and, often, regional championships; international matches at U.14, U.15 and U.16 level (these include U.16 Triangular and Home Counties Quadrangular matches, U.16 Copenhagen Invitation event and U.14 European Nations generally as team and individual events) summer coaching courses, and the Barclays Bank National Schools Championship which replaced 'Top Schools'.

The highlight is perhaps a mammoth U.16 Inter-County Championship, held at Easter in centrally situated University of Nottingham's twelve-court hall (once an aircraft hangar). It now involves forty counties, each playing ten matches over four days. For winners and runners-up in the latter, the Gannon and Povey-Richards trophies are awarded. News of these events is circulated in a monthly newsletter, part of an intensified publicity drive by PRO Mike Stringer.

ESBA is a team effort but it is hard not to mention such long-serving names as Tom Bowker, Netta and Pip Capon, coaches Ian Graham, Eric Brown and now retired Allon Horrocks and Frank New, and new – and equally enthusiastic – workers such as Geoff Bedford, Anne Dale, Paddy Donkin, Mike Stringer, Gary Walters and Tony Bristow, to name but a few.

So great has become the volume of work that a permanent, professional secretariat has been established at Milton Keynes National Badminton Centre under lynch-pin Barbara Stanton.

Liaison is encouraged at all levels: in the counties between schools and senior associations; at national level with the BAE, with two members of each on the other's council; and even internationally.

1. Inter-Counties Tournament Results

1966	1. Cumberland	2.	Lancashire
1967	1. Cumberland	2.	Essex
1968	1. Essex	2.	Cumberland
1969	1. Essex	2.	Surrey
1970	1. Lancashire	2.	Nottinghamshire
1971	1. Lancashire	2.	Nottinghamshire
1972	1. Lancashire	2.	Ulster
1973	1. Yorkshire	2.	Lancashire
1974	1. Surrey	2.	Essex
1975	1. Yorkshire	2.	Warwickshire
1976	1. Yorkshire	2.	Surrey
1977	1. Surrey	2.	Yorkshire
1978	1. Merseyside	2.	Yorkshire
1979	1. Surrey	2.	Warwickshire
1980	1. Surrey	2.	Edinburgh
1981	1. Derbyshire	2.	Yorkshire
1982	1. Surrey	2.	Derbyshire
1983	1. Sussex	2.	Essex
1984	1. Sussex	2.	Essex
1985	1. Essex	2.	Nottinghamshire
1986	1. Essex	2.	Kent

2. Under 16 National Individual Championships

	Boys' Singles	Girls' Singles
1970	J. Stretch	N. Gardner
1971	P. Kidger	K. Redhead
1972	P. Wood	K. Redhead
1973	J. Unwin	S. Coates
1974	K. Jolly	K. Bridge
1975	N. Tier	K. Bridge
1976	A. Goode	K. Bridge
1977	C. Back	G. Clark
1978	S. Wassell	G. Clark
1979	S. Butler	W. Poulton
1980	C. Dobson	H. Troke

1981	D. Hall	D. Simpson
1982	D. Hall	N. Roope
1983	P. Edevane	S. Halsall
1984	P. Bush	S. Halsall
1985	G. Brocklesby	F. Gallup
1986	R. Harmsworth	J. Munday

Boys' Doubles

1970	R. Wallace/L. Stevens
1971	A. Fish/I. Loten
1972	P. Wood/G. Scott
1973	S. Stranks/J. Virdee
1974	J. Wallace/G. Reeves
1975	G. Reeves/N. Tier
1976	C. Featherstone/D. Roebuck
1977	D. Burden/A. Pryce
1978	M. Cattermole/A. Plater
1979	D. Tailor/A. Wood
1980	M. Parker/D. Tailor
1981	D. Hall/S. Spurling
1982	D. Hall/A. Downes
1983	A. Nielsen/A. Willey
1984	S. Adams/M. Pallant
1985	A. Fairhurst/C. Hunt
1986	J. Horrocks/R. Hennity

Girls' Doubles

1970	N. Gardner/C. Beer
1971	S. Stuart/D. Hurst
1972	G. Scholey/C. Kelly
1973	P. Kilvington/L. Fowler
1974	L. Gaston/K. Shaw
1975	K. Bridge/K. Puttick
1976	T. Bass/K. Bridge
1977	S. Leadbeater/N. Rollason
1978	G. Clark/K. Coates
1979	L. Campbell/K. Lister
1980	G. Gowers/S. Morrice
1981	L. Chapman/L. Salmon
1982	L. Chapman/L. Salmon
1983	S. Halsall/A. Roope
1984	S. Halsall/L. Midgelow
1985	J. Muggeridge/T. Salmon
1986	J. Munday/T. Dineen

Mixed Doubles

1970	T. Wing/C. Salmon
1971	G. Roberts/S. Coates
1972	P. Littlewood/J. Mawdsley
1973	R. Marshall/J. Bush
1974	D. Bridge/A. Maine
1975	G. Reeves/C. Bairstow
1976	A. Goode/K. Bridge
1977	N. Yates/S. Leadbeater
1978	S. Wassell/G. Clark
1979	C. Wood/S. Leeves
1980	D. Tailor/G. Gowers
1981	R. Baddeley/L. Chapman
1984	S. Adams/T. Cooke
1985	P. Beckett/T. Salmon
1986	R. Harmsworth/T. Dineen

3. Under 14 National Championships

Boys' Singles		Girls' Singles
1976	C. Wood	S. Leeves
1977	S. Butler	G. Gowers
1978	I. Beckett	H. Troke
1979	R. Baddeley	N. Roope
1980	A. Nielsen	C. Johnson
1981	D. Robinson	S. Halsall
1982	G. Brocklesby	T. Salmon
1984	R. Harmsworth	F. Gallup
1985	A. Bush	K. Egerton
1986	A. Griffin	J. Hunt

Boys' Doubles
1976	C. Wood/D. Power
1977	D. Tailor/M. Parker
1978	I. Beckett/M. Fraser
1979	R. Baddeley/J. Prior
1980	P. Isherwood/J. Leather
1981	S. Adams/R. Silk
1982	J. Andrews/M. Bennett
1984	S. Day/R. Harmsworth
1985	A. Bush/A. Spencer
1986	N. Cottrill/A. Griffin

Girls' Doubles
1976	M. Leeves/S. Leeves
1977	G. Gowers/J. Edwards
1978	H. Troke/A. Cartwright
1979	N. Roope/A. Fisher
1980	D. Buddle/D. Hore
1981	S. Halsall/K. Pearson
1982	K. Batten/T. Cooke
1984	T. Dineen/J. Munday
1985	K. Egerton/J.T. Groves
1986	L. Day/J. Hunt

4. Under 13 National Championships

Boys' Singles		Girls' Singles
1979	D. Hall	B. Blair
1980	A. Nielsen	C. Palmer
1981	S. Laskey	S. Halsall
1982	M. Ellis	T. Salmon
	Under 13 Discontinued	

Boys' Doubles
1979	D. Hall/A. Downes
1980	P. Isherwood/J. Leather
1981	S. Laskey/D. Robinson
1982	M. Lyne/N. Prior
	Under 13 Discontinued

Girls' Doubles
1979	L. Thomas/D. Thomas
1980	D. Buddle/D. Hore
1981	S. Halsall/K. Pearson
1982	T. Salmon/K. Rogers
	Under 13 Discontinued

5. Under 12 National Championships

Boys' Singles		Girls' Singles
1981	G. Brocklesby	T. Salmon
1982	R. Harmsworth	F. Gallup
1983	W. Mellersh	T. Groves
1984	P. McGlinchey	J. Hunt
1985	A. Robertson	E. Herrity

1986	K. Jones	E. Keeling

Boys' Doubles
1981	M. Lyne/N. Prior
1982	G. Campbell/A. Spencer
1983	A. Bush/A. Spencer
1984	P. McGlinchey/N. Cottrill
1985	S. Archer/A. Robertson
1986	K. Jones/O. Robinson

Girls' Doubles
1981	T. Salmon/K. Rogers
1982	T. Groves/P. Laskey
1983	K. Egerton/T. Groves
1984	L. Day/J. Hunt
1985	N. Groves/K. Wilson
1986	L. Atkinson/T. Hallam

ESBA COMPETITORS' CODE OF CONDUCT

1. In attitude be serious, pleasant and well-mannered.
2. Always there will be stronger and weaker players than yourself. Treat all with respect and courtesy.
3. Win or lose graciously, accepting your victory or defeat with dignity. Bad temper and melodrama have no place in our sport.
4. Irritating time-wasting, off-putting tactics are totally unacceptable.
5. Bad line calls and fault-serving create ill-feeling very quickly. Make sure YOU are always scrupulously fair.
6. Make sure you know and understand the 'Laws'. A few are obscure but most are entirely straightforward.
7. Should you be faulted by an umpire or service judge and you genuinely do not know why – politely ask. At the end of a match, as well as thanking your opponent, always thank both the umpire and service judge. Should you also have linesmen, a cheery wave of thanks is a pleasant gesture.
8. In a game without an umpire, should you feel that you are being cheated by your opponent, DO NOT GET ANGRY. Quietly report to the referee and explain your problem.
9. Always remember that many eyes and ears are watching and listening. Your reputation is in your own hands but never forget that you are an advertisement not only for yourself but for parents, teachers and coaches.
10. One further essential – ENJOY YOUR SPORT.

ETIQUETTE

Badminton, like the other racket games, has its own etiquette:

1. A courteous player *DOES NOT*:
   (a) Carelessly scoop the shuttle under the net to return it to his opponent at the end of a rally; he hits it or throws it carefully to him.
   (b) Leave his opponent to retrieve the shuttle when he, the striker, has hit it into the net.
   (c) Query line decisions given by his opponent when the shuttle falls on the latter's side of the net.
   (d) Shout noisily or distractingly during play (except to 'call' (q.v.).
   (e) Damagingly hit the shuttle on the half-volley.
   (f) Walk across or behind another court while a rally is in progress.
   (g) 'Poach' (q.v.).
2. He *Does:*
   (a) At the end of a match-game shake hands with his opponent(s).
   (b) Shake hands also with umpire and service judge (if any).
   (c) Encourage his partner.
   (d) Declare any 'slings' (q.v.) (unless there is an umpire) or if the shuttle has touched his body, clothing, hair or racket before being hit by his partner (when the umpire has not observed it).
   (e) Tries to maintain the spirit and the letter of the Laws dealing with service and its return (q.v.).

EUROPE CUP

A competition for the champion clubs of each affiliated EBU member country instituted in 1978. A Challenge Cup was presented by the President, Dr Herman Valken. It was initially won by Gentofte BK of Copenhagen, Denmark at Göppingen, FR Germany.

Since then they have been beaten only once – by BMK Aura in 1984. The next year they returned the compliment with a searing 7-0 victory. Not surprising as their team included Frost, Kjeldsen, Nierhoff, Charlotte Hattens and Kirsten Larsen. Surprising though, that Aarhus BK beat them for a place in the 1986 competition.

Results
1978 Gentofte BK – BV Mulheim – (Ranked)
1979 Gentofte BK 6 – BC Duinjwijck 1
1980 Wimbledon BC 4 – Hvidovre BK 1
1981 Gentofte BK 7 – BMK Aura Malmö 0
1982 Gentofte BK 6 – Duinjwijck 1
1983 Gentofte BK 7 – BMK Aura Malmö 0
1984 BMK Aura Malmö 5 – Gentofte BK 2
1985 Gentofte BK 7 – BMK Aura Malmö 0

Venues
1978 Göppingen
1979 Haarlem
1980 Mulheim
1981 Copenhagen
1982 Edegem (Belgium)
1983 Paris
1984 Malmö
1985 Mulheim

EUROPEAN BADMINTON UNION

The EBU was founded in 1967 at a meeting in Frankfurt-am-Main of Austria, Belgium, Czechoslovakia, Denmark, England, Finland, FR of Germany, Netherlands, Norway, Sweden and Switzerland. This number has increased to twenty-seven with the addition of France, Ireland, Scotland, Wales and Yugoslavia (1968), German DR (1971), Malta (1972), Hungary (1973), USSR (1975), Portugal, Italy and Poland (1977), Iceland (1978), Luxembourg (1981), Faroe Islands and Spain (1982).

Its first President, H.P. Kunz, and S. Mohlin and H. Brohl were key figures in organizing the first European Championship in 1968. A Junior Championship followed in 1969 at Voorburg (Netherlands). These events are played in alternate years. The Helvetia Cup (for teams not ranked in Europe's top six) was taken over in 1975 from Switzerland BA, who pioneered it; the Europe Cup, for national champion clubs, started in 1978; and three Europe v. Asia fixtures were arranged. The junior Finlandia Cup (q.v.) alternates with the Helvetia.

In addition, umpiring co-ordination seminars and summer coaching schools have been held. More help, financial and coaching, including a youth scholarship is now being given to emergent associations who are encouraged to participate in La Plume d'Or competition (q.v.).

EUROPEAN CHAMPIONSHIPS

The EBU (q.v.) was formed in September 1967. At the initial meeting, largely on the initiative of the FR of Germany, it was decided to hold biennial European Championships (Individuals) the following year. In April 1968 the first such event was held at Bochum in W. Germany.

Team championships were added in 1972 at Karlskrona. From twelve (1972) to twenty-one (1980) countries compete. In 1984 nineteen countries were divided into three groups, each sub-divided into two sub-groups of three (or four). The latter played for 1, 2 or 3 ranking on a round-robin basis. 1's, 2's, and 3's then played each other to determine ranking for the whole group. Finally a promotion and relegation tie was played between the bottom team in Group I and the top team in Group II, and similarly between Groups II and III. The top six teams are then considered ineligible to play in the Helvetia Cup (q.v.).

The most astonishing result was in 1976. England and Denmark had each won two ties and lost one; both had won nine matches. England's winning twenty-one games to Denmark's twenty caused them to be announced the winners but, on protest by Denmark, this was nullified by England's losing fifteen games to Denmark's fourteen. Eventually a jubilant Denmark team was awarded the title as they had beaten England 3-2 in the last vital tie.

EUROPEAN SENIOR CHAMPIONSHIPS

Date/Venue
1968	Bochum
1970	Port Talbot
1972	Karlskrona
1974	Vienna
1976	Dublin
1978	Preston
1980	Groningen
1982	Böblingen
1984	Preston
1986	Uppsala

Men's Singles
1968	S. Johnsson
1970	S. Johnsson
1972	W. Bochow
1974	S. Johnsson
1976	F. Delfs
1978	F. Delfs
1980	F. Delfs
1982	J.P. Nierhoff
1984	M. Frost
1986	M. Frost

Ladies' Singles
1968	I. Latz
1970	E. Twedberg
1972	M. Beck
1974	G. Gilks
1976	G. Gilks
1978	L. Køppen
1980	L. Blumer
1982	L. Køppen
1984	H. Troke
1986	H. Troke

Men's Doubles
1968	J.D. Eddy/R. Powell
1970	E. Hansen/P. Walsoe
1972	W. Braun/R. Maywald
1974	W. Braun/R. Maywald
1976	R.P. Stevens/M. Tredgett
1978	R.P. Stevens/M. Tredgett
1980	C. Nordin/S. Karlsson
1982	T. Kihlström/S. Karlsson
1984	M. Dew/M. Tredgett
1986	S. Fladberg/J. Helledie

Ladies' Doubles
1968	M.B. Boxall/S. Whetnall
1970	M.B. Boxall/S. Whetnall
1972	G. Gilks/J. Hashman
1974	G. Gilks/M. Beck
1976	G. Gilks/S. Whetnall
1978	N. Perry/A. Statt
1980	N. Perry/J. Webster
1982	G. Gilks/G. Clark
1984	K. Chapman/G. Clark
1986	G. Clark/G. Gowers

Mixed Doubles
1968	A.D. Jordan/S. Whetnall
1970	J.D. Eddy/S. Whetnall
1972	D. Talbot/G. Gilks
1974	D. Talbot/G. Gilks
1976	D. Talbot/G. Gilks
1978	M. Tredgett/N. Perry
1980	M. Tredgett/N. Perry
1982	M. Dew/G. Gilks
1984	M. Dew/G. Gilks
1986	M. Dew/G. Gilks

EUROPEAN TEAM CHAMPIONSHIP (Senior)

Year/Venue		Winner	Runner-up
1972	Karlskrona	England	Denmark
1974	Vienna	England	Denmark
1976	Dublin	Denmark	England
1978	Preston	England	Denmark
1980	Groningen	Denmark	England
1982	Böblingen	England	Sweden
1984	Preston	England	Denmark
1986	Uppsala	Denmark	England

EUROPEAN JUNIOR CHAMPIONSHIPS

These were speedily instituted in 1969 at Voorburg, Netherlands as individual championships the year following the first EC. A team championship was added in

1975 at Copenhagen. Entrants in the latter have varied from eleven to nineteen.

1983   A. Nielsen/G. Paulsen
1985   J. Paulsen/M. Christiansen

Date/Venue
1969   Voorburg
1971   Gottwaldov
1973   Edinburgh
1975   Copenhagen
1977   Ta Qali (Malta)
1979   Mulheim
1981   Edinburgh
1983   Helsinki
1985   Pressbaum

Boys' Singles
1969   F. Delfs
1971   R. Ridder
1973   J. Helledie
1975   B. Wackfeldt
1977   A. Goode
1979   J.P. Nierhoff
1981   M. Kjeldsen
1983   K. Thomsen
1985   M. Smith

Girls' Singles
1969   A. Berglund
1971   A. Berglund
1973   M Nyhre
1975   P. Nielsen
1977   K. Bridge
1979   K. Larsen
1981   H. Troke
1983   H. Troke
1985   L. Stuer-Lauridsen

Boys' Doubles
1969   K.P. Arthur/R.P. Stevens
1971   P.J. Gardner/R.C. Stretch
1973   S. Karlsson/W. Nilsson
1975   B. Wackfeldt/G. Sterner
1977   J. Johansson/S. Karlsson
1979   J. Antonsson/P. Isaakson
1981   M. Kjeldsen/M. Christiansen
1983   C. Rees/L. Williams
1985   J. Paulsen/L. Petersen

Girls' Doubles
1969   J. van Beusekom/M. Luesken
1971   A. Berglund/L. Køppen
1973   A. Forrest/K. Whiting
1975   L. Gottsche/L.B. Pedersen
1977   K. Bridge/K. Puttick
1979   S. Leadbeater/G. Clark
1981   D. Kjaer/N. Nielsen
1983   J. Shipman/L. Chapman
1985   L. Stuer-Lauridsen/L. Olsen

Mixed Doubles
1969   G. Perneklo/K. Lindquist
1971   P.J. Gardner/B. Giles
1973   J. Helledie/S. Johansen
1975   T. Stokes/K. Puttick
1977   N. Tier/K. Puttick
1979   J.P. Nierhoff/L. Pilgaard
1981   D. Tailor/M. Leeves

EUROPEAN TEAM CHAMPIONSHIP (Junior)

Date/Venue		Winners	Runners-up
1975	Copenhagen	Denmark	England
1977	Malta	England	Denmark
1979	Mulheim	Denmark	England
1981	Edinburgh	Denmark	England
1983	Helsinki	England	Denmark
1985	Pressbaum	Denmark	England

EUROPEAN SUMMER SCHOOL

An annual, week-long international school run by the EBU Deveopment sub-committee. Its curriculum includes the three 'Ts': technique, tactics and training, as well as planning and motivation, and social and cultural activities. It has been held at Pressbaum (Austria) 1982, Lilleshall Hall (UK) 1983 and Ribe (Denmark) 1984. Some fifty juniors and twenty coaches attend from up to seventeen different Associations as far apart as the Faroes and Portugal.

In 1985 it was held in Scheessel, W. Germany. For the first time, eleven non-European coaches were invited, from countries as far afield as Argentina, Nigeria and Sri Lanka. In 1986, in Basel.

EUROPEAN U.14 EIGHT NATIONS CHAMPIONSHIPS

Since the U.14 Championships started in 1977, countries participating have increased from four to the current eight. In 1984, it was played in two divisions with a one team promotion/relegation play-off.

Results

	Division I	Division II
1977	England	—
1978	F.R. of Germany	—
1979	England	—
1980	England	—
1981	England	—
1982	England	—
1983	England	—
1984	England	Austria
1985	England	Austria

The 1985 Championships were sponsored by Carlton.

Final positions were:

Division I: 1. England; 2. Netherlands; 3. F.R. of Germany; 4. Scotland.

Division II: 1. Austria; 2. Wales; 3. Belgium; 4. Switzerland.

F

FAMOUS GROUSE

Nothing to do with the 'Glorious 12th'! A well-known Scottish whisky firm who, recognizing badminton 'as a major racket sport of fascinating skill', impartially sponsor the Scottish National and Open Championships, and the English ICC (1983/4-1984/5). They also backed one-off productions of English Masters and World Badminton Doubles Challenge.

FAROE ISLANDS –
Badmintonsamband Foroya

BF was established in 1981 and joined the IBF in 1982, although the game had been played for some twenty-five years. BF fielded a team in 1985 in a tripartite match with Greenland and Iceland, and scored only 29 points in sixteen games against Iceland! Quite undeterred they hope shortly to enter Nordic and European Championships. Its 800 members play enthusiastically in ten halls, one built exclusively for badminton.

FAULT

Error in play leading to the loss of a rally. (These are covered by no fewer than twelve sub-sections in Law 14.) A fault by the serving, or 'in', side results in the loss of a serve; by the receiving or 'out' side, to a point for the 'in' side.

FEATHER

(a) Colloquial term for a shuttlecock, originally always made of feathers, now often of synthetic material; (b) essential constituent of a shuttlecock (q.v.).

FEDERAL REPUBLIC OF GERMANY – Deutscher Badminton Verband EV

Founded in 1953, the DBV already boasts 87,500 members (only 56,000 in 1980) in twelve regional associations. Its President, Dr Heinz Barge, held the same office for the EBU and was an IBF Council member (1978-83). Despite such a reservoir of players and thorough administration, the DBV's current team members have not won European titles as did their predecessors of the 1970s. Wolfgang Bochow (men's singles, 1972); Willy Braun and Roland Maywald (men's doubles, 1972 and 1974); Irma Latz (ladies' singles, 1968) and her runner-up, Marie-Luise Zizman, who together were defeated in the 1970 ladies' doubles final.

DBV won the Helvetia Cup ten times 1962-71 and again in 1983 after relegation from the European Championships.

FERRY SONNEVILLE COACHING FUND

A fund, IBF administered, that gives financial help to emergent badminton nations to set up coaching facilities. It is supported by the interest from 'an interesting donation' given in 1976 by Ferry Sonneville (q.v.).

FINLANDIA CUP

Conceived and first played during heavy snow, this is a junior team competition run on the lines of the senior Helvetia Cup (q.v.) except that two girls' and two boys' singles are played. The first competition (January 1984), opened by IOC President Juan Samaranch and played in the sixteen-court Badminton Centre in Lausanne, resulted: 1. Norway, 2. Finland, 3. Poland, 4. Wales, 5. Ireland, 6. Austria, 7. Iceland, 8. Hungary, 9. Switzerland, 10. Belgium. The first four placings in the 1986 competition were: 1. USSR, 2. Finland, 3. Ireland, 4. Poland. The trophy was donated by Finland's Anders Segercrantz. The competition alternates with European Junior Championships.

FINNISH BADMINTON ASSOCIATION

Strangely, badminton came to Finland as rehabilitation therapy for World War II wounded. The FBA now has some sixty clubs spawned from the 1944 Helsingfors BK, (2,700 players). They nevertheless ran the 1983 European Junior Championships most efficiently in Helsinki when they were ranked fourteenth out of seventeen; improved to twelfth out of twenty-three in 1985. They came an excellent second in the 1984 Finlandia Cup.

FISHER, Alison (Essex)
Born 13 October 1965

Alison Fisher may be one of the smallest players in the game but by 1985 she had already won the Essex Senior and Junior, National U.21, European Six Nations U.18 LS titles, and been on U.19 tour of Korea and China. Already with four U.23 caps, she is now ranked as England's No. 8. Coached by Ray Stevens and sponsored by local estate agents, she should go far – especially as part of the deal was a Talbot Samba!

FLICK

Deceptive form of service (q.v.)

FOLLOW-THROUGH

The path of the racket after impact with the shuttle. Used in power and touch shots alike, it helps achieve control, and accuracy if it is kept in line with the target area.

It should never be so long as to prevent quick return of the racket-head to the position of readiness or result in hitting the net.

FOOT FAULT

Under Laws 14(c) and 16 a player is penalized if, as server or receiver: (a) his foot is on or touching a line; (b) part of both feet are not in contact with the floor, stationary until impact, and within the correct service court.

FOOTWORK

In a sport where the shuttle must be volleyed and where, in order to attack, the shuttle must be taken at least at tape-height (five feet), speed to the shuttle is essential.

When waiting to return serve, the receiver is poised for instant movement backwards or forwards. In a wide-ish, sideways stance, knees bent, body weight a little forward in a slightly crouched position, he is ready for quick, aggressive action.

Even in between strokes static body inertia is never allowed to take over. Players, knees slightly bent, on the balls of the feet, with a little bounce or shuffle, are more easily able to accelerate forward or backward in a split second. Feet are never still.

Movement forward is by normal running, terminated, near the net, by a long, braking, right-footed lunge, or, if split-second movement is needed to make a net-kill, by a leap. After the lunge, a driving push on the bent front leg swiftly powers the player back to base or to anticipated shuttle-fall.

Movement backward is either by chasséing (skipping) or, more often, by short running steps. As with the forward lunge, the last longer step back onto the right foot acts as brake and then forward drive. Under pressure, it may be onto the left foot with a scissor-kick recovery action. Athletic and agile players frequently terminate the run-back with a vertical jump in order to pressure their opponent by taking the shuttle still earlier and to obtain greater downward angle. Balanced landing gives quick recovery.

Movement across the court is often a sideways chasséing ended by a longer stride with the right foot. If the shuttle has already been struck cross-court, the player may immediately turn and *run*. If the shuttle has not yet been struck, the player will chassé towards his base, not fully committing himself, in case the shuttle is returned to the side he has just left.

In all movement, balance must be maintained if (1) the shot is to be played accurately; (2) over-running the shuttle or falling back way from it is to be avoided; and (3) a fast, driving recovery is to be made.

Good footwork is the basis of all good badminton.

FORECOURT

Generally regarded as the front part of the court, the area (6½ by 20 feet, 1.98 by 6 metres) lying between net and short service line.

FOREHAND

The side to the right of a right-handed player (the left of a left-hander). So called because the front (or palm) of the hand is to the net when strokes are played forehanded.

FORGIE, Hugh

A chunky Canadian whose boyhood aspirations to be an ice-hockey international were thwarted by lack of inches – but he became World Professional Badminton Champion for eleven years and later put the game on stage – and even *on ice*.

Before the war he appeared in a Royal Command Performance at the London Coliseum with that other great trick-shot expert Ken Davidson (q.v.). During the war he entertained tens of thousands of troops; after it, hundreds of thousands of spectators, as, on world-wide tours in such spectaculars as *Holiday on Ice*, he put the thrills of fast-moving, phenomenally accurate badminton, laced with rip-roaring humour, onto ice, under appalling conditions of light and 'drift' (q.v.).

In his act, seen live and on TV by an estimated billion viewers, he rallies with another World Professional Champion, his son Reg, and American Uber Cup trialist, long-legged Shirley Marie who provides the glamour as well as skill.

He is over seventy – and still on skates!

FRANCE – Fédération Française de Badminton

Although today numbering only 6,000 players in 170 clubs, French badminton history stretches back to 1898, when at Saint-Servan J.E. Jones, a British Army crammer, built a four-court hall. On its closure, play continued in a Paramé hotel dining-room, despite its centrally placed candelabra. Dieppe BC affiliated to the Badminton Association, ousted indoor tennis from a local garage and in 1908 held the first-ever Continental tournament, which attracted England's leading players until 1914.

Equally popular were the pre-World War II championships held several floors up in the prestigious Racing Club de Paris. RSL director René Gathier had much to do with their success and insisted on their being held even during the 1940 'phoney war'.

Only in 1979 did FFB regain its independence from the French Lawn Tennis Association. The game's resurgence owed much to the drive and enthusiasm of France-domiciled Roger Grimwood, who also ran a vast entry Championships in two halls simultaneously.

French players are classified according to ability.

FREDERIKSEN, Ib (Denmark)
Born 1964

Shot to the fore in 1985. At the World Championships he took a game from Yang Yang. A semi-finalist in the English Masters, he next reinforced his potential by ousting Frost as Danish National Champion.

Reached the finals of the Canadian Open (1985) and the Japanese Open (defeating Prakash but losing again to Yang Yang) and won the Dutch Open (1986).

In the 1986 AEC he showed his fighting powers and heavy smash by beating Yates after game down. Then took the first game in the quarters from losing finalist M. Sidek.

Strongly athletic, Ib lives, surely inappropriately, at Skive.

FREEMAN, Dr David Guthrie (USA)
Born 1921

From Pasadena, California, a neurosurgeon and friend of tennis star Jack Kramer, he came to Britain in the AEC Golden Jubilee Year in 1949 with a ten-year unbeaten singles record behind him. In the first ever Thomas Cup semi-final he played Malayan Champion Wong Peng Soon (q.v.), advancing inexorably from 4-4 to 15-4, 15-1, and also defeated Ooi Teik Hock (q.v.) 15-10, 10-15, 15-4. In the following AEC he again beat Wong, 2 and 4, and Ooi Teik Hock, 1 and 6 in the final. He won the title, having dropped only 24 points in 120 in the last four rounds.

After six weeks' intensive medical study and virtually no practice, he won the Danish Championships, beating Wong Peng Soon in the semi-final and Ooi in a gruelling three-setter 15-11, 14-18, 17-15 final.

For four years he dedicated himself to further study before making a final, last-minute competitive foray in the Canadian Strathgowan Invitation Singles which he won, beating both 1951 US Champion Joe Alston and reigning Canadian Champion Don Smythe; and in winning his 7th US Open title. In all he was unbeaten at singles from just before his nineteenth birthday to his retirement at thirty-three.

His skills included tight and deceptive drops; a steep, meticulously placed smash; a brick wall defence; dancing feet allied to an uncanny ability to 'read' (q.v.) his opponents' strokes; 100 per cent concentration; a rooted – and sometimes noisy – dislike of his own – rare – unforced errors; and a relentless determination to win.

FROST, Morten (Denmark)
Born 4 April 1958,
Copenhagen

Originally Morten Frost Hansen, publicity-minded, he dropped the Smith-common 'Hansen'. First playing when eight years old, he won the Danish Junior titles at 14-16 (once) and 16-18 (twice) levels, having learnt by watching others rather than by formal coaching.

He became a member of the great Gentofte BK, playing many tournaments, and was fortunate to be able to practise with Prakash Padukone who settled temporarily in Copenhagen to train. In 1981 he lost narrowly to Chen Changjie in the World Games. His major breakthrough came a year later when he beat China's Luan Jin (q.v.) at the AEC – and victory-rolled under the net. Although he easily headed the 1983 Pro-Kennex preliminary points ladder, he lost to Jin in the final, 2 & 6. He lost also, surprisingly, to winner Sugiarto in the 1983 World Championships, 5 & 3. 1984 saw him recover superbly in the AEC final against thrice-champion Liem Swie King from 9-15, 5-10 to 15-10, 15-10 to win a seventy-minute thriller.

1984 was to become a highlight with victories also in the Scandinavian Cup, English Masters, European Games, Danish, Chinese Taipei and Japanese Opens, and the Pro-Kennex GP. He was unbeaten by a European player from April 1980 to 1985. Then in 1985, his hopes of three AEC titles in succession were dashed by gangling, unknown Zhao Jianhua who had beaten him in preliminary Scottish and Japanese Open finals. After a nervous first game 6-15, Zhao smashed his way to 15-10, 8-1, 13-5 before Frost fought back to a desperately close 13-15. Worse still befell him in the World Championships when after conceding only 44 points in ten games, including an 8 and 5 win against Yang Yang, he lost 18-14, 10-15, 8-15 to Han Jian, losing the last twelve points in succession from 8-3 up!

December 1985, however, saw his record sixth successive Danish Open Singles victory. He defeated partisan-encouraged Misbun Sidek in the heat of the Malaysian Masters but lost to a back-to-World-Champion-form Sugiarto in the Alba Quartz. Despite handsomely heading the Pro Kennex Points Table, he was startlingly defeated in the semis by unseeded Sze Yu, a Hong Kong emigrant to Australia, who could muster only 6 and 3 in the final against Han Jian. He beat Yang Yang, however, for third place.

In 1986, comfortably beat M. Sidek for his 3rd AEC title. And in TC gained revenge on Han Jian – despite seeking to reverse unfair decision against the latter.

Six feet two inches (1.87 metres) tall, crinkly haired, craggy, laser-lean, 'Twinkle Toes' greatest asset is his lithe mobility, perfect balance and ability to take the shuttle early. (As an amateur athlete he jumped his own height until disqualified for taking badminton prize-money!) Ally this with patience, delicacy of touch, imperturbability and a hard-worked-on, sharper smash, and the reason for only one defeat prior to 1985 in fifty matches becomes clear. Unassuming, popular and very determined. In the 1984 Pro-Kennex, in stifling heat, he outlasted Misbun Sidek after having had a bucket of cold water thrown over him!

Frost has written *Play It My Way* and an anti-smoking booklet for Danish Cancer Research. Sponsored by Carlton and Carlsberg, he is a history graduate who likes Danish classics and 'who dunits'. He attributes his success to his dentist wife Ulla-Brit, with whom he won the 1983/4 Danish Licensed Players National mixed doubles, and who 'has fantastic capability to get my wheels turning again'.

Allergic to cats, grasses and nineteen other things, he is permitted to use, as part of his asthma cure, a drug normally prohibited.

Migrated to Enfield, UK (next door to Steve Baddeley), in 1985 to make tax-savings which would enable him to take his wife with him on some of the 265 days a year when he is 'globe-trotting'. Welcomed to the English training squad – but still playing for Denmark.

FRYING-PAN GRIP

Grip in which the racket is held square to the net with the *palm* on the main back bevel.

Because it somewhat inhibits the use of the wrist, it should be used only at the net. There it has the advantage of being able to be used on forehand or backhand without change of grip.

Often automatically adopted by beginners, it is so called because of its similarity to that adopted on occasion by irate cooks.

G

GALLO, Melissa

Symbol of badminton determination? Having lost repeatedly to Ingrid Fairbrother, was demolished 0-11 by her in Ontario U.19 final first game – but psyched herself back to win at 37th attempt 11-4, 12-10.

GAME POINT

The point before the final point, i.e. 14 in 15 up, 10 in 11 up, and similarly in setting (q.v.). A player (or pair) at such a score, serving four times before winning, or losing, is said to have *had*, or held, four game points. A player or pair 10-14 down who put out their opponents three times without the latter scoring are said to have *saved* three game points.

Game point becomes the still more critical *match point* when the game is the deciding one.

GENTOFTE BK

Currently perhaps the best known of the Danish super-clubs. Among its famous players it has numbered Poul Holm, S. Skovgaard, J.P. Nierhoff, Morten Frost, S. Fladberg, M. Christiansen and M. Kjeldsen; Tonny Ahm, Aase Jacobsen, Lene Koppen, Pia Nielsen and Kirsten Larsen. They have won the Europe Cup for clubs on six out of seven appearances.

Other famous clubs are Skovshoved IF, Københavns BK and Hvidovre BC, who play in specially built, multi-court halls with a membership of up to 600 playing from early morning to late evening.

GET THE LIFT

The basic strategy of attempting to force opponents to hit the shuttle upwards, so maintaining the attack and getting another chance to obtain an outright winner.

GILKS, Gillian M., MBE (Surrey and England)
Born 20 June 1950

Records speak volumes (see below) but cannot say everything. Gillian, who as a spindle-shanked $12\frac{1}{2}$-year-old won the AEC U.15 singles title (1963) is today a still playing legend with a record 108 caps.

She won the latter title for two more years and as a fourteen-year-old won also the U.18 title for good measure (1964-5), a title she was to win for another three years. At sixteen, she won the first of her 108 caps for England but not until nineteen her first of twenty-six National titles (eight-singles, seven ladies, eleven mixed). Over 600 championship titles were to follow. In 1984 she won sixteen world-class titles and was a Uber Cup silver medallist.

First entering for the AEC singles in 1965, it was not until 1970 that she got through the first round and not until 1976 that she won the first of her two AEC singles titles – after three successive finals appearances. Nerves and lack of confidence were her bugbears. Meantime, however, in 1969 she had won, with Roger Mills, the first of six mixed doubles titles and, in 1974, the first of three ladies' doubles titles. In all, a tally of eleven AEC titles to match her eleven European Championship titles. These, together with a host of others, including two silvers in the first World Championships, not surprisingly gained her Sportswoman of the Year Award (twice), BBC Super Star and the final accolade of MBE. She was a treble Triple Champion: at the 1974 Commonwealth Games and at the 1976 AEC and European Championships!

Sadly, pairing again with Nora Perry, England's two famous ladies failed to do themselves justice in a last bow 1985 World Championships, losing 7 and 9 to unseeded Koreans, H.S. Kang and S.A. Hwang. She also lost in the quarters of the mixed with Martin Dew with whom she had become nearly unbeatable. Worse was to follow. A totally ruptured Achilles tendon in the 1985 English Masters landed her in the same hospital as her coach Mike Goodwin – where she also learnt her house had been burgled!

Gilks maintained desultory warfare with the BAE over her wish to choose her own partners and fixtures. She thought them stuffy and archaic in the dawning era of Open badminton; they thought her dictatorial, obstinate. Outlawed, and with golden opportunities lost, she became known as 'the gentle blonde with the hard centre'.

Today the rift is warily healed. Singles are wisely no longer for her. But those long legs Mistinguet might have envied still bestride the court; the body that boxer John Conteh's physical trainer toughened is still resilient; the strokes are grooved; the experience is monumental; and she is still 'awesome' in mixed doubles as evidenced by her 1986 European Mixed gold.

Never has there been a more talented all-rounder.

GILLILAND, W.A. (Billy) (Scotland)
Born 27 March 1957, Greenock

A full time licensed player, Jordanhill PE College trained, and Scotland's No. 1 (twenty national titles (ten mixed and nine men's doubles in succession) and sixty-five caps, just two short of McCoig's record). He strengthened his game with unflagging practice with his brother, after hard days of vacation work as groundsmen at Scotland's Sports Council Inverclyde Centre at Largs.

He has a distinguished record: 1977 World Championships mixed doubles bronze; 1978 Commonwealth Games mixed doubles silver; 1981 World Games

men's doubles bronze with regular partner, fellow Scot Dan Travers; 1982 AEC men's doubles runners-up (8-15, 15-9, 15-10) to the brothers Sidek; and also runner-up with Karen Chapman in the mixed doubles to Dew and G. Gilks, 10-15, 17-14, 7-15. In 1985, with Nora Perry, he won the AEC to become the first Scottish title-holder. It was a feat not repeated in the World Championships as both he and Nora had to play with partners of their own nationality.

Six feet three inches, he has a tape-skimming flat serve, a lethal return of serve, low or flick, and a steep smash. Quiet, modest and sporting – hates watching himself on video replays.

He has been President of the BPF (q.v.) and is now a keen coach.

GOODE, Andrew B. (Herts and England)
Born 30 January 1960

Currently England's No. 5 with forty-seven caps to his credit, Andy is the son of a talented father and is in sports shop collaboration with younger brother Nick.

English National junior men's singles and mixed doubles in 1977/8; European junior men's singles in 1977; U.21 men's singles in 1978 and men's doubles in 1981; English National men's singles 1983/4 and runner-up 1984/5 after a close fight with Steve Baddeley.

Best results: beating, with N. Tier, Frost and Nierhoff in 1984/5 to win Scottish Open; twice beating Zhao Jianhua in doubles, and winning the 1985/6 English Masters and Nationals with N. Tier. Sixty-six caps.

GOWERS, Gillian C. (Sussex and England)
Born 9 April 1964

Winner of National U.15 mixed doubles in 1978-9, U.18 ladies' doubles and mixed doubles in 1981-2, and of the U.21 L.D. in 1983, Gowers was chosen to tour Australasia. In the Melbourne Silver Bowl she beat Gillian Clark in the singles but lost in the finals with her in the doubles: results which were reversed in New Zealand.

She has an impressive AEC mixed record. With Nigel Tier, in 1983 and 1985 she reached the semis, and in 1984 the final, all going to three hard games. In

1985, partnering Billy Gilliland, she was a finalist in Taipei and Hong Kong, and winner in Japan when they beat Dew/Gilks; with Tier, in the World Championships, she beat Kihlstrom and Magnusson to reach the semis where they lost 4 and 8 to ultimate winners Park/Yoo and was runner-up in the Indonesian Open. In the English Nationals she won the doubles with Gillian Clark and might have won the mixed but for a prolonged nose-bleed!

More recently Gowers has pushed Larsen to three close games in the World Championships and won the Malaysian Ladies' singles and doubles and the Danish Open mixed. In 1986, won both National ladies' doubles, with Helen Troke, and mixed doubles with Tier. With sixteen U.23 and eleven England caps, she ranks No. 5. Currently studying for a sports science degree in her native Sussex.

GRACE, W.G.

The bearded giant of turn-of-the-century cricket – and an interested spectator at the 1902 AEC held in the Crystal Palace transept. Sadly, he appears never to have been an active player, though his cricketing successor J.B. Hobbs certainly was.

GRIPS

A correct grip is necessary for correct strokes. There are four main grips, though all strokes can be played with the basic grip.
1. *Basic.* This is a shake-hands, finger-grip with (a) the handle held at the bottom for maximum leverage, power and reach, though a number of Eastern players do use a shorter grip; (b) the fingers spread out, not bunched; (c) the V between index-finger and thumb roughly in line with shaft and frame.
2. *Backhand.* The racket is rolled by the fingers thirty degrees to the right so that the thumb is flat along the *back* bevel for added power and control.
3. *Backhand variant.* Instead of putting the thumb flat on the bevel, it is placed on the top edge of the bevel, so allowing greater wrist flexibility.
4. *Frying-pan.* Analogously named, the racket is held square to the net with the palm behind the back bevel. As it restricts the full use of the wrist, it

should be used only at the net or in rushing (q.v.) serves. In the former case it obviates change of grip for backhand strokes but necessitates it for upward net-shots.

The grip may be relaxed (but never sloppy) between strokes, in delicate net-shots and in low serves. At impact, it must be firm but never so tight that wrist flexibility is lost.

GUILD HALL, Preston

Preston's Queen's Hall was the venue of the first-ever Thomas Cup Final in 1949. Since then major badminton events including the 1978 European Championships and a 1982 Thomas Cup semi-final have been held in the Guild Hall, a multi-entertainment complex which includes a Grand Hall seating 2,100, theatre, restaurant and seven bars, all set over a shopping arcade with direct access to Europe's largest bus station.

GUNALAN, Punch (Malaysia)

Gunalan started playing at the age of four and won his first of many titles (Negri Sembilan State) whilst still in the third form!

He won the 1970 Commonwealth Games doubles with Ng Boon Bee and also the 1971 AEC; and the 1974 CG Singles, 15-1, 15-6 against J. Paulson (Canada). Remembered particularly for superb play in the 1974 AEC final against Hartono (though losing a third game cliffhanger after having been 15-8, 7-1 in the first two) he is aptly nicknamed 'Panther' for his speed, deadly attack and adventurousness.

Having earned a degree at Sussex University, he coached Malaysia's Thomas Cup teams and Scottish Inverclyde (q.v.) courses and now acts as a Far East manager for Carlton and Malaysian Team Manager.

GUT, Manufacture of

When buying a new racket, most players look searchingly at its attractively anodized frame, carbon or steel shaft and leather or towelling grip. Too few pay enough attention to the stringing, which is even more important, since it is this which makes contact with the shuttle in power smashes and delicate touch-shots.

Natural Gut

Many think of gut as coming from cats, but the term 'cat-gut' is derived from 'kit' (later 'kat'), a small violin carried by itinerant dancing-masters!

The best gut is made from the intestines of sheep or cows. Australia produces possibly the best because its cattle are in fine condition and the gut is treated within twenty-four hours of slaughter. The intestines are cut into strips, twisted and, under heat, annealed in that twist. They are made into different gauges according to the numer of strands incorporated.

The resultant gut should be semi-transparent and of a whitish colour. Its great advantages are that tightness of stringing is maintained and that, because of this thinness, it expands and contracts on impact with the shuttle more quickly than synthetic, and so gives greater responsiveness. Its disadvantages are that thinness can lead to breakage and it is affected by damp. The latter can be countered temporarily by coating with a waterproof varnish.

Synthetic gut

This is generally a derivative of nylon. It is extruded under heat as a mono-filament not so much in the finer gauges as in the medium to heavy gauges. The thicker the string, the slower its recovery after impact, its responsiveness; this can be obviated to some degree by reducing stringing tension.

Today there is an almost bewildering number of improved variants on the monofilament. The 'wrapped' is a mono-filament wrapped round with one or two much thinner guts. (Synthetic does not anneal.) This is recognizable by the horizontal grain and gives a good grip-surface to the shuttle base. In other types, the monofilament is a hollow cylinder filled either with *oil* or with many hair-thin fibres. Or there is the more expensive graphite core, carbon wrapped, distinguishable by its black colouring.

Stringing

Formerly, much depended on the expertise of experienced and graded stringers. Today, with the advent of machines, stringing is much less individualistic. Among the major faults to look for are over-or-under-tensioning, uneven tensioning, slight cutting of string and slack knotting off. As a rough guide, fine natural gut should be strung at 13 lb, medium or heavy, according to thickness, at 12-10 lbs.

H

HADINATA, Christian (Indonesia)
Born 11 December 1949, Purwokerto

Eye-catchingly programmed merely as 'Christian', Hadinata has shown little meekness in a long and versatile career. As a shrewd eleven-year-old, he turned from Indonesian soccer, as offering little chance of world fame, to badminton's greater glory.

With AEC titles in 1972 and 1973 with 'Big Ade' Chandra, the men's doubles world was at their feet until even more brilliant fellow Indonesians Tjun Tjun and Wahjudi made them play second fiddle. With Tjun Tjun injured in 1980, the World Championship (and the English FP Masters) was theirs at last (after a 3 and 4 finals defeat in 1977). When burly Chandra became too slow, Christian teamed up with Liem Swie King. In powerful combination they won – though unavailingly – both Thomas Cup finals doubles against China's best in 1982, and also the Asian Games team title.

Indonesians generally husband their resources for one event. Not so Christian. In 1973 he reached the AEC Singles final only to perish before Hartono at his best, 4-15, 2-15. Wisely but most unusually, he turned to mixed doubles in 1975. He shattered the Western stranglehold on that event by beating, with Imelda Wigoeno, the incomparable Tredgett-Perry combination, 15-1, 18-17 to win the AEC Mixed in 1979. Although he lost to them in both the 1980 and 1981 AEC finals, he beat them again when it mattered most – in the 1980 World Championships. He has since had numerous victories with Ivana Lie, including the 1985 Alba Quartz WC.

At the net he employed quicksilver movement and gun-draw reflexes for outright winners, and delicate touch to set them up for his partner. Fast and powerful at the back and strong in defence, he nevertheless unorthodoxedly raided the net in mixed, secure in Imelda's fleet footedness and pin-pointed attack behind him.

Quiet, unassuming, a magnificent doubles all-rounder.

HALF-COURT PUSH

A side-arm cross between net-shot and a drive, played flat, and deceptively, with apparent fast-drive action, that confusingly places the shuttle between net and back players into the 'divorce area' (q.v.). Used mainly in mixed by the men as they probe for an opening or as a return of serve.

HALL, Darren (Essex and England)
Born 25 October 1965, Chingford

The 1980/81 U.15 National Triple Champion who in 1984 was labelled 'a better prospect than ever Kevin Jolly was'.

In 1982 he and his coach-uncle, England's No. 1, Ray Stevens, won the Portuguese Open by beating Gilliland/-Travers, 3 and 8. Later he won the men's singles of both the Melbourne Silver Bowl and the New Zealand Open. After winning the Danish U.18, he was rewarded with an 'apprentice' trip to the Far East in 1984 by the EBU as 'Most

King by name; King by talent! Liem Swie King (Indonesia) keeps his eyes on the shuttle as he plays an attacking clear

Ray Sharp (Kent and England) lunges determinedly to play a perfectly balanced backhand lob

Denmark's Morten Frost, one of the world's finest ever Singles players, shows that even champions can be under pressure as he stretches for a sideline smash

Left-hander Steve Baddeley (Sussex and England) exemplifies the game's grace as he executes a perfectly controlled backhand lob

A wristy smash by Nick Yates (Kent and England), who is already moving in to maintain the attack

China's Zhao Jianhua shows he's got what it takes to be a champion: a towering, steeply-angled, jump smash, that helped him to a first-appearance AEC title

Tang Hsien Hu, first of the great Chinese masters, illustrates the secret of success: 'take the shuttle early'

Two Great Danes — and characters. Svend Pri (*left*) and Erland Kops, both AEC winners, make a formidable pair as they go for 'the one down the middle'

Japan's Atsuko Tokuda races in for a net-kill; Mikiko Takada is poised to finish off any return. Not for nothing known as TNT!

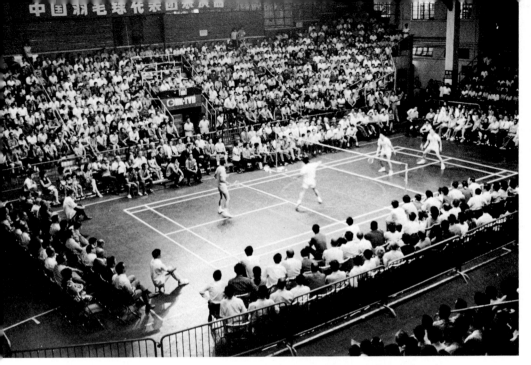

Serried rows of shirt-sleeved spectators show that badminton is just as keenly —
and much more vociferously — followed in Hong Kong and the Far East as at
Wembley's All-England Championships, below

Gillian Gilks crouches to return Mike Tredgett's cross-court smash: Nora Perry
and Derek Talbot are equally alert. 1977 — and both ladies still going strong!

Doubly talented Sang Yee Hoo (South Korea): 1985 World Championship Mixed winner *and* Ladies' Doubles semi-finalist

Kim Yun Ja (South Korea) makes the most of her fewer inches by reaching out to take the shuttle high

Long name — long reach: Indonesia's petite Lie Ing Hoa Ivana in action in the 1980 English Masters at the Albert Hall

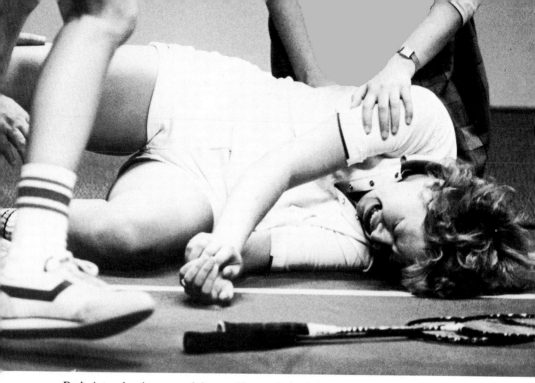

Badminton has its ups and downs. Here a thrice injured Gillian Clark (England) writhes in agony with a snapped Achilles tendon

Gillian Gilks (Surrey and England), the world's greatest all-rounder, caught in elegant mid-flight playing a round-the-head stroke

Helen Troke (Hampshire and England), England's riposte to the Chinese, shows her youthful athleticism and determination

Grace and charm exemplified by one half of the famous Danish Rasmussen sisters, Karin Jorgensen

Promising Player'. He reached the quarters of the Chinese-Taipei Masters in singles and doubles but lost 2 and 0 to Frost, and, with Yates, 1 and 1 to Kartono and Heryanto. But he took a game off Frost in the 1985 Scottish Open.

U.21 National men's singles champion in 1983 and 1984, he has sixteen U.23 caps, and twenty-two senior caps, and ranks joint No. 3 with his close friend Steve Butler.

In 1986 beat Butler in 'probably the best ever final seen at an English National' by 15-5, 9-15, 18-17, after 11-5 up in the third had become 11-13 down.

As relaxation, he enjoys pool at the 'Crooked Billet' and disco dancing.

HALLS, DATA FOR

The following are the requirements for a top-class badminton hall. (Doubtless they will cause a pang to badminton's majority, who play – but still thoroughly enjoy the game – in often highly unsuitable school halls and gyms, drill halls and church halls.

Height: At international level, a clear height of 30 feet (9.14 metres); at club level, 25 feet (7.62 metres).

Clear space round the court: 5 feet (1.52 metres) minimum at the ends of the court; 4 feet (1.22 metres) at the sides; 3 feet (0.91 metres) between parallel courts.

Background: Preferably walls should be without windows and of a dark colour, often green, with a matt finish. If there are windows, they should be curtained; natural light should be from roof-lights on the north or east side to avoid glare.

Floor: Should preferably be of wood, though composition is acceptable. Both should be in no way slippery or shiny. When this does not pertain, HOVA (q.v.) plastic courts should be securely laid on them.

Artificial lighting: Tungsten lighting of not less than 2 kw per court: 5 × 200 w fittings on each side; or two twin-lamp 5-foot fluorescent fittings (minimum) mounted end to end. These should be centred on the net, 3 feet outside the side-lines, and 16-19 feet above the floor. Many variations are met but in all cases lights should be shielded or enclosed to reduce glare to an absolute minimum.

Markings: Painted matt white lines or adhesive plastic tape.

Posts: Preferably screwed into floor on the sideline.

Ventilation: Must not be such as to cause 'drift' (q.v.).

Temperature: Not more than 50°F unless essential for spectator comfort.

HALLS, FAMOUS

Probably the most famous badminton halls are Wembley Arena (London), Senayan Stadium (Jakarta), Stadium Negara (Kuala Lumpur), Brondby Hallen (Copenhagen), Municipal Gym (Tokyo), Guild Hall (Preston, UK), Albert Hall (London), Kelvin Hall (Glasgow), Mountbatten SC (Portsmouth, UK), Duinjiwick (Holland), Wimbledon S & BC (London), Indraprastha Stadium (New Delhi) and the Saddledome (Calgary, Canada).

HALSALL, Sara (Lancashire and England)
Born 29 September, 1967

A teenage (seventeen) début victory against an even younger Korean débutante, fourteen-year-old Cho Young Sook, was the start of a swift rise to No. 6 ranking. In March 1985 Sara became English Junior Champion and after defeating England's No. 4, Gillian Gowers, was runner-up in the Senior National. She failed to do herself justice in the European Junior but was runner-up in the girls' doubles, rounding off a fine season in China with two ladies' doubles victories with Karen Beckman. With her she won not only the 1985/6 Bell's LD but also beat the two Gillians, Gowers and Clark, to take the British Masters title. Twenty caps.

Received a salutary 0 and 1 hammering from Troke in the National quarters.

Despite her 'I don't like mixed' she won the Bell's mixed with M. Brown.

Playing tennis for Lancashire at $16\frac{1}{2}$ may have helped develop a whole-hearted smash. Beat Fiona Elliott in vital ICC final and Denmark's Kjaer/Nielsen in UC.

HAN, Jian (China)
Born 6 July 1956, Liaoning

A child football-fanatic converted by waterlogged pitches to indoor badminton only at the badminton-late age of sixteen. He rose meteorically in Chinese ranking but had to wait until 1981 for China's admission to world-wide competition. After relentless physical training in an 82°F humidity diving-pool, he beat Swie King in the 'match of the century' China-Indonesia clash but Prakash Padukone later outmanoeuvred him in three defeats.

1982 was his highlight. With two singles victories in the 1982 Thomas Cup final, including a key 15-12, 11-15, 17-14 win over arch-rival Swie King, he was the architect of China's triumph. He also won 'gold' in the Asian Games singles and team events, both at King's expense.

In 1983 he beat Arbi 4 and 13 in the Alba Quartz but, suffering from a back injury, lost disappointingly to Swie King 9 & 3 in the World Championship semi-final. In 1984 injury again forced his withdrawal from an eagerly awaited AEC semi-final clash with a rampant Morten Frost. In the 1984 Thomas Cup he won all his games except that vital one in the final against Arbi, which lost China the match – and trophy. But he more than made up for this by winning the 1985 World Championships from 3-8 down in the third with twelve consecutive winners against arch rival Frost. And thrashed up-and-coming compatriot Yang Yang 8 & 2 to win the Pro-Kennex.

Concentration and determination, power, placement, agility and rock-like defence were the keystones of his success. Off court, known as 'Mr Snow', he has a yen to learn English and a puckish sense of clowning which made him don the Duke of Beaufort's deer-stalker hat during a tour of Badminton House.

Still saying 'Getting too old for singles' – and convincingly disproving it.

HAND

Term for a run of successive serves by one player: as in 'he scored 8 points in his first hand'.

Used also in connection with handicap doubles. When a pair is handicapped 'owe one hand', only one player (in the right court), not both, serves in one innings. This is held to be roughly equivalent to owe 12.

The opponents of a pair who are 'give a hand' have three hands of serve not the customary two in each innings.

In 1899 at the AEC Miss M.C. Hardy scored 30 ponts in *one* hand. A feat repeated by Betty Uber and Bill White in 1933 against Denmark's best pair. In a handicap event at Cheltenham in 1908, Hazel Hogarth scored 35 points in one hand.

HANDICAPS

Each player or pair

(a) is 'scratch', starting normally, at 'love';

(b) receives anything from 1-12 points, starting at the given figure if opponent(s) is 'scratch' or 'owing';

(c) 'owes' anything from 1-12 points; starting at, say, 'owe 10' each point won reduces his owed score to 9, 8, 7 ... down to love, when he then scores normally.

A pair may be alternatively or additionally handicapped by being 'owe a hand' or 'give a hand', e.g.; owe a hand −8, or give a hand −6, or even, though rarely (but horrifyingly) owe a hand, give a hand, −4. (See *Hand*.)

As handicaps are based on the assumption of a 15-point game, setting is not permitted in handicap events. Nor may they be altered during the course of the event.

Pairs when both receive or both owe points do not start at those figures. To prevent unduly shortened or prolonged games, they start at an equitably calculated geometrical proportion to the original odds based on a game of 11, 15 or 21 points.

Handicaps

The formula for received odds is

Z × the difference between the handicaps

Z − the smaller of the handicaps
Z = points to be played. In resultant, $\frac{1}{2}$ or more counts as 1.

So with A + 12 and B + 8   15 up.

$$\frac{15 \times (12 - 8)}{15 - (8)} = \frac{15 \times 4}{7} = \frac{60}{7} = 8\frac{4}{7}$$

A starts at +9; B at 0.

The formula for owed odds is

$$\frac{Z \times (Z + \text{the longer odds})}{Z + \text{the shorter odds}} - Z$$

So with A − 10 and B − 4

$$\frac{15 \times (15 + 10)}{15 + 4} = \frac{15 \times 25}{19} = \frac{375}{19} = 20$$

$$- 15 = -5$$

A starts at −5; B at 0.

Fortunately the BAE Handbook contains comprehensive tables of such differentials.

HARTONO, Rudy (Indonesia) Born (Rudi Nio) 18 August 1951

Lithe, with dark, fringed hair, Indonesia's eighteen-year-old National Champion and No. 1 came to Wembley in 1968. From a field that contained seven-times champion Erland Kops, he joined that élite band, Tan Joe Hok, Conny Jepsen and Dave Freeman, of first-time winners by finally overcoming 1966 champion Tan Aik Huang.

1969-74 saw him win the title six more times consecutively. In doing so, he was a law unto himself, scoring in the 1969-73 finals 150 points against 40. An average of 8 points conceded per final! In one game against him it took Christian thirteen serves before he scored the first of his 4 points.

In 1972, a week before the AEC, Hartono lost to Pri 15-1, 9-15, 5-15 but beat him comfortably 15-9, 15-4 in the AEC final. In 1974 'Black Panther' Gunalan had him by the throat 8-15, 1-7 down but still lost as Hartono, with seven consecutive wins, equalled Kops record of an overall seven (8-15, 15-9, 15-10). The following year a super-fit Pri joyously beat him. But in 1976 it was Hartono yet again against a suspiciously lack-lustre Liem Swie King (15-7, 15-7), creating a new record.

In a Thomas Cup match in 1979 Hartono could still win 10 and 2 against Delfs, who had taken over Hartono's old AEC mantle in 1977. And in 1980, perhaps spurred on by the familiar 14,000-throat roar of 'Rudy! Rudy!' came probably his greatest win − in the World Championships, against Swie King, 9 and 9.

Surely that should have been enough. But two years later panic-stricken Indonesian selectors begged him to come out of retirement to help retain the Thomas Cup against Chinese threat. With only ten weeks training he played twenty-three-year-old Luan Jin in a crucial tie but, conceding eight years, lost gracefully 9-15, 15-1, 9-15.

Where lay Hartono's strength? Physically, in power of smash from the base-line and speed of balanced recovery and follow-in, supple ease of jump and round-the-head shots. Mentally, in cool consistency and shrewd opponent analysis, in a morale-destroying knack of starting in top gear, of emerging unruffled from the tightest corners and of peaking overwhelmingly for AEC finals, and in dedicated professionalism and national pride.

A sportsman of charm and modesty, who is now an 'elder statesman' on the IBF Council.

With ever greater international depth of strength building up, Hartono's record is likely to be unassailable. So is the £1,800 paid at auction for one of his rackets!

HASHMAN, née Devlin, Judy (USA and England) Born 1936, Canada

A father with eighteen AEC and innumerable Irish titles and a Wimbledon tennis mother gave chunky, auburn-haired Judy Devlin a flying start. For America, she played in no fewer than five Uber Cup series, losing only one match in fourteen years − and won thirty-one US Open titles (twelve ladies' singles, twelve ladies' doubles and seven mixed doubles. In 1954, in just three weeks, she won two US Open, two AEC and three US junior national titles − as well as becoming a US lacrosse international.

For all that, AEC titles are perhaps her greatest claim to fame. In 1954, aged eighteen, on her first appearance, she and her sister Sue (twenty, later Peard) won the first of their record six doubles titles. And she beat England's Iris Cooley to win the singles. In 1955 and 1956 she lost to Texan Margaret Varner but beat her in 1957 and 1958. 1959 saw Varner too busy playing tennis and squash for USA to compete, but Devlin lost to a nineteen-year-old English girl, Heather Ward − and announced her engagement to Middlesex player Dick Hashman. 1960 saw Varner's final appearance − and defeat. 1961-4 produced four more victories, including a thirteen-minute demolition job of England's Ursula Smith, who was to win the title in 1965. Family affairs had prevented much competitive play in 1964, and she lost in the fourth round to an astonished New Zealander, Sonia Cox.

Triumphant in 1966, in 1967 she set her sights on double figures. After a sleepless night, she was 1-5 down in the third to diminutive but fleet-footed 'runner' Noriko Takagi (Japan). Somehow she found her stamina and indomitable will to win, 12-10 – and so made it ten. With seven doubles titles (six with Sue), she was still just one behind her father's eighteen tally but had equalled Meriel Lucas's record.

'Little Red Dev' learned tactics from her father, ruthless determination from America and pin-point accuracy, consistency and deception by herself. Naturalized in 1970, she captained and played eight times for England between 1970 and 1972. Appointed England's 'Supremo' in 1977, she saw her team win the 1978 European Championships – only to receive her dismissal the same day.

HAVERS, John (Essex and England)

Enthusiastic player and administrator. Played seventy-eight county matches for Essex – and was for many years their Match Secretary. He won seven England caps (1963-6), BAE Council Member (1966); Chairman of Selectors 1977-84; England Team Captain for Thomas Cup, Commonwealth Games and international matches; and, currently, Deputy Chairman of the BAE Council.

HAWTHORN, Edward (Kent and England)
Born 1878

A 6-foot-6-inch (1.98 metres) giant who played delicate and deceptive dropshots but rarely a powerful smash. He won two AEC titles and eight caps. The last of the latter he won in 1925 when he was forty-eight, an AEC mixed doubles semi-finalist, and winner, not surprisingly, of the AEC Veterans' men's doubles. (He won again in 1926 and caused the age limit to be raised to fifty.)

To his meticulous and mathematical brain, harassed tournament referees owe today's time-saving handicap tables (see *Handicaps*). BAE Vice-President 1929-51.

HELVETIA CUP

Named after the powerful Celtic tribe who settled in central Switzerland, and donated by Mr H.P. Kunz, Swiss President of the EBU. A team competition for the less strong European nations, first played in Zurich in 1962. It was held annually, then from 1971 biennially, alternating with the European Championships, at different centres.

The FR of Germany won it ten times successively (1962-71), with the Netherlands seven times runner-up. With both countries then given European Championship status, it was won by Czechoslovakia, Norway, USSR (twice) and Ireland until, now relegated from the European Championships, the FR of Germany won again in 1983 and the Netherlands in 1985.

The top six teams in the European Championships are not allowed to participate.

Date/Venue		Winner	Runner-up
1962	Zurich	West Germany	Netherlands
1963	Munich	West Germany	Austria
1964	Haarlem	West Germany	Belgium
1965	Graz	West Germany	Netherlands
1966	Bruxelles	West Germany	Netherlands
1967	Lausanne	West Germany	Netherlands
1968	Oslo	West Germany	Norway
1969	Prague	West Germany	Netherlands
1970	Neuss	West Germany	Netherlands
1971	Heerlen	West Germany	Netherlands
1973	Graz	Czechoslovakia	Norway
1975	Antwerp	Norway	Yugoslavia
1977	Leningrad	USSR	Ireland
1979	Klagenfurt	USSR	Ireland
1981	Sandefjord	Ireland	Norway
1983	Basel	West Germany	Wales
1985	Warsaw	Netherlands	Wales

HERBERT SCHEELE AWARD

A top award instituted by the BAE in memory of Herbert Scheele, OBE, BAE and IBF Secretary for many years. The engraved silver medal is given on an 80 per cent Council majority, for 'extremely meritorious service to the game of badminton'.

The first recipient, in 1984, was a Swede, Stellan Mohlin, IBF President (q.v.), who healed the East-West split. The second (1985) was Peter Birtwistle, international player and tireless administrator for Lancashire BA and the BAE for some forty years.

HERYANTO, Rudy, and KARTONO, Hariamento (Indonesia)
Born 19 October 1954, Tasikmalaya; 8 August 1954, Tegal

Not easily distinguishable on court by the Western eye and always thought of as a pair, so paired together here.

In 1980, in the World Championship, they did well to take Chandra and Christian to three games (7-15, 15-5, 5-15), having lost disastrously in the AEC to the unseeded Sideks. 1981 was perhaps their highlight, when they proved themselves Indonesia's best by beating Chandra and Christian in the AEC semi-final, and holders Tjun Tjun and Wahjudi 9 and 8 in the final.

For two years they were in AEC doldrums. In 1982 they lost again (semi-final) to the again unseeded Sideks, who went on to take the title. 1983 was even more disastrous, when they lost in the third round to 'unknowns' Teong and Chup (M.) – and so, almost unprecedented, left no Indonesian pair in the 'semis' – and were not paired for the World Championships.

1984 they bounced back like fire-crackers with relentless speed and flat, fast shots to the body to put paid in the AEC final to England's hopes (Tredgett and Dew) of a first Men's Doubles title since 1938. With Swie King, Kartono won the 1985 Alba Quartz.

Sadly, in the 1982 Thomas Cup final against the Chinese Sun Zhian and Yao Ximing, it was they who, having lost narrowly 14-17, swept triumphantly through to 15-3 – only to reap the whirlwind in the third, a five-minute 1-15 débâcle, which yielded the long-held trophy to China.

HICKSON, F.W.

An eager ping-pong player who turned to badminton administration: Alexandra Palace BC official; founder of London League (1908) and Middlesex BA; BAE's first paid Secretary (1927-37) and Honorary Treasurer; IBF Secretary (1934-7). His memory is perpetuated in the F.W. Hickson Permanent Memorial Trophy awarded to the AEC's men's singles winner.

HILL, Colonel Arthur

Rugby for Blackheath, cricket for the Gentlemen, but only club standard badminton was his sporting background. (He travelled 120 miles a week to play for Southsea BC – until he was eighty.) A meticulous administrator, he was BAE Hon. Secretary and Treasurer (1910-27) and President (1927-50) – forty years of service. He died at the age of ninety-nine.

HOGARTH, Hazel (England)

Expert Frank Devlin (q.v.) regarded her as 'murder at the net'. As such, she won the first of six AEC mixed titles (four in succession with Sir George Thomas (1914-22) in 1905, and the last of her five ladies' doubles titles in 1927. Played thirteen times for England (1904-29). Contrary to popular opinion, she, not a Malayan, was the first to serve back-handed.

HOLDING A SHOT

A deceptive ploy, underhand or overhead, in which the wrist is kept cocked and the shot is delayed, hoping the opponent will advance too far forward and, off-balance, be wrong-footed, when the wrist is uncocked to flick the shuttle just over his head to rear-court.

HOLWILL, H.

'Uncle Bill' was former City of London policeman, throughout the Blitz, and RSL representative at all major tournaments in England for nearly thirty years. He could well boast he had seen more top-class play and met more top-class players than almost any other living man. He did innumerable kindnesses and was honoured with a presentation at the AEC in 1976. He died in 1985, shortly after attending the last of his many All-Englands.

HOOPER, Brian (Hampshire)
Born 16 November 1939, Portsmouth

The failed county coach who helped thirteen-year-old Helen Troke to world class. He played men's singles and mixed for Hants BA until 1972, when he started group coaching. Amongst others, he took Maggie Boxall and Anne Statt (both England) under his wing.

In 1979 he picked out young Helen Troke from a group 'who couldn't win a raffle'. Quietly dedicated, he coaches six or seven nights a week. In 1979 the BAE appointed him team coach of the England U.23 Ladies, then, recently, of the senior ladies.

'Give me someone with a 100 per cent – and I'll give 100 per cent' is his watchword.

HORNER, Nancy (Middlesex and Scotland)

A Scot who won fifteen caps and Scottish National and Open titles in all three events (including a 1953 Open Triple Crown) and reached both the 1953 AEC ladies' singles and mixed doubles semis.

As first BAE Coaching Secretary, later Director of Coaching, she got English post-war badminton on the move. For this she was honoured by being made the only BAE female Vice-President (1967-75) in an otherwise male, eighty-strong list of past and present officers.

On her own heath she ran memorable summer coaching courses at St Andrews and Inverclyde, Largs. Her straight-forward, no frills approach is evidenced in the crisp style of 'the Little Red Book', the BAE's manual for coaches.

She retired from coaching to give more time to her mother but herself died on 20 November 1984 after a long illness stoically borne.

HORTICULTURAL HALL

Situated in Vincent Square, quite close to Westminster Abbey, it was the venue for the AEC and international matches in the halcyon era of English badminton (1910-39). (See also *All-England Championships*.)

HOU, Chia Chang and TANG, Hsien Hou (China)

The first Chinese 'dragons', linked here because it was they who fired the imagination when China first emerged from behind the 'Bamboo Curtain', courteously to demolish the Danish and Canadian teams from whom they had 'come to learn'.

It was the same tale when China played – and won, without dropping a men's game (420 points to 170) – all four matches in England in 1973. That they

showed dumbfounded spectators a new dimension is evidenced by the fact that Tang and Hou, both in their later twenties, beat the unfortunate English National Champion, Ray Stevens, to 1 and 1, and together beat D. Talbot and E. Stuart, also National Champions, 2 and 5. No wonder the English players' party song was rueful:

> We'd like to learn to play the game
> The way the Chinese do.
> To smash and bang like Fang and Tang
> And drop like Hou and Liu.

Exciting, fast, accurate, deceptive and, on demand, powerful. The pundits held that either could have beaten the unbeatable Rudy Hartono but, sadly, politics prevented such an epic encounter.

Hou won both the Asian Games title (1974) and the Asian BC title (1976) when he beat Swie King. He is presently one of China's leading coaches.

HOUR-GLASS COURT

Prior to 1901 the court had a 15-foot (4.5 metres) waist at the net. The posts were continued up a further 5 feet (1.5 metres) like miniature Rugby posts, so that invalid shots passing outside them but landing in-court could be more easily observed. This shape, used also in tennis until 1877, is said to have originated in a Poona hall which had inward-opening doors on either side at post level.

HOVA COURT

Ready marked, green plastic, non-slip court surface often laid on slippery floors for major events. It was invented post-War by Hove Borough Surveyor T.R. Humble. The first trial strip (6 by 3 feet, 1.8 by 0.9 metres), was made from an old indoor tennis surface and tested by Sussex BA President's wife *throwing* shuttles at English international F.C. Sharp!

It rolls up into halves that must be firmly secured with broad adhesive tape when in use. A good-looking boon used world-wide.

HUME, Donald C. (Middlesex and England)

Hard-hitting, fast-moving English international (twenty-four caps, 1928-48), never renowned for on-court smartness. He won AEC singles in 1930 but was more effective in men's doubles (1932-5)

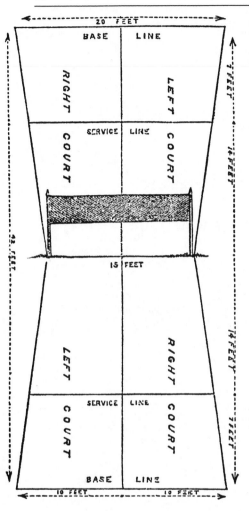

with even harder-hitting R.M. White, and was virtually unbeatable in mixed with Betty Uber (1933-6). Died 3 May 1986.

HWANG, Sun Ai (S. Korea) Born 1962

Strikingly Oriental in looks and masculinely built. Unheralded, Sun Ai Hwang caused a furore by winning both the Taipei Open and the Japanese Cup in 1981. Coming to Europe, in the Danish Open 'quarters' she fell 8-11, 10-12 to Canadian Wendy Carter but made amends in the Swedish by annihilating Indonesia's Lie Ivana ('Ivana mauled by Korean tigress' headlined the papers). They met again in the AEC, and Hwang was 5-11, 2-5 down before storming out 11-7, 11-0.

And so to the final against Europe's darling, Lene Koppen, expected to make it 'three in a row': Instead, Hwang allowed her just 3 points in all to take a 'first appearance' title.

Fleet Street found rumour as exciting as Hwang's own play: she had trained for four years in a convent, been chastised if one of her scheduled practice drop-shots found the net, and was later found to be an insurance clerk.

With China's acceptance by the IBF, she met Zhang Ailing in the World Games final. Two super-fit girls battled it out in a 7-11, 11-9, 12-9 marathon that favoured Ailing.

Spurred to a still tougher training regimen, Hwang fell and fractured ankle and playing-hand thumb. Re-emerging for the 1982 AEC, she lost to Song Youping by an incredible 11-9, 2-11, 0-11. Later that year, in a record 125-minute doubles, she and Kang Heung Sook beat compatriots Yun Ja Kim and Yoo Sang Hee to win the Asian Games title. But it was only as second-string doubles that she played in the 1984 TC finals. With Kang, she ruthlessly disposed of England's Perry and Gilks in the 1985 World Championships but lost to Ying and Dixi in the semis.

Intrigued spectators by greeting her best winning shots with a clamant martial cry.

HYBART, Maureen (Welsh BU Secretary and Development Officer)

A petite blonde whose drive is out of all proportion to her size. Her efficiency springs from a University of Wales honours degree and ICI experience. Capped for Wales at netball but not badminton, she has made up for this by producing a son (junior) and a daughter who have both sported the 'Red Dragon'.

I

IBF AWARDS

Instituted in 1985, they consist of:

1) *The Meritorious Service Award* given to players and/or administrators for at least fifteen years' service in assisting the growth of sport in a national organization. First recipients were:

C.A. Baxter, Australia
R.O. Fyfe, Australia
W.R. Hindson, Australia
Miss E.R. Robert, Australia
Mrs C.A. Rowlands, Falkland Islands
R. Neyns, Belgium
R.E. Servais, Belgium
C.Y. Wong, Chinese Taipei
P. Razso, Hungary
E. Fodor, Hungary
N. Worley, Malta
Miss N.M. Fleming, New Zealand
E. Jørgensen, Denmark
J. Skaarup, Denmark

2) *The Distinguished Service Award* given for long (fifteen years) and/or distinguished service in an international context. The Council's decision must be unanimous.

First recipients were:

E.S. Jarrett, USA
Zhu Ze, China
O. Mertz, Denmark
Mrs B. Scheele, England
J. Benes, Czechoslovakia
A. Segercrantz, Finland
Mrs L. Køppen, Denmark
Christian Hadinata, Indonesia
Khir Johari, Malaysia
J.F. Devlin, USA
Mrs J. Hashman, England
E. Kops, Denmark
Wong Peng Soon, Singapore
Eddy Choong, Malaysia

IBF MEMBERSHIP NUMBERS

Unfortunately these figures do not give an accurate idea of the numbers actually playing the game. In Indonesia and Malaysia, for example, tens of thousands play in the open on makeshift courts. In, the UK and Ireland many clubs never affiliate to the national organization, and their large numbers of players are never added to the strength. The IBF considers that numbers actually playing could be ten times these numbers.

The palms for rapid growth over the last six years must go to the USSR (50,000-160,000), Korea (2,500-14,856) and Chinese Taipei (39,00-62,167). It is extraordinary to see the Indonesian decline from 153,500-50,000 – one that surely must be only nominal.

LARGEST MEMBERSHIPS

	1980	1985
Denmark	145,000	171,049
USSR	50,000	160,000
England	113,000	103,543
China	100,000	101,000
	(1981)	
Japan	71,000	91,033
German FR	56,000	87,500
Netherlands	70,000	82,788
Chinese Taipei	39,000	62,167
Canada	55,000	60,000
Indonesia	153,500	50,000
Sweden	22,000	42,389
Ireland	24,500	24,500
Malaysia	15,000	20,350

SMALLEST MEMBERSHIPS
(*Associate Members, i.e. fewer than 500 registered players*)

	1985
St Helena	22
Barbados	35

Antigua	50
Fiji	50
Seychelles	50
Gibraltar	50
Kuwait	70
Bermuda	100
Grenada	100
Brazil	150

ICELAND –
Badmintonsamband Islands

The game started before World War II in Iceland, and its first National Championship was held in 1949. (The winner, Einar Jonsson, now aged seventy, still plays singles.) Thanks to attendance at Danish coaching courses, and the visit of a Chinese coach, standards of its 5,000 players have improved enough for them to enter the Nordic Championships, the Helvetia Cup and, bravely, the European Championships. They have also organized a biennial competition with Greenland and the Faroe Islands and now have a purpose-built hall in Reykjavik.

IMAKITA, Motoo
Born 1937, Hokkaido

When his Olympic ski-ing dreams were shattered at fourteen by illness, he played and organized badminton through school and university. As a Tokyo-based, BSc (engineering) executive, he travelled widely with little time for badminton until, in 1970, he took over the international affairs of Nippon BA, of which he is now its Secretary.

In 1979 he joined the IBF Council and within two years was responsible for the Tokyo Uber Cup finals and the organization of the all-important IBF/WBF unification meeting. He now runs one of the world's biggest tournaments, the Japanese Open.

Founder-member of the International Disaster Club.

INDIA – Badminton Association of India

Possible country of origin of the game and among the earliest IBF affiliates (1935), it was not until after World War II that India took to badminton as a major sport, when the 8th Indian Championships gave it a great fillip.

Today Prakash Padukone (the only Indian ever to win an AEC title – 1980 men's singles) is a household name for graceful skill and sportsmanship. Other wristy and deceptive (but seldom powerful) players who achieved international repute were N.M. Natekar, T.N. Seth, Dipu and Roman Ghosh, Suresh Goel (1982 CG Singles champion, S. Modi) and, alone perhaps among the women, Ami Ghia.

INDIAN OCEAN ISLAND GAMES

Badminton is played – and enjoyed – in even the most far-flung places. The first Games were held in the tiny volcanic island of Reunion, 15,000 kilometres from Paris (1979). The second in much larger Mauritius (1985).

Players are as used to playing outdoors as indoors, and ladies so reluctant to take up the game that neither individual ladies' doubles nor a ladies' team event have been played. The men's team event is played on Thomas Cup lines.

1985 Results
MS   P. Richard (Maur)
LS   Marie Claude Hurree (Maur)
MD   P. Lesage and P. Richard (Maur)
Mxd D J. and C. Foo Kune (Maur)
Team Event
1979 1. Mauritius
        2. Reunion
        3. Maldives
        4. Seychelles
1985 1. Mauritius
        2. Maldives
        3. Reunion
        4. Seychelles

INDONESIA – Persatuan Bulutangkis Seluruh Indonesia

Badminton owes much to Singapore merchants who took the game, in the late 1920s, to Indonesia, fifth largest country in the world, an archipelago of thousands of islands.

Despite problems of size and transport, badminton has become the national sport, with 150,000 affiliated members in 2,000 clubs and a vast 3-5 million playing unofficially on any spare patch of land. Television and Press coverage is on a scale undreamt of in Europe. After Indonesia's 1975-6 Thomas Cup victory, President Suharto put 30 million rupeahs (£43,000) into the team's bank account as 'an incentive to keep them playing as amateurs'.

With such numbers and enthusiasm, it is not surprising that Indonesia has achieved so much. With 8 wins out of 11 since its first appearance, between 1958 and 1986, it has almost monopolized the Thomas Cup – a fact not surprising when one remembers the early brilliance of Ferry Sonneville and Tan Joe Hok, followed by that of Iie Sumirat, the incomparable Rudy Hartono, Liem Swie King, Icuk Sugiarto and Hastomo Arbi; and doubles pairs such as Tjun Tjun and Wahjudi, Hadinata and Chandra, Kartono and Heryanto. And it was Christian who brilliantly trespassed on European preserves to win the AEC and World mixed titles.

Indonesia has produced women of World class too: the great Minarni, Retno Koestijah and, more recently, Imelda Wigoeno (now Kurniawan) and the majestic Verawaty (now Fajrin). Five times runners-up in the Uber Cup, they won it in 1974-5, each time fighting it out with Japan until they fell to China in 1986.

Indonesia has done much for the game off-court too. Their President, Ferry Sonneville, generously provided the money to fund the coaching scheme for emergent nations that bears his name. PBSI has sent its own coaches to Mexico, Kampuchea, Hong Kong, W. Germany and Canada as well as opening its own specialized training camps to European rivals. In the IBF it has been a moderating force.

For twenty years the world's greatest badminton nation, but today rather in the shadow of near neighbour China despite a gallant 1984 recapture of the Thomas Cup.

Men's Singles
1982   I. Sugiarto
1983   L.S. King
1984   L. Pongoh
1985   Han Jian
1986   I. Sugiarto

Ladies' Singles
1982   V. Fajrin
1983   Ivana Lie
1984   Li Lingwei
1985   Li Lingwei
1986   Shi Wen

Men's Doubles
1982   Kartono/Heryanto
1983   Kartono/Heryanto
1984   C. Hadinata/Hadibowo
1985   L.S. King/Kartono
1986   L.S. King/Kartono

Ladies' Doubles
1982   G. Gilks/G.M. Clark
1983   R. Damayanti/R. Francisca
1984   N. Perry/J. Webster
1985   Han Aiping/Li Lingwei
1986   V. Fajrin/Ivana Lie

Mixed Doubles
1982   M. Dew/G. Gilks
1983   C. Hadinata/Ivana Lie
1984   C. Hadinata/Ivana Lie
1985   M. Dew/G. Gilks
1986   S. Fladberg/G. Glark

INTER-CITY CHAMPIONSHIP

Instituted in February 1985, a men's event (three men's singles, two doubles), in which home team Kuala Lumpur 'A' beat Jakarta 5-0. Other teams competing were Bangkok, Tokyo, Seoul and Kuala Lumpur 'B'.

INTER-COUNTY CHAMPIONSHIP

This, the official BAE county competition, is not restricted to English counties: groups or branches from Scotland, Ireland and Wales as well as Guernsey and the Isle of Man take part. Where travelling conditions are arduous or expensive, competitors have to be prepared to play their 'home' matches 'away'. In 1985/6, 110 I, II and III teams, split into seven divisions, competed.

Divisions I and II are each split into two sections, basically North and South. In Division I semi-finals (Winner Section A v. Runner-up Section B) and a final are held to decide who will hold the trophy presented by the Cheshire clubs, Chester, Claughton, Grosvenor and Wallasey. (In addition, in 1985, the losing finalist challenged the winner for the newly awarded Famous Grouse Challenge Trophy, won 8-3 by Surrey against Lancashire.) In Division II the section winners play off for the trophy presented in 1937/8 by Brigadier R. Bruce Hay DSO; until 1948 solely for second teams.

Divisions III to VI are split into four sections of five teams, regionalized to minimize travelling: Division VII into two sections. All ties consist of seventeen matches (three men's singles, two ladies' singles, four men's, four women's and four mixed doubles) played on a home and away basis.

Relegation and promotion ensue but on a basic complicated by the fact that two teams from one county are not allowed in the same section. (See *BAE Handbook ICC regulations.*)

Middlesex, largely pre-war (ten) and Surrey post-war (twenty-three), have monopolised Division I with sporadic Northern resistance from Lancashire (six) and Cheshire (five) who were also runners-up twelve times. Surrey II (eight) have been a force in Division II.

The first recorded county match was Surrey v. Hampshire (12-4) in 1899. Such matches were mainly in the South but a Lancashire team did daringly but unsuccessfully challenge an English team returning triumphantly from an 8-1 defeat of Ireland in 1905. Lancashire and Cheshire (then powerfully amalgamated) recorded: 'We played for fun with never a Cup at the end.'

With the growth of county associations, the first official ICC was inaugurated in 1928/9 but with no arrangement for a championship play-off. This was rectified in 1930/31 when Middlesex, with almost an international side, won the first of their seven pre-war finals. After the war they scored two more victories, and Cheshire, previously five times runner-up, three. In 1946/7 they shared the title when unable to agree a play-off date. Middlesex's 1930-47 record makes astounding reading. Their thirty-three players (eighteen internationals) won fifty-four of fifty-six ties, scoring 605 points to 168.

1954/5 saw the start of Surrey's even more complete domination: nineteen victories in twenty-one years. Lancashire then took over the title with five wins and Essex with two. The only other winner had been Kent (twice). Surrey, with victories in the last three years, seems all-conquering again.

In 1937/8 a second team competition was started. In 1948/9 this became a Division II competition open to first and second teams. Winners have been much more varied, but Surrey 2nd has won it eight times in all and six successively (1938-63).

1955 saw the entry of third teams, used largely as 'nurseries', and the formation of further divisions.

The format of each tie, and of the championship as a whole, has frequently changed to suit changing conditions. Unfortunately, recently, the pressures of Open badminton have been such as to prevent the regular appearance of internationals for their counties.

Sponsorship from Bowring Shipton, Friends Provident and Famous Grouse has done much to alleviate soaring costs, and currently the Royal Bank of Scotland have added £15,000 prize-money in an overall £60,000 spread over 3 years.

DIVISION ONE
Results of Final Ties

1930-1	MIDDLESEX beat Northumberland, 13-2
1931-2	MIDDLESEX beat Cheshire, 11-5
1932-3	MIDDLESEX beat Northumberland, 13-3
1933-4	CHESHIRE beat Middlesex, 9-7
1934-5	MIDDLESEX beat Cheshire, 13-3
1935-6	MIDDLESEX beat Cheshire, 12-4
1936-7	MIDDLESEX beat Cheshire, 11-5
1937-8	LANCASHIRE beat Sussex, 8-8

(19 games to 18)
1938-9 MIDDLESEX beat Cheshire, 8-8
(21 games to 18)
1939 to 1946 *No Competition*
1946-7 Cheshire and Middlesex divided
(unplayed)
1947-8 YORKSHIRE beat Surrey, 9-7
1948-9 CHESHIRE beat Surrey, 11-5
1949-50 CHESHIRE beat Surrey, 8-8 (21
games to 17)
1950-1 MIDDLESEX beat Cheshire, 9-6
1951-2 CHESHIRE beat Middlesex, 11-4
1952-3 MIDDLESEX beat Cheshire, 9-6
1953-4 KENT beat Cheshire, 9-6
1954-5 SURREY beat Cheshire, 12-3
1955-6 SURREY beat Lancashire, 10-5
1956-7 SURREY beat Lancashire, 13-2
1957-8 SURREY beat West of Scotland,
9-6
1958-9 SURREY beat Cheshire, 12-3
1959-60 KENT beat West of Scotland, 13-2
1960-1 SURREY beat Lancashire, 11-4
1961-2 SURREY beat West of Scotland,
12-3
1962-3 SURREY beat Lancashire, 12-3
1963-4 ESSEX beat West of Scotland, 10-5
1964-5 SURREY beat Cheshire, 11-4
1965-6 SURREY beat Lancashire, 15-0
1966-7 SURREY beat Yorkshire, 13-2
1967-8 SURREY beat Yorkshire, 15-0
1968-9 SURREY beat Cheshire, 10-5
1969-70 SURREY beat West of Scotland,
14-1
1970-1 SURREY beat West of Scotland,
14-3
1971-2 SURREY beat Essex, 9-8
1972-3 SURREY beat Essex, 12-5
1973-4 SURREY beat Essex, 9-8
1974-5 SURREY beat Kent, 9-8
1975-6 LANCASHIRE beat Kent, 10-7
1976-7 ESSEX beat Lancashire, 10-7
1977-8 ESSEX beat Hampshire, 9-8
1978-9 LANCASHIRE beat Yorkshire,
10-7
1979-80 LANCASHIRE beat Yorkshire,
11-6
1980-1 LANCASHIRE beat Kent, 9-8
1981-2 SURREY beat Yorkshire, 11-6
1982-3 SURREY beat Lancashire, 10-7
1983-4/1984-5 *No final tie* SURREY
1985-6 LANCASHIRE beat Surrey, 9-8

DIVISION TWO
(Until 1948 this was contested between county
2nd teams only)
1937-8 SUSSEX 2nd beat Yorkshire 2nd,
11-5
1938-9 SUSSEX 2nd beat Yorkshire 2nd,
8-8 (20 games to 18)
1939-1946 *No Competition*
1946-7 KENT 2nd beat Cheshire 2nd, 9-5
1947-8 CHESHIRE 2nd beat Middlesex
2nd, 9-6
1948-9 CHESHIRE 2nd beat Somerset,
11-5
1949-50 ESSEX* beat Cheshire 2nd, 8-8 (21

games to 19)
1950-1 HERTFORDSHIRE beat Cheshire
2nd, 9-6
1951-2 CHESHIRE 2nd beat
Gloucestershire, 14-1
1952-3 BERKS, BUCKS & OXON* beat
Cheshire 2nd, 9-6
1953-4 SOMERSET beat Derbyshire, 11-4
1954-5 CHESHIRE 2nd beat Kent 2nd,
11-4
1955-6 DERBYSHIRE* beat Hertfordshire,
12-3
1956-7 KENT 2nd beat Northamptonshire,
11-4
1957-8 SURREY 2nd beat Isle of Man, 9-6
1958-9 SURREY 2nd beat Isle of Man*, 8-7
1959-60 SURREY 2nd beat Lancashire 2nd,
13-2
1960-1 SURREY 2nd beat Lancashire 2nd,
9-6
1961-2 SURREY 2nd beat Lancashire 2nd,
8-7
1962-3 SURREY 2nd beat Lancashire 2nd,
8-7
1963-4 MIDDLESEX* beat Lancashire
2nd, 9-6
1964-5 HERTFORDSHIRE beat
Nottinghamshire*, 10-5
1965-6 HAMPSHIRE* beat Yorkshire 2nd,
10-5
1966-7 MIDDLESEX* beat Yorkshire 2nd,
11-4
1967-8 HAMPSHIRE beat
Nottinghamshire, 13-2
1968-9 BERKSHIRE beat Yorkshire 2nd,
10-5
1969-70 BERKSHIRE beat Derbyshire, 9-6
1970-1 NORTHUMBERLAND* beat
Berkshire*, 10-7
1971-2 DERBYSHIRE beat Glamorgan,
15-2
1972-3 HAMPSHIRE* beat Staffordshire,
12-5
1973-4 KENT* beat Durham, 16-1
1974-5 STAFFORDSHIRE* beat Surrey
2nd, 9-8
1975-6 MIDDLESEX beat Yorkshire*, 9-8
1976-7 SURREY 2nd beat Lancashire 2nd,
11-6
1977-8 WARWICKSHIRE beat
Gloucestershire*, 11-6
1978-9 DERBYSHIRE beat Middlesex,
10-7
1979-80 KENT* beat Yorkshire, 14-3
1980-1 ESSEX* beat Durham*, 10-7
1981-2 SURREY 2nd beat Lothian*, 11-6
1982-3 DURHAM beat Middlesex, 13-4
1983-4 *No final tie.* MIDDLESEX
1984-5 LOTHIAN beat Essex 2nd, 13-14*
1985-6 DERBYSHIRE beat Middlesex,
12-5

* Also gained promotion to Division 1.

THE INTER-COUNTY CHAMPIONSHIP 'LINE-UP' FOR 1985/86

DIVISION I
Section A	*Section B*
Cheshire	Essex
Lancashire	Hampshire
Lothian	Kent
Yorkshire	Surrey

DIVISION II
Section A	*Section B*
Derbyshire	Devon
Durham	Essex 2
East Strathclyde	Glamorgan
Lancashire 2	Middlesex
Leinster	Surrey 2

DIVISION III
Section A	*Section B*
Avon & Somerset	Cheshire 2
Cornwall	Nottinghamshire
Dorset	Upper Strathclyde
Wiltshire	West Strathclyde
Gwent	Yorkshire 2

Section C	*Section D*
Northamptonshire	Essex 3
Staffordshire	Kent 2
Warwickshire	Middlesex 2
Gloucestershire	Suffolk
Worcestershire	Sussex

DIVISION IV
Section A	*Section B*
Cumbria	Cheshire 3
Northumberland	Derbyshire 2
Lancashire 3	Leicestershire
Scottish Midlands	Lincolnshire
Yorkshire 3	Nottinghamshire 2

Section C	*Section D*
Avon & Somerset 2	Hampshire 2
Devon 2	Buckinghamshire
Dorset 2	Northamptonshire 2
Glamorgan 2	Kent 3
Berkshire	Oxfordshire

DIVISION V
Section A	*Section B*
Lincolnshire 2	Cornwall 2
Durham 2	Gloucestershire 2
Lothian 2	Guernsey
Shropshire	West Glamorgan
Staffordshire 2	Wiltshire 2

Section C	*Section D*
Bedfordshire	Berkshire 2
Buckinghamshire 2	Leicestershire 2
Hertfordshire	Oxfordshire 2
Norfolk	Warwickshire 2
Cambridgeshire	Worcestershire 2

DIVISION VI
Section A	*Section B*
Buckinghamshire 3	Staffordshire 3
Devon 3	Isle of Man
Hampshire 3	Cumbria 2
Isle of Wight	Northumberland 2
Sussex 2	Nottinghamshire 3

Section C	*Section D*
Herefordshire	Bedfordshire 2
Leicestershire 3	Cambridgeshire 2
Northamptonshire 3	Hertfordshire 2
Warwickshire 3	Norfolk 2
Worcestershire 3	Suffolk 2

DIVISION VII
Section A	*Section B*
Gwent 2	Cambridgeshire 3
Cornwall 3	Hertfordshire 3
Dorset 3	Lincolnshire 3
Isle of Wight 2	Herefordshire 2
Wiltshire 3	Shropshire 2
Avon & Somerset 3	

INTERNATIONAL BADMINTON FEDERATION

Rumblings of discontent with the Badminton Association's (q.v.) benevolent despotism were first heard in 1932 during the Welsh Championships. Ireland, Scotland and Wales, each having only one vote on the twenty-two-strong BA Committee, put their case to the BA's most influential figure, Sir George Thomas. He, A.D. Prebble and J. Plunkett Dillon worked farsightedly and persuasively to reverse the BA's first appalled reaction to such heresy.

On 5 July 1934 the IBF was founded, with Sir George as President; Canada, Denmark, England, France, Ireland, Netherlands, New Zealand, Scotland and Wales as the nine founder members; and a not ungenerous £200 christening present from the BA, who now gracefully relinquished control after forty-one years. Nevertheless, only two of the thirteen-strong executive came from outside the UK.

Fittingly India, where the game may have originated, was the first new member of the forty-nine who were to follow. From 1938-76 IBF affairs were run from his home by a modestly paid Secretary, Herbert Scheele. A London AGM finished promptly on time for an early lunch followed by Wimbledon tennis, men's singles semi-finals, at Sir George Thomas's expense.

Today the IBF organizes the World Championships and the Thomas and Uber Cup competitions, co-ordinates championship and open events world-wide, encourages development in smaller countries, publishes *World Badminton* quarterly and controls the Laws of badminton. All this is carried out by four committees (Finance; Rules and Laws; International Championships; Open badminton), and the resultant work is processed at the IBF's office (24 Winchcombe House, Winchcombe Street, Cheltenham, GL52, 2NA, UK) under the control of a General Secretary, Mrs V.S. (Ronnie) Rowan (q.v.).

The Council consists of the President, Immediate Past President and President-elect, Hon Secretary/Treasurer, up to seven Vice-Presidents, twelve Council members, and Continental representatives. Overall 1984 membership was fifty-nine full members and twenty-five associate members.

Each affiliated national organization may send to General Meetings two delegates, one of whom casts his organization's vote(s). These are allotted (a) one for affiliation (b) one for 10,000+ players; two for 50,000+ players (c) one for entry in two of the three most recently concluded Thomas Cup or Uber Cup events: i.e. a maximum of four. On membership issues, however, it is 'one nation – one vote'.

The IBF is financed by members' fees (based on playing numbers), Open badminton levies, its own competition receipts and interest on reserves.

IBF HANDBOOK

Badminton's *Wisden* – now sadly defunct. Herbert Scheele's brainchild – the only single book ever to embrace virtually all badminton's records. Sadly killed by ever-rising costs and player-pur-chaser apathy.

It contained general articles and 'Topics of the Day' from Mr Scheele's pen; Annals of the IBF; detailed records of all Thomas and Uber Cup matches, regulations and players; the Laws of badminton; IBF Rules; tournament regulations; recommendations to umpires; and full details of every affiliated association. The latter included a comprehensive international match summary, international players and appearances; open championship winners; inter-provincial results etc.

Some thirty issues, growing from fewer than fifty pages to 420 were published.

A mammoth task – yet a labour of love. The game today sadly lacks such a book.

INVERCLYDE, Largs, Ayrshire

Formerly Hills Hotel, and 1st Army HQ prior to the invasion of N. Africa (when the author had his last glimpse of Britain for four years); now, the Scottish Sports Council's National Sports Training Centre with excellent facilities and a superb view over the Firth of Clyde characterized by Everest's conqueror Sir John Hunt as 'the finest in Britain'.

Summer courses were originally organized here by Scot Nancy Horner for the BAE. And joyous Hogmanay ones run by Pat Davis. Now it is regularly used by the Scottish BU for squad training, and very popular summer coaches and performance courses.

J. Blane and R. Altham-Turner (Wardens), Secretary Judy Budge (later SBU Administrator) and groundsman Hugh McColl did much for its early success.

IRELAND – BADMINTON UNION OF IRELAND

A body that has transcended the religious and political differences of North and South.

Limavady, in 1892, had the first club, closely followed by Derry, Coleraine, Wicklow and Dundrum. A dispute between the two latter was the cause of the BUI's founding in 1899. It quickly insisted on a vote in the Badminton Association's (q.v.) Council. In 1902 the Irish Open came hot on the heels of the All-England, and England were challenged in 1903 – though a win was never recorded in fifty-six encounters – now discontinued. Scotland was first played in 1910, and the Ulster (Northern) Branch was formed in 1911.

The BUI's Hon Secretary, J. Plunkett Dillon, played a leading role in the 1934 formation of the IBF. Major J.D. McCallum's Strollers cheerfully put the game on court in Europe, and he himself was the Northern Branch's Hon. Secretary for fifty-two years.

For a small country its roll of honour is surprisingly long: the incomparable Frank Devlin and 'Curly' Mack; 6-foot-4-inch giant Ian Maconachie; inseparable pairs Tom Boyle and Jim Rankin, Frank Peard and Jim Fitzgibbon; the Hamilton family, five-strong; and Mary O'Sullivan (now Bryan) and Yvonne Kelly, both with over fifty caps and as lively off court as on. The Irish ladies reached the final of the European Zone in the first three Uber Cup competitions. Recent years have failed to produce such giants – but eighty-four-year-old Frank Devlin is still coaching back in Co. Wicklow.

Famous halls in Ireland include Dublin's 1930s Elm Park Hall and the present Leinster Branch Hall at Terenure (1954). Belfast used Queen's University's fine Sans Souci hall and now has the commemorative six-court McCallum Hall. Lisburn's Alpha Club has been used recently for international matches.

Ireland hosted the 1976 European Championships in Dublin and won the Helvetia Cup in 1981.

IRISH NATIONAL CHAMPIONSHIP WINNERS

Men's Singles

1911-2	R.H. Lambert
1912-3	—
1913-4	F.A. Kennedy
1914-9	No Competition
1919-20	G.S.B. Mack
1920-1	—
1921-2	G.S.B. Mack
1922-3	F.A. Kennedy
1923-4	—
1924-5	G.S.B. Mack
1925-6	No Competition
1926-7	W. Hamilton
1927-31	No Competition
1931-2	A. Hamilton
1932-3	A. Hamilton
1933-4	W. Hamilton
1934-5	W. Hamilton
1935-6	R. Hanna
1936-7	A.G. Trapnell
1937-47	No Competition
1947-8	D.B. Green
1948-9	J.J. FitzGibbon
1949-50	F.W. Peard
1950-1	F.W. Peard
1951-2	F.W. Peard
1952-3	F.W. Peard
1953-4	J.P. Doyle
1954-5	J.P. Doyle
1955-6	J.P. Doyle
1956-7	J.P. Doyle
1957-8	J.P. Doyle
1958-9	J.P. Doyle
1959-60	J.P. Doyle
1960-1	J.P. Doyle
1961-2	C.W. Wilkinson
1962-3	R. Harris
1963-4	R. Harris
1964-5	R. Harris
1965-6	R. Harris
1966-7	J.J. McCloy
1967-8	R. Harris
1968-9	P. Moore
1969-70	R. Harris
1970-1	M. Morrow
1971-2	P. Moore
1972-3	C. Bell
1973-4	J. Taylor
1974-5	J. Taylor
1975-6	A. Bell
1976-7	J. Scott
1977-8	C. Bell
1978-9	B. Thompson
1979-80	C. Bell
1980-1	J. Taylor
1981-2	W. Thompson
1982-3	J. Taylor
1983-4	J. Taylor
1984-5	P. Marron
1985-6	W. Thompson

Ladies' Singles

1911-2	Miss H. Pigot
1912-3	Mrs R.H. Plews
1913-4	Miss E.F. Stewart
1914-9	No Competition
1919-20	Mrs Beattie
1920-1	Miss E.F. Stewart
1921-2	No Competition
1922-3	Miss D. Pilkington
1923-4	Miss D. Pilkington
1924-5	Miss D. Pilkington

1925-6	No Competition
1926-7	Mrs T.D. Good
1927-31	No Competition
1931-2	Miss M. Hamilton([1])
1932-3	Miss M. Hamilton([1])
1933-4	Miss M. Hamilton([1])
1934-5	Mrs M. Macnaughton
1935-6	Mrs M. Macnaughton
1936-7	Miss N. Stoker
1937-47	No Competition
1947-8	Miss B.J. Good
1948-9	Miss B.J. Good
1949-50	Miss B. Curran
1950-1	Mrs B.I. Donaldson
1951-2	Miss J.C. Lawless([2])
1952-3	Miss S. Moore([3])
1953-4	Miss E. Abraham([4])
1954-5	Miss E. Abraham([4])
1955-6	Miss Y.W. Kelly
1956-7	Miss Y.W. Kelly
1957-8	Miss Y.W. Kelly
1958-9	Miss M.U. O'Sullivan([5])
1959-60	Miss M.U. O'Sullivan([5])
1960-1	Miss Y.W. Kelly
1961-2	Miss M.U. O'Sullivan([5])
1962-3	Miss M.U. O'Sullivan([5])
1963-4	Miss M.U. O'Sullivan([5])
1964-5	Miss Y.W. Kelly
1965-6	Mrs E.T. Bryan
1966-7	Miss Y.W. Kelly
1967-8	Mrs E.T. Bryan
1968-9	Mrs E.T. Bryan
1969-70	Mrs A.J. Mockford
1970-1	Mrs E.T. Bryan
1971-2	Mrs E.T. Bryan
1972-3	Miss B. Beckett
1973-4	Miss B. Beckett
1974-5	Miss B. Beckett
1975-6	Miss B. Beckett
1976-7	Ms B. Beckett
1977-8	Mrs D. Cunningham
1978-9	Ms B. Beckett
1979-80	Ms B. Beckett
1980-1	Mrs I. McCrave
1981-2	Mrs D. Underwood
1982-3	Mrs D. Underwood
1983-4	Ms B. Beckett
1984-5	Miss C. Doheny
1985-6	Miss C. Doheny

Men's Doubles

1911-2	F.A. Kennedy/F.O'B. Kennedy
1912-3	Rev. A.M. Cave/T.D. Good
1913-4	F.A. Kennedy/F. O'B. Kennedy
1914-22	No Competition
1922-3	R.A.J. Goff/R.H. Hastings
1923-4	–
1924-5	R.A.J. Goff/G.S.B. Mack
1925-6	No Competition
1926-7	R.A.J. Goff/W. Hamilton
1927-31	No Competition
1931-2	A. Hamilton/B. Hamilton
1932-3	W. Hamilton/N.D. Good
1933-4	W. Hamilton/N.D. Good
1934-5	T.H. Boyle/J.L. Rankin
1935-6	C.H. Maidment/E.L. Warren

1936-7	G. Paltridge/J. Killen
1937-47	No Competition
1947-8	D.B. Green/T.T. Majury
1948-9	J.J. FitzGibbon/F.W. Peard
1949-50	J.J. FitzGibbon/F.W. Peard
1950-1	J.J. FitzGibbon/F.W. Peard
1951-2	J.J. FitzGibbon/F.W. Peard
1952-3	J.J. FitzGibbon/F.W. Peard
1953-4	J.J. FitzGibbon/F.W. Peard
1954-5	J.J. FitzGibbon/F.W. Peard
1955-6	J.K.D. Lacey/J.P. Doyle
1956-7	R.S. Love/K. Carlisle
1957-8	G. Henderson/R.C. McCormack
1958-9	G. Henderson/R.C. McCormack
1959-60	G. Henderson/R.C. McCormack
1960-1	J.J. FitzGibbon/F.W. Peard
1961-2	J.J. FitzGibbon/F.W. Peard
1962-3	C.W. Wilkinson/J.P. Doyle
1963-4	C.W. Wilkinson/J.P. Doyle
1964-5	C.W. Wilkinson/S. Blair
1965-6	C.W. Wilkinson/S. Blair
1966-7	C.W. Wilkinson/S. Blair
1967-8	C.W. Wilkinson/S. Blair
1968-9	C.W. Wilkinson/S. Blair
1969-70	C.W. Wilkinson/S. Blair
1970-1	P. Moore/A.R. Reddick
1971-2	D. Doherty/C. McIlwaine
1972-3	D. Doherty/C. McIlwaine
1973-4	D. Doherty/C. McIlwaine
1974-5	A. Bell/C. Bell
1975-6	A. Bell/C. Bell
1976-7	J. Scott/F. Evans
1977-8	J. Scott/F. Evans
1978-9	B. Thompson/C. McIlwaine
1979-80	F. Evans/B. McKee
1980-1	F. Evans/B. McKee
1981-2	W. Thompson/C. McIlwaine
1982-3	W. Thompson/R. Keag
1983-4	B. Coffey/J. McArdle
1984-5	B. Coffey/J. McArdle
1985-6	W. Thompson/R. Keag

Ladies' Doubles

1922-3	Miss M. Homan([6])/Miss Stoney
1923-4	Mrs Anderson/Miss D. Pilkington
1924-5	Mrs T.D. Good/Mrs R.H. Plews
1925-6	No Competition
1926-7	Miss M. Homan([6])/Miss D. Pilkington
1927-31	No Competition
1931-2	Miss D. Good([7])/Miss M. Hamilton([1])
1932-3	Miss D. Good([7])/Miss M. Hamilton([1])
1933-4	Miss N. Stoker/Miss M. Hamilton
1934-5	Miss N. Stoker/Mrs M. Macnaughton
1935-6	Miss N. Stoker/Mrs M. Macnaughton
1936-7	Miss N. Stoker/Mrs M. Macnaughton
1937-47	No Competition
1947-8	Miss N.M. Conway/Miss B.J. Good
1948-9	Miss N.M. Conway/Miss B.J. Good
1949-50	Miss N.M. Conway/Miss B.J. Good
1950-1	Miss N.M. Conway/Miss B.J. Good

1951-2	Miss N.M. Conway/Miss B.J. Good
1952-3	Mrs B.I. Donaldson/Miss J.C. Lawless([2])
1953-4	Mrs R. Gibson/Miss Y. Kelly
1954-5	Mrs B.I. Donaldson/Miss J.C. Lawless([2])
1955-6	Mrs B.I. Donaldson/Miss J.C. Lawless([2])
1956-7	Miss Y.W. Kelly/Miss M.U. O'Sullivan([5])
1957-8	Miss Y.W. Kelly/Miss M.U. O'Sullivan([5])
1958-9	Miss Y.W. Kelly/Miss M.U. O'Sullivan([5])
1959-60	Miss Y.W. Kelly/Miss M.U. O'Sullivan([5])
1960-1	Miss Y.W. Kelly/Mrs F.W. Peard
1961-2	Mrs L. McAleese/Miss M.U. O'Sullivan([5])
1962-3	Miss Y.W. Kelly/Miss M.U. O'Sullivan([5])
1963-4	Mrs L. McAleese/Mrs F.W. Peard
1964-5	Miss Y.W. Kelly/Mrs E.T. Bryan
1965-6	Miss Y.W. Kelly/Mrs E.T. Bryan
1966-7	Miss Y.W. Kelly/Mrs J. Leslie
1967-8	Mrs L. McAleese/Mrs J.J. McCloy
1968-9	Mrs L. McAleese/Mrs J.J. McCloy
1969-70	Mrs L. McAleese/Mrs J.J. McCloy
1970-1	Mrs E.T. Bryan/Miss Y.W. Kelly
1971-2	Mrs E.T. Bryan/Miss Y.W. Kelly
1972-3	Mrs L. McAleese/Mrs F.W. Peard
1973-4	Miss B. Beckett/Mrs L. McAleese
1974-5	Miss B. Beckett/Mrs F. Cunningham
1975-6	Miss B. Beckett/Mrs F. Cunningham
1976-7	Miss B. Beckett/Mrs F. Cunningham
1977-8	Mrs M. Dinan/Ms W. Orr([10])
1978-9	Mrs M. Dinan/Ms W. Orr([10])
1979-80	Ms B. Beckett/Mrs D. Underwood
1980-1	Mrs M. Dinan/Ms N. Lane
1981-2	Mrs M. Dinan/Ms W. Orr
1982-3	Mrs M. Dinan/Mrs W. Donnelly
1983-4	Miss B. Beckett/Miss D. Freeman
1984-5	Miss C. Doheny/Miss N. Lane
1985-6	Miss A. O'Sullivan/Miss E. Doyle

Mixed Doubles

1912-3	R.H. Lambert/Miss N. Lambert([8])
1913-4	R.H. Lambert/Miss N. Lambert([8])
1914-22	No Competition
1922-3	R.H. Lambert/Miss M. Homan([6])
1923-4	—
1924-5	G.S.B. Mack/Miss F. Stewart
1925-6	No Competition
1926-7	W. Hamilton/Mrs T.D. Good
1927-31	No Competition
1931-2	A. Hamilton/Miss M. Hamilton([1])
1932-3	W. Hamilton/Miss D. Good([7])
1933-4	M.D. Good/Miss M. Hamilton([1])
1934-5	T.H. Boyle/Miss O. Wilson
1935-6	L. Green/Miss G. Carty
1936-7	C.H. Maidment/Miss N. Stoker
1937-47	No Competition
1947-8	D.B. Green/Miss V.H. Gillespie
1948-9	J.J. FitzGibbon/Miss B.J. Good

1949-50	F.W. Peard/Mrs B.I. Donaldson
1950-1	F.W. Peard/Mrs B.I. Donaldson
1951-2	F.W. Peard/Mrs B.I. Donaldson
1952-3	F.W. Peard/Mrs B.I. Donaldson
1953-4	J.J. FitzGibbon/Miss B.J. Good
1954-5	F.W. Peard/Mrs B.I. Donaldson
1955-6	J.K.D. Lacey/Miss J.C. Lawless([2])
1956-7	K. Carlisle/Miss J. Duncan
1957-8	G. Henderson/Mrs P. Sharkey
1958-9	K. Carlisle/Miss L. Rea([9])
1959-60	K. Carlisle/Miss L. Rea([9])
1960-1	K. Carlisle/Miss L. Rea([9])
1961-2	C.W. Wilkinson/Miss Y.W. Kelly
1962-3	C.W. Wilkinson/Miss Y.W. Kelly
1963-4	S. Blair/Miss M.U. O'Sullivan([5])
1964-5	S. Blair/Mrs E.T. Bryan
1965-6	C.W. Wilkinson/Miss Y.W. Kelly
1966-7	C.W. Wilkinson/Miss Y.W. Kelly
1967-8	K. Carlisle/Mrs L. McAleese
1968-9	C.W. Wilkinson/Miss Y.W. Kelly
1969-70	C.W. Wilkinson/Miss Y.W. Kelly
1970-1	C.W. Wilkinson/Miss Y.W. Kelly
1971-2	J. McCloy/Mrs E.T. Bryan
1972-3	A. Bell/Miss B. Beckett
1973-4	A. Bell/Miss B. Beckett
1974-5	R. Reddick/Miss B. Beckett
1975-6	J. Scott/Miss B. Beckett
1976-7	J. Scott/Mrs D. Cunningham
1977-8	J. Scott/Mrs D. Cunningham
1978-9	B. Thompson/Ms B. Beckett
1979-80	B. Thompson/Ms B. Beckett
1980-1	W. Cameron/Mrs L. McCrave
1981-2	W. Cameron/Mrs M. Dinan
1982-3	J. Scott/Miss N. Lane
1983-4	J. Scott/Miss N. Lane
1984-5	G. Henderson/Miss N. Lane
1985-6	G. Henderson/Miss N. Lane

([1]) Now Mrs M. Macnaughton
([2]) Now Mrs P. Sharkey
([3]) Now Mrs R. Smyth
([4]) Now Mrs H.B. Mercer
([5]) Now Mrs E.T. Bryan
([6]) Now Mrs Thorpe
([7]) Now Mrs W.M. Hutton
([8]) Now Mrs Anderson
([9]) Now Mrs McAleese
([10]) Now Mrs Donnelly

IRISH OPEN WINNERS

Men's Singles

1902	B. Hamilton
1903	B. Hamilton
1904	B. Hamilton
1905	H.N. Marrett
1906	H.N. Marrett
1907	A.M. Cave
1908	A.M. Cave
1909	A.M. Cave
1910	F. Chesterton
1911	G.A. Thomas
1912	G.A. Sautter
1913	G.A. Thomas
1914	G.A. Thomas
1915-19	No Competition
1920	Sir G.A. Thomas, Bt.

1921	Sir G.A. Thomas, Bt.		1906	No Competition
1922	G.A. Sautter		1907	No Competition
1923	G.S.B. Mack		1908	No Competition
1924	J.F. Devlin		1909	No Competition
1925	G.S.B. Mack		1910	No Competition
1926	J.F. Devlin		1911	No Competition
1927	Sir G.A. Thomas, Bt.		1912	No Competition
1928	A.E. Harbot		1913	No Competition
1929	W. Hamilton		1914	No Competition
1930	W. Hamilton		1915-19	No Competition
1931	W. Hamilton		1920	No Competition
1932	R.M. White		1921	No Competition
1933	W. Hamilton		1922	No Competition
1934	R.M. White		1923	No Competition
1935	J.L. Rankin		1924	Mrs R.J. Horsley
1936	R.C.F. Nichols		1925	Mrs R.C. Tragett
1937	J.L. Rankin		1926	Mrs R.C. Tragett
1938	T.H. Boyle		1927	Miss D. Pilkington
1939	A.S. Samuel		1928	Mrs F.G. Barrett
1940-6	No Competition		1929	Miss D. Good[1]
1947	N.B. Radford		1930	Mrs H.S. Uber
1948	N.B. Radford		1931	Mrs R.J. Horsley
1949	Ong Poh Lim		1932	Mrs H.S. Uber
1950	F.W. Peard		1933	Miss O. Wilson
1951	E.B. Choong		1934	Miss T. Kingsbury[2]
1952	E.B. Choong		1935	Mrs R.J. Teague
1953	E.B. Choong		1936	Miss T. Kingsbury[2]
1954	J.E. Robson		1937	Miss E.A.R. Anderson[1]
1955	A.D. Jordan		1938	Miss D.M.C. Young[4]
1956	J.P. Doyle		1939	Mrs Macnaughton
1957	E.B. Choong		1940-6	No Competition
1958	Oon Chong Jin		1947	Miss Q.M. Allen[5]
1959	C.T. Coates		1948	Miss Q.M. Allen[5]
1960	R.S. McCoig		1949	Miss Q.M. Allen[5]
1961	C.T. Coates		1950	Mrs A.M. Horner
1962	C. Wattanasin		1951	Miss I.E. O'Beirne[6]
1963	C.J. Beacom		1952	Miss J.C. Lawless[7]
1964	R.S. McCoig		1953	Miss I.L. Cooley[8]
1965	R.H. Purser		1954	Mrs J.F. Robson
1966	Lee Kin Tat		1955	Miss I.L. Cooley[8]
1967	A. Parsons		1956	Miss M. O'Sullivan[9]
1968	Lee Kin Tat		1957	Mrs W.C.E. Rogers
1969	R.J. Sharp		1958	Miss Y.W. Kelly
1970	R.S. McCoig		1959	Miss H.M. Ward[10]
1971	D. Talbot		1960	Miss M.O'Sullivan[9]
1972	C. Bell		1961	Miss U.H. Smith[11]
1973	C. Bell		1962	Miss U.H. Smith[11]
1974	R.S. McCoig		1963	Miss U.H. Smith[11]
1975	P. Ridder		1964	Mrs G.C.K. Hashman
1976	M. Wilkes		1965	Miss A.M. Bairstow[12]
1977	T. Goode		1966	Mrs E.T. Bryan
1978	R. Purser		1967	Miss A.M. Bairstow[12]
1979	B. Wallwork		1968	Mrs E.T. Bryan
1980	D. Travers		1969	Miss G.M. Perrin[13]
1981	A. Goode		1970	Miss Y.W. Kelly
1982	M. Maly		1971	Miss M. Beck[14]
1983	J. Ford		1972	Miss Y.W. Kelly
1984	K. Jolly		1973	Miss B. Beckett
1985	K. Jolly		1974	Miss D. Tyghe
1986	A. White		1975	Miss J. van Beusekom
			1976	Miss B. Beckett

Ladies' Singles

1902	No Competition		1977	Miss P. Hamilton
1903	No Competition		1978	Mrs D. Cunningham
1904	No Competition		1979	Miss S. Leadbetter
1905	No Competition		1980	Miss E. Thoresen
			1981	Miss H. Troke

1982	Miss P. Hamilton
1983	Miss P. Hamilton
1984	Mrs S. Podger
1985	Miss F. Elliott
1986	Miss A. Fisher

Men's Doubles

1902	W.J. Hamilton/B. Hamilton
1903	G. Lucas/R.D. Marshal
1904	B. Hamilton/T.D. Good
1905	H.N. Marrett/A.D. Prebble
1906	H.N. Marrett/A.D. Prebble
1907	B. Hamilton/T.D. Good
1908	B. Hamilton/T.D. Good
1909	F. Chesterton/G.A. Thomas
1910	F. Chesterton/G.A. Thomas
1911	G.A. Sautter/G.A. Thomas
1912	G.A. Sautter/G.A. Thomas
1913	G.A. Sautter/G.A. Thomas
1914	R.H. Plews/G.A. Thomas
1915-19	No Competition
1920	F.A. Kennedy/R.H. Lambert
1921	J.F. Devlin/R.H. Plews
1922	G.S.B. Mack/Sir G.A. Thomas, Bt.
1923	G.S.B. Mack/Sir G.A. Thomas, Bt.
1924	G.S.B. Mack/Sir G.A. Thomas, Bt.
1925	G.S.B. Mack/R.A. Goff
1926	R. du Roveray/Sir G.A. Thomas, Bt.
1927	G.S.B. Mack/Sir G.A. Thomas, Bt.
1928	A.F. Harbot/Sir G.A. Thomas, Bt.
1929	J.B.H. McCallum/Sir G.A. Thomas, Bt.
1930	H.S. Uber/D.C. Hume
1931	G.S.B. Mack/J.F. Devlin
1932	D.C. Hume/R.C.F. Nichols
1933	T.H. Boyle/J.L. Rankin
1934	I. Maconachie/W. Hamilton
1935	I. Maconachie/J.L. Rankin
1936	I. Maconachie/J.L. Rankin
1937	I. Maconachie/J.L. Rankin
1938	K.L. Wilson/A. Titherley
1939	T.H. Boyle/J.L. Rankin
1940-6	No Competition
1947	T.H. Boyle/J.L. Rankin
1948	N.B. Radford/F.W. Peard
1949	Ong Poh Lim/Lim Kee Fong
1950	F.W. Peard/J.J. FitzGibbon
1951	H.R. Marsland/K.R. Greasley
1952	E.L. Choong/E.B. Choong
1953	E.L. Choong/E.B. Choong
1954	F.W. Peard/J.J. FitzGibbon
1955	W. Shute/J.R. Best
1956	J.A. Russell/A.I. McIntyre
1957	E.B. Choong/Oon Chong Teik
1958	Oon Chong Jin/C.L. Oon
1959	A.D. Jordan/R.J. Lockwood
1960	R.S. McCoig/W.F. Shannon
1961	H.T. Findlay/R.J. Lockwood
1962	R.S. McCoig/W.F. Shannon
1963	A.D. Jordan/P.J. Waddell
1964	R.S. McCoig/W.F. Shannon
1965	R.J. Mills/D.O. Horton
1966	R.S. McCoig/M. Henderson
1967	R.J. Mills/D.O. Horton
1968	I. Hume/J.K. McNeillage
1969	J.D. Eddy/R.A. Powell

1970	R.S. McCoig/F.D. Gow
1971	E.C. Stuart/D. Talbot
1972	A. Bell/P. Moore
1973	A. Bell/C. Bell
1974	J. Ansari/J. Britton
1975	W. Kerr/K. Parsons
1976	P. Bullivant/M. Wilkes
1977	T. Goode/D. Bridge
1978	R. Purser/B. Purser
1979	D. Bridge/R. Rofe
1980	D. Travers/G. Hamilton
1981	A. Goode/G. Scott
1982	W. Gilliland/D. Travers
1983	W. Gilliland/D. Travers
1984	D. Tailor/C. Dobson
1985	W. Gilliland/D. Travers
1986	D. Travers/A. White

Ladies' Doubles

1902	No Competition
1903	Miss M. Lucas/Miss M. Hardy[15]
1904	Miss M. Lucas/Miss E. Thomson[16]
1905	Miss M. Lucas/Miss E. Thomson[16]
1906	No Competition
1907	Miss M. Hogarth/Miss M.K. Bateman[17]
1908	Miss M. Lucas/Miss M. Larminie[18]
1909	Miss M. Hogarth/Miss M.K. Bateman[17]
1910	Miss M.K. Bateman[17]/Miss M. Larminie[18]
1911	Miss M. Larminie[18]/Miss L.C. Radeglia
1912	Mrs R.C. Tragett/Miss L.C. Radeglia
1913	Mrs R.C. Tragett/Mrs Plews
1914	Miss L.C. Radeglia/Mrs Pearson
1915-19	No Competition
1920	Miss H. Hogarth/Miss L.C. Radeglia
1921	Miss H. Hogarth/Miss F.F. Stewart
1922	Mrs F.G. Barrett/Miss K. McKane[19]
1923	Mrs Anderson/Miss D. Pilkington
1924	Mrs A.M. Head/Miss K. McKane[19]
1925	Mrs A.M. Head/Miss A. Homan[20]
1926	Mrs R.J. Horsley/Miss V. Elton
1927	Mrs Good/Miss D. Pilkington
1928	Mrs F.G. Barrett/Miss V. Elton
1929	Mrs Good/Miss D. Pilkington
1930	Mrs R.J. Horsley/Mrs H.S. Uber
1931	Mrs R.J. Horsley/Miss C.T. Duncan
1932	Mrs R.J. Horsley/Mrs H.S. Uber
1933	Mrs R.J. Horsley/Miss O. Wilson
1934	Mrs R.J. Horsley/Mrs H.S. Uber
1935	Mrs R.J. Horsley/Miss O. Wilson
1936	Mrs R.J. Horsley/Mrs H.S. Uber
1937	Mrs M. Macnaughton/Miss N. Stoker
1938	Miss D.M.C. Young[4]/Miss N. Stoker
1939	Mrs Macnaughton/Miss O. Wilson
1940-6	No Competition
1947	Miss Q.M. Allen[5]/Mrs H.J. Uber
1948	Miss N.M. Conway/Miss B.J. Good
1949	Miss Q.M. Allen[5]/Mrs H.S. Uber
1950	Miss N.M. Conway/Mrs B. Potter
1951	Miss I.E. O'Beirne[6]/Miss A. Choong[21]
1952	Miss J.C. Lawless[7]/Miss B.J. Good
1953	Miss I.L. Cooley[8]/Miss J.R.

1954	Miss I.L. Cooley[8]/Miss J.R. White[22]		

1954   Miss I.L. Cooley[8]/Miss J.R.
        White[22]
1955   Miss I.L. Cooley[8]/Miss J.R.
        White[22]
1956   Miss M.B. Forrester[23]/Miss M.
        McIntosh
1957   Mrs W.C.E. Rogers/Mrs E.J.
        Timperley
1958   Miss C.E. Dunglison/Miss G.
        Massie[24]
1959   Mrs W.C.E. Rogers/Mrs E.J.
        Timperley
1960   Miss Y.W. Kelly/Miss M.U.
        O'Sullivan[9]
1961   Mrs F.W. Peard/Miss L. Rea[25]
1962   Miss Y.W. Kelly/Miss M.U.
        O'Sullivan[9]
1963   Mrs E. Parr/Miss H.J. Pritchard[26]
1964   Mrs F.W. Peard/Mrs G.C.K.
        Hashman
1965   Miss U.H. Smith[11]/Miss H.J.
        Pritchard
1966   Miss Y.W. Kelly/Mrs E.T. Bryan
1967   Miss M.B. Boxall[27]/Miss S.D.
        Pound[28]
1968   Miss Y.W. Kelly/Mrs E.T. Bryan
1969   Miss M.B. Boxall[27]/Mrs P.E.
        Whetnall
1970   Miss Y.W. Kelly/Mrs F.W. Peard
1971   Miss M. Beck[14]/Mrs W. Rickard
1972   Mrs E.T. Bryan/Miss Y.W. Kelly
1973   Miss B. Beckett/Mrs W. McAleese
1974   Miss B. Lord/Miss D. Tyghe
1975   Miss M. Luesken[29]/Miss J. van
        Beusekom
1976   Miss B. Beckett/Miss Y.W. Kelly
1977   Mrs M. Dinan/Miss W. Orr
1978   Miss C. Stewart/Miss A. Johnston
1979   Miss K. Redhead/Miss D. Simpson
1980   Miss C. Heatley/Miss J. Reid
1981   Miss J. Pringle/Miss M. Leeves
1982   Miss P. Hamilton/Miss A. Fulton
1983   Miss F. Elliott/Miss J. Pringle
1984   Mrs S. Podger/Mrs B. Sutton
1985   Miss F. Elliott/Miss A. Fisher
1986   Miss A. Fisher/Miss C. Gay

Mixed Doubles
1902   B. Hamilton/Mrs Goff
1903   L.U. Ranford/Miss M. Hardy[30]
1904   L.U. Ranford/Miss M. Hardy[30]
1905   N. Wood/Miss H. Hogarth
1906   N. Wood/Miss H. Hogarth
1907   N. Wood/Miss H. Hogarth
1908   B. Hamilton/Miss M. Lucas
1909   G.A. Thomas/Miss H. Hogarth
1910   G.A. Thomas/Miss M. Larminie[18]
1911   G.A. Thomas/Miss M. Larminie[18]
1912   G.A. Thomas/Mrs R.C. Tragett
1913   G.A. Sautter/Miss H. Hogarth
1914   G.A. Thomas/Miss H. Hogarth
1915-19 No Competition
1920   Sir G.A. Thomas, Bt./Miss H.
        Hogarth
1921   Sir G.A. Thomas, Bt./Miss H.
        Hogarth
1922   G.A. Sautter/Miss E.G. Peterson
1923   J.F. Devlin/Miss E.F. Stewart
1924   G.S.B. Mack/Mrs R.C. Tragett
1925   G.S.B. Mack/Mrs R.C. Tragett
1926   F. Hodge/Miss V. Elton
1927   G.S.B. Mack/Mrs A.M. Head
1928   A.E. Harbot/Miss V. Elton
1929   J. Barr/Miss C.T. Duncan
1930   H.S. Uber/Mrs H.S. Uber
1931   J.F. Devlin/Mrs R.J. Horsley
1932   D.C. Hume/Mrs H.S. Uber
1933   J.L. Rankin/Miss M. Hamilton[31]
1934   D.C. Hume/Mrs H.S. Uber
1935   I. Maconachie/Mrs R.J. Horsley
1936   D.C. Hume/Mrs H.S. Uber
1937   J.L. Rankin/Miss O. Wilson
1938   T.H. Boyle/Miss O. Wilson
1939   T.H. Boyle/Miss O. Wilson
1940-6 No Competition
1947   R.C.F. Nichols/Mrs J.B. Shearlaw
1948   H.J. Wingfield/Mrs V.E. Duringer[32]
1949   H.R. Marsland/Miss Q.M. Allen[5]
1950   J.C. Mackay/Mrs A.M. Horner
1951   E.B. Choong/Miss A. Choong[21]
1952   H.A. Heah/Mrs G.F. Saunders
1953   E.B. Choong/Miss J.R. White[22]
1954   W.A. Robinson/Mrs A.M. Horner
1955   A.D. Jordan/Miss J.R. White[22]
1956   R. Smyth/Mrs Smyth
1957   A.D. Jordan/Mrs E.J. Timperley
1958   M. Henderson/Miss M. McIntosh
1959   A.D. Jordan/Mrs E.J. Timperley
1960   R.S. McCoig/Miss W. Tyre[33]
1961   A.D. Jordan/Mrs E.J. Timperley
1962   R.S. McCoig and Miss W. Tyre[33]
1963   K.R. Derrick/Mrs G.W. Barrand
1964   R.S. McCoig/Mrs G.C.K. Hashman
1965   J.N. Havers/Mrs G.W. Barrand
1966   M. Henderson/Miss C.F. Dunglison
1967   R.J. Mills/Mrs W.C.E. Rogers
1968   R.S. McCoig/Miss M.D. Thompson
1969   A.D. Jordan/Mrs P.E. Whetnall
1970   R.S. McCoig/Miss H.T. Kelly[34]
1971   D. Talbot/Mrs M.A. Gilks
1972   J. McCloy/Mrs E.T. Bryan
1973   A. Bell/Miss B. Beckett
1974   F. Gow/Miss C. Stewart
1975   R. Ridder/Miss M. Ridder
1976   J. Scott/Miss B. Beckett
1977   J. Scott/Miss P. Hamilton
1978   B. Giebland/Mrs J. Flockhart
1979   D. Bridge/Miss K. Redhead
1980   E. Evans/Mrs D. Underwood
1981   R. Ridder/Mrs M. Ridder
1982   W. Gilliland/Miss C. Heatly
1983   W. Gilliland/Miss C. Heatly
1984   W. Gilliland/Miss C. Heatly
1985   W. Gilliland/Miss E. Allen
1986   D. Travers/Mrs M. McKay

[1] Now Mrs W.M. Hutton
[2] Now Mrs E.G. Scovil and Mrs C.W. Welcome
[3] Now Mrs J.A.S. Armstrong
[4] Now Mrs J. Warrington
[5] Now Mrs F.G. Webber
[6] Now Mrs R.C.F. Nichols

(7) Now Mrs P. Sharkey
(8) Now Mrs W.C.E. Rogers
(9) Now Mrs E.T. Bryan
(10) Now Mrs E.B. Nielsen
(11) Now Mrs L. Oakley
(12) Now Mrs A.M. Palmer
(13) Now Mrs M.A. Gilks
(14) Now Mrs R.J. Lockwood
(15) Now Mrs Lionel Smith
(16) Now Mrs D.R. Larcombe
(17) Now Mrs Flaxman
(18) Now Mrs R.C. Tragett
(19) Now Mrs L.A. Godfree
(20) Now Mrs Thorpe
(21) Now Mrs H.A. Heah
(22) Now Mrs E.J. Timperley
(23) Now Mrs J.A. Russell
(24) Now Mrs W.J. Allen
(25) Now Mrs McAleese
(26) Now Mrs D.O. Horton
(27) Now Mrs E.J. Allen
(28) Now Mrs P.E. Whetnall
(29) Now Mrs M. Ridder
(30) Now Mrs Lionel Smith
(31) Now Mrs M. Macnaughton
(32) Now Mrs Kingston
(33) Now Mrs Reid
(34) Now Mrs T. McIntosh

ISLE OF MAN BA

Although cut off from mainland competition by a stormy Irish Sea, the IOM has always been a hotbed of enthusiastic audiences and players, including top-class men such as P. Kniveton and D. Jones. It has regularly participated in the ICC, although frequently having to play its 'home' matches in England as well as its away ones.

In 1985 a unique Festival of Badminton was held, with £10,000 prize money in all for separate tournaments for veterans, juniors and moderates and for players in each separate ICC division. It culminated in the final of an England v. Korea international series, won 3-2 by Korea.

ISRAEL – Badminton Association of Israel

First played during the British Mandate of Palestine, badminton progressed slowly, despite the enthusiasm of current President Yosef Geffen.

Five clubs, with Maccabi Ashdod in the lead (already an IBF Associate Member), founded BAI in 1976. It became IBF affiliated, established a National League and took part in Plume d'Or and Maccabiah Games.

In the latter, in 1985, it was a brothers' final when the Spurlings (GB) beat the Rabins (USA). The Moses family currently dominates junior badminton. Amir (U.14) won a title in all three age-groups; Sigalit won the U.13 and U.18 girls' singles; Reuven won all three senior titles, including the mixed with sister Aliza, a previous triple champion herself.

ITALY – Associazione Italiano Badminton

Conceived in Rome by Commendatore A. Chiappero in 1961, then nurtured almost solely in Merano and now spreading south as far as Civitavecchia and Rome.

Italy bravely entered the 1983 European Junior only to be castigated for poor standard by *Badminton Now*'s infamous '*Snooper*'.

Italy still operates its own peculiar but not unattractive 'relay' scoring system. With teams of five players or pairs in opposition, first pairs play fifteen points, say 9-6, second pairs then play a further fifteen points from this score to, say, 19-11. Third pairs, with 1-14, may take the team scores to 20-25. And so on to a total of seventy-five.

J

JAKARTA

(Formerly spelt Djakarta.) Home of the Indonesian BA and Senayan Stadium, the hotbed of Indonesian badminton. Within a few degrees of the Equator, it is feared by Europeans for its debilitating steamy heat.

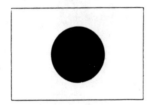

JAPAN – NIPPON BA

Japan's badminton origins may be mist-shrouded as Fuji itself but its women's international successes are clear cut. Play *may* have been started just after World War I but Yokohama certainly had a YMCA club in 1937. NBA was formed in 1946; within a year the first All-Japan Championships were held (1947) and IBF affiliation followed in 1951.

On its first appearance, in 1965/6, Japan won the Uber Cup for the first of six consecutive finals appearances and five convincing victories. Only the advent of the Chinese halted the success story of Japan's long list of great players: Hiroe Yuki, Noriko Nakayama, Etsuko Takenaka (unseeded) were AEC singles winners, and tomboy Saori Kondo, twice a losing but cheerful finalist. Japan also produced great doubles pairs such as Takagi and Yuki together, Aizawa and Takenaka, and Takada and Tokuda

(T'NT), all AEC winners, as well as the 1977 World Champions Toganoo (formerly Takenaka) and Ueno. All are unforgettable for sheer determination and a non-stop on-court 'twitter' of instruction and encouragement.

Japanese men have never fared so well, though Iino and Tsuchida might have been AEC finalists (1979) had not their disqualified semi-final opponents been reinstated.

Its Open championship is the richest on the Pro-Kennex circuit – and the only one played in two centres, first Kinyu and the Tokyo.

91,000 affiliated players.

Men's Singles
1981 R. Hartono
1982 T. Kihlström
1983 Han Jian
1984 M. Frost
1985 Zhao Jianhua
1986 Yang Yang

Ladies' Singles
1981 Sun Ai Hwang
1982 Li Lingwei
1983 Han Aiping
1984 Zheng Yuli
1985 Wu Jianqiu
1986 Li Lingwei

Men's Doubles
1981 C. Hadinata/L. Pongoh
1982 H. Kartono/R. Heryanto
1983 T. Kihlström/S. Karlsson
1984 T. Kihlström/S. Karlsson
1985 Joo Bong Park/Moon Soo Kim
1986 R. Sidek/J. Sidek

Ladies' Doubles
1981 Y. Yonekura/A. Tokuda
1982 N. Perry/J. Webster
1983 G.M. Clark/G. Gilks
1984 K. Beckman/G. Gilks

1985   Yun Ja Kim/Sang Hee Yoo
1986   Lin Ying/Wu Dixi

Mixed Doubles
1981   —
1982   M. Tredgett/N. Perry
1983   T. Kihlström/N. Perry
1984   M. Dew/G. Gilks
1985   W. Gilliland/G. Gowers
1986   W. Gilliland/N. Perry

JARRETT, Edwin S. ('Ted')

Graduate of Princeton and Harvard
Business School, he first played in 1931
in the 17 feet high basement courts of
New York's Presbyterian Church – and
has played and administered ever since,
over fifty years. When forty-five, played
twenty-two games in a single day to win
New York Metropolitan Singles.

As USBA delegate first attended an
IBF Council meeting in the latter's
anniversay twenty-fifth year – and
continued as such for twenty-three years
and twenty-seven Atlantic crossings (at
his own expense).

By 1983, he had attended all three
World Championships; five All-
Englands; six Canadian Opens; seven
Thomas and twelve Uber Cup ties; as
well as ten USA Junior championships;
more, he had played thirty-eight times in
the USA National – thirty-six times
successively!

President of USBA 1959-61; Vice
President IBF since 1969.

Fit, friendly and highly efficient.

JOLLY, Kevin R. (Essex and England)
Born 9 July 1959

Triple AE Junior Champion in 1976-7,
Jolly might well have also achieved that
distinction in the 1977 Malta European
Junior Championships had not an
unnecessary 'Jolly jump' fractured his
ankle. Quickly winning sixty caps and,
amongst other titles, the 1982-3 English
National singles, he might have taken
over Ray Stevens England No. 1 spot had
not Baddeley and Yates, developing
unusually fast, overhauled him.

Having blotted his copy-book on
occasion with stormy behaviour, he is
currently ranked No. 6 but injury and
some disagreement with the BAE have
damped his enthusiasm. He lost in the
1985 National 'quarters' to Andy Goode,
5 and 11.

JONES, Arthur E.
Born 1922

His active badminton career was curtailed by war-time Arctic convoys and
Pacific submarines – but it is recorded he
won the Middlesex Handicap Singles! He
more than made up administratively in
the game's fastest growing and Open
periods. Chairman, Hon. Secretary and
Treasurer of Essex BA, he was known as
something of a rebel on the IBF Council
(1956). Of this he was later to become an
efficient Chairman (1975-84) and Vice-
President (1973-). He did much to help
create the National Badminton Centre
and to build up its professional staff.

An excellent umpire and former
chairman of the BUAE, he has refereed
the 1983 Copenhagen World Championships and the 1984 Uber and
Thomas Cup Kuala Lumpur finals. With
T. Bacher (Denmark) and R. Johannsson
(Sweden), he master-minded the successful new format for the latter.

He joined the IBF Council in 1976,
and in 1984 was elected a Vice-President
and Chairman of the International
Championships and Tournament Committee.

JORDAN, A.D., OBE (England)

Jordan more than lived up to 'the best
seventeen-year-old ever' tag, achieved
when, in 1952, having earlier beaten
master-tactician David Choong in an
adult mixed with his mother, he became
AE Junior Triple Champion.

He was the first England player to win
a hundred caps (ninety-seven consecutively), 1951-70; won the AEC mixed
doubles four times (1956-1968), and the
European Championships once, always
in contention with Finn Kobbero (q.v.),
with three different partners: June
Timperley, née White, Sue Pound (later
Whetnall) and Jenny Pritchard (later
Horton); and played in seven Thomas
Cup series. He won thirteen English
Invitation titles and five National titles
(1953/4-1967/8).

A fine all-rounder, he excelled in mixed
doubles through ruthless receiving, subtle
variations of pace, and round-the-head
'bite'. Tony delighted in practical jokes.

JUMP SMASH

A stroke pioneered by small but agile Malaysians, Indonesians and Chinese. Among its first users in England was Malaya's Eddy Choong in the 1950s.

Its advantages are two-fold. (1) The shuttle is met earlier, thus hurrying an opponent seeking to regain position or cover a gap. (2) With greater height comes greater angle or steepness, making the return more difficult and more steeply lifted. It can be demoralizing too!

To play it, the striker should be in the basic sideways-on stance with right knee bent and shoulder dipped. A strong push off from that foot gets him airborne, whilst in the forward swing phase shoulders and hips turn strongly and square. Balanced landing is essential for quick recovery.

Even 6-foot-plus (1.8 metres) Zhao Jianhua used it most effectively to win the 1985 AEC with steeply angled smashes to the side-lines that left Frost groping.

K

KARLSSON, Stefan (Sweden)
Born 5 November 1955

'Pinocchio' to his many friends, this modest, English-speaking fireman, helped by rigorous job fitness training, has set Swedish badminton ablaze.

Originally a men's doubles specialist, he won the 1973 European Junior BD, was 1979 AEC runner-up, 1980 European winner with Claes Nordin, and English Masters runner-up in both 1980 and 1981. Won the European again in 1982, the AEC in 1983, and the Nordic title in 1984 beating both Helledie and Fladberg and Frost and Nierhoff *en route*, each time partnering Kihlstrom with whom he made one of the best and most exciting pairs in the world.

An opportunist, he has speed, anticipation and aggressive defence, all of which helped him become a surprise though deserving 1985 World Championship mixed doubles runner-up with Maria Bengtsson, narrowly losing a titanic match against Park and Yoo, 10-15, 15-12, 12-15.

KELVIN HALL

Glasgow's 3,000 seater hall, famous as venue for the first-ever Thomas Cup semi-final in 1949 (USA v. Malaya) and for a long succession of World Invitation Tournaments (q.v.) which started in 1951.

KIHLSTROM, Thomas (Sweden)
Born 11 December 1948

Kihlstrom shadowed Sweden's other great, Sture Johnsson, before taking over his No. 1 mantle. A chiropractor by profession, he showed scant respect for his own body by playing – successfully – all three events until he was thirty-two.

Major singles titles narrowly eluded him. But in 1976 with Bengt Froman he received a Wembley standing ovation when they became the only Europeans to break what was to become a Malaysian/-Indonesian near stranglehold on the event (1971-84). In 1983, with fireman Stefan Karlsson, with whom he had won the European Championship in 1982, he repeated the AEC victory. Five wins over Heryanto and Kartono and other top pairs set them among the giants.

His mixed doubles skills were recognized by shrewd Nora Perry. After her long partnership with Mike Tredgett, in 1983 she struck up a winning combination with Kihlstrom in the Victor Cup, Scandinavian, Swedish and Japanese Opens, the AEC and the World Championships. They won the Alba Quartz World Cup in 1984.

Lost the 1986 AEC MD semi 2 & 2 to winners Kim & Park but was European MD runner-up 12-15, 17-18 to Fladberg & Helledie.

Agile, a tight server, a lethal receiver, he tempers aggressive defence with deceptive, pin-pointed attack. Thoughtful, cool, calm and collected.

KILL, TO

To score a decisive, outright winner by a power-stroke. Often chanted by excited Indonesian spectators as they urge on their favourites: 'Kill! Kill! Kill!'

KILLER INSTINCT

The inborn urge essential to champions to meet the shuttle early, to hit down, to maintain the attack no matter how exhausted, and to beat one's opponent without slackening effort, without mercy. Often allied with a stubborn 'refusal' to let the shuttle land on their side of the net.

KIM, Yun Ja (South Korea)
Born 15 May 1963

Hastily pushed into the front line when the injured Sun Ai Hwang lost form and face, Kim made her mark by beating Yonekura, and by winning the Asian BC junior mixed title and being runner-up in the senior singles.

In the 1983 World Championships she beat Lene Koppen on her own courts 11-4, 6-11, 11-7 before losing narrowly in the quarters to runner-up Han Aiping, 12-10, 3-11, 10-12. In the 1984 AEC, seeded 5/8, she lost ingloriously to Quian Ping (China) 8-11, 3-11 but more than made amends in the doubles semi-final with Sang Hee Yoo by beating holders Xu Rong and Wu Jianqiu 5-15, 15-7, 15-13. In one of the most exciting ever finals, against Wu Dixi and Lin Ying, 8-15, 15-8, they clawed back from 9-14 to 14 all but bravely lost the 57-minute final of 30 and 40 shot rallies, 14-17. In the 1985 World Championships they lost in the semis by the narrowest of margins, 10-15, 15-9, 17-18, to eventual winners Aiping/Lingwei. But in the Alba Quartz final they crashed 4 and 5 to Lin Ying and Wu Dixi after beating Aiping and Lingwei 15-11, 11-15, 15-3.

Won the 1986 AEC Singles but, wearily lost the LD final to Korean 2nd string Chung & Hwang. With Yoo mustered only 7 points against Li & Han in TC semi.

A rather solemn face hides massive determination in a small frame that will run and defend for ever. Her smash lacks absolutely cutting-edge against her peers.

KINGSBURY, Leonie and Thelma (Hampshire and England)

Second only in fame to the Devlin sisters, the Hampshire girls dominated English badminton in the 1930s but seldom teamed up together. In the 1932 AEC Leonie, with Mrs F.G. Barrett, holder 1928-30, won the ladies' doubles; in 1933, left-handed Thelma with Marjorie Bell (later Henderson) gained the first of four consecutive victories, a feat not performed since 1904-10 when Meriel Lucas won seven in succession.

In the singles it was Leonie who won in 1932 and 1934 while fleet-footed Thelma (although maintaining, 'Singles are too strenuous to be enjoyable') won in 1936 and 1937.

In 1938 Thelma joined Ken Davidson's act in America, then turned to free-lance coaching. With Janet Wright she won the USA Open (1941; 1947-50). Between 1940 and 1950 they never lost a tournament match.

KJAER, Dorte (Denmark)
Born 6 February 1964,
Roskilde

When only sixteen, badminton precocious, she played in the Uber Cup and reached the semis of the 1980 European Senior Championships (with Anne Skovgaard); a year later won the ladies' doubles and was runner-up (with M. Christiansen) in mixed doubles of the 1981 European Junior; again reached the semis of the Senior ladies' doubles in 1982; and the final in 1986.

Has formed a most effective partnership with Nettie Nielsen with whom she also won the 1982 and 1983 Nordic Championships and the 1986 Danish (Open)

Petite Dorte is a member of Greve Strand BC.

KJELDSEN, Michael (Denmark)
Born 13 November 1962,
Søborg

A fast and clever left-hander, five feet nine inches (1.75 metres) eleven stone (69 kg) Kjeldsen is perhaps the most promising of Denmark's new generation, with international potential in both singles and doubles. He made his mark in junior badminton, rounding things off very satisfactorily by winning both the doubles and the singles at the Edinburgh European Championships in 1981.

The difficult transition from junior to senior top-flight play was bridged in 1984 when he won the Canadian Open singles; was runner-up in the Nordic Championships men's doubles and the Scandinavian Cup men's doubles; was Danish National men's doubles champion; and selected for the Thomas Cup finals.

In 1985 he very definitely arrived. He and regular partner Mark Christiansen reached the AEC final, beating the Sideks, fellow Scandinavians Kihlstrom and Karlsson, and England's Dew and Baddeley, and then taking winners Kim and Park to 15-7, 10-15, 9-15. That performance was underlined by their reaching the World Championship semis where against China's Yongbo and Bingyi they fought magnificently, 16-18, 18-14 before caving in 3-15.

A wristy and aggressive player (for Gentofte BC), he snaps up the fleeting chance at the back with a jump smash as readily as he does a net return with a lunge leap.

KNIVETON, Peter

A versatile 1950s player from the Isle of Man, a fanatical badminton stronghold, who nearly out-rivals Brian White's record (fifty-one) with fifty IOM restricted titles (fifteen men's singles, seventeen men's doubles and eighteen mixed doubles).

KOBBERO, Finn (Denmark)

A wayward genius who loved parties – and disliked training – he had every shot in the book, including a flashing backhand; he flaunted deception and excelled in the forecourt. This complemented Hammergaard Hansen's heavy smash from rear-court, when they won six AEC men's titles, four in succession (1955-64). With Kirsten Thorndahl (four) and Ulla Rasmussen, later Strand (four), he took a further eight mixed titles (1955-66).

In the 1950s it was not uncommon to play all three events. Kobbero did reach three AEC singles finals but lost all, caught between the upper and nether millstones of Eddy Choong's agility (1956) and Erland Kops' power (1958 and 1961).

Tall, good-looking, is now a TV commentator.

KONDO (now KOHMOTO), Saori (Japan)
Born 18 March 1956

Fate often deals unkindly with the nicest people. Saori Kondo was a case in point. Her rolling sailor-gait, on short and sturdy legs, her expressive face, her bouncing play on court and bouncing sense of humour off, endeared her immediately to Wembley crowds. So too did her gift of mimicry, her willingness to side-line restring the rackets of her more successful compatriots, her partner-encouraging bottom-whacking that far outdid Nora Perry's gentle tap.

In 1978, on her second visit to Wembley, Saori bounced her way through to the final only to fall to Gillian Gilks at her best (1-11, 9-11). The next year it was again the final – and again defeat, this time against Lene Køppen: Saori faltered at 9-9, swept triumphantly to 11-1 but could not clinch the decider, 8-11. That was heartbreaking enough, but in the 1980 quarters she lost to the lanky Kirsten Larsen, on the crest of a wave having beaten Gillian Gilks 11-4, 11-6; and in 1981, unseeded, she was first drawn against holder Lene Køppen. 10-1 up in the first, she might have made history but finally it was 12-10, 9-11, 3-11.

If at the AEC it was always 'yet so near', it was triumph in the tense 1981 Uber Cup final when, with three victories, including a vital 11-6, 11-8 against Verawaty with the score 2-2, she inspired her team-mates to a fifth victory in six competitions.

Three short years underlined the New Order. In the 1984 Uber Cup, China's Zhaing Ailing gave her no respite, 11-2, 11-3, but against Xu Rong and Wu Jianqiu the old fighting Kondo (with Takada) emerged to lose narrowly, 6-15, 15-11, 13-18.

KØPPEN, Lene (Denmark)
Born 5 May 1953

Denmark's No. 1 for a decade; Europe's darling even longer; the only dentist you would gladly visit.

Determined, a runner, a lissom athlete who could miraculously return shots inches from the floor or feet behind her with thigh-splitting lunges and back-breaking clears, singles were her forte. In 1977 she beat Gillian Gilks in the World Championship final, 12-9, 12-11, but only after six attempts did she win the AEC title – in 1979 and 1980. Her hopes of winning the trophy outright were blasted by an unheard-of newcomer, Sun Ai Hwang, who left her stunned (1-11, 2-11).

In 1982 she was alone amidst seven Chinese quarter-finalists and lost in the semis to Ling Wei, 8-11, 0-11. In 1983 it was 3-11, 0-11 to Xu Rong in the quarters. She announced she would retire after the third World Championships – and there, on her own courts, the day before her thirtieth birthday, she was beaten by another Korean, Yun Ja Kim, in the second round.

Liking the back of the court, she won numerous ladies' doubles titles and – more surprisingly – mixed, with the giant Skovgaard, though never the coveted AEC ones. Among many others she won a remarkable twenty-five Nordic Championships events (1973-81), being Triple Champion for seven successive years (1975-81). Unbeaten by a fellow Dane for eleven years.

But it was more than her play or her looks (brown eyes, cap of black hair, a 116 lb (53 kg) 5-foot-5-inches (1.63 metres) figure, and dentist's dream teeth) that endeared her to worldwide crowds. She won modestly; she lost smilingly and generously. She had charisma. That she outvoted by 200 per cent the Danish Soccer XI and out-pointed Bjorn Borg in popularity polls says it all!

KOPS, Erland (Denmark)

The very name Kops suggests a picture of its sturdy, piercing-eyed, bald-pated, bearded owner. But he started as a fiery unknown, E. Olsen, in the 1956 AEC when he beat Ferry Sonneville.

In 1957 he was still unseeded but beat Kobbero in a seventy-five-minute battle that (despite training in a weighted waistcoat) took such heavy toll that he (now Kops) 'kopped it' in the final with Eddy Choong. In 1958 defender became attacker with a new-found weightier smash, beating Choong, then Kobbero again in the final.

For two years Kops (with Kobbero) trained and practised in Bangkok – and returned, with Oriental inscrutability, ruthlessness, delicate drops and net-shots, and new skilled defence to take four AEC titles 1960-63. In 1964, one game and 14-9 up, he lost to Singapore's Dr Lee Kin Tat; in 1965, with power and precision, he beat nineteen-year-old Tan Aik Huang; in 1966 he lost in the first round to Malaya's great doubles-player Tan Yee Khan, 15-11, 11-15, 13-15, but

was back in 1967 to beat Tan (the holder) and make it a record seven titles in a decade (so beating J.F. Devlin's six).

With singles supremacy and the memory of a 1958 AEC doubles victory with P.E. Nielsen fading, with Henning Borch he took on the Kobbero-Hansen doubles mantle, winning the AEC trophy outright (1967-9) virtually the last Danes to withstand the Asian whirlwind. He returned in 1982 to win the AE Veterans doubles with Scot Ian Hume. A generous paunch betokened his skill as chef and restaurateur and his delight in Copenhagen lager.

A great character!

KOREA BADMINTON ASSOCIATION

Badminton was introduced quite by chance. In 1957 the Government delegation visiting Tokyo watched a tournament and so liked the game that they decided to start it in their country.

Affiliated to the IBF in 1962, they still had only 500 members in 1970 – mainly from educational and commercial groups. Then small clubs, often playing outdoors, mushroomed. Numbers rose from 2,500 in 1980 to 14,856 in 1985. Little was heard of Korea's top players until 1981, when Sun Ai Hwang appeared out of the blue to win Japanese, Swedish and AEC titles and be World Games runner-up!

Since then they have toured worldwide with ever-growing successes. In 1982 Joo Bong Park and En Kum Lee (now a coach) reached the AEC semis. The England touring team lost 1-5 in 1983, and in England in 1984 Korea gave the home country a hard fight.

Korean highlights have been Yun Ja Kim and Sang Hee Yoo's magnificent fight in the 1984 AEC final, Joo Bong Park and Moon Soo Kim's great victory in the 1985 AEC, and Park's outstanding double in the 1985 World Championships and in the 1986 AEC.

Fourth in the Thomas Cup and third in the Uber Cup in 1984, and a 3-2 1985 victory in England show how high 'the Land of the Morning Calm' now ranks in World badminton. A record that smacks of China's rapid emergence into the very top flight.

L

LADIES' SINGLES

These, like men's singles, were 15 up until 1907. Then they were reduced to 11 but with setting at 9 and 10 to 5 and 3 respectively. The latter anomaly was reduced in 1937 to conform roughly with men's singles with setting at 9 and 10 reduced to 3 and 2 respectively.

From time to time a change back to 15 is mooted (unsuccessfully) on the grounds of the modern woman's much greater mobility and athleticism.

LAMB, G.C. ('Larry')

'Best Rugby referee of the lot' who became badminton's first Chief Executive – from a 400-strong field (1978).

'Unafraid of change', he kept an equally firm – and meticulous – hand on the BAE helm through the sometimes choppy 1980s. But it was RAF rather than RU which won him the job: Air Vice-Marshal CB, CBE, AFC, FBIM, he flew sixty different types of aircraft, researched jet-icing, organized Nimrod sea patrols, rescued troops from behind Borneo rebel lines and crossed the Atlantic in a submarine.

Among his major achievements as Chief Executive have been (1) creation of a National Badminton Centre at Milton Keynes; (2) the concept of a permanent team manager which, in the person of Ciro Ciniglio, brought England great national success which in turn stimulated the game at all levels; (3) a rationalized and streamlined administration with an eye for detail.

LARSEN, Kirsten (Denmark)
Born 14 March 1962

Six feet (1.8 metres) tall, 1979 European Junior Champion, Larsen hit the international headlines in the 1980 'Battle of the Legs' when she electrified Wembley and shocked equally leggy 1978 Champion Gillian Gilks by an incredible first round, 11-4, 11-6 and demolished Ghia (India) and Kondo (Japan) in straight games, only to be put agonizingly and relentlessly in her place in the semi-final, 11-0, 11-0, by Denmark's No. 1 (and ultimate winner) Lene Køppen.

She did not recapture that form until the 1983 Pro-Kennex, when she creditably fought Zhang Ailing to 11-4, 7-11, 5-11 in Senayan heat but capitulated to her in the 3/4 play-off, 3-11, 1-11.

In the 1984 Uber Cup, she gained a fine 11-2, 11-8 win over Ivana Lie but lost a key match for a place in the final against Helen Troke (11-8, 7-11, 4-11) with whom she practises and often battles it out for European supremacy. She had her revenge in the English Masters and again in the Danish Open, she beat Li Lingwei in 1985 Japanese Open and lost only narrowly to Wu Dixi in the final.

Now Lene Køppen's successor as Denmark's No. 1, she has tremendous reach and unusual power but the deep backhand corner is sometimes vulnerable to attack.

LAWS

See under 'Rules' and in Appendix 1

LEE KIN TAT, Dr (Singapore)

'Patrick' or 'Leaking Tap' as he was popularly known as a student in England, was one of the finest players who never represented his country. Indeed, in the 1964 AEC he beat the holder Erland Kops before losing to the ultimate winner K.A. Nielsen, and he was Singapore Singles Champion in 1961 and National Champion in 1968.

He has been President of Singapore BA and is currently Secretary of the Asian Badminton Confederation.

LEFT-HANDERS

Left-handers are very much in the minority but they have nevertheless produced some outstanding champions. None had won the AEC men's singles until Zhao Jianhua in 1985 but three have won the ladies' singles: Mrs F.G. Barrett, Thelma Kingsbury and Kirsten Thorndahl. Sue Devlin (now Peard), Poul-Erik Nielsen and Margaret Boxall were left-handed AEC doubles-winners up to the 1970s. Since then England has produced Jane Webster and three distinguished male left-handers in Mike Tredgett, Martin Dew and Steve Baddeley.

It is recorded that all four players in a Tasmanian pennant game were left-handers. In the 1985 AEC men's doubles semi-final, Baddeley, Dew and Kjeldsen were all left-handers – only Christiansen broke the sequence. And in the 1985 AEC men's singles three of the four seeds in the bottom half were left-handers: Baddeley, Yang Yang and Jianhua.

In 1911 Calcutta BC ran a 'left-handers only' tournament – for 'right handers'. English international Geoff Fish could play ambidextrously!

LET

Replay of a rally generally (a) when the shuttle strikes an agreed obstruction such as girder or light: not the ceiling, as this could be deliberately hit under pressure; (b) when players (or, occasionally, umpires) are undecided on a line decision.

It is no longer given, as in tennis, when the shuttle strikes the tape in course of a service.

LI, Ling Wei (China)
Born 4 January 1964

She seems to have a great future ahead of her, provided she suffers no recurrence of knee trouble. She made her mark in the 1981 AQ World Cup, losing to Chen Ruizhen, 10-12, 11-2, 7-11, after holding match point in the first game. Thereafter she was in the shadow of Zhang Ailing but took the 1983 World Championship title after Aiping had conveniently removed the former. With Aiping she also won the AQ World Cup Doubles title. In the Pro-Kennex (1983) she again beat Aiping, taking the first game to 'love'. And it was Aiping, now her only real rival, who, despite the umpire's three times confusing their scores, was to fall to her in the 1984 AEC final, 5-11, 8-11.

It was a record that seemed to make her incontestable World No. 1 but Aiping still had other ideas, beating her first in the 1985 AEC, 11-7, 12-10. In the World Championship semis she lost to Wu Jianqiu, 7-11, 9-12, but with Aiping won both ladies' doubles events, defeating the holders, Wu Dixi and Lin Ying, in the latter. She won the Alba Quartz singles (though losing in the semis of the doubles) and the Pro-Kennex to stop a Grand Slam by Aiping.

In 1983/4 Uber Cup she won all her five matches without dropping a game and conceding only 42 points.

She owes much to her fleetness of foot, doggedness and deception.

An expert volley-ball player.

LICENSED PLAYERS

They may register, for an annual fee, with the BAE, who must give approval for all commercial contracts etc undertaken. They may then:
(a) receive assistance and accept any prize money above the amateur limit (£300), provided it is first paid to the BAE;
(b) accept up to £300 for playing in an exhibition match.
But they may *not*:
(a) accept appearance money at tournaments;
(b) play in any tournament, match or exhibition outside England without BAE permission;
(c) take part in the Olympic Games. (Subject to possible revision.)

Breach of such provisions can result in their being deemed professionals, and so unable to take part in virtually all major events. No reinstatement is permitted until twelve months after application.

LIE, Ing Hoa Ivana (Indonesia)
Born 1960

Petite and feminine as her name but with
dancing pony-tail and feet and a
deceptively powerful smash she has
followed a switchback road to become
Indonesia's female Swie King.

Her game can be as mercurial as her
temperament. In 1980, after losing 1-11,
1-11 to ultimate AEC winner Lene
Koppen, she also lost in the World
Championships final to compatriot Verawaty 1-11, 3-11. In 1981 in the AEC
semis she had ultimate winner Sun Ai
Hwang at her mercy, 11-5, 5-2, but was
beaten in a David-and-Goliath game
(7-11, 0-11). Worse was to come for in
1982 she had to undergo an Achilles
tendon operation.

Dogged training had its reward. With
Christian she won the Asian Games
mixed and in the SEAP Games she won
both the mixed doubles and the singles. In
the stronger 1983 Alba Quartz context
she reached the singles semis, losing to
Ailing, and the mixed final, losing a
three-setter to Dew and Gilks.

With such a fillip, in the following
weeks she reached her peak in the
Indonesian Open. Fighting back from
first-game deficits, she won the singles,
defeating Wu Jianqiu (AEC runner-up)
12-11, 11-0, and in the final Quian Ping,
12-11, 11-2 – cheered on in 'vocal
bedlam' by the crowd who had jeered her
off court in 1980. She crowned her
performance by also winning the mixed
with Christian against Dew and Gilks –
with a 1984 repeat.

But in the 1984 Uber Cup her surprise
2-11, 8-11 defeat by Kirsten Larsen
ended Indonesia's hopes of a semi-final
place, and in the 1985 AEC, seeded 5/8,
lost in the first round to Guan Weizhen.
She was not selected for the World
Championships and lost in the Alba
Quartz singles final to Li 3 & 2, and to
Latie 12-11, 12-11 in the SE Asia Games
but won the AG mixed with Hadinata.

LIEM, Swie King (Indonesia)
Born 28 February 1956

King by name and king by nature.
Always in for the early take but missed
by a day a Leap Year birthday that
would have been highly appropriate for
the game's highest jumper. A bullet-like
smash, dancing feet, tight net-shots and
stamina were the attributes that made
him a worthy successor to the 'Great
Rudy'.

First taught by his international sisters
Inawati and Idawati, he won the junior
National singles title in 1973 and the
senior in 1974. His international début
was in Teheran, at the Asian Games,
where, although annihilated by the
legendary Hou and Tang in turn, he
learnt much.

He reached the AEC singles final every
year from 1976 to 1981. 1976 saw a
lack-lustre showing against Hartono, bent
on his eighth title. In 1978 he got his
revenge – and the title – against an
equally off-form Hartono. Were they
under orders? In 1979 he outspeeded
Delfs, who had beaten him in 1977. In
1980 he was out-manoeuvred by the wily
Padukone, whom he outlasted the
following year. In 1984, now a veteran
twenty-eight, it seemed that at 15-9, then
5-0 and 9-5, he would make a grand
finale. But impregnable Morten Frost
wore him down 15-10, and, from 8 all,
15-10 again. In 1985, perhaps as a
worthy swansong, Liem made a fighting
recovery against Yang Yang, ten years
his junior, before being beaten by
whirlwind Jianhua in the semis.

Hopes of a World Championship were
bitterly disappointed. In 1980 an ageing
Hartono, brought out of retirement by
King's own AEC failure, beat him 15-9,
15-9. And in 1985, after one of the
longest (a hundred minutes) and most
brilliantly exciting finals, he was inched
out, 8-15, 15-12, 16-17, by lower-ranked
compatriot Sugiarto. In 1985 he was
entered only in men's doubles, losing to
Park and Kim 11-15, 15-17.

Sadly, he felt that his long run of
Thomas Cup victories had been negated
by his failure to beat Han Jian in the
crucial 1982 Thomas Cup match – and
this despite his three other victories. Two
were with Christian, their complementary
skills making them a formidable combination. In the 1984 Thomas Cup he lost to
Luan Jin but won his doubles with
Kartono to help Indonesia, to whom he
had given so much, regain the trophy 3-2.
With Kartono he won the 1985 Alba
Quartz but lost both his matches in the
TC Final.

As a national hero, he had a statue
erected to him in his home-town, Kudus –

only to see it torn down when he failed. Now owner of a cinema, a hotel and a sports outfitters, he is ready for retirement.

LILLESHALL HALL

Formerly the stately home of Dukes of Sutherland near Newport, Staffs. Backed by a South African post-war gift, it was converted into a superb Central Council of Physical Recreation National Sports Centre, where many badminton events, including Midland Counties Junior Championships and international coaching and trials have been held.

LINESMAN

An official appointed to assist the umpire by giving 'in' or 'out' decisions on his allotted line. Such decisions, unlike those in lawn tennis, may not be over-ruled by the umpire. 'Out' shuttles are indicated by a call of 'Out!' and wide-flung arms; 'in' by pointing to the line; 'unsighted' by placing hands over eyes. (Shuttles on or touching the line are 'in'.)

At the AEC, when seven courts are in action, some 140 linesmen are needed. There, the basic number per court is eight (ten for finals): (three at each end cover side- and centre-lines, two on each side of the net, opposite the umpire, the service and base-lines.) Fewer are used in minor tournaments, and none in basic ICC matches, where decisions are left to the player(s) on the shuttle-fall side of the court. Line decisions (again thankfully unlike tennis) are seldom queried.

At the All-England, linesmen and women, uniformly red-sweatered, march out in ordered ritual behind umpire and service judge. The mammoth task of organizing and assembling was undertaken for twenty-seven years by Kent player, 6-foot-6-inch (1.98 metres) R.S. 'Tiny' Lucas. Today they are controlled by Dr J.B. Alexander – and his computer. (See diagrams p.100).

LOB

Defensive, underhand stroke played from the forecourt when the shuttle is low after opponents' drop- or net-shot. The shuttle is returned high and deep to the base-line with a lunge and well-timed wrist flick. (High to give time for recovery; deep to nullify smashing.) It can be made 'attacking' by hitting less high. If the shuttle is very close to the net, a pronounced follow-through is necessary to obtain height and therefore maximum possible distance.

LOCKWOOD, Margaret (née Beck) (Middlesex and England)

A teenage international, Margaret left depressed W. Cumberland for greater badminton opportunity in London. For over a decade she and Gillian Gilks vied for supremacy. She started winning her forty-six caps when still a junior, and her long string of successes included English National (five), All-England (two), World Invitation (one), European Championships (two) and Commonwealth Games (two) titles (1969-78). She was voted 'Sportswoman of the Year' in 1973 by Sports Writers Association.

After reaching two 1977 World Championships semi-finals, she was forced to retire with serious knee injuries, probably brought about by long periods of over-zealous training – even shuttle-runs on the pavement outside her flat! A fluent stroke producer and mover, her play was sometimes marred by lapses of concentration.

She married England selector Ron Lockwood (thirteen caps) and is now playing county golf.

LOVE

Term employed for 'no score'. Possibly derived from 'real tennis' where a chalked-up elliptical 'O' looked rather like an egg – in French, *l'oeuf*.

LUAN, Jin (China)
Born 20 July 1958, Jiangsu (Fujian)

Strong-faced, superbly developed, Jin looks the aggressive player he is once he has a full head of steam. Knowing little English, he is quiet off-court – and an impeccable sportsman on.

He started playing when he was five and, though he later flirted with table tennis, fortunately was faithful to badminton. His first major success was a victory over Padukone in the 1978 Bangkok Asiad. 1980 saw him win both Chinese National singles and doubles. 1982 found him good enough to run

Shuttle is in

Shuttle is out

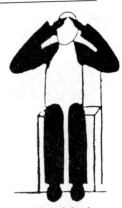

If unsighted

Frost to 15-11, 2-15, 7-15 in the AEC final. He turned the AEC tables on Frost in 1983 with an amazing 15-2, 12-15, 15-4, lost to Padukone in the World Championships 'quarters' equally amazingly 3 and 9 and bounced back, having beaten Swie King 15-13, 15-8 and Padukone 15-6 and 15-11, to allow Frost in the Pro-Kennex final only 2 and 6.

His erratic course continued in the 1984 AEC, when he had the doubtful distinction of being the first holder for years to lose on the first day (9-15, 15-5) and (after 11-9 up) 11-15 to the youthful England No. 2 Nick Yates. ('Mr Yates played very well,' impassively commented the Chinese manager.) But he won four of his five Thomas Cup singles, including a splendid win over Swie King in the final.

Highlights of his career? Standing down in 1976 Asian Championships semi-final to allow his idol Hou Chia Chang a breathing-space before meeting – and beating – Swie King 17-16, 15-8. Beating eight times AEC champion Rudy Hartono 15-9, 1-15, 15-9 in the 1982 Thomas Cup to keep 1-3 down China in contention with Indonesia.

He prefers singles but turns in good doubles results. A very physical player, he out-grunts Jimmy Connors in all-out attack. His form slumped in 1984-5 and he was not nominated for the AEC or World Championships.

LUCAS, Meriel (England)

One of the earliest 'greats' – from Devon. She was awarded only seven caps in the era of few internationals but between 1899 and 1910 won seventeen AEC titles (six ladies' singles, ten ladies' doubles, one mixed doubles), a record exceeded only by Sir George Thomas and J.F. Devlin. She and Miss E. Thomson (later Mrs Dudley Larcombe, Wimbledon singles champion, 1912) shared the singles title from 1900 to 1910 and together won the doubles four times. In 1907-8 she won the Triple Crown in England, Ireland and Scotland.

LUCAS, R.S. (Kent)
Born 30 May 1913, Forest Hill, London

Six feet six inches, sixteen stone (1.98 metres, 101 kg) he was not unnaturally nicknamed 'Tiny', as well as *der Englische skyscraper*' and 'the man with the vertical smash'.

A leading umpire and BUAE administrator, he organized AEC linesmen for twenty-seven years and is now a BUAE Hon. Life Member. He often played, to the crowd's delight, with 4-foot-11½-inch (1.5 metres) Siow Watt Soon, later to become President of Singapore BA.

M

MACFARLANE, N.R.J. ('Nev')

MacFarlane has been in the engine-room of the English Schools' Badminton Association almost since its inception in 1958; on the bridge as Chairman for thirteen years.

His varied background (BSA draughtsman, Para at Arnhem, PE teacher, motor-bike scrambler and, after a year's Adolescent Psychology study, a school counsellor) made him ideal not merely as ESBA Chairman but also as team manager, and a driving force with the BAE England Youth Squad.

He is a man of unusual sympathy, insight and drive. Through his hands have passed most of today's leading players as well as, indirectly, hundreds of thousands of much less talented schoolchildren who nevertheless obtain great enjoyment from the game. And all this voluntarily!

MACK, G.S.B. – 'Curly' (Ireland)

One of the greats of the 'Golden Twenties' who was also an Irish Davis Cup (tennis) player and a double first Scholar of Trinity College, Dublin.

Elegant and ice-cool (he would play a hard match without removing his sweater), he stylishly won six Irish Open titles: four with Sir George Thomas, on whom he admitted modelling himself; the 1924 AEC singles title and six AEC doubles titles (1923, 1926-7, 1929-31) with his contrastingly fiery compatriot, Frank Devlin. As a pair, they were described as 'confusing, exhausting and devastating'.

Had he ever bothered to practise or train, he might have been *the* 'greatest'. His leisurely glide resulted from inspired anticipation. He was a classic stylist with an unhurried smash and a wide range of fluent strokes. When he won the 1923 AEC mixed title with Mrs Tragett, he was epitomized as 'the poetry of motion'.

A few days before he emigrated to Canada, he was persuaded to play a farewell last-minute tournament by Ian Maconachie. Totally out of practice and with borrowed clothes, shoes and racket, he played 'like a dream'. In Canada he used his great talents to coach and teach for some years before, tragically, he committed suicide.

MACONACHIE, Ian (Ireland)

A jovial giant (6-feet-4-inches, 17 stone, 1.93 metres, 108 kg), Geordie-born but of Irish descent, he represented his country many times and, with Thelma Kingsbury, won the 1937 AEC mixed titles. More important perhaps, as works manager for RSL (q.v.) for fifty years he produced many million, best-in-the-world 'Tourney' shuttles. Most important, he personified on court the joy of badminton.

An MCC cricketer, he also drove golf balls (+3) – and express trains during the General Strike.

Awarded the IBF Distinguished Service Award.

MAGNUSSON, Christine (Sweden)
Born 21 November 1964

Born at Toro, Uganda, but moved when she was ten to Sweden (Stockholm) to avoid Idi Amin's purge.

Won the Swedish U.18 singles three times and the girls' doubles twice. Took all three senior national titles in 1983,

1984 and 1985!

Sprang a surprise by beating Kirsten Larsen in 1985 World Championships before losing 6 and 8 to Li Lingwei in the quarters. With Bengtsson, reached the final of the 1985 Danish Open losing only to Yun Ja Kim and Sang Yee Hoo, and won the 1986 Scottish Open Singles by beating Ricki Sørensen. In the 1985 Norid Championships won the singles, and was runner-up in LD and Mx D.

The first coloured girl to reach the top, she has a sturdy defence and a beaming smile on court as well as off.

MALAYSIA – Badminton Association of Malaysia

From 'badminton on the lawn' at the tea-parties of the *towkays* (wealthy businessmen) in the 1920s, to Malaysian post-World War II domination is a spectacular jump. Friendly matches led to inter-state competition until in 1934 Selangor, Penang and Perak (playing for the Leong Sin Nam and Permaisuri team trophies for men and women respectively) invited Johore and Singapore to join them in forming the Malaysian Badminton Association (which in 1964 became BAM).

With players of the calibre of Wong Peng Soon, Ooi Teik Hock, Ong Poh Lim and Law Teik Hock to be followed by David and Eddy Choong, Ng Boon Bee, the brothers Tan, Aik Huang and Aik Mong, and 'Punch' Gunalan, Malaya's and Malaysia's names are inscribed four times (1949, 1952, 1955 and 1967) on the Thomas Cup and, often, those of its players on the men's singles and doubles trophies of the AEC. Recently Malaysian teams have not evidenced the same strength in depth: the Sidek brothers, Misbun, Jalani and Razif, have shown themselves world-class – but erratic. Sylvia Ng, Malaysia's 1975 Sportswoman of the Year, is the only really well-known woman player.

MBA played a leading role in the formation of the Asian Badminton Confederation (1959), organized the first ABC championships (1962) and hosted the first joint Thomas-Uber Cup competition at Kuala Lumpur in 1984. It now boasts some 20,000 registered players.

Men's Singles
1983   L. King
1984   I. Sugiarto
1985   M. Sidek

Ladies' Singles
1983   Pan Zhenli
1984   Li Lingwei
1985   G. Gowers

Men's Doubles
1983   C. Hadinata/R. Ertanto
1984   Moon Soo Kim/D.C. Lee
1985   R. Sidek/J. Sidek

Ladies' Doubles
1983   Yun Ja Kim/Sang Hee Yoo
1984   Wu Jianqiu/Guan Weizhen
1985   G.M. Clark/G. Gowers

Mixed Doubles
1983   M. Dew/N. Perry
1984   M. Dew/G. Gilks
1985   Cancelled

MALDIVE ISLANDS – Badminton Association of the Maldives

Even 2,000 coral islands (200 inhabited) seem an unlikely hotbed for badminton. Yet BAM was formed in 1982 by *Presidential decree* to become the Maldives' first internationally affiliated sports organization.

A crash coaching course by English-born, French-resident Roger Grimwood enabled them to take part in the first Indian Ocean Games and later in the 1982 Asian Games in distant New Delhi.

National Championships were organized in 1983 for over fifty men and eight women; eight clubs took part in an inter-club event, and a Sri Lankan team toured. The Association now has 300 affiliated members.

MALTA – Badminton Association of Malta

Interest in the game was originally engendered by British Servicemen but waned after World War II. It was revived in the 1970s by the enthusiasm and drive of Joe Zammit-Lewis and Norman Worley. Although boasting only a handful of clubs, BAM conceived the idea of a Mediterranean Championship; staged the 1977 European Junior Championships; brought in a stream of foreign coaches; runs a friendly and very popular International Championship tournament (held in Malta's delightful early summer weather); and prints *BADMINTON*, a lively, illustrated mixture of local and international events edited by new live-wire Joe Seychell.

MARATHON

On 29 May 1984 three Nottinghamshire BA teams of four, backed up by fifty-four helpers and supervised by BUAE umpires, set out in simultaneous attempts to beat the existing record of seventy-four hours forty-one minutes continuous play set up in Swansea in May 1981.

After some sixty hours play, eight players dropped out, suffering from severe hallucinations and mental and physical exhaustion. The remaining four carried on to beat the previous record by playing for seventy-seven hours one minute. Their success, accompanied by TV and radio broadcasts, as well as the Mayor of Broxtowe and the Beeston Pipe Band, raised £3,000 for mentally handicapped children and a hall extension.

The record breakers were: Ben Smith, Paul Farmer, Loraine Storey and Andy Hood. Other participants were Barry Smith, A. Dumelow, N. Woodward. C. Ward, A. Tongue, A. Attewell, Bev Kippax, M. Attewell.

MARRS, Tommy (Cumbria)

A Cumbrian county player (1957-74) and Hon. Secretary for seventeen years – with a flair for organization, a real sense of humour and burning enthusiasm. In 1978 he was appointed BAE Promotions Manager and since then has boosted the prestige of major international events such as the Masters, the All-England Championships, European Championships and Thomas Cup final with the professional and polished presentation essential for TV coverage. In his 'spare' time, he has edited *Badminton Now*.

Marrs was the first man to use the Albert Hall, London as a badminton court!

MASTERS GAMES

A multi-sport world event held for the first time in Toronto, 7-25 August 1985. To be held quadrennially thereafter.

RESULTS
Men (40+)
Ladies (35+)

MS	J. Mortensen
LS	J. Youngberg
MD	C. Ratanaseansuang/ R. Kanchanaraphi
LD	B. Cousins/ J. Youngberg
Mxd D	V. Sukanake/ S. Gadd

	Men (50+)	Men (60+)
	Ladies (45+)	Ladies (55+)
MS	J. Poole	K. Grierson
LS	S. Gadd	J. Jones
MD	J. Poole/A. Shaikh	D. Adams/ K. Grierson
LD	F. Salazar/ S. Gadd	J. Jones C. Bowyer
Mxd D	J. Poole/ J. Jones	K. Grierson K. Hoffman

MATCH POINT

The point before the ultimate winning point of the *final* game: 14-9. A player 9-14 down who catches up to 14 all is said to have 'saved five match points'. A player who serves fruitlessly four times at 14 and then loses is said to have 'held four match points'.

McCALLUM, Major Johnnie, CBE, DSO (Ireland)

Affectionately known as 'the Wee Major', he not only played eight times for Ireland but also kept wicket for them and was a Rugby trialist. Fifty-two years Hon. Secretary of the BUI Northern Branch,

President of the BUI, President of the IBF (1961-3) and, signal honour, elected Hon. Life Vice-President. He is best known perhaps for his international 'Strollers' who initiated Denmark and other European countries into the joys of badminton.

McCARRY, John J. (Scotland) Died April 1977

Glaswegian 'Honest John' played nineteen times (1930-47) for Scotland and was good enough to be picked for the Combined Team (Ireland, Scotland and Wales) v. England in 1932/3 and 1935/6.

He made an even bigger mark off-court by his wit (he condensed Shakespeare's Seven Ages of Man into four with a final 'By God, Sir, you're looking well!'); his administrative wisdom as SBU President and IBF Vice-President; and his part in organizing the first-ever Thomas Cup semi-final (1949) and the subsequent World Invitation Tournaments in Glasgow's famous Kelvin Hall.

McCOIG, Robert S., MBE (Scotland)

Born in Greenock, which has had continuous Scottish representation from 1935 to 1985, and with an uncle who had risen from shipyard social club player to international, McCoig became a Scots legend. He won thirty-nine Scottish National titles (winning one at least in nineteen successive years) and a record sixty-seven caps and was the only Scot ever to win the Scottish and Irish Open Singles.

He won thirty-seven major titles, including the World Invitation Mixed twice, and the Welsh Open, with his wife Sheila, and had over 350 other British tournament successes. He won the Commonwealth Games Mixed Bronze in 1966, but his finest performance was runner-up in 1968 AEC mixed although unseeded. He was captain (and flag-bearer) of the entire Scottish 1974 Commonwealth Games team.

McCoig was a determined player who used speed, strong defence and cool serving in a crisis in all three events. A career of more than twenty years carried him through seven Thomas Cup campaigns (1957-76) and twenty countries to a well-earned MBE (1975). He is still

winning Veterans' events!

His frequent spectacle-polishing and shoelace-retieing made him a caricaturists' delight.

McKANE, later Godfree, Kitty (England)
Born c. 1898, London

In a class of her own, agile, lynx-eyed and with a long reach, she queened the badminton – and tennis – courts of the 1920s. Without peer in singles, she won the AEC four times (1920-22 and 1924), the ladies' doubles twice (1921 and 1924) with her sister M. McKane (later Stocks) and the mixed twice, 1924 and 1925, with J.F. Devlin who, in a normally male-dominated game, was happy for her to play 'sides' (q.v.).

At Wimbledon in 1923 she was runner-up to the legendary Suzanne Lenglen. In 1924 she won the title, inflicting her only Wimbledon defeat on 'Little Poker Face' Helen Wills Moody, who later took the title eight times (not dropping a single set between 1927 and 1932. In 1926 Kitty and her husband, Leslie Godfree (the first man to strike a ball on Wimbledon's then new Centre Court), became the first married pair to win the mixed title. She won the singles title as well that year.

Lively and alert as ever at eighty-plus.

McTAGGART, D.F. (Canada)

Canadian Open singles champion 1956-8, he gave up badminton to become a dollar millionaire – and a driving force behind 'Greenpeace'. He made a 7,000-mile voyage through the 'Roaring Forties' to penetrate the French Navy cordon around Muroa Atoll just before an atomic explosion vaporized everything within four cubic miles.

MEN'S AND LADIES' DOUBLES

This type of game, between two pairs of men or two pairs of women, is probably that played most in the average club.

For serve and return both pairs take up an attacking *back and front* formation with the server near the front service line and his partner mid-court behind him astride the centre line. The receiver stands as near his front service line as is compatible with being able also to move back to attack high serves while his partner stands a couple of yards behind him just in his own half-court.

The server by tape-skimming low serves and deceptive flicks seek to force an initial 'lift', a lob or clear. The receiver, equally determined, seeks to seize the attack with the first stroke by hitting down, with dab or smash, or by playing a very tight net shot.

Positions thereafter will change (sometimes once or twice in a rally) as the pairs gain the attack (i.e. their strokes, downwards, flat, or very tightly upwards to the net, force their opponents to lift the shuttle) or have to defend. When attacking, the *back and front formation* is maintained; when defending, the *side-by-side* formation.

The attackers may use drop shots or accurate net shots to force a short lob which will be met with the main attacking stroke, the smash. The flat, attacking clear will be used occasionally as a deceptive variant of the latter. The lob and clear will be little used as these are defensive strokes giving the attack to the opponents. The attacking net player will dab crisply down into a gap or the body or, more gently, half-court.

The defenders' reply to the drop shot is an early take net shot or a fast, low lob to the opponent's weaker backhand. The smash and dabs will be returned with flat drives or pushes. The aim of course, is to turn defence into attack by forcing their opponents to hit up rather than down.

Ladies' Doubles were once called by spectators 'glassy-eye' because of rallies of interminable, deep defensive clears and lobs which neither side had the ability to smash effectively. Today, in an era of fast, hard-hitting ladies their form of doubles is much the same as the man's though their smashes will always lack the latter's power.

The most famous men's pair have been the unruffled Sir George Thomas with a variety of partners; Ireland's Frank Devlin and 'Curly' Mack; England's hard-hitting Don Hume and Bill White; Malaysia's bounding Choong brothers; Denmark's elegant Finn Kobbero and Hammergaard Hansen; Indonesia's whiplash Tjun Tjun and Wahjudi; and today's lightning reflexed Koreans Joo Bong Park and Moon Soo Kim.

Among memorable ladies' pairs (both with a variety of partners) Meriel Lucas was supreme in long-skirted days, Margaret Tragett in the mid-twenties; immediately pre-war, Thelma Kingsbury and Majorie Henderson; post-war, Denmark's delightful Toni Olsen and Kirsten Thorndahl; the powerful USA Devlin sisters; more recently England's 'golden girls' Nora Perry and Gillian Gilks, and bouncing, tireless Asian combinations with rock-like defences such as Japan's Aizawa and Takenaka, China's Ling Ying and Wu Dixi, and Li Lingwei and Han Aiping – and Korea's Yun Ja Kim and Sang Hee Yoo.

ter METZ, Emile

Inspired by the pleasure his international daughters Margot and Lilli got from badminton, Metz decided to put as much back into the game.

He organized foreign visits to Denmark and England for the Duinwijck BC of Haarlem and administered national teams and tournaments for the Netherlands BA.

By 1973 his organizing efficiency had earned him the still-held EBU secretaryship and saw him EBU delegate to the IBF. He was immediately elected to the tournament and international championships committees which, joined in 1976, he has chaired since 1978. Two of his major successes have been the inauguration of the Europe Cup (q.v.) and the bringing of Czechoslovakia and USSR into the European badminton fold.

MILLS, Roger J. (Surrey and England)

A talented all-rounder who between 1960 and 1971, helped by nimble feet, a strong smash, fluent strokes and controlled touch, won forty-four caps and ninety-one titles. Additionally he won the English National singles (three times), the men's (twice) and the mixed (four times) and a gold medal for the 1966 Commonwealth Games mixed with Angela Bairstow.

In 1971 he was appointed BAE's second chief coach. With a lively and original approach, he made his mark but unfortunately was dismissed for breach of contract. His appeal to the Industrial Dispute Court was upheld and he was awarded damages – reduced because of his own intransigence.

Currently coaching at the University of Surrey.

MINARNI, later Soedaryanto (Indonesia)

Probably Indonesia's nearest female equivalent to Rudy Hartono. At fifteen she played in Indonesia's first Uber Cup tie (second series, 1959/60) which was lost 2-5 to Australia. (Also playing were Swie King's two sisters.) On Indonesia's first Challenge Round appearance (fifth series 1968/9) she beat H. Yuki 11-6, 11-2 in the second single, scoring Indonesia's sole victory; such tactical positioning caused bitter comment as she was undoubtedly the best singles player on either side. In 1962 she won the Asian Championship singles.

As Mrs Soedaryanto, mother of twin boys and a girl, she returned to the courts to win the 1974 World Invitation ladies' doubles with Regina Masli and, with two fine doubles victories, to clinch Indonesia's 5-2 1974/5 Uber Cup victory over Japan which broke the latter's run of three successive victories.

Known as 'the Magnificent Minarni'.

MITCHELL, Stanley

The first Englishman to be honoured as President of the EBU (1984). Prior to that he was BAE Deputy Chairman of the Council and a Vice-President. His particular interest is the development of the game in emergent badminton nations.

MIXED DOUBLES

A fascinating branch of the game demanding speed, delicacy of touch, accuracy of placement, deception and tactical expertise rather than the sheer power and defence of men's or ladies' doubles.

Largely a prerogative of European players, the AEC mixed title has, since 1947, been won by Danish pairs eighteen times (all between 1947 and 1972); sixteen times by English pairs (ten times between 1973 and 1984); once by Americans (the husband/wife Stephens combination); twice by Asians (Hadinata & Imelda Wigoeno, as late as 1979, were the first ever); and thrice by English ladies partnered respectively by a Malaysian (David Choong), a Swede (Thomas Kihlstrom) and a Scot (Billy Gilliland).

Hadinata and Imelda Wigoeno in 1979 were the only all-Asian pair to win until Park and Chung prevailed in 1986.

The most successful men have been Finn Kobbero (eight) and Tony Jordan (four), S. Pri, M. Tredgett and D. Talbot (three); 'the ladies' Ulla Strand, née Rasmussen (seven), Gillian Gilks (six), Nora Perry, née Gardner (six) and Kirsten Thorndahl (five).

Despite this, Asian pairs Hadinata and Wigoeno (1980) and Joo Bong Park and Yoo Sang Hee (1985) have won the World Mixed title.

Positional Play

Because a woman cannot run as fast or hit as hard as a man of the same general standard, at club level, she covers 'the front' or forecourt ($6\frac{1}{4}$ feet by 20) whilst the man covers the 'back', or mid- and rear-court ($15\frac{1}{2}$ feet by 20). The latter thus covers an area more than double that of the woman, but this is compensated for by the fact that the woman has half the time to hit a shuttle which is often travelling twice as fast as when the man plays it.

With a pair thus spaced apart, and in the centre of the court, the shuttle is mainly hit flat and down the side-line into the back 'boxes' (q.v.), between the two partners, or tightly to the net.

Woman's role

The following are essential qualities for the skilled woman; a grooved low serve that is difficult to rush and its complementary deceptive flick serve (q.v.); the ability to meet the served shuttle early and hit it down (from rear-court as well as fore) or tightly up to the tape; at the net to dab crisply down (not flat) to gaps or body and not to give away the attack by lifting net-shots to rear-court; to cut off cross-court drives or half-court pushes; to counter smashes with crouch defence dabs; and above all not to attempt to intercept too fast or too high shots which she cannot control and which are more easily and effectively taken by the man.

Man's role

At club level, the man's first aim is to attempt to dominate the woman by deceptive serve and net-shots, by aggressive return of serve, and by forcing the comparatively weak woman to a deeper, more vulnerable position.

If he cannot do that, he duels with the opposing man by pushes to the 'divorce area' (q.v.), fast, flat drives to the back 'boxes' (q.v.), or cross-court, or fast, low lifts to the backhand. Generally cross-court shots should be played only when opponents have been moved from a central position to the side-line and the shuttle can be hit down or flat. Shuttles lifted short he will smash down the side-line or at the body; those hit deep he will counter with fast drops, again to the 'divorce areas'.

In the last fifteen years, with women fitter and stronger, in top-level play they often not merely drop back to 'sides' in defence but will effectively cover the back if their partner is caught out of position, off-balance, or is raiding the net.

Playing as a pair

Although the man's and woman's roles are fairly clear cut, they play not as individuals but as a pair, each helping to set up winners for the other. The woman's tight net-shots may force a short lob her partner can kill; the man's straight smash to the body often elicits a weak return to the net that the woman can dab down for a winner. Equally important is the avoidance of shots that put their partners under pressure, e.g. the woman's short lob or the man's attempted cross-court net-shot to a centrally positioned opponent.

MOHLIN, Stellan (Sweden)

A prodigious worker who, fittingly, was the first recipient of the Herbert Scheele Medal (q.v.) for 'outstanding meritorious service' to badminton, and an IBF Life Vice-President.

After compulsory military service, he became an air-line pilot, then businessman. Having won twenty-three Swedish 'caps' and eleven National titles, he played in two Thomas Cup competitions (1951/2 and 1954/5) and reached the 1953 semi-final of the AEC men's doubles. Then he turned to administration: 1954, Swedish BA Committee; 1964, IBF Council; 1969-77, President of the still fledgling EBU, whose championships, as an expert linguist, he always opened in the language of the host country. 1969-76 IBF Vice-President; 1976-81 IBF President. As such he was a prime mover in the creation of the official World Championships, the first of which, in tribute to him, were played at Malmö in 1977.

His greatest success lay in the patience and diplomacy he used to bring together the warring IBF and WBF (1981) after their disastrous rift in 1978.

In all, fifty years' commitment to badminton.

MØLLER, Hans Christian
Born 12 March 1925, Aarhus, Jutland

With such Christian names, he should have been a spinner of fairy stories. In fact, he is known the world over as the Danish News Agency's very knowledgeable badminton reporter – with thirty years' experience – and co-editor of *Badminton*. He perfected his English during an eighteen-month stint as salesman at Selfridges and has now attended twenty successive AECs. Made an Honorary Member of the Danish BF in 1985, he says 'Today, Badminton on court is faster; off court, less sociable.'

MONEY, Ken

Canadian Olympic high-jumper in 1956 – jumping still higher in 1967 as an astronaut. His demanding standard of fitness has been achieved by playing six badminton singles a day under pressure – in his mid-fifties.

MORILD, Carsten (Denmark)
Born Aalborg, Jutland

Denmark's successor to Hans Svendsen as National Coach and Chief Coach. As the latter post was only on a part-time basis, he resigned in 1985 and applied unsuccessfully for appointment as BAE Team Manager.

With Erland Kops he won the Danish national in 1964/5. Unusually, he was also a fine cricketer, captaining Denmark, as had other members of his family.

MOZAMBIQUE – Federaçao Mozambicana de Badminton

Founded only in 1975, FMB showed great initiative by holding international championships at Beira in 1978, junior championships in 1981, and enlisting the coaching services of Denmark's Torsten Berg and China's Li Chen Peao. 825 registered players.

MULTI-FEEDER

A coaching device that makes thirty-forty shuttles quickly available one after another to a coach engaged in multi-shuttle speedwork routines.

MULASARTSATHORN, Ladawan (Thailand)

Surely one of the youngest-ever internationals. When still only twelve, she won the ladies' singles and doubles and was runner-up in the mixed doubles of the Indonesian Junior Open. At thirteen she beat three of Thailand's top women 'in rapid-fire succession like clay pigeons' to win the TBF Gosen Masters. And she represented her country in the 1984 Uber Cup. She allies a cool precocity and control with power and fierce attack. Ranked No. 4.

Her father, a former Thai boxer and a current MP, is grooming her for politics rather than badminton!

N

NAME, LONGEST

Channarongratanasaengsuang not only claimed sixteen Thailand caps (1960-67) but also the game's longest name (twenty-six letters) which *he* maintained needed no hyphens although these were often shown in programmes.

NAMES FOR BADMINTON

Bulutangkis (Indonesia)
Federball (East Germany)
Pluimbal (South Africa)
Sulkapallo (Finland)
Tollaslabda (Hungary)

NATIONAL BADMINTON CENTRE

Until 1968, when the BAE office moved to rather cramped quarters in Palace Road, Bromley, Kent, all post-war BAE business, as well as that of the IBF and the *Badminton Gazette*, was conducted from 4 Madeira Avenue, Bromley, the home of that dedicated two-man band Secretary Herbert Scheele and his wife Betty (q.v.).

When, in 1978, Larry Lamb took over as the BAE's Chief Executive, he saw the desirability of a more central HQ. New Town Milton Keynes was chosen. There, with the help of the Development Corporation's ninety-nine-year lease at peppercorn rent, a hundred-per-cent, twenty-five-year mortgage from sponsors Friends' Provident Life, and a Sports Council grant (£75,000), derelict $1\frac{1}{2}$ acre Loughton Lodge Farm was bought.

With limited resources, the BAE had to phase development. Converting the farmhouse into offices for a rapidly growing game and expanding staff was the first priority, completed on 28 July 1980. Phase II, the building of a three-court hall for use by local clubs as well as England A & B squads and youth squads, and of ancillary changing accommodation (£165,000) was completed in 1982. Phase III saw the building of a money-saving hostel for overnight and weekend courses. Phase IV provides stewards' accommodation and Phase V, conference hall, meeting-rooms, library, museum and film studio. Landscaping of the site was undertaken with badminton enthusiasts donating trees and shrubs.

Prince Andrew, the game's Patron, formally opened the Centre in April, 1986.

The National Badminton Centre

NAT WEST INTER-REGIONAL JUNIOR COMPETITION

A sponsored competition between the eight coaching regions. It is played off in a single day on an American basis with a seeded team in each of the two groups.

1985   Eastern 4 – S. Midlands 1
1986   S. East 4 – East 1

NEPAL BADMINTON ASSOCIATION

Introduced by a young Indian in the 1930s, badminton was popularized by Professor Rishikesh Shah, Professor Narendra Bahadur Bashyat and Dr T.N. Uprety. Minor tournaments were soon held but the only official one, in 1933/4, was disrupted by an earthquake.

Participation in the N. Indian Championships, a journey to the 1954/5 Singapore Thomas Cup matches, visits by leading Malaysian players and overseas coaches, participation in the Asian Games, and royal patronage have much improved playing standards.

2,200 registered players.

NET

This is generally 20 feet (6.10 metres) in length, $2\frac{1}{2}$ feet (76 cm) in depth, and is edged with a 3-inch (75 mm) doubled white tape, through which runs the supporting cord. It should be of fine dark cord or artificial fibre (nylon) in a mesh between $\frac{5}{8}$ inch and $\frac{3}{4}$ inch (15-20 mm). It should be kept taut at a height of 5 feet (1.5 metres) in the centre and 5 feet 1 inch (1.55 metres) at the posts.

NET CORD

(1) The cord inside the white net-tape which strains the net between the posts.
(2) A legal but fortuitous shot in the course of which the shuttle hits the tape and cord and topples over into the opponents' court. Even if the shot is a serve, unlike in tennis, a let cannot be claimed.

NET-SHOTS

As the name implies, these are shots played from, or to, near the net. They require either delicacy of touch or quick reflexes – or both. They may roughly be divided into two simple categories: downwards or upwards.

Downwards Net-Shots

Any shuttle near the net should, if possible, be met early while it is still above the tape and can therefore be hit downwards for a winner or to gain or maintain the attack.

(1) *The dab* is used when the shuttle is between 2 inches and 2 feet (5cm and 0.6 metre) above the tape. It is played with virtually no back-swing, and a minimum of follow-through to obviate hitting the net, a fault. The closely bent forearm is extended and the wrist uncocked to dab the shuttle *steeply* and firmly down; if it is hit flat, it may well fly over the base-line.

(2) *The tap* is similar to (1) but hit more gently.

(3) *The brush shot:* If the shuttle is very close to the net, a semi-circular motion is used to prevent racket hitting net in the follow-through. The rotary movement also adds deception to the shot. Often used in returning serve to the net or half-court just before the shuttle drops below tape level.

(4) *Dead racket shot:* With the grip almost completely relaxed, the shuttle drops close to the net from a stationary racket.

Upward Net-shots

Any shuttle below the tape lifted to the rear-court straightaway gives the opponents clear-cut attack. It is better to play a delicate upward net-shot, away from the opposing net player, that rises so little above the tape that it is impossible to 'kill'.

(1) *Upward:* A perfect shot if played early may travel upwards only one or two inches (2.5 or 5 centimetres) before striking the tape and tumbling vertically downwards, almost touching the net. Delicacy of touch, a correctly angled racket-face and a relaxed grip are essentials. The only hope of returning this perfect net-shot is to let the shuttle fall below the bottom of the net and then play a cross-court net-shot.

(2) *Hair-pin:* A shot played in difficulties when the shuttle is very tight to the net and 2 to 3 feet (0.6 to 0.9 metres) below the tape. The shuttle is hit vertically upwards to just loop over the tape and drop straight down. Unless very accurate, it is dangerous against a net-raider.

(3) *Stab* is played by stabbing the racket forward under the base of the shuttle, so making it turn 'cork over feathers'. To ensure a clean return, the opponent is

forced to let the shuttle drop until the base only can be cleanly hit.

(4) *Spin:* In this, the racket face following a curved path and striking feathers and base spins the shuttle on its axis. Best played back along original line of flight. In both tight spin and stab net-shots often the shuttle is forced against the net-cord and tumbles down the other side very close to the net.

NETHERLANDS – Netherlands Badminton Bond

Enthusiastically formed in 1931, its growth was delayed by the war. Today the NBB boasts over 82,000 players in 800 clubs. The high average club membership is due to the farsighted building of a number of fine purpose-built Pelikan halls.

Early advances owed much to Kent's Ken Brock and Bill Holwill, Emile ter Matz's administrative drive, and the foundation of the now famous Duinwijck BC in Haarlem. The 1970s was a golden era which produced an excellent trio in Rob Ridder, Marjan Luesken-Ridder and Joké van Beusekom, who was European singles semi-finalist three times and, with Marjan, doubles semi-finalist twice.

Lack of depth, however, has prevented TC or UC successes. The 1983 opening of a magnificent ten-court NBB Centre at Nieuwegein, venue of the long-popular international Championships of the Netherlands, will certainly be a stimulus.

NEW YORK BC

Possibly the earliest established of all clubs – 1878. Its membership carried more social than badminton distinction. With a 300-long waiting-list – many were débutantes – its committee was reputed to select them on face and figure rather than playing-potential. Prizes were lavish ranging from silverware to US Steel stock – and diplomatically apportioned.

Women were rendered virtually immobile by trains and huge hats; men played solemnly in top hats, chokers and long-tailed Prince Albert coats; one who so far exerted and forgot himself as to take off his jacket was expelled!

NEW ZEALAND BADMINTON FEDERATION

Play started as far back as the 1900s with the formation of the Auckland BC but the first NZ Open (at Wanganui) was not played until 1927, when the NZBF was also formed with NZ Champion Arch-deacon Creed-Meredith as President. The first club in Wellington was formed by J.R. Marshall, later to become Prime Minister.

Play was given a boost by the presentation of the Wisden Cup for District Association competition and the Whyte Trophy for biennial contest between NZ and Australia. A coaching visit by the legendary Frank Devlin also helped. Today there are a number of well equipped multi-court halls and over 20,000 players.

NZBF, through Nancy Fleming (who played for NZ for twenty-five years), can claim to have had a big hand in promoting the Uber Cup and was second only to Denmark in creating a National Umpires' Association.

Isolated, NZ's leading players have been unable to make world class but Jeff and Heather Robson, Nancy Fleming and Sonia Cox (who once beat Judy Hashman) and Richard and Brian Purser made a very definite mark when they sought competition in England.

NICHOLS, Ralph C.F.
(Middlesex and England)

The last of the AEC-dominating Englishmen, he won, with brother Leslie, the AEC doubles, 1936-8, the mixed once, 1939, and the singles five times. His reign ended – and that of the Danes and other overseas competitors began – in 1939, when he was beaten by a young Dane, Tage Madsen, 15-10, 13-18, 7-15.

He was a player who spurned brute force, preferring accurate placement and deception. Excellent anticipation, a steely wrist and a rock-like defence were his armaments in the wars of attrition he relished.

He won thirty-six 'caps' (1930-51) and at one time pre-war his international record over twenty-four matches read singles 22-0, men's doubles 22-2, mixed doubles 2-0.

Nichols married Elizabeth O'Beirne (fourteen England caps).

NIELSEN, née Ward, Heather (Surrey and England)
Born 1940

Heroine of one of England's all too rare post-war fairy stories.

Heather clearly announced the shape of things to come by four consecutive English National Junior singles victories (1953/4-1956/7), three girls' doubles and three mixed doubles.

In 1958 eighteen-year-old Heather reached the AEC singles semis to take a game, after 5-10 down, from Judy Devlin, the first lost in two years, and lost 9-12 only after an inch-out serve and an adverse net-cord.

Then, playing for the first time with Texan Margaret Varner, she beat twice former holders, the Devlin sisters, in the semis, and 1953 and 1955 winners June White and Iris Cooley in the final, 12 and 2.

Still greater things to come: in 1959, fleet of foot, defensive and playing to plan, she beat Judy Devlin eager to annex the famous cup permanently after three previous victories (11-7, 3-11, 11-4). She also stretched the Devlin sisters to three games in the doubles.

Sadly for England, Heather settled in S. Africa, moved on to Australia and married. She played again for England on her return (eighteen caps in all) and is currently BAE Council member and selector. In 1985 won yet another AEC title – the Veterans' ladies' doubles. Cheerfully unassuming.

Her son Anders, aged nineteen, is bidding fair to follow in his mother's footsteps.

NIELSEN, Nettie Hyldborg (Denmark)
Born 23 July 1964, Tølløse

Lene Köppen's successor in charm and talent? This Hvidovre BC junior played in the Uber Cup when only sixteen; won the European Junior ladies' doubles title with regular partner Dorte Kjaer in 1981; only a year later lost narrowly in the Senior semis to England's very experienced Perry and Webster 9-15, 17-14, 11-15; and improved on that in 1986, losing only in the final 11-15, 12-15 to Clark and Gowers.

Won both ladies' singles and ladies' doubles in the 1982 and 1983 Nordic Championships, and the 1986 (Danish (Open) ladies' doubles.

Has also won German (1983), New Zealand and Australian Singles (1982) titles as well as the Scottish Open mixed doubles with Morten Frost (1983).

A lively and versatile player.

NIELSEN, Poul Erik (Denmark)

With a trained legal mind, today's President of the IBF holds high position in Denmark's not over-popular Ministry of Taxes.

Not just a penetrating mind but an ex-international player (thirty-three caps between 1954 and 1954), he won four national titles and doubtless would have won many more had he not played in the era of Finn Kobbero's genius. More than that, he won the AEC doubles twice, with Kops (1958) and Kobbero (1960), and the mixed with Inge Hansen (1959), when he interposed in the eleven-year Kobbero-Jordan duel.

As a reminder that he is still very much in touch with the modern game and 'mens sana in sano corpore', he recently successfully defended his Danish Veterans' titles (48+) with Ole Mertz and Inge Hansen. A left-hander, he still adds tight and thoughtful serving and cast-iron defence to shrewd tactical play.

As active off-court as on, he has been Hon. Secretary of the Danish BF; Vice President of the EBU; IBF Vice-President (1979) and Chairman of its Rules and Laws Committee; and Editorial Committee member of World Badminton.

NIERHOFF, Jens-Peter (Denmark)
Born 2 September 1960, Aalborg

Blonde, 6-feet-2-inches (1.87 metres), strongly built, with a whiplash backhand and probably the heaviest smash in the business, Nierhoff is undoubtedly Flemming Delf's successor.

As a junior member of the famous Triton BK, he won the singles and mixed titles in the 1979 European Junior Championships. Within two years he had improved sufficiently to win the Danish National men's singles (1981/2) and doubles (with Helledie) in 1981/2 and 1982/3, to be runner-up in the Nordic Singles and to win the W. German Open title. He also gained a 15-9, 15-8 victory over Padukone on the latter's home ground in the first Indian Masters, the German title again, and, to crown all, the 1982 European singles title.

In the latter event Frost was beaten not by the Nierhoff smash but by a restraining injunction after a legal wrangle between rival racket manufacturers as to whose rackets he would endorse and use. Frost is still Nierhoff's bogy man: 8-15, 2-15 in the 1984 European Championships, but the latter was runner-up *with* Frost in the doubles. So too is England's tireless 'runner' Nick Yates, who got the better of him in four successive clashes. But, unseeded, in the 1984 AEC he gave Han Jian an electrifying shock when he took him to the limit 15-7, 5-15, 16-17.

Scratched from the 1985 AEC but playing in the World Championships, he reached the semis, losing to Han Jian, 9-15, 14-17.

Reserved but not without a sense of humour, Nierhoff came on court in the 1983 Alba Quartz with a strip of black velvet fixed down his hair, an amusing riposte to opponent Misbun Sidek's recently adopted tinted blonde streak in his black hair.

NIGERIA – Amateur Badminton Association of Nigeria

Nigeria's size and climate might appear unfavourable to badminton growth but ABAN, formed only in 1974, already has 10,000 affiliated players overall in Nigeria's nineteen states. Three Chinese coaches are employed and, with Commonwealth Games and Thomas Cup experience, its playing standard is probably the best in Central Africa.

NORDIC CHAMPIONSHIPS

Individual championships instituted between Denmark, Norway and Sweden in 1962. Since then Finland, Iceland and the Faroe Islands have joined in. Senior events are held in November, junior ones in March.

Sture Johnsson (three) and Eva Twedberg (three) are the only non-Danish singles winners, and only in 1983 did Swedish pairs win the ladies' and mixed doubles for the first time. Lene Koppen has established a hard-to-beat record of twenty-five victories.

Men's Singles

1962	K.A. Nielsen
1963	K.A. Nielsen
1964	E. Kops
1965	E. Kops
1966	E. Kops
1967	E. Kops
1968	E. Kops
1969	S. Johnsson (SW)
1970	J. Mortensen
1971	S. Pri
1972	S. Johnsson (SW)
1973	S. Pri
1974	S. Pri
1975	S. Johnsson (SW)
1976	F. Delfs
1977	S. Pri
1978	M. Frost
1979	M. Frost
1980	M. Frost
1981	M. Frost
1982	M. Frost
1983	M. Frost
1984	M. Frost
1985	I. Frederiksen

Ladies' Singles

1962	K. Jorgensen
1963	U. Rasmussen
1964	U. Rasmussen
1965	U. Rasmussen
1966	U. Strand
1967	E. Twedberg (SW)
1968	J. Föge
1969	I.R. Nielsen
1970	L. von Barnekow
1971	E. Twedberg (SW)
1972	E. Twedberg (SW)
1973	L. Køppen
1974	L. Køppen
1975	L. Køppen
1976	L. Køppen

1977	L. Køppen
1978	L. Køppen
1979	L. Køppen
1980	L. Køppen
1981	L. Køppen
1982	N. Nielsen
1983	K. Larsen
1984	K. Larsen
1985	C. Magnusson (SW)

Men's Doubles

1962	B. Glans/G. Wahlquist (SW)
1963	K.A. Nielsen/H. Borch
1964	O. Mertz/J. Sandvad
1965	E. Kops/K. Kaagaard
1966	E. Kops/H. Borch
1967	E. Kops/H. Borch
1968	S. Pri/P. Walsoe
1969	S. Pri/P. Walsoe
1970	S. Pri/P. Walsoe
1971	S. Pri/P. Walsoe
1972	S. Pri/P. Petersen
1973	E. Hansen/F. Delfs
1974	S. Pri/P. Petersen
1975	T. Kihlström/B. Fröman (SW)
1976	T. Kihlström/B. Fröman (SW)
1977	T. Kihlström/B. Fröman (SW)
1978	F. Delfs/S. Skovgaard
1979	T. Kihlström/B. Fröman (SW)
1980	M. Frost/S. Fladberg
1981	M. Frost/S. Fladberg
1982	M. Frost/S. Fladberg
1983	T. Kihlström/S. Karlsson (SW)
1984	T. Kihlström/S. Karlsson (SW)
1985	T. Kihlström/S. Karlsson (SW)

Ladies' Doubles

1962	U. Rasmussen/K. Jorgensen
1963	U. Rasmussen/K. Jorgensen
1964	L. von Barnekow/P. Molgaard Hansen
1965	U. Rasmussen/K. Jorgensen
1966	U. Strand/K. Jorgensen
1967	U. Strand/L. von Barnekow
1968	A. Flindt/P. Molgaard Hansen
1969	A. Flindt/P. Molgaard Hansen
1970	A. Flindt/P. Molgaard Hansen
1971	A. Flindt/P. Molgaard Hansen
1972	L. Køppen/A. Berglund
1973	U. Strand/P. Kaagaard
1974	L. Køppen/I.R. Nielsen
1975	L. Køppen/I. Borgstrom
1976	L. Køppen/P. Nielsen
1977	L. Køppen/I. Borgstrom
1978	L. Køppen/S. Berg
1979	L. Køppen/I. Borgstrom
1980	L. Køppen/P. Nielsen
1981	L. Køppen/P. Nielsen
1982	N. Nielsen/D. Kjaer
1983	C. Magnusson/M. Bengtsson (SW)
1984	K. Larsen/D. Kjaer
1985	D. Kjaer/N. Nielsen

Mixed Doubles

1962	P.E. Nielsen/U. Rasmussen
1963	H. Borch/U. Rasmussen
1964	F. Kobberø/U. Rasmussen
1965	E. Kops/U. Rasmussen
1966	P. Walsoe/U. Strand
1967	E. Kops/U. Strand
1968	P.E. Nielsen/P. Molgaard Hansen
1969	P. Walsoe/P. Molgaard Hansen
1970	S. Pri/U. Strand
1971	P. Walsoe/P. Kaagaard
1972	E. Hansen/U. Strand
1973	E. Hansen/U. Strand
1974	E. Hansen/P. Kaagaard
1975	S. Skovgaard/L. Køppen
1976	S. Skovgaard/L. Køppen
1977	S. Skovgaard/L. Køppen
1978	S. Skovgaard/L. Køppen
1979	S. Skovgaard/L. Køppen
1980	S. Skovgaard/L. Køppen
1981	S. Skovgaard/L. Køppen
1982	S. Skovgaard/H. Adsbol
1983	T. Kihlström/M. Bengtsson (SW)
1984	J. Helledie/D. Kjaer
1985	S. Karlsson/M. Bengtsson (SW)

Note: All winners are Danish except those marked (SW), Swedish.

NORDISK BADMINTON KONGRES

NBK held its first championships in 1962, since almost completely dominated by Denmark, and was elected to the IBF in 1967. Its members are Denmark, Faroe Islands, Finland, Iceland, Norway and Sweden.

(See also *Nordic Championships*.)

NORWAY – Norges Badminton Forbund

Norway owes its badminton to a British consul, Hudson, who brought his racket north with him. He formed the Aalesund BC in 1929, but there were only four more clubs in 1938 when NBF was formed. (Joined IBF 1939.) Snow, fjords and mountains hampered development but 1965's thirteen clubs have had beanstalk growth to a steadily increasing 145, with over 7,000 affiliated players.

ODDS

Term used in handicap events to denote actual handicaps: e.g. +6 or −7 (See also under *Handicaps* for Tables of Differentiated Odds.)

OFFICE CLEANING SERVICES SPORTS SCHOLARSHIPS

Three scholarships are awarded annually to students qualified for admission to the University of Bath. They enable the student to extend his academic course by a year and offer financial help with equipment and training. He/she also receives full technical back-up in training, including physiological and psychological testing, medical and dietary screening, video technique analysis and conditioning advice for international competition.

OLYMPIC GAMES

The accolade of inclusion in the Olympic Games has since 1965 been the ambition of the IBF and its former Secretary Herbert Scheele. Competition was fierce but badminton was a 'Demonstration Game' at the fateful 1972 Munich Games when Palestinian terrorists massacred the Israeli team. The WBF-IBF dispute, 1977-81, rendered inclusion impossible.

However, indefatigable lobbying led to the anouncement at the 90th International Olympic Committee session on 5 June 1985 that Badminton had unanimously been voted one of the twenty-four full-medal sports accepted for the 1992 Games. (Also that Seoul OOC had requested its inclusion as an Exhibition Sport in 1988.) The IOC flag was presented to the IBF at the World Championships in Calgary.

A new eligibility code (based perhaps on that of lawn tennis in 1988) will almost certainly abolish the outdated licensed player. The IBF will have to plan how the permitted 144 players will qualify – and with what reasonable geographical spread.

The venue? *Perhaps* Paris, Barcelona, Amsterdam or Birmingham.

Apart from sheer prestige, badminton may benefit in several ways: (1) direct Olympic revenue; (2) Olympic Solidarity Development grants: (3) new drug-testing facilities; (4) individual government assistance through their own national Olympic Committees.

In 1972 twenty-five players from eleven countries, organized by the Deutscher BV and IBF, brilliantly demonstrated the game's qualities.

Results

Men's Singles
   Rudy Hartono (I) beat S. Pri (D) 15-6, 15-1
Ladies' Singles
   N. Nakayama (J) beat U. Dewi (I) 11-5, 11-3
Men's Doubles
   Chandra and Hadinata (I) beat Ng Boon Bee and P. Gunalan (M) 15-4, 2-15, 15-11.
Mixed Doubles
   D. Talbot and G. Gilks (E) beat S. Pri and U. Strand (D) 15-6, 18-16.

ONG, POH LIM (Singapore)

Lim was born in the wilds of Sarawak, at Kuching, but the date (1926) is uncertain as his birth certificate was falsified by a Japanese officer so that Lim could avoid conscription and continue to play badminton with him!

He reigned from 1949 to 1963, winning three hundred trophies. His first triumph (15-9, 15-8) was in Paris, against Wong Peng Soon – but after game and 12-9 up, he lost to him in the 1951 AEC final. He was so tired that he lost also (with Ismail bin Marjan) to the Choongs in the men's doubles but gained his revenge, with Ooi Teik Hock in 1954, when he beat them (winners for the previous three years) not only in a spectacular AEC final but also in the Glasgow World Invitation and US Open. He played in the first three TC series and won all his nine finals matches.

Pan-handled, he had a powerful if flat smash, completely unorthodox strokes, rock-like crouch defence which often seized the attack, lightning reflexes and, his speciality, a quickly dipping low serve, christened 'crocodile' after the crafty denizens of Sarawak swamps.

Now a devoted antique collector.

OPEN BADMINTON

For many years, winners of the AEC, then virtually regarded as world champions, took home vouchers for 2 guineas, later raised extravagantly to 5 guineas. Badminton was a strictly amateur game; professionals were a mere handful who lived largely on coaching fees.

With ever-growing prize-money pouring into the bank accounts of millionaire tennis and golf champions, their European badminton counterparts urged that badminton 'go Open', so that they might get a well-deserved share of the apparently limitless sponsorship money. National Associations and the IBF, naturally fearful of the difficulties that had dogged lawn tennis, inched forward until finally in 1979 at the AGM in Jakarta the IBF announced: 'Badminton has gone Open!'

New regulations governing tournaments and amateurism had been framed. A new 'licensed player' category had been created: 'professionals' were still outside the IBF fold. Such licensed players could now accept cash prizes exceeding the amateur £300 limit, more generous support grants, and advertising contracts. The latter were, however, subject to National Association scrutiny, and prize money, in the first place, to avoid currency and taxation pitfalls, was payable only through them. But to gain such benefits they had to sacrifice eligibility for multi-sport gatherings such as the Olympic Games.

'Open' tournament organizers had to obtain IBF sanction, pay a fee for a sacrosanct date and submit a detailed report (through which the IBF hoped to iron out latent problems).

Joanna Flockhart (Scotland) was the first to take the licensed player plunge; many others stood on the edge hesitant as to the full or likely implications. In September 1979 the Friends' Provident Masters, pre-Jakarta, planned and brilliantly staged in the prestigious Albert Hall, with £20,000 prize money and an international cast, was the first such new and major event. Though early rounds were sparsely attended, it was a success. Both singles winners, Lene Køppen (D) and Prakash Padukone (Ind.) had to hand their prizes (£3,000) back to their National Associations as neither had registered. Bell's Scotch Whisky Highlands Championship, on a smaller (£2,000) scale, was equally successful but the first Danish 'Open', the Randers, had teething troubles.

Since then 'Open' tournaments have multiplied world-wide and in 1983 culminated in the first Grand Prix circuit, the Pro-Kennex (q.v.). Star badminton players probably now earn, for the handful of years they are at the top, some £40,000 a year. But as tournaments still lack worthwhile TV coverage, sponsorship is modest, and prize money, by tennis and golf standards, a 'bell-hop's' tip. As a result the greater part of that sum comes from racket and clothing endorsement.

OPEN CHAMPIONSHIPS

Until 1980 'Open championships' signified that they could be entered by players from any other region or country. 'Open' is now used to denote those events where increased prize money is involved. Other major events are known simply as 'international'.

OPEN RACKET FACE

Term applied when the face of the racket is tilted upwards to hit the shuttle upwards; the opposite of 'closed', tilted downwards.

OVER 50's CHAMPIONSHIPS

A championship for Over 50's clubs in the Sports Council's Southern Region inaugurated in 1983. One final saw 153 years on one side of the net and 110 on the other!

1985 Winners
Veterans' Cup
   J. Rumble and P. Watts
Grand Dames' Cup
   W. Miles and E. Bridges
Darby and Joan Cup
   D. Ovenden and W. Miles

OWE

A term used in handicap events to indicate that a good player has to score the allotted number of owed points before his score is called as 'zero' or 'love' and he can start scoring normally to 11, 15 or 21 (e.g. 'owe seven' means he must score seven points before starting at 'love').

A player, solely or additionally, may 'owe a hand'. In doubles, this means that only one player of a pair is allowed to serve in each 'innings', not the normal two.

In singles, a little-known and rarely used handicap is the apparent paradox of 'owe a hand'. Since in singles a player has no partner it might seem that with such a handicap he could never serve. In fact, such a handicap is translated into 'give a hand', and his opponent thus has two, not one, innings.

P

PADUKONE, Prakash (India)
Born 10 June 1955

Six feet (1.8 metres) and eleven stone (70 kg) of sinuous speed earned the good-looking Indian bank clerk the title of 'Bangalore Torpedo'. As a small fire-cracker, he performed the remarkable feat in 1972 of winning both the Indian National junior and senior singles titles – at the age of sixteen. The latter he was to hold for nine successive years. A singles specialist.

In the 1978 AEC he had a long lead in the quarters against Flemming Delfs – and lost 15-5, 8-15, 11-15, this despite weeks of torrid training in Jakarta with Indonesians. But he made amends by getting a gold medal at the Commonwealth Games in Edmonton, when he dropped a total of only 33 points in the last 90. Some four months later, at a Wembley Arena 'Evening of Champions', he gained revenge, out-manoeuvring Delfs 15-8, 15-7. In the first Friends' Provident Masters (1979) he beat Kihlstrom, Pri, Talbot and, in the final, Frost, without dropping a game – and with only three double-figure scores against him. Sadly, this first-ever major prize money (£3,000) went not direct to his pocket but to the Indian BA, since he had not registered as a licensed player.

In the 1980 AEC, having scythed through a strong field without dropping a game, he mesmerized Swie King with deception to shatter his hopes of winning the trophy outright (15-3, 15-10), despite having forecast of the Indonesian whirlwind: 'It is almost impossible to stop him.' No wonder a grateful India awarded its first-ever champion the high honour of 'Padma Shri' for his 'noble and gentlemanlike manners' as much as for his on-court talents. In 1981 he won the first Alba Quartz without dropping a game, defeating Han Jian, 15-0, 15-13.

Later, in bitter weather, he became Member 1,401 of Denmark's Hvidovre club: a two-way benefit in that he coached the Danish club and national players, and himself obtained vital top-class play. Homesick, he said: 'I care more for Danish badminton than Danish weather.' Since then has not kept apace of Frost and Han Jian.

PALMER, Ian (Surrey)

A Surrey county player who made his mark as an outstanding women's coach at international level. Among his most famous protégées were Iris Rogers (née Cooley), June Timperley (née White), Gillian Gilks (née Perrin) and Angela Palmer (née Bairstow) – top English internationals, between 1952 and 1985.

PALMER, Ian

First President of the Wellington BA (NZ); Chairman of the Wellington Hall Building Committee; Assistant Manager to NZ Commonwealth Games team to Edinburgh (1970); President of the NZBF (elected 1973/4); Vice-President IBF (1981); player, umpire and Uber Cup referee (1981). No mean record for New Zealand's leading administrator, who is often up in the air – as an executive member of the NZ Gliding Association. Elected IBF President in 1986; the first New Zealander ever to become President of any international sports association.

PAN-AMERICAN BADMINTON CONFEDERATION

Largely through the efforts of Mexico's Victor Jaramillo Villalobos of Mexico, the PBC was formed in 1976 with Canada, Curaçao, Guyana, Jamaica, Mexico, Netherlands Antilles, Peru, Surinam, Trinidad/Tobago and the USA as founder members. Pan-american junior and senior championships were played until, in 1981, PBC's activities virtually ceased. The Canadian and Peruvian BAs are making efforts to revive it.

PARK, Joo Bong (S. Korea)

Few players can boast of playing in the Thomas Cup (1982) while still at school — *and* winning all first four games, two singles and two doubles, as well as the only two games won against Thailand in the next round. Park did just that.

Only nineteen, he did even better in the 1984 series when, although not surprisingly losing three of his five top singles encounters (though running Frost and King close), he and Moon Soo Kim won all five doubles played. These included Korea's only wins against China and Indonesia, and the win that tipped the scales against Denmark (3-2) for a semi-final place.

Prior to that, in the 1983 Alba Quartz, Park had shown his tremendous potential when, with Kim (playing his first major tournament), he won the event. They claimed famous scalps *en route*: world champions Helledie and Fladberg (D), Dew and Baddeley (E), the Sideks (M) and, in the final, Ertanto and Hadinata (I), 15-6, 15-11, to whom they had narrowly lost in the round-robin 17-18, 14-18.

Tall, rangy, hatchet-faced Park moves with raw speed to use a whiplash smash at the back and annihilate even the slightest inaccuracy at the net. Aggressive, point-hungry, he fights to the last rally, can adapt his game and combines perfectly with Kim, an unusual and brilliant backhand server.

He reached his peak in 1985, when he and Moon Soo Kim decisively defeated Denmark, China and Indonesia's best to win both the AEC and the World Men's Doubles titles. In mixed, he and Sang Hee Yoo lost easily in the AEC quarters (7 and 9) to ultimate winners Gilliland and Perry, but in Calgary, now unseeded, they sprang a major surprise by beating Karlsson/Bengtsson 15-10, 12-15, 15-12 to win the title.

Park withdrew from Alba Quartz at last minute having previously won the Indian Open.

In 1986 he was the clear star of the AEC, winning two titles by beating the Sideks 2 and 11, and, seeded 5 and 8, trouncing compatriots Lee and Chung in the mixed.

PEARD, Frank (Ireland)

Ireland's post-war equivalent of Frank Devlin?

A thoughtful and consistent player, tigerishly quick and with a wide range of strokes, he was skilled in singles, men's doubles and mixed. He won all three Irish National titles for four years consecutively, making a tally of eighteen in all, and also both singles and men's doubles in the 1950 Irish Open.

He played regularly for Ireland for eleven years (thirty caps) winning his singles eight times against full-strength England teams. He and wily Jim Fitzgibbon were ranked for two years as Europe's best and the world's eighth best; they reached the AEC doubles semis in 1952, losing only to the ultimate winners, the Choongs, 15-12, 6-15, 6-15. The *Gazette* described them as 'the magnetic, energetic, ever-attractive pair from Dublin'.

Peard played a big part in creating Ireland's Terenure Hall. He now writes on coaching matters: for example, 'The Mathematics of Badminton', a paper given to the 4th European Coaches Seminar in 1984, and 'Factors affecting Performance' at the 4th World Championships in 1985.

He was Deputy Managing Director of Guinness and is married to the former Sue Devlin (q.v.).

PEARD, Sue, née Devlin (USA and Ireland)

Rather overshadowed by the ten AEC ladies' singles successes of her $4\frac{1}{2}$ older sister, Judy Hashman, q.v., Sue Devlin was nevertheless a fine player in her own right.

London-born, Baltimore-bred, she won innumerable doubles titles with her sister, and shared with her in US Uber Cup victories, winning six AEC, ten USA Open (and junior) ladies' doubles titles. She had stubborn defence and a telling 'surprise' left-hand, especially at the net. In their last AEC victory, one of the toughest of their career (15-5, 14-17, 15-12, against the former Rasmussen sisters), it was Sue who won the vital points. In the 1961 AEC singles she beat second seed H. Jensen, then succumbed 3 and 1 to Ursula Smith – but was avenged in the final by Judy.

She married Ireland's Frank Peard and there won three Open and two National ladies' doubles titles in the era of the all-conquering Kelly-O'Sullivan combination.

She won a coveted senior scholarship and her BSc in Physiology and Bacteriology at Goucher College, USA.

PEARSON, J.P. ('Pip') (Essex)

Super salesman! A small man with great drive. Pearson joined Carlton as a sales rep in 1962, an era of nylon shuttles and metal-framed rackets. Responsible for the whole UK, he covered it in a suitably small mini-van.

1970 saw the start of his annual Far Eastern and round-the-world trips, which cover thousands of miles and sell tens of thousands of shuttles and rackets. He is now Carlton's Marketing Director.

Pearson nearly became a Geordie soccer pro but instead played badminton for Durham and Essex and was ranked tenth for England.

PERRY, née Gardner, Nora, MBE (Essex and England)
Born 15 June 1954

Starting badminton at the ripe old age of twelve Nora Perry was a late developer. U.15 English National junior titles eluded her, and 'N.C. Gardner' does not appear in the U.18 records until 1970/71, when she won ladies' singles and ladies'

doubles, and 1971/2 when she was Triple Champion; she was also runner-up in both doubles events in the European Junior Championships. She has never looked back – and few championship doubles trophies do not bear her name. (Among others she won seventeen Bell's Scotch Whisky events out of seventeen entered in seven years.)

Fate had a hand in her rapid advance to stardom. Twice Warwickshire's Ann MacFarlane gave Nora Gardner her chance when accidents forced her to scratch; twice she stepped in as substitute partner and won, beating no lesser players than Margaret Beck and Judy Hashman. Since then she has won ten English National titles, five mixed doubles in succession with Mike Tredgett (1976/7-1980/81) and five ladies' doubles. European Championship titles were won in ladies' and mixed doubles in 1978 and 1980. In addition she won both Commonwealth Games doubles titles at Edmonton in 1978.

She celebrated her majority in 1975 by unexpectedly winning (with Elliott Stuart) the first of six AEC mixed titles. In 1980, in an all too short partnership with Gillian Gilks, she won the AEC doubles title, and again in 1981 with Jane Webster.

In the 1977 World Championships she won a bronze medal with Tredgett and with Margaret Lockwood; in 1980 it was silver with Tredgett and gold with Webster, and in 1983 silver with Jane and gold with Sweden's Thomas Kihlstrom (with whom she won the 1984 Alba Quartz World Cup).

Famous for her bob-curtsey and encouraging bottom-tap, the 5-foot-9-inch, 10-stone, grey-blue eyed blonde, who plays croquet with badminton determination and fizzes like her favourite champagne drink, has long been both TV and Pressman's dream, and crowd-puller extraordinary.

Probably the finest net-player of all time, her success has stemmed from a metronome-grooved low serve and perfectly disguised flick, aggressive return of serve, dancing feet, lightning reflex and gossamer touch at the net, and an ability to turn defence into attack against even the strongest man.

She gained a double prize in 1984 when she was awarded a well-earned MBE and gave birth to Gemma. Three months later she was helping England to a steamy Kuala Lumpur Uber Cup final by winning all her matches except that against China. In 1985 she won another AEC mixed title – with a third partner, Scotland's Billy Gilliland. Unfortunately, in the World Championships, in a revived partnership with Gillian Gilks and with Dipak Tailor, her great career (ninety caps) did not end in a last blaze of glory.

However, she struck up yet another mixed partnership – with Steen Fladberg – to win the Malaysian Masters and lose only narrowly to Hadinata/Lie in the Alba Quartz. And in 1986 added Japanese and Chinese–Taipei mixed titles to her long list of badminton honours. Received the BWA award (q.v.), as 'Player of the Year', 1985-6. Ninety caps.

PHILIP, Prince

As Lt Mountbatten RN, he played regularly at Corsham (Wilts). He was assessed 'Energetic and enthusiastic but lacking skill'. He should have made prize presentation at 1953 AEC but more official duties in Germany prevented this. However, he made amends, with the Queen, as spectator at the cliff-hanger China v. Indonesia Thomas Cup final in the Albert Hall (1982). His son Prince Andrew is now the BAE Patron.

PHOTOGRAPHY

Badminton long suffered from being played in what to the lay eye might be called Stygian gloom; to the photographic, 'low light intensity'.

It was not until 1953 that the first crop of action photos, dark and distant, appeared in the *Gazette*. The pioneers were John Newland, R.W. Butler and Pat M. Turner. After the war, improved hall-lighting, high-speed films and better accessories gave the photographer greater scope. But it is badminton itself rather than Fleet Street which has produced the great photographers.

As an indoor game it obviously lacks the sunshine of tennis and cricket, and dazzling 'flash' is strictly taboo. It was only the photographer's expert knowledge of his game's technique and tactics, aided by better equipment, that enabled him to capture split-second, pin-sharp action. Leaders in the post-war field have been Graham Habbin, the indefatigable Louis Ross ('Mr Lens' himself, who world-wide has taken tens of thousands of shots, as

he crouches for hours on his little courtside stool), Mervyn Rees, Peter Richardson, Chris Bewick, Preben Seborg and Tommy Handley (the only professional).

Equipment used varies according to the photographer and his particular approach. Generally speaking, a 35 mm single-lens reflex camera is used. Now that colour prints and transparencies are in demand, it is essential to have two or three easily interchangeable bodies. 50 mm, 85 mm, 135 mm and 200 mm lenses are needed if a zoom lens is not used.

In order to overcome lighting deficiencies, apertures are set as wide as fl.4 −2.0. If even this is not sufficient, the commonly used 400 ASA black-and-white film can be 'souped up' to 800 or even 1,600 ASA equivalent. Each photographer naturally has his own preference but Tri-X (b/w) and Ektachrome transparencies are successfully used. A shutter speed of 1/250 sec. is commonly employed but the interplay of that, film speed and aperture depends on individual style. Off court or at prize presentation, flash with 125 ASA film is used.

Much depends on the photographer's equipment and his knowledge of it, and of play and players – and, sometimes, sheer luck. To catch dramatic impact action may need a hundred abortive shots. In skilled hands, the camera brings out badminton's speed, agility and power to the full.

PIONEER EAST SEA CHAMPION RABBIT

A brand of Far Eastern shuttlecocks!

PLAY

R. Stanton Hales, President of USBA, in *World Badminton* quoted the following statistics not to denigrate lawn tennis but to show badminton as an even more demanding sport worthy of at least equal publicity and popular support.

In the Wimbledon final Boris Becker (WG) defeated Kevin Curren (USA) 6-3, 6-7, 7-6, 6-4. The game lasted 198 minutes during which the ball was in play for eighteen minutes, or a nine per cent intensity. 1,004 shots were played in 299 rallies, i.e. 3.4 shots per rally including missed first serves, or 5.1 shots per elapsed minute.

In the World Championship badminton final Han Jian (China) beat Morten Frost 14-18, 15-10, 15-8. This encounter lasted seventy-six minutes during which the shuttle was actually in play for thirty-seven minutes, or a forty-eight per cent intensity. 1972 shots were played in 146 rallies, i.e. 13.5 shots per rally, or 25.9 shots per elapsed minute.

Hales also calculated that the tennis players ran two miles (3.2 km); the badminton players four miles (6.4 km) (but based on an estimated twenty-two (6.6 metres) feet travelled per shot this may unduly favour badminton).

It is extremely difficult to quantify weight of racket and exertion in stroke-production, i.e. to compare energy used in a tennis serve and a badminton smash, especially a jump smash – or in a last-ditch lob.

PLAYERS' APPRECIATION CUP

A cup purchased by American players and presented by them to a person who 'has devoted endless years of time and energy to furthering our game behind the scenes at National level'. Jack van Praag was the first recipient.

PLUME D'OR

The 'Golden Feather' competition was inaugurated in Brussels in May 1973 by the Belgian BF. Smaller badminton nations, France, Portugal, Czechoslovakia and Switzerland, competed on a round-robin basis, each tie consisting of three singles and four doubles. Under the Presidency of A.A. Verstoep, it was agreed to make it an annual, late-season weekend event. It is not under EBU jurisdiction.

Thirteen competitions have now been held, new participants as far separated as Spain and Israel, Malta and Austria welcomed and preliminary and classification rounds instituted.

1972 Czechoslovakia
1973 Czechoslovakia
1974 Belgium
1975 No competition
1976 Switzerland
1977 Yugoslavia
1978 Yugoslavia
1979 Belgium
1980 Belgium
1981 Belgium
1982 Austria
1982 Austria
1982 Austria
1985 Austria
1986 Austria

POACHING

Action of taking shots that normally should be returned by one's partner. Done either through over-enthusiasm (forgivable), greed (unforgivable) or lack of confidence in partner's ability (unforgivable except *in extremis*).

PODGER, Sally (Guernsey and England)
Born 8 February 1962

The only Channel Islander ever to play for England.

She won English National junior girls' singles and doubles (with Gillian Clark) in 1978/9 and 1979/80, and European Junior girls' doubles in 1979. In the 1982 Commonwealth Games she was runner-up to Helen Troke and again in the 1984 European Championships. She won thirty-eight caps (1980-84) and achieved No. 2 Ranking.

Podger boosted English morale on-court with frequent 'retrieval' splits and off with bubbly good humour. In hot but friendly contention with Helen Troke for top European honours, she retired rather than endanger her marriage by long absences on tour.

POETRY

Badminton for all its grace and balletic qualities has only occasionally inspired verse from its adherents. The following, on account of its humour and recording of an AEC final incident, rather than for its prosody, deserves recognition.

They also serve who only stand and wait

The singles final's stage was set
when, almost underneath the net,
the lady champion found a spot;
though whether it was there or not
I could not tell, because to me
there was not anything to see.

Thereafter there was some delay
and so, in hope of starting play,
officials had to search about
for means to wipe the damn thing out.

A mop, made wetter than it 'oughter'
by former player's casual water
was then applied on champion's order
to middle court as well as border.

The consequence, as you may guess
was merely to produce a mess,
which made the lady champion cry
'I cannot play until it be dry'.

Miss Bairstow then essayed relief
by getting out her handkerchief
and hands and knees upon the floor
rubbed hard, as on a family chore,
but not enough; and I must state
that some grew tired of this long wait.

Now, showing little sign of nerves,
Miss Bairstow tries some practice serves
and to and fro her way she wends
continually changing ends,
as if she'd solve her rival's troubles
by partnering her in ladies' doubles.

When all the champions who appear
produce the same results each year
and none are English, let's take pride
that we can see the funny side.

C.H.C

from *The Badminton Gazette*, May 1963.

POINT OF IMPACT

The precise point at which the racket-face
strikes the shuttle-base. In general (for
control, effective use of weight, and
balance) it is just in front of the leading
foot. Only strong-wristed, highly skilled
players can effectively play shuttles far
behind the head with power and control.

Variations are slight but important.
For the defensive (upward) clear the
shuttle is (roughly) struck over the right
shoulder; for the flat attacking clear, over
the forehead; for the drop-shot, 12 inches
(30 centimetres) in front; and for the
smash, some 18 inches (45 centimetres) in
front. The straight drive is played just in
front of the leading foot; the cross-court
18 inches (45 centimetres) further
forward.

In overheads, if the point of impact is
too far forward, the shuttle will be hit into
the net; if too far back, skied uncontrol-
lably. In a drive, the shuttle, if taken
behind the body, will generally be hit out.

Correct impact is essential for correct
stroking.

POLAND – Polski Zwiazek Badmintona

Small is beautiful when as enthusiastically
organized as PZB.

Between 1972 and 1977 badminton
made great strides. Sports centres were
used, local leagues formed and senior and
junior   championship   organized.
Additionally, periodicals were published,
Sweden's Anders Lindberg trained coaches and Owe Wikström, umpires.

Some eighty clubs with over two
thousand players have been established.
The 1984 Polish Championships attracted over a hundred entries from fourteen
countries. PZB achieved a very creditable
eleventh place (nineteen) in the 1984
European Championships and thirteenth
(twenty-four) in the 1985 European
Junior.

POPMOBILITY

Fitness exercises performed to 'pop'
music. Pioneered by Ken Woollcott, an
AAA coach sponsored by Robinson's
Barley Water, and demonstrated by his
team of girls to many clubs and counties.
Lively beat and group participation made
exercising less arduous and so of longer
duration. Now it is known by the more
serious and scientific title of 'aerobics'.

POSITION OF READINESS

The position taken up at the outset of a
rally or between strokes during a rally.
Thoughtful positioning of feet and racket
is essential for quick movement and reflex
stroke necessitated by a fast-flying
shuttle. It varies according to situation.

For the receiver, it is a threatening
sideways, half-crouching stance near the
front-service line with racket at tape level.
The server's partner, astride the centre
line, crouches more squarely, with
racket-head defensively in front of the
likely target – the stomach. The net

player stands square to the net, knees only slightly bent, on the balls of his feet, with racket constantly tape-high. During rallies, when on the attack, players stand much as the receiver, though rather less crouched; in defence, like the server's partner but a little less square; some players prefer a backhand stance.

POSTS

Of wood or metal 5-feet-1-inch (1.55 metres) in height, these should be firmly fixed *on* the doubles side-line by a screw-device or heavy weight. If posts are not on the line, a white lath should be fixed from that line to the net-cord to indicate continuation of the line.

They should be channelled on the top; they should have hooks on the inside face (so that the net can be secured across the full width of the court) and one on the outside over which the end of a looped net-cord end can be slipped. If straining ropes are necessary, it is essential to affix red warning 'flags' to prevent possible decapitation.

Prior to 1922, posts were placed 2-feet (0.6 metres) outside the doubles side-line. With the post thereafter *on* the line, there was nothing in the Laws to prevent a player, had arm and racket together measured $3\frac{1}{2}$-4 feet (1.08-1.2 metres), serving *round* the post until the Law was purposely amended in the late 1970s.

PRESS, A

A mechanical, portable, spring or screw clamp into which one or more wood-framed rackets were inserted to prevent warping. Metal-framed rackets rendered them obsolete.

PRESS DOUBLES CHAMPIONSHIP

An interesting event held among the world's Press during the World Championships. In 1985, it was won by 6-foot-plus (1.8 metres), handle-bar moustached Pujzant Kassabian of badminton fledgling Bulgaria. He played with Supardi, who sadly claimed, 'I'm the only Indonesian going back to Jakarta with a title.'

Kassabian also won the Press Singles at Malmö in 1977 and the doubles in Copenhagen in 1983.

PRESS, The

Badminton has long and justifiedly complained that the Press has never given it a tithe of tennis's coverage and publicity. In the 1900s badminton played a poor third fiddle in *Lawn Tennis and Croquet!*

After World War II it was very much 'also ran' in *Lawn Tennis and Badminton*, when the latter was allotted just five columns in thirteen issues. Even in the Wong Peng Soon era, tennis-player and reporter John Oliff in the *Daily Mail* labelled it 'a poetic pastime for the parish hall'! And that paper's sports artist had previously penned in a tennis ball on a missileless action photo of England's Daphne Young – to give it greater reality!

Right through to the 1980s the game's main upholders were Dickie Rutnagur (*Daily Telegraph*) and Christina Wood (*Manchester Guardian*). The 'popular' Press didn't want to know. But with the advent of Open badminton and prize money (and Gilks controversy!), coverage grew wider, with *Times* cricket correspondent Richard Streeton leading the way, followed by William Kings of the *London Standard*, Eric Brown of *The Sunday Times*, Richard Eaton of *The Sunday Times* and Peter Jessup of the *London Evening Standard*. But, overall, coverage is still much too scant.

PRI, Svend (Denmark)

Born only a shuttle hit from a badminton hall, he first played at eight and was a Danish Junior Champion from thirteen to eighteen. In a thirty-year long career, the successor to Kops, the forerunner of Delfs, he won seventeen National titles (eight men's singles, five men's doubles, four mixed doubles) and eleven Nordic (four men's singles, six men's doubles, one mixed doubles): the tip of the iceberg, for he won innumerable titles – and popularity – world-wide. In 1975 he wrote his aptly titled book *Ten Years at the Top*.

First of these victories was the AEC 1967 mixed title when he took on Kobbero's eight-win mantle as well as his petite partner Ulla Strand. He was to repeat that win in 1971 and 1972.

But Pri's greatest triumphs – and disappointments – were in singles. In the 1973 Thomas Cup final in the steaming heat of Jakarta, which he was then the only European to overcome, he beat Rudy Hartono in one of the tensest-ever matches. Having won the first and 'thrown' the second, he saw Hartono in the third race from 8-11 to 14-11 in a single hand, saved four match points to set, and won 17-15 after 73 steam-bath minutes. Elated, he threw his three rackets to the 12,000 cheering Indonesians who had tremendous admiration for his sheer guts. In all, he took part in no fewer than six Thomas Cup series.

Only after ten years did he win the AEC title in 1975 by breaking Rudy Hartono's hoped for record-breaking eighth successive victory, 15-11, 17-14.

Magnificent quadriceps testified to his training with top Danish cyclists. As strong in last-ditch defence as in attack, he was a master of the trick shot, 'a Nastase without the nastiness'. A livewire entertainer, he loved pubs and parties and made a moving retiral speech after the 1977 World Championships to the strains of Frank Sinatra's *My Way*. Later he played his farewell game outside his shop in a packed arcade!

Appointed Danish National Coach, he shortly after suffered renal failure, recovering only to die in 1983 aged thirty-seven.

PRIZE MONEY

Since the first Open Masters event in 1979, with its total of £21,000 prize money, players' rewards have varied according to TV coverage and sponsorship, inflation and geographical situation. The 1984 Portsmouth British Airways sponsored Masters offered only £15,000 but from the Far East came news of an extra $250,000 for the 1985 Pro-Kennex Grand Prix, making a total *overall* sponsorship of £2.7 million spread over three years, as compared with Yonex's European sponsorship of the AEC £100,000 each of three years.

Though still playing only 11 up in singles, women were disappointed that their Portsmouth Masters singles winner got roughly half the men's prize money. In general, prize-money is much bigger in the Far East, where quarter-finalists and juniors can sometimes pick up as much as a European winner.

Badminton's highly skilled, extremely fit and much-travelled top players still earn a pittance compared with top golfers

and tennis-players, or even darts and bowls experts. Chris Kinard, six times USA Singles Champion, worked out that in 1982/3, IBF's twenty-seven licensed players, who earned £77,583 between them, would take forty-three years to accumulate Martina Navratilova's career earnings (then) of £3,485,161.

The answer lies mainly in increased TV coverage, which will result perhaps only when *all* club players and enthusiasts write to the BBC demanding greater coverage – and then watching it.

PRO-KENNEX GRAND PRIX

The first major Grand Prix series – sponsored by Taiwan racket manufacturers Pro-Kennex. It was based on the 1983 AEC, Japanese, Swedish, Indonesian, Canadian, Dutch, Indian, Malaysian and Hong Kong Championships. These were divided into four categories according to total prize money offered and so strength of entry. Category 1 AEC and World Championships; Category 2 £11,200 min.; Category 3 £8,400 min.; Category 4 £5,700 min. Points were awarded to competitors in these events on the following scale.

CATEGORY

	(1)	(2)	(3)	(4)
Winner	250	175	150	125
Runner-up	200	140	120	95
Losing SF	160	110	90	70
Losing QF	120	80	60	40
Losing Round of 16	80	50	35	20
Losing Round of 32	40	25	20	10
Losing Round of 64	15	10	5	–

Subject to having played at least three of the above events, the top twelve men and eight women qualified for the finals held at Jakarta, 14-18 December 1983. Play was first on a round-robin basis with the men in four groups of three arranged on current form and the women in two or four. Group winners played off on a knock-out basis for prize money of £26,000 (men) and £12,800 (women) with bonus pools of £5,570 (men) and £4,400 (women) divided on a sliding scale according to position for the next thirteen men and twelve women.

In 1985, Pro-Kennex increased the number of qualifying tournaments to fifteen; announced sponsorship of £2.7 million over 1985-7; and agreed the inclusion of doubles to give the 1986 finals greater variety.

Some disquiet was felt by European

players after the 1985 semi-finals. Unusually easy semi-final wins by Han Jian over Yang Yang (8 and 12) and by Li Lingwei over Wu Jianqiu (2 and 3) suggested these games had been 'arranged'.

The reasons? (1) To preserve pecking order? (2) To achieve a shared distribution of titles? (3) To ensure freshness of one Chinese player in the final against a player of another nationality who might well have had a gruelling three-game semi? No comment was made by Chinese officials.

The final points table below is interesting but the key factor is 'events played' rather than 'points scored'. Han Jian, for example, in six events scored twice as many as Darren Hall in fourteen. Similarly, Han Aiping in five events scored only some 300 fewer than Helen Troke in twelve. Asian players do not have as many tournament opportunities as European ones, and are 'peaked' more exactly.

The seventeenth and final event in the 1985 Pro-Kennex Badminton Grand Prix took place in Edinburgh, Scotland during the week ending 24 November 1985. The final points standings were as follows:

Men's Singles

		Points	Events Played
1.	Morten Frost (Denmark)	1,690	10
2.	Han Jian (China)	1,300	6
3.	Steve Baddeley (England)	1,080	13
4.	Michael Kjeldsen (Denmark)	945	13
5.	Ib Frederiksen (Denmark)	925	14
6.	Nick Yates (England)	910	11
7.	Lius Pongoh (Indonesia)	905	8
8.	Sze Yu (Australia)	835	13
9.	Misbun Sidek (Malaysia)	830	11
10.	Torben Carlsen (Denmark)	765	15
11.	Zhao Jianhua (China)	720	4
12.	Darren Hall (England)	665	14

Ladies' Singles

		Points	Events Played
1.	Kirsten Larsen (Denmark)	1,740	11
2.	Helen Troke (England)	1,645	12
3.	Han Aiping (China)	1,330	5
	Wu Jianqiu (China)	1,330	7
5.	Li Lingwei (China)	1,000	5
6.	Zheng Yuli (China)	980	7
7.	Gillian Gowers (England)	890	14
8.	Qian Ping (China)	880	6
9.	Denyse Julien (Canada)	785	15
10.	Fiona Elliott (England)	695	10
11.	Rikke V. Sørensen (Denmark)	605	12
12.	Eline Coene (Netherlands)	565	12

The first fourteen men and first ten women in the above listings were therefore invited to take part in the 1985 Pro-Kennex Grand Prix finals held in Tokyo, Japan, 12-15 December 1985.

RESULTS

Men's Singles

1983 Luan Jin beat Morten Frost 15-2, 15-6

1984 Morten Frost beat Liem Swie King 15-5, 15-4

1985 Han Jian beat Sze Yu 15-6, 15-3

Ladies' Singles

1983 L. Lingwei beat Han Aiping 11-0, 4-11, 11-4

1984 Han Aiping beat Ivana Lie 11-3, 11-2

1985 Li Lingwei beat Han Aiping 11-3, 11-3

VENUES

1983 Jakarta

1984 Kuala Lumpur

1985 Tokyo

GRAND PRIX TOURNAMENT
Pro-Kennex RESULTS 1985

Championship	Men's Singles	Ladies' Singles	Men's Doubles	Ladies' Doubles	Mixed Doubles
Hong Kong 10-13 January	Yang Yang	Han Aiping	J. Helledie/ S. Fladberg	Han Aiping/ Xu Rong	M. Dew/ G. Gilks
Chinese/Taipei 17-20 January	L. Pongoh	H. Troke	Kartono/ R. Heryanto	G. Clark/ N. Perry	M. Dew/ G. Gilks
Japanese 22-27 January	Zhao Jianhua	Wu Jianqiu	Park Joo Bong/ Moon Soo Kim	Yun Ja Kim/ Sang Hee Yoo	W. Gilliland/ G. Gowers
Dutch 8-10 February	M. Kjeldsen	K. Larsen	J. Helledis/ S. Fladberg	G. Clark/ G. Gowers	S. Fladberg/ G. Paulsen
German 1-3 March	N. Yates	Gian Ping	Li Yongbo/ Q. Ding	Wu Jianqiu/ Guan Weizhen	M. Dew/ G. Gilks
Danish 7-10 March	M. Frost	Zheng Yuli	Li Yongbo/ B. Tian	Yun Ja Kim/ Sang Hee Yoo	D. Tailor/ N. Perry
Swedish 14-17 March	Han Jian	Han Aiping	Li Yongbo/ Q. Ding	Li Lingwei/ Han Aiping	S. Karlsson/ M. Bengtsson
All-England 20-24 March	Zhao Jianhua	Han Aiping	Joo Bong Park/ Moon Soo Kim	Li Lingwei/ Han Aiping	W. Gilliland/ N. Perry
Thailand 10-14 July	I. Sugiarto	Wu Jianqiu	B. Ertanto/ R. Heryanto	Wu Jianqiu/ Guan Weizhen	—
Malaysian 16-21 July	M. Sidek	G. Gowers	R. Sidek/ J. Sidek	G. Clark/ G. Gowers	—
Indonesian 23-28 July	Han Jian	Li Lingwei	L.S. King/ Kartono	Han Aiping/ Li Lingwei	M. Dew/ G. Gilks
Indian 18-22 September	S. Baddeley	H. Troke	Joo Bong Park/ Moon Soo Kim	Hang Suk Kang/ Sun Ai Hwang	S. Baddeley/ G. Gowers
Victor 13 October	Cancelled	Cancelled	Cancelled	Cancelled	Cancelled
Scandinavian 27 October	M. Frost	Yun Ja Kim	S. Fladberg/ J. Helledie	Yun Ja Kim/ Sang Hee Yoo	N. Tier/ G. Gowers
Canadian 1-3 November	J.P. Nierhoff	C. Backhouse	J.P. Nierhoff/ J. Helledie	J. Fallardeau/ D. Julien	W. Gilliland/ N. Perry
Scottish 24 November	Sze Yu	C. Magnusson	M. Christiansen/ M. Kjeldsen	D. Kjaer/ N. Nielsen	W. Gilliland/ G. Gowers

PROVERBS

A bird in the hand is worth two in the net.
Fine feathers make fine birds.
Look after the points and the games will look after themselves.
Every court has a white lining.
As one rally closes, another opens.
Birds of a feather go on court together.

PUSH-SHOT

A side-arm stroke used much in mixed, mainly by the man, when the shuttle is just at or slightly below tape-height. It may be used gently and accurately as a drop-shot against a slow-moving or off-balance net-player, or hit rather harder and flatter as a teasing, probing shot to the 'divorce area' between man and woman to cause indecision between them or to force a lift. Slow shuttle flight must be safeguarded by a fast and deceptive drive-like initial action.

QUARTER FINALS
(abbreviated 'quarters')

The stage reached when eight pairs, or players, are left in an event.

The four winning pairs or players are then in the semi-finals ('semis').

change ends. Finding that the other end is even worse than I thought, can I change my decision and stay where I was?' – Letter to *World Badminton*.

'Somebody shut the door!' – Sven Pri to the audience as he suffered the Wembley Arena drift.

1st Round	2nd Round	3rd Round	Quarter-Finals	Semi-Finals	Final	Winner
64	32	L	L			
		M		L		
P L A Y E R S	P L A Y E R S	N	N		P	
		O				
		P	P			
		Q		P		
		R	R			
		S				Y
32	16	T	U			
		U		U		
M A T C H E S	M A T C H E S	V	W		Y	
		W				
		X	Y			
		Y		Y		
		Z	Z			
		A				

QUOTES

'All players participating in this honourable Championships I hope all of you will give full play to your skill ... and be careful of your health' – Governor of Tokyo.

'After my opponent has won the toss and decided to serve, I then decide to

'Every year I go to the IBF meetings and every year they try to kick me out' – C.Y Wong (Taiwan BA)

'I take it as it comes. I don't argue. After all, where does it get you?' – Dipak Tailor (England)

'Your foot will not get well as long as there is a horse standing on it' – Lorne Wortman, *World Badminton* editor, on the IBF-WBF dispute.

R

RFA *RELIANT*

Royal Navy supply ship to the Falkland Islands, with possibly the only floating badminton court, marked out in the hold. South Atlantic rollers add their own unique difficulties!

RACKET

Until ˜ 1984 there was no binding definition of 'racket' in the Laws. It could have a head as big as a dustbin lid and a shaft as long as a broomstick. A player could – and still can – use two rackets simultaneously if he wished.

Rackets are, of course, descended from the earliest battledores (q.v.), simply shaped pieces of wood. These eventually evolved into a circular, light wood head covered with velvet ribbon (which also extended down the shaft-cum-handle) 'strung' with vellum. They varied in length from 2 feet (0.6 metres) to a miniature one foot (0.3 metres).

Chardin's (1699-1779) painting in the Ufizzi Gallery, Florence, *The Shuttlecock* shows a young girl holding an ovoid, heavily framed racket with slack, wide-spaced stringing, rather like a small tennis racket. The young Earl of Dysart has been depicted with a similar racket (*c.* 1740).

In the game proper's infancy, many rackets were Indian imports, often from Sealkot, costing about 3s. 6d, sturdily made but suffering, so a contemporary asserted, from 'Eastern lassitude' in their stringing.

At the turn of the century, the heavy, rather lifeless racket slowly started to evolve into today's lightweight piece of dynamic modern engineering that weighs a mere $3\frac{1}{2}$ oz (99 gm). Shaft and shoulders were strengthened with binding; the head became more rounded. Prossers claimed their rackets were 'scientifically built'; Ayres that theirs were 'highly strung'.

By pre-World War I standards, F.A. Davis rackets at $5\frac{1}{2}$-$5\frac{3}{4}$ oz (155-162 gm) were 'light as a feather' compared with a few used at up to $7\frac{1}{2}$-oz (213 gm). The *Swallow* was the first to offer 'good balance'. A much more radical advance was the *Birmal* – metal-framed and wire-strung, it took heavy toll of shuttles as 'it threw itself heart and soul into the game' (1924).

As far back as 1913, the *ADP (rebble)* was the first endorsed racket. In the 1920s the *GAT [homas]* and *MRT [ragget]* followed. The former had a reinforced shaft, the latter a double ash-bend to reduce warping. It was not until 1936 that a revolutionary development was made with the *Hazell Streamline* with slim 'supports' running from central shaft to head to give 'effortless follow-through'. Much more effective was Ayres *Silvershaft* which set the trend for a whippier, stronger, *steel* shaft. These in turn were adapted for even greater power – and sales: Ayres made it oval, then tapered it, whilst Carlton 'squeezed' it. *Silver Fox* had an open throat and shock-absorbers in the frame. Muller made *Resilite*'s steel shaft stronger still with a coating of fibreglass.

In 1967 Carlton, 'using space technology', made a yet lighter, tougher head to take still higher tensioned stringing. Yonex produced the 'slenderest-ever' shaft and a pointed head to give a larger sweet-spot. Suggiyama offered a twin-shaft. So did Sondico, with an 'extruded lightweight frame' which John Mott claimed to better with the *Feather*, 'lightest in the world'.

Carlton went for a smaller head. And ex-international Derek Talbot, for greater power, devised the Grip-shaft that ran the full length of a synthetic handle of consistent weight and gave greater power.

Technology is constantly on the move, adding ever-increasing permutations and combinations of frame and shaft construction.

Aluminium gives a light head; steel, a tough one; and carbon fibre coating on steel, or on its own, or with the addition of boron, makes for added strength and lightness in either head or shaft. The latter, formerly separate components united by a tee-piece, are being increasingly made as a single one-piece entity. Today's superbly crafted rackets, weighing less than a chocolate block, are sleek, whippy and tough.

In 1984 the IBF undertook the unenviable task of defining a racket (Law 4(e)):

(1) The hitting surface to be flat, of uniformly crossed strings, not less dense in the centre than elsewhere.

(2) The whole racket *not to exceed* 680 mm in length; 230 mm in width; similarly, the strung surface, 280 mm and 200 mm; and the actual head 290 mm in length.

(3) The frame to be free of any device which makes it possible for the player to change materially the shape of the racket.

RACKET, Manufacture of

Like its counterpart, the shuttle, today's racket is light (96 gm-120 gm) a mere 3.4 oz compared with a tennis racket's 13.5 or 15 oz (383 or 425 gm), and yet with all the strength of space-age materials.

Head

This, ovoid in shape, is made of steel, aluminium or carbon-graphite and boron. It is thin and channelled or grooved so that the strings are not rubbed if the racket-head is scraped along the floor. To prevent abrasion of strings in the frame itself, smooth plastic eyelets or grommets are inserted in the stringing holes. Carbon graphite, made of thin hair-like strands of polyacrylonite, is five times stronger than its fibre-glass predecessor. It adds to the strength of other materials (e.g. in helicopter blades), withstands knocks and

enables higher tension stringing without distortion, dampens undue vibration and has less chance of metal fatigue. It is now sometimes used layered with boron.

T-Piece

The head has long been secured to the shaft at the throat by a joining T-piece. The latest development, however, is a one-piece head and shaft which it is claimed gives greater transfer of power.

Stringing

The racket head is strung with natural or synthetic gut (q.v.), generally without trebling. Stringing is standardized in mass-produced rackets. Individual stringing is preferable, for an experienced stringer will take into consideration durability, racket construction, personal style of play, type of shuttle used – feathered or plastic, cork or synthetic base, playing conditions, hot or cold, dry or humid.

Shaft

Like the head, the shaft, light and strong, is made in an almost bewildering range of materials and shapes. Steel, stainless steel, chrome molybdenum steel, carbon-coated steel or pure graphite (and boron) are all used. Shafts may be roughly circular, tapered, flattened or waisted, each seeking to generate a little more power.

Handle

The other end of the shaft is inserted, and firmly secured, through a ferrule, into the handle. This is hollow and made of wood. Roughly octagonal in shape, it is bevelled with a broad face on either side for ease of grip and six narrower faces between the broader ones. The butt end is slightly splayed and capped to render it more difficult for the racket to slip through the hand.

Grip

Round the handle is a diagonally wound grip of leather. It is slightly ridged and perforated to give tiny perspiration drainage and suction holes. Towelling is sometimes used instead of leather for hot-handed players who want a firmer grip. In rare cases, for additional safety, a looped thong is attached to the handle through which the player puts his hand as he holds the handle. The latter are generally available in two or three sizes ranging from $3\frac{3}{8}$ in to $3\frac{5}{8}$ inches (8.57 to 9.20 centimetres).

Racket dimensions were standardized for the first time in 1984 under Law 4 (e).

Inscrutable Chinese? Not a bit of it! Trophy laden winners of the 1985
All-England Singles are Zhao Jianhua and Han Aiping

The Greatest! Indonesia's unforgettable Rudy Hartono who won the All-England Singles a record eight times

A youthful Eddy Choong (Malaysia) proudly displays the All-England Singles trophy (*left*) he has wrested from compatriot Wong Peng Soon (1953), and will win outright in 1957

England's ladies (1974), more adept with rackets, are coached in the delicate art of chopsticks prior to the first ever China tour. *Left to right:* Heather Nielsen, Nora Perry, Margaret Beck, Gillian Gilks, Sue Whetnall and Margaret Boxall

England's victorious 1972 European Championship team. *Left to right, front row:* Derek Talbot, Julie Rickard, Margaret Beck, Gillian Gilks, Elliott Stuart; *back row:* John Havers (Team Captain), Judy Hashman (Manager), David Eddy and Ray Stevens

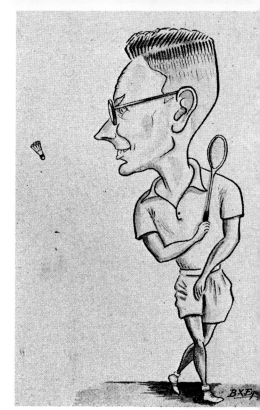

J.F. Devlin (Ireland) who 'steamed like
mother's copper'
The wily Jim Fitzgibbon: 'I'm good for
years yet.' (1960)

Frank Peard (Ireland) (1960):
'tigerishly quick'

Charoen Wattanasin (Thailand):
'Human Machine', who coached a l

Athletic and supple, Denmark's Kirsten Larsen jumps to it for a superb
round-the-head shot

China's Han Jian ('Mr Snow' to his English friends), 1985 World Champion, shows power and speed

Saori Kondo (Japan), for all her sturdy build, seems to coax, rather than hit, the shuttle over the net

Court Jester 'Whimp' had a shrewd eye
and lively pen for badminton foibles in
the '70s

YOURS!!!

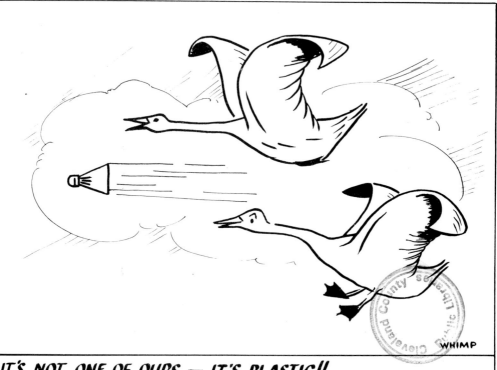

IT'S NOT ONE OF OURS — IT'S PLASTIC!!

Six times AEC champions (1974–80) Tjun Tjun and Wahjudi. The former demonstrates his murderous receiving while Chandra, wisely 'going to ground', leaves it to Christian

RAHMAN, Tunku Abdul, Al Haj

Seventh son of the Sultan of Kedah, he became known as Bapa Malaysia (Father of Malaysia) when elected as first Prime Minister of an independent Malaysia in 1957 (in gratitude for which event he made the pilgrimage to Mecca).

A patron of all sports, he took a decisive step for badminton in 1959 when, after BA of Malaysia initiative, he inaugurated a meeting that formed the Asian Badminton Confederation.

RALLY

An unbroken sequence of strokes from the opening service until a player fails to make a valid return. A beginner's rally often consists of only three or four strokes; in a top man's singles or ladies' doubles it may consist of forty to fifty (or occasionally more than sixty) played inside a minute.

RANKING LIST

Most countries now publish an annual, pre-season ranking list, based on the previous season's results for singles to show, in order, their ten best players. Such lists are of general interest and an aid of seeding committees (q.v.). (The IBF now do the seeding of major events.)

As players do not always play with the same doubles partner, doubles lists are much more rarely published. With the international season now extended throughout twelve months, some countries are producing bi-annual lists.

RANKINGS, ENGLISH SENIOR, 1985-6

Men's Singles
1. Steve Baddeley
2. Nick Yates
3. Steve Butler
   Darren Hall
5. Glen Miltone
6. Andy Goode
7. Miles Johnson
8. Anders Nielsen
9. Matthew Smith
10. Joe Ford

Ladies' Singles
1. Helen Troke
2. Fiona Elliott
3. Gillian Gowers
4. Karen Beckman
5. Gillian Clark
6. Alison Fisher
7. Caroline Gay
   Sara Halsall
9. Wendy Massam
   Claire Palmer

RASMUSSEN SISTERS (Denmark)

Two Danish girls who brought charm and talent to badminton in the 1960s. With hair boyishly cut, they announced at the All-England 'We are de Beadles!'

Petite blonde Ulla (later Strand) won ten AEC titles: three ladies' doubles, two with sister Karin Jorgensen, and seven mixed doubles, four with Kobbero, three with Svend Pri (one short of Betty Uber's record); twenty-one Danish National (three ladies' singles, ten ladies' doubles, seven with Karin, and eight mixed doubles); and seven Danish Open, one ladies' doubles and six mixed doubles.

READING A STROKE

A child slowly learns to weave individual letters into a word. A player similarly learns subconsciously to observe the varied characteristics of an opponent's action: position on court, body posture, arm and therefore racket action, with particular regard to speed (fast or slow), direction (to forehand or backhand), trajectory (up, down or flat) of racket-head at impact.

This, unless his opponent uses last fraction of a second deception, enables him to assess the kind of stroke likely to be played, just before or as the shuttle is hit, and so start moving to the shuttle well before it crosses the net. The beginner often cannot assess this until, too late, the shuttle is on his side of the net. If the shuttle is even reached, a hurried stroke results. Experienced players on the other hand appear unhurried simply because they move *early*.

A player is said to 'read the game well' when he is able quickly to assess his opponent's tactics and strategy and adapt his own accordingly throughout a game.

RECEIVER

The player to whom the shuttle is served. He should be dominating, alertly poised, racket up-raised, able to spring forward or backwards to attack low, high or flick serves. He stands as near the front service line as is concomitant with getting back to attack 'flick' serves. In the right court he is near the centre line; in the left, more centrally placed.

His aim is to score an outright winner or to secure the attack by hitting down or very tightly up to the net. Aggressive receiving can demoralize the server and make scoring difficult for opponents.

RECOVERY

1. Movement back to base or direct to the shuttle upon completion of a stroke. Ideally this should be instantaneous (in overheard shots part of the stroke itself). Strong legs, good balance, drive and a quick brain are essential if a player is to be on base before his opponent hits the shuttle, or be moving to it as the shuttle travels to his opponent.
2. To make up a deficit of points, say from 3-11 down to win 15-12: 'a good recovery'.
3. Sometimes the return of a single difficult shot.

RED BOOK, Little

Affectionate term for the slender BAE Coaches Manual written largely by Nancy Horner. So called because of its cover and publication in the era of Chinese leader Mao Tse Tung's similarly titled, rather more philosophical writings.

REEDIE, Craig
Born 6 May 1941, Stirling

A middle-of-the-road player who became a top-of-the-tree administrator. He studied Law successfully at Glasgow University but failed to set the Clyde alight with badminton. He turned to insurance broking with David Bloomer (IBF President, 1965-9) and badminton administration.

Reedie was Hon. Secretary and Hon. Treasurer as well as Vice-President and President of the Scottish BU; Vice-President European BU (1974-80); IBF Council member (1970-77), Vice-President (1977-81), Chairman (1980) and twelfth President (1981-4).

In between he helped mastermind World Invitation tournaments at Kelvin Hall, Glasgow (1960-76) and organize the 2nd Commonwealth Games at Edinburgh in 1970, and the 3rd European Junior Championships, Edinburgh again, in 1973, as well as refereeing them in 1977 in Malta. He helped create SBU's Cockburn Centre and institute the Alba Quartz World Cup, for which he donated the Craig Reedie Trophy (men's singles).

With a friendly and encouraging nature, he brought a younger outlook to IBF deliberations, seeking to expand the licensed player circuit and to plant grass-roots badminton in the 'desert' areas of the Americas and Africa.

REES, Chris (Wales) Age: 20

One of the young 'Dragons' currently making Wales an international force. Club play with his father, starting at nine, set him on the road to the Glamorgan U.14 county team, many junior titles and, at sixteen, the first of his thirty-five caps.

His greatest successes include a victory over Wales No. 1 Phil Sutton, and winning the 1983 European Junior title with Lyndon Williams – with whom he seldom has the opportunity to practise. He has been most influenced by Morten Frost's play and Ray Stevens' practical top-level 'under-pressure' advice. Persistent in training, hard-hitting, fast-moving, he aims to become a full-time licensed player and has moved to London.

Mixed is not his game, but lost only narrowly in last sixteen of 1986 European Games to Tier & Gowers (runners-up).

REFEREE

The umpire is in control of a game during play. The referee is in charge of a match, cup tie or tournament. His basic function is to see that general regulations are adhered to, such as correct speed of shuttles used, scratching of late-comers without excuse, and substitution of players in accordance with tournament regulations, and to adjudicate on any points of *Law* – not of fact – that may be raised.

In most tournaments he will also be responsible for the programming and recording of play; in some, this is done by a match controller. Tact, diplomacy, firmness and and encyclopaedic knowledge of the game are needed. Herbert Scheele was the AEC referee for thirty-four years.

REINFORCED SHUTTLECOCKS LTD

Since 1930 RSL have been making feathered shuttles. Their No. 1 Tourney was used annually in the AEC from 1947 to 1984 when, with Yonex sponsoring the event, Yonex shuttles replaced it.

The firm was started by René Gathier and G.P. Thomson, importers of gut from France, and R.W. Webber, who ran a small football and cricket ball factory in South Norwood. Extending his repertoire, he made shuttles at home, washing the feathers in the bath and drying them in the kitchen with his wife's help.

Amalgamating, the three opened a South Norwood factory where shuttles were made first by hand, then by machine. The firm took its name from a praiseworthy but impracticable idea of protecting each delicate quill with a plastic sleeve. Came the War: production ceased and the factory was bomb-damaged. Work was transferred to Altoona, USA, and kept going by orders for shuttles for recreational use by the US Armed Forces.

When peace came, Ian Maconachie, 6-foot-4-inch (1.93 metres) Irish international (q.v.) became works manager, improved upon the American machinery and set up a production line at the ancient Cinque Port of Sandwich (1947). Constant advances, including a second glued strengthening thread and availability in thirteen speeds, led to RSL No. 1 Tourney becoming the automatic choice worldwide for major championships, and a household name.

In 1981 the soaring price and falling quality of imported feathers, and cheap Asian shuttle imports forced the closure of the Sandwich factory. Its machinery was sent to China, where with good-quality feathers and skilled labour available under regular RSL supervision, the No. 1 Tourney world-wide saga continued. In 1984 Managing Director Murray Maxton received an MBE for Services to Exports.

RSL has consistently broken new ground: Hova courts (q.v.), synthetic 'Competition Tourney' shuttles and, recently, their own range of rackets and bags. Also introduced were 'cold' shuttles made of a special material that did not become brittle in cold weather; and 'gold', so coloured to give better visibility against light-coloured backgrounds.

REVERSE CUT SPIN SERVE

A novel serve pioneered and practised by the youthful Malaysian Sidek brothers in 1980. With a backhand action the racket strings were cut across the side of the shuttles held *with the feathers downwards* – not, as always hitherto, upwards. This caused the shuttle to spin, veer in flight and dip quickly after crossing the net.

Its erratic flight, sometimes feathers first, often made the receiver mis-hit, or even 'miss', in an attempted 'rush', or forced him to let the shuttle drop to right itself with no alternative then but to lift, so immediately yielding the attack.

Highly effective, it was copied by many players but by none so effectively as China's Wu Dixi (q.v.). Drastically shortening the length of rallies and expensively demanding a new shuttle's crispness of feather for maximum effect, it was outlawed in 1982 by the IBF. (See Law 14(a)(i).)

RICHARDS, Gordon

Poly-athlete: Folkestone-Paris (200 miles) canoeist; inventor of 'centre of excellence'; trainer of representative English tennis, hockey and skiing teams; Principal of Moray and Aberdovey Outward Bound Schools; the man behind Jim Fox, who took Pentathlon gold in the 1976 Montreal Olympics.

All of which omits badminton. This for years he regarded as 'a game fit only for poufters'. But in 1980 he put all his physiological and psychological experience behind top badminton players. Wales' Phil Sutton lived with him, Gordon acting as his trainer and father figure. Ray Stevens, after a Richards-devised twelve-minute circuit, done at 80-90°F (27-32°C) in the Stevens sauna prior to the 1980 World Championships, said, 'I can now blow out in a power-situation and recover in seconds.' Karen Bridge (now Beckman) averred, 'He strengthened my legs and I'm much quicker off the mark.'

As a trainer, motivator and individual scheduler, Gordon was in a class of his own.

ROBSON, Jeffrey E. (New Zealand)

A racket player and administrator of distinction, he has represented New Zealand at both badminton and lawn tennis and been elected President of both Associations, as well as life member.

He shares the record (with Richard Purser) of nine NZ singles titles and has won seven men's and five mixed doubles. For a player so 'isolated', he showed great talent on his one visit (1953/4) to Europe. In the Glasgow World Invitation Tournament he beat Malaya's Ooi Teik Hock, 6 and 7 T.N. Seth 6 and 0, and ran ultimate winner and later AEC champion Eddy Choong to three games.

His tennis record was nearly equally distinguished: three times men's singles, seven men's doubles, two mixed doubles, and he played in the Davis Cup 1947-64. He saw Wimbledon more frequently than Wembley, making four appearances there, in the first of which he reached the last sixteen. Also a member of ICT.

He was an IBF Council member in 1979 and is currently Deputy Chairman of their Open Badminton committee. He refereed the 1985 World Championships.

His wife Heather was a talented badminton player in her own right, and his son Graeme, runner-up in the 1985 Auckland International men's singles, bids fair to do the same.

ROGERS, née Cooley, Iris (Surrey and England)

Her power at the back of the court was the perfect foil for June Timperley's velvet touch at the net. Together they won the AEC title three times 1953, 1955 and 1959) in the heyday of the Devlin sisters and the Danes. They were also a formidable part of the virtually unbeatable Surrey team in the ICC (1954/5-74/5).

With John Best, she won the 1954 AEC mixed doubles, mastering not only Finn Kobbero but also the gale-like drift across court which worried Kobbero. She also coached BBC actors and actresses taking part in a village drama – at badminton.

She won fifty-two caps (1952-69).

ROSS, Louis C.H.

Possibly the best, certainly the most prolific, badminton photographer. Starting photography purely as a hobby in the mid-1970s, Ross has since travelled the world for photos and now professionally publishes postcards, posters and books.

Generous, ingenious, cheerful and very popular, he is part and parcel of the tournament scene as he crouches for hours on his little stool, courtside, camera ever at the ready. Ably assisted backstage by his wife, Kath, he must have taken a hundred thousand photos!

His 1982 *Picture Book* of action and character studies is in its second edition, and his *Badminton in Europe* shows 300 players in some thousand photos.

ROSSIA HOTEL, Moscow

Largest hotel ever used to accommodate tournament (USSR International Championships) competitors: 5,738 beds.

ROUGH OR SMOOTH?

The three bottom horizontal rows of stringing were for many years of thinner, coloured gut known as 'trebling'. Their function was basically to prevent the vertical strings shifting apart or bunching together.

However, they were so woven that one side was 'smooth' to the touch, the other 'rough'. This provided a ready 'heads or tails' means of deciding which player had choice of ends, of serving first, or doing neither (Law 6). This leaves his opponent with choice of one of the two remaining options.

Today, because of better stringing, trebling is rarely used, and players are forced to resort to printed names or logos on frame or handle.

ROUND-THE-HEAD STROKES

These are smashes, clears and drop-shots played to the left of the head, the backhand side, with a forehand action. At low playing levels they are an excellent way of avoiding use of a weak backhand. At higher levels they are more powerful than backhand strokes and have the added advantage, if balance is maintained, of quicker recovery.

Basically they are played by placing the left foot well out to the left. The player, thus well balanced, leans supplely out towards the shuttle falling, say, a couple of feet (0.6 metres) to his left. At the same time the racket is drawn back normally but, instead of then being thrown straight up again over the right shoulder, it is brought up to the left, slightly behind and round the head to impact outside the left shoulder. If a smash is hit at head-height – for example, in returning a drive serve – the forearm actually brushes across the top of the head.

ROWAN, née Brock, Veronica Born 20 July 1942, Lee, London

Finding anyone with Secretary Herbert Scheele's encyclopaedic knowledge of the badminton world and gargantuan appetite for work was never on the cards. Realizing the future beanstalk growth of badminton, the IBF delegated his work to three committees, looked around for an efficient co-ordinating General Secretary to be directly responsible to the President and the Committee Chairmen and found 'Ronnie' Brock (1976).

Her badminton pedigree was impeccable. Her father and mother, Ken and Sidney, were both Kent county players, and Ronnie followed so successfully in their footsteps that she was seeded 5/8 with Sue Pound (later Whetnall) in the 1965 AEC and won her way to the quarters, only to be beaten by 3/4 Scottish seeds C. Dunglison and M. Ferguson. (Sidney, now seventy-plus still plays doubles – and tennis singles!)

Veronica Brock emigrated to Canada, married and was involved in a car crash with resultant back injuries that would have ended a less hardy player's career. She returned to Britain, settled in Cheltenham, played for Gloucestershire and was appointed IBF General Secretary.

She has proved popular round the world and as capable of doggedly and cheerfully ploughing through mounds of AGM paperwork as she was of ploughing through ladies' doubles opposition.

RUBBER

Term, now little used, for the best of three games.

RUBBER GAME

The deciding game when scores are level at one game each.

RULES, Early

Knowledge of the early rules is somewhat vague. However, in 1876 a pamphlet,

showing neither author nor publisher, was printed entitled 'Rules for the New Games of Tennis and Badminton'. The Badminton section, prefaced by the inscription 'The Anglo-Indian Game of Badminton or Lawn Rackets', was only five pages of the twenty-three. It decreed that (a) the distance between the 'poles' be 12 feet (3.65 metres); the net 3 inches (7.6 centimetres) deep; the game for four or eight players; the front line 5 feet (1.52 metres) from the net and the rear line 9 feet (2.7 metres) further back.

In the accompanying diagram of the hour-glass court (a tennis court was similarly shaped but made rectangular for the first Wimbledon in 1877), the distances shown are not those quoted above.

In 1878 there appeared a pamphlet of rules apparently drawn up by H. Day, Racquet Master, at the Oval, Kennington, London, who gave demonstrations at 5 guineas a night. Three particularly interesting features were that (a) 'the player is "out" if he fails to serve the shuttle in *three* attempts'; (b) 'at "game-ball" the "out" side may choose their best player to take it'; (c) '15 or 21 makes a good game'.

In 1911 S.M. Massey, an English international, claimed that the first real *Laws* had been drawn up in book form by Colonel (then Lieutenant) H.O. Selby RE in 1877, probably in Poona (India) where the game was known as 'fashionable badminton' or, by the Indians, as 'tomfool', derived from '*tam tam*' a native game and '*phul*' a flower (the shuttlecock). On the title page was the Shakespearean quotation 'Here's law and warrant, lady.' Whether this means they were drawn up at the request of a woman or because women players were often 'laws unto themselves' is not known.

These rules were revised by J.H.E. Hart in 1887 and again, with the help of Mr Bagnel-Wild, in 1890. On them were based the rules first adopted in 1893 when Colonel Dolby formed the BAE. Courts were then hourglass-shaped (amended 1901) with three, four or even five aside (amended 1907) but the rules printed in Massey's book were in form and word not dissimilar from today's.

Coincidentally 1877 was a red-letter year in sporting annals because it heralded the first England v. Australia Test Match and the first Wimbledon

Championships.

Later in that year, a New York sports goods firm, Peck & Snyder, published 'Guide to Shooting with Bow and Arrow, also playing Rules of Lawn Tennis and Badminton'!

RUSH, to

To move forward quickly and aggressively to attack a low serve as early as possible before it drops below tape-height. The shuttle is hit with a strong, downward dab straight through or into the advancing server, his partner's stomach, a gap or towards the back 'boxes'.

RUTNAGUR, D.J.

England's most prolific badminton correspondent who has written for the *Daily Telegraph* since 1966 (and fills in the summer reporting county and Test cricket). He maintains he was destined for badminton as his parents, students at Bombay's Elphinstone College, formed a lasting partnership when they were drawn out of the hat together for a mixed doubles tournament!

His greatest game? Hartono's 1974 AEC singles victory when 'Black Panther' Paddy Gunalan adventurously led 15-8, 7-1, held Rudy for five hands at 11 all in the third, and finally lost 11-15 – in a single hand.

S

SADDLEDOME

The venue of the 1985 World Badminton Championships is sited in Calgary, Alberta, Canada, in the once dinosaur-frequented 'Bad Lands', only 30 miles from the Rockies. One of the world's most modern sports complexes, it is appropriately saddle-shaped and can accommodate 19,600 spectators — though only 6,000 attended the World Championship finals.

and touch. With drop-shots and net-shots of uncanny accuracy, he hit innumerable 'net-cords'.

His wife (née Cecilia Chan) won the All-Malayan Open ladies' singles nine times (1939-55), the ladies doubles, with a variety of partners, nine times (1947-61) and the mixed doubles four times.

SAUTTER, Guy (Switzerland)

Comte Sautter de Beauregard is the only

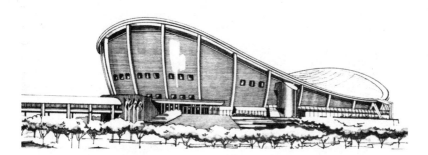

SAMUEL, A.S. (Malaya)

First winner of the Malayan Open singles and men's doubles (1937), 'Sammy' came to Britain as a student and entered the 1939 AEC. Having virtually never played indoors or with shuttles of correct speed in Malaya and despite being so affected by the cold that he wore pyjama trousers under his white ones and six sweaters, he narrowly lost in the semi-final (after 10-0 up) to the eventual winner, a young Dane, Tage Madsen. With no backhand, Samuel relied solely on craft, placement

Swiss ever to have won an AEC title. He won the singles in 1911, 1913 and 1914. Despite ill-health engendered by imprisonment as an early French Resistance suspect, he returned in 1922, hoping to win the coveted trophy outright with a fourth victory. He was foiled by Sir George Thomas, who, by gaining a third successive victory, himself won the cup.

Before his time in tough fitness training, Sautter had a fine round-the-head smash and often played (when he should have been learning the restaurant trade) under the entirely inappropriate *nom-de-guerre* of 'un lapin' (a rabbit!).

SCHEELE, Betty

Wife and PA of Herbert Scheele but a badminton 'great' in her own right not only in behind-the-scenes work at the All-England Championships and English National Championships, for the IBF and the BAE, but also as the writer of the popular gossip feature 'Off the Court' under the pen-name 'Velma'.

She met her husband, then a Civil Servant, whilst fire-watching during the war in Bournemouth, and worked side-by-side with him until his death. She was honoured by the BAE as a Life Individual Associate Member and by the IBF with the Distinguished Service Award.

Turned players into personalities.

SCHEELE, Herbert A.E., OBE

Mr Badminton: two words that sum up a man and his world-wide reputation.

He was educated firstly at Montclair Academy, USA, then Dulwich College, UK. His love of sport was soon apparent and he played good club tennis and hockey; at badminton he was a Kent county player and England trialist (1946-8).

Administratively he made his mark as a tireless Hon. Secretary and Treasurer *and* Match Secretary for Kent BA. In 1945, realizing his enthusiasm and dedication, the BAE selected him as its first paid Secretary. 'Paid' should mislead no one: the BAE struggled to make ends meet, and a single room in his Bromley house, and his wife, Betty (q.v.), had to suffice as office and staff for a task that invariably saw him working into the small hours. It was a position he was to hold until he 'retired' in 1970, together with the editorship of the *Badminton Gazette* (1946-70) to which he himself contributed vigorously under Kent's motto '*Invicta*'.

But it was as Secretary of the IBF that Scheele made a still wider and deeper mark. He had been appointed in 1938, after the death of its first Secretary, F.W. Hickson, and remained in office as such until 1976, when he became Advisory Vice-President. During his tenure of office, IBF membership rose from fourteen to fifty-five, the Thomas and Uber Cups were instituted, the WBF-IBF rift occurred, World Championships were planned and Open badminton posed questions. In addition to having a large part in these developments, Herbert edited the IBF Handbook (a monumental compendium of records that grew to over 400 pages), instituted *World Badminton* and edited it 1972-8. His forthright editorials were not always well received, especially in the Far East, by readers who did not appreciate that these were his personal opinions as editor and individual, not as IBF spokesman. Unfortunately he never found time to put his vast knowledge into a book.

In addition, his knowledge, efficiency and fearlessness brought him invitations to referee major international events all over the world. That fearlessness was exemplified in the 1966/7 Challenge Round in Jakarta's Senayan Stadium, when, with Malaysia poised for victory, Indonesian spectator interference grew to such a pitch of unfairness that he suspended play in the face of the fury of 10,000 over-zealous partisans. And yet he was to return there, much moved, some years later to a standing ovation from the same spectators.

His courage was shown too when he discharged himself from hospital to make his twenty-fifth consecutive appearance at the AEC (twenty-four times as referee), and when he continued painfully to travel the world despite the same back affliction.

His other love was cricket. A staunch Kent supporter and one-time Secretary of the Club Cricket Conference, he had a fine collection of cricket prints and Wisden's Almanacks.

Scheele's leonine head of grey hair, horn-rimmed spectacles and lip-dangling cigarette will long be remembered by those who saw him rise painfully from the referee's table to limp across court to congratulate or commiserate with finalists. Danish BF paid a rare tribute to the man who specially learnt their language to help them better, by making him an Honorary Member. And he received, proudly, a richly deserved OBE from the Queen only four months before he died – almost exactly as the AEC Men's singles final started on 29 March 1981.

BAE President Stuart Wyatt paid him just tribute: 'The greatest administrator ever in any game; a man of honesty and singleness of purpose.'

SCORE-BOARDS, Electronic

Score-boards have advanced far from the hand-inserted or roller number days.

Today, at major events, the umpire operates a computerized panel which actuates an electronic board behind him. The main panel indicates players' names and their respective scores. On the left, red lights indicate the server: one for singles and doubles 'first server', two for 'second server'. On the right, under 'Set', is a 0 which changes to 2, 3 or 5 if setting (q.v.) is chosen; and the score on the main panel automatically reverts to 0-0. If setting is not chosen, the 0 remains and the main panel continues normally to 11 or 15.

The original design concept was developed by Hans Paulsen. Two students of Aberdeen's Institute of Technology appropriately Shuttleworth, and Moss, further developed it for the Scottish Open, 1986.

SCORING

Normally badminton is played as the best of three games, each of 15 points.

In doubles, the pair (A and B) choosing to serve first have only *one* server in their *first* innings: the player (A) in the right court. As long as that pair win rallies, they score a point *and* change sides (so that the same opponent is not served to continuously). When they lose a rally, the server loses his right to serve. Then (since in the very first innings they have only *one* server) the serve passes to their opponents (C and D).

Again, the player in the *right* court (C) serves first and, like A, continues to serve, (scoring points and changing sides) until C and D lose a rally. The serve then passes to D, who serves in similar fashion. When C and D lose a second rally, their innings is completed.

The serve therefore passes back to A and B. Whoever is in the right-hand court serves first (say B). Play continues as above (with points scored and sides changed for each winning rally) until a rally is lost and the serve passes to A, no matter in which court he is.

When another rally is lost, the serve, as before, passes to the opponent in the right-hand court. And play continues in this manner throughout the game until one pair scores the necessary points.

If the score reaches 13 all, the side which scored 13 first has a choice of procedures: (1) They may elect to play 'straight through', i.e. to 15 in the usual way; (2) or they may elect 'to set', i.e. to play a further 5 points to 18. The score is now called as 'love all' and so on to 5.

The same procedure applies at 14 all, except that then only three further points, to 17 are played. If a pair elects to play 'straight through' at thirteen, this does not preclude their setting at fourteen if they wish.

To prevent possible later dispute, the score should be called *clearly* at the end of *each* rally. The score of the pair actually serving is called first. If they have two points and their opponents seven, the score is 2-7. When a rally (and therefore a serve) is lost, 'second server' must be added and called in each succeeding rally; thus, 2-7, second server; 3-7 second server. When the serve reverts to their opponents, the latter's score is put first, 7-3.

Ladies' singles are only eleven up and setting is at nine (three points) and ten (two points).

On occasions a single game of twenty-one may be agreed. Setting is then at nineteen (five points) and twenty (three points).

SCOTTISH BADMINTON UNION

St Andrews is the birthplace of Scottish badminton as well as world-wide golf. Play started there in the 1880s, promoted by retired Indian Army officers and a Dr McTier. 1900 saw the first club match: St Andrews v. Aberdeen, the new centre. Due largely to T.L. Adam, the Scottish Open (1907), formation of the SBU, and regular matches against Ireland (1910) were inaugurated. Matches against England commenced in 1922 but Scotland has yet to beat the Auld Enemy after fifty-six encounters.

In 1927/8 the Inter-Group competition was inaugurated to precede the BAE's ICC competition by three years and be the first of its kind in the world.

A World Invitation Tournament was successfully run at Glasgow's Kelvin Hall by David Bloomer and, later, Craig Reedie, both destined to become IBF Presidents. And it was Scotland that produced *World Badminton* 1980-84. An enthusiastic Council aided by able Executive Administrators Judy Budge and Anne Smillie and Coach Allan Cambell (1980), have seen playing standards and numbers (more than 500 clubs and 13,000 players) rapidly increase, and the opening of the six-court National Cockburn Centre (1980) converted from an old warehouse.

In addition to W. Gilliland, D. Travers, R. McCoig, K.R. Davidson and Nancy Horner (q.v.), Scotland's top players have included J. Barr, E.W. Wilson, J.A. Russell, H.E.B. Neilsen (who represented Scotland at five sports), Rugby international R.W. 'Jumbo' Stevenson, milkmaid Wilma Reid (née Tyre), Muriel Woodcock (née Ferguson) and Maths Honours graduate Joanna Flockhart. Today's names to conjure with are Charlie Gallagher, Alex White, Kenny Middlemiss, Pam Hamilton, Jenny Allen, Gillian Martin, Susan Bell, Aileen Nairn and Alison Fulton.

SCOTTISH RANKING LIST 1986

Men's Singles:
1   Dan Travers
2   Alex White
3   Charlie Gallagher
4   Kenny Middlemiss
5   Anthony Gallagher
6   Alan McMillan
7   Kevin Scott
8   Gordon Hamilton
9   Ross Gladwin
10 Brian Stewart
11 Iain Pringle
12 Steven Clarke
Ladies' Singles:
1   Jennifer Allen
2   Pam Hamilton
3   Anne Gibson
4   Gillian Martin
5   Aileen Nairn
6   Susan Bell
7   Alison Fulton
8   Elinor Allen
9   Jill Barrie
10 Christine Heatly
    Fiona Stark
12 Alison Gordon

SCOTTISH NATIONAL CHAMPIONSHIPS

Men's Singles
1949-50 A.I. McIntyre
1950-1   J.A. Russell
1951-2   J.A. Russell
1952-3   J.A. Russell
1953-4   J.A. Russell
1954-5   J.A. Russell
1955-6   R.M. Fowlis
1956-7   J.A. Russell
1957-8   R.S. McCoig
1958-9   R.S. McCoig
1959-60 R.S. McCoig
1960-1   R.S. McCoig
1961-2   R.S. McCoig
1962-3   R.S. McGoig
1963-4   R.S. McCoig
1964-5   R.S. McCoig
1965-6   J.R. Sydie
1966-7   R.S. McCoig
1967-8   R.S. McCoig
1968-9   R.S. McCoig
1969-70 R.S. McCoig
1970-1   R.S. McCoig
1971-2   R.S. McCoig
1972-3   R.S. McCoig
1973-4   N.H. McCloy
1974-5   N.H. McCloy
1975-6   N.H. McCloy
1976-7   N.H. McCloy
1977-8   R. Conway
1978-9   W.A. Gilliland
1979-80 C. M. Gallagher
1980-1   C.M. Gallagher
1981-2   C.M. Gallagher
1982-3   C.M. Gallagher
1983-4   A. White
1984-5   A. White
1985-6   D. Travers

Ladies' Singles
1949-50 Mrs A.M. Horner
1950-1   Mrs A.M. Horner
1951-2   Mrs M. Robertson
1952-3   Mrs A.M. Horner
1953-4   Mrs A.M. Horner
1954-5   Miss W. Tyre
1955-6   Miss W. Tyre
1956-7   Miss C.E. Dunglison
1957-8   Miss C.E. Dunglison
1958-9   Miss W. Tyre
1959-60 Miss W. Tyre
1960-1   Miss W. Tyre
1961-2   Miss M. Ferguson
1962-3   Miss M. Ferguson

1963-4	Miss M. Ferguson
1964-5	Miss M. Ferguson
1965-6	Miss M. Ferguson
1966-7	Miss M. Ferguson
1967-8	Miss M. Ferguson
1968-9	Mrs M. Hume
1969-70	Mrs M. Hume
1970-1	Mrs M. Hume
1971-2	Miss H.T. Kelly
1972-3	Mrs J.D. Flockhart
1973-4	Mrs J.D. Flockhart
1974-5	Miss A. Johnstone
1975-6	Mrs J.D. Flockhart
1976-7	Mrs J.D. Flockhart
1977-8	Mrs J.D. Flockhart
1978-9	Mrs J.D. Flockhart
1979-80	Mrs J.D. Flockhart
1980-1	Miss P. Hamilton
1981-2	Miss P. Hamilton
1982-3	Mrs A. Fulton
1983-4	Mrs A. Fulton
1984-5	Miss J. Allen
1985-6	Miss P. Hamilton

Men's Doubles

1909	J.H. Cochrane/W. Cochrane
1910	Dr J. Crombie/H.J.H. Inglis
1911	Dr J. Crombie/H.J.H. Inglis
1912	Dr J. Crombie/H.J.H. Inglis
1913	Dr J. Crombie/H.J.H. Inglis
1914	Dr J. Crombie/H.J.H. Inglis
1915-20	No Competition
1921	W.T. Henderson/J.W. Millar
1922	W.K. Tillie/J.W. Henderson
1923	R.R. Herbertson/H.E.B. Neilson
1924	E.R. Butcher/R.S. Jackson
1925	J. Barr/H.E.B. Neilson
1926	E.R. Butcher/H.E.B. Neilson
1927	J. Barr/H.E.B. Neilson
1928	J. Barr/H.E.B. Neilson
1929	J. Barr/H.E.B. Neilson
1930	J. Barr/H.E.B. Neilson
1931	J. Barr/T.G. Dempster
1932	J. Barr/T.G. Dempster
1933	J.J. McCarry/M. MacLean
1934	E.R. Butcher/E.W. Wilson
1934-5	E.R. Butcher/E.W. Wilson
1935-6	E.D. Ballantine/C. Skirving
1936-7	R.W. Stevenson Jnr/G.M. Crabbie
1937-8	R.W. Stevenson Jnr/G.M. Crabbie
1938-9	J.C. MacKay/E.W. Wilson
1939-47	No Competition
1947-8	J.C. MacKay/E.W. Wilson
1948-9	J.C. MacKay/E.W. Wilson
1949-50	J.C. MacKay/E.W. Wilson
1950-1	W.M. Williams/J. Stevenson
1951-2	J.C. MacKay/J.B. Leslie
1952-3	J.C. MacKay/W.A. Robinson
1953-4	J.A. Russell/A.I. McIntyre
1954-5	J.A. Russell/A.I. McIntyre
1955-6	D. Ross/W.F. Shannon
1956-7	J.A. Russell/A.I. McIntyre
1957-8	D. Ross/J.L. Young
1958-9	D. Ross/A.W. Horden
1959-60	D. Ross/A.A.S. Morgan
1960-1	R.S. McCoig/W.F. Shannon

1961-2	R.S. McCoig/W.F. Shannon
1962-3	R.S. McCoig/W.F. Shannon
1963-4	R.S. McCoig/W.F. Shannon
1964-5	R.S. McCoig/W.F. Shannon
1965-6	R.S. McCoig/W.F. Shannon
1966-7	R.S. McCoig/J. Campbell
1967-8	R.S. McCoig/J. Campbell
1968-9	I. Hume/J.K. McNeillage
1969-70	R.S. McCoig/M. Henderson
1970-1	R.S. McCoig/F.D. Gow
1971-2	R.S. McCoig/F.D. Gow
1972-3	R.S. McCoig/F.D. Gow
1973-4	R.S. McCoig/F.D. Gow
1974-5	J. Ansari/A.J. Britton
1975-6	J. Ansari/A.J. Britton
1976-7	F.D. Gow/W.A. Gilliland
1977-8	F.D. Gow/W.A. Gilliland
1978-9	F.D. Gow/W.A. Gilliland
1979-80	W.A. Gilliland/D. Travers
1980-1	W.A. Gilliland/D. Travers
1981-2	W.A. Gilliland/D. Travers
1982-3	W.A. Gilliland/D. Travers
1983-4	W.A. Gilliland/D. Travers
1984-5	W.A. Gilliland/D. Travers
1985-6	W.A. Gilliland/D. Travers

Ladies' Doubles

1922	Mrs O'Connor/Mrs MacLehose
1923	Mrs O'Connor/Mrs MacLehose
1924	Miss E.C.F. MacDonald/Miss K.M. Cochrane
1925	Miss M.C.F. MacFarlane/Miss M. Armstrong
1926	Miss E.C.F. MacDonald/Miss K.M. Cochrane
1927	Miss G.H. Dempster/Miss B.S. Dempster
1928	Miss M.K. King-Clark/Miss D.H. Ramage
1929	Miss M.K. King-Clark/Miss D.H. Ramage
1930	Miss M.K. King-Clark/Miss D.H. Ramage
1931	Miss D.H. Stenhouse/Miss J.M. Cassils
1932	Miss D.H. Stenhouse/Miss J.M. Cassils
1933	Miss E.F. Ogilvie/Miss E.A.R. Anderson
1934	Miss E.F. Ogilvie/Miss E.A.R. Anderson
1934-5	Miss E.W. Greenwood/Miss A.J. Gilzean
1935-6	Miss G.A. Matheson/Miss C.B. Alison
1936-7	Miss C.P.R. Montgomery/Miss E. Smart
1937-8	Miss E.F. Ogilvie/Miss E.A.R. Anderson
1938-9	Miss C.P.R. Montgomery/Miss E. Smart
1939-47	No Competition
1947-8	Mrs J.B. Shearlaw/Miss C.B. Alison
1948-9	Mrs J.A.S. Armstrong/Miss E.W. Greenwood
1949-50	Mrs J.A.S. Armstrong/Miss E.W.

	Greenwood
1950-1	Mrs A.M. Horner/Miss J.H. McGregor
1951-2	Miss J.H. McGregor/Miss I.S. Vallance
1952-3	Mrs A.M. Horner/Mrs J.A.S. Armstrong
1953-4	Miss J. Smart/Miss I.S. Vallance
1954-5	Miss J.M. Dunglison/Miss C.E. Dunglison
1955-6	Miss Forrester/Miss M. McIntosh
1956-7	Miss W. Tyre/Miss E. Tyre
1957-8	Miss C.E. Dunglison/Mrs Gordon
1958-9	Miss C.E. Dunglison/Mrs Gordon
1959-60	Miss W. Tyre/Miss M. McIntosh
1960-1	Miss W. Tyre/Miss M. McIntosh
1961-2	Miss W. Tyre/Mrs D.G. Calder
1962-3	Miss C.E. Dunglison/Miss M. Ferguson
1963-4	Miss E.A. Anderson/Miss M. Ferguson
1964-5	Miss C.E. Dunglison/Mrs W. Reid
1965-6	Miss C.E.Dunglison/Mrs W. Reid
1966-7	Miss C.E. Dunglison/Miss M. Ferguson
1967-8	Mrs W. Reid/Miss M. Ferguson
1968-9	Mrs W. Reid/Mrs M. Woodcock
1969-70	Mrs W. Reid/Mrs M. Gibson
1970-1	Miss C. Evans/Mrs M. Hume
1971-2	Miss H.T. Kelly/Mrs J.D. Flockhart
1972-3	Miss H.T. Kelly/Mrs J.D. Flockhart
1973-4	Miss H.T. Kelly/Mrs J.D. Flockhart
1974-5	Mrs H.T. McIntosh/Mrs C. Stewart
1975-6	Mrs H.T. McIntosh/Mrs C. Stewart
1976-7	Mrs J.D. Flockhart/Mrs C. Stewart
1977-8	Mrs C. Stewart/Miss A. Johnstone
1978-9	Mrs J.D. Flockhart/Mrs C. Stewart
1979-80	Miss C. Heatly/Miss J. Reid
1980-1	Mrs A. Fulton/Miss P. Hamilton
1981-2	Mrs A. Fulton/Miss P. Hamilton
1982-3	Mrs A. Fulton/Miss P. Hamilton
1983-4	Mrs A. Fulton/Miss M. Johnson
1984-5	Miss P. Hamilton/Mrs M. Johnson
1985-6	Miss J. Allen/Miss E. Allen

Mixed Doubles

1908	H.J.H. Inglis/Miss Balfour
1909	Dr J. Crombie/Miss V.I. Todd
1910	J.H. Cochrane/Miss V. Lamb
1911	Dr J. Crombie/Miss V.I. Todd
1912	J.E. Crabbie/Miss D. Addis
1913	Dr J. Crombie/Miss M. Findlay
1914	H.J.H. Inglis/Miss H.C.A. Longmuir
1915-20	No Competition
1921	Dr J. Crombie/Miss E.C.F. MacDonald
1922	E.R. Butcher/Miss M.C.F. MacFarlane
1923	Dr J. Crombie/Miss E.C.F. MacDonald
1924	R.S. Jackson/Mrs Herriot
1925	R.S. Jackson/Mrs Herriot
1926	E.R. Butcher/Miss M.C.F. MacFarlane
1927	J. Barr/Miss C.T. Duncan
1928	J. Barr/Miss C.T. Duncan

1929	J. Barr/Miss C.T. Duncan
1930	J. Barr/Miss M.K. King-Clark
1931	J. Barr/Miss M.K. King-Clark
1932	E.D. Ballantine/Miss M. Langmuir
1933	E.D. Ballantine/Miss M. Langmuir
1934	K.R. Davidson/Miss J.R. Stewart
1934-5	N.M. McIntosh/Miss G.A. Matheson
1935-6	E.W. Wilson/Miss M.G. Bingham
1936-7	E.W. Wilson/Mrs B.H. Cuthbertson
1937-8	M. MacLean/Miss E.A.R. Anderson
1938-9	E.W. Wilson/Mrs J. Holmes
1939-47	No Competition
1947-8	J.C. MacKay/Miss C.B. Alison
1948-9	J.C. MacKay/Miss C.B. Alison
1949-50	J.S. Millar/Mrs J.A.S. Armstrong
1950-1	J.C. MacKay/Mrs A.M. Horner
1951-2	J.C. MacKay/Miss J.H. McGregor
1952-3	J.A. Russell/Miss I.G. Montgomerie
1953-4	J.A. Russell/Miss I.G. Montgomerie
1954-5	A.I. McIntyre/Miss MacKenzie
1955-6	D. Ross/Mrs Greig
1956-7	R.S. McCoig/Miss W. Tyre
1957-8	R.S. McCoig/Miss W. Tyre
1958-9	M. Henderson/Miss M. McIntosh
1959-60	R.S. McCoig/Miss W. Tyre
1960-1	R.M. Fowlis/Miss A. Barclay
1961-2	R.S. McCoig/Miss W. Tyre
1962-3	M. Henderson/Miss C.E. Dunglison
1963-4	R.S. McCoig/Mrs W. Reid
1964-5	R.S. McCoig/Mrs W. Reid
1965-6	M. Henderson/Miss C.E. Dunglison
1966-7	R.S. McCoig/Miss M. Tait
1967-8	R.S. McCoig/Mrs W. Reid
1968-9	R.S. McCoig/Mrs W. Reid
1969-70	R.S. McCoig/Mrs W. Reid
1970-1	R.S. McCoig/Mrs W. Reid
1971-2	I. Hume/Mrs M. Odell
1972-3	F.D. Gow/Mrs C. Stewart
1973-4	A.J. Britton/Mrs C. Weir
1974-5	F.D. Gow/Mrs C. Stewart
1975-6	W.A. Gilliland/Mrs J.D. Flockhart
1976-7	W.A. Gilliland/Mrs J.D. Flockhart
1977-8	W.A. Gilliland/Mrs J.D. Flockhart
1978-9	W.A. Gilliland/Mrs J.D. Flockhart
1979-80	W.A. Gilliland/Mrs J.D. Flockhart
1980-1	W.A. Gilliland/Miss C. Heatly
1981-2	W.A. Gilliland/Miss C. Heatly
1982-3	W.A. Gilliland/Miss C. Heatly
1983-4	W.A. Gilliland/Miss C. Heatly
1984-5	W.A. Gilliland/Miss C. Heatly
1985-6	W.A. Gilliland/Miss C. Heatly

SCOTTISH OPEN CHAMPIONSHIPS

Men's Singles

1907	G.A. Thomas
1908	F. Chesterton
1909	G.A. Thomas
1910	G.A. Thomas
1911	G.A. Thomas
1912	G.A. Thomas
1913	G.A. Thomas

1914	G.A. Thomas
1915-20	No Competition
1921	Sir G.A. Thomas, Bt.
1922	Sir G.A. Thomas, Bt.
1923	W.M. Swinden
1924	G.S.B. Mack
1925	Sir G.A. Thomas, Bt.
1926	Sir G.A. Thomas, Bt.
1927	A.E. Harbot
1928	I. Maconachie
1929	T.P. Dick
1930	W. Hamilton
1931	R.M. White
1932	W. Hamilton
1933	D.C. Hume
1934	W. Hamilton
1935	C.H. Whittaker
1936	C.H. Whittaker
1937	R.C.F. Nichols
1938	T.H. Boyle
1939	R.C.F. Nichols
1940-6	No Competition
1947	N.B. Radford
1948	N.B. Radford
1949	F.W. Peard
1950	F.W. Peard
1951	E.B. Choong
1952	H.A. Heah
1953	E.B. Choong
1954	J.E. Robson
1955	J.P. Doyle
1956	J.D. McColl
1957	E.B. Choong
1958	Oon Choong Jin
1959	R.S. McCoig
1960	C.T. Coates
1961	C. Wattanasin
1962	C. Wattanasin
1963	R.S. McCoig
1964	R.S. McCoig
1965	R.H. Purser
1966	Lee Kin Tat
1967	Lee Kin Tat
1968	R.S. McCoig
1969	Oon Chong Hau
1970	P.E. Whetnall
1971	D. Talbot
1972	R.P. Stevens
1973	C.J. Beacom
1974	P.E. Whetnall
1975	R. Livingston
1976	P.E. Whetnall
1977	R. Ridder
1978	D. Talbot
1979	A. Goode
1980	P.E. Whetnall
1981	N. Yates
1982	M. Frost
1983	M. Frost
1984	M. Frost
1985	Z. Jianhua
1986	Sze Yu

Ladies' Singles

1907-12	No Competition
1913	Miss L.C. Radeglia

1914	Miss L.C. Radeglia
1915-20	No Competition
1921	Miss L.C. Radeglia
1922-3	No Competition
1924	Mrs R.C. Tragett
1925	Mrs R.C. Tragett
1926	Mrs R.C. Tragett
1927	Mrs F.G. Barrett
1928	Mrs R.C. Tragett
1929	Mrs F.G. Barrett
1930	Mrs R.J. Horsley
1931	Mrs H.S. Uber
1932	Miss M. Hamilton
1933	Miss A. Woodroffe
1934	Miss M. Hamilton
1935	Miss T. Kingsbury
1936	Miss T. Kingsbury
1937	Miss D.M.C. Young
1938	Mrs H.S. Uber
1939	Mrs H.S. Uber
1940-6	No Competition
1947	Miss M.G. Welsh
1948	Miss Q.M. Allen
1949	Miss Q.M. Allen
1950	Miss Q.M. Allen
1951	Miss I.E. O'Beirne
1952	Miss I.E. O'Beirne
1953	Miss A.M. Horner
1954	Miss I.L. Cooley
1955	Miss I.L. Cooley
1956	Miss I.L. Cooley
1957	Mrs T. Ahm
1958	Miss H.M. Ward
1959	Miss W. Tyre
1960	Miss I. Hasselsteen
1961	Mrs G.C.K. Hashman
1962	Miss U.H. Smith
1963	Miss M.U. O'Sullivan
1964	Miss U.H. Smith
1965	Miss M. Ferguson
1966	Miss A.M. Bairstow
1967	Miss M. Ferguson
1968	Miss U.H. Smith
1969	Miss M.B. Boxall
1970	Miss M.B. Boxall
1971	Mrs M.A. Gilks
1972	Miss M. Beck
1973	Mrs J.D. Flockhart
1974	Miss M. Beck
1975	Miss M. Luesken
1976	Mrs M.A. Gilks
1977	Mrs M. Ridder
1978	Miss J. Webster
1979	Miss J. Webster
1980	Miss P. Kilvington
1981	Mrs G. Gilks
1982	Miss L. Køppen
1983	Mrs S. Podger
1984	Mrs S. Podger
1985	Miss K. Larsen
1986	Miss C. Magnusson

Men's Doubles

1907	G.A. Thomas/R.G.P. Hunter
1908	F. Chesterton/H. Comyn
1909	G.A. Thomas/H. Comyn

1910	G.A. Thomas/H. Comyn
1911	E. Hawthorn/G.A. Sautter
1912	G.A. Thomas/S.M. Massey
1913	Dr J. Crombie/H.J.H. Inglis
1914	G.A. Thomas/F. Chesterton
1915-20	No Competition
1921	R.A.J. Goff/J.F. Devlin
1922	R.A.J. Goff/J.F. Devlin
1923	Sir G.A. Thomas, Bt./H.S. Uber
1924	G.S.B. Mack/R.A.J. Goff
1925	Sir G.A. Thomas, Bt./H.S. Uber
1926	Sir G.A. Thomas, Bt./H.S. Uber
1927	Sir G.A. Thomas, Bt./H.S. Uber
1928	I. Maconachie/H.E.B. Neilson
1929	T.P. Dick/F. Hodge
1930	A. Hamilton/W. Hamilton
1931	K.G. Livingstone/R.M. White
1932	A. Hamilton/W. Hamilton
1933	T.H. Boyle/J.L. Rankin
1934	W. Hamilton/I. Maconachie
1935	D.C. Hume/R.M. White
1936	T.H. Boyle/J.L. Rankin
1937	R.C.F. Nichols/I. Maconachie
1938	T.H. Boyle/J.L. Rankin
1939	T.H. Boyle/J.W. McGarry
1940-6	No Competition
1947	R.C.F. Nichols/I. Maconachie
1948	T.L. Henry/F.W. Peard
1949	T.L. Henry/F.W. Peard
1950	R.C.F. Nichols/A. Barron Renton
1951	E.L. Choong/E.B. Choong
1952	E.L. Choong/E.B. Choong
1953	E.L. Choong/E.B. Choong
1954	J.D. McColl/A.D. Jordan
1955	F.W. Peard/J.J. Fitzgibbon
1956	W. Shute/J.R. Best
1957	E.B. Choong/Oon Chong Teik
1958	H.T. Findlay/Oon Chong Jin
1959	A.W. Horden/D. Ross
1960	H.T. Findlay/R.J. Lockwood
1961	R.S. McCoig/W.F. Shannon
1962	C. Wattanasin/J. Lim
1963	R.S. McCoig/W.F. Shannon
1964	C.J. Beacom/K.R. Derrick
1965	R.S. McCoig/W.F. Shannon
1966	R.J. Mills/D.O. Horton
1967	R.S. McCoig/M. Henderson
1968	J.D. Eddy/R.A. Powell
1969	R.J. Sharp/P.E. Whetnall
1970	D.O. Horton/E.C. Stuart
1971	D.O. Horton/E.C. Stuart
1972	R.S. McCoig/F. Gow
1973	J. Ansari/A.J. Britton
1974	P. Gunalan/T. Bacher
1975	D. Talbot/E.C. Stuart
1976	R.P. Stevens/M.G. Tredgett
1977	R. Ridder/P. Ridder
1978	D. Talbot/M.G. Tredgett
1979	A.J. Britton/G. Higgins
1980	R.P. Stevens/M.G. Tredgett
1981	A.B. Goode/G. Scott
1982	W.A. Gilliland/D. Travers
1983	W.A. Gilliland/D. Travers
1984	M. Frost/J. Helledie
1985	A.B. Goode/N. Tier
1986	M. Christiansen/M. Kjeldsen

Ladies' Doubles

1907	Miss F.A. Todd/Miss V.I. Todd
1908	Miss M. Lucas/Miss G.L. Murray
1909	Miss M. Lucas/Miss G.L. Murray
1910	Miss M. Lucas/Miss G.L. Murray
1911	Miss V.I. Todd/Miss H.C.A. Longmuir
1912	Miss V.I. Todd/Miss H.C.A. Longmuir
1913	Mrs W.S. Gill/Miss L.C. Radeglia
1914	Miss L.C. Radeglia/Miss K.M. Cochrane
1915-20	No Competition
1921	Miss E.G. Peterson/Miss D.M. Aitken
1922	Miss E.G. Peterson/Miss D.M. Aitken
1923	Miss H. Hogarth/Miss K. McKane
1924	Mrs R.C. Tragett/Miss E.F. Stewart
1925	Mrs R.C. Tragett/Mrs F.G. Barrett
1926	Mrs R.C. Tragett/Miss C.T. Duncan
1927	Miss V. Elton/Mrs F.G. Barrett
1928	Mrs R.C. Tragett/Miss E.C.F. MacDonald
1929	Mrs F.G. Barrett/Mrs R.J. Horsley
1930	Mrs R.C. Tragett/Miss C.T. Duncan
1931	Mrs R.J. Horsley/Mrs H.S. Uber
1932	Mrs R.C. Tragett/Miss C.T. Duncan
1933	Mrs R.J. Horsley/Miss B.E. Speaight
1934	Mrs R.J. Horsley/Miss B.E. Speaight
1935	Mrs M. Henderson/Miss T. Kingsbury
1936	Mrs M. Henderson/Miss T. Kingsbury
1937	Mrs M. Henderson/Miss T. Kingsbury
1938	Miss O. Wilson/Mrs H.S. Uber
1939	Miss D. Doveton/Mrs H.S. Uber
1940-6	No Competition
1947	Mrs J.B. Shearlaw/Miss C.B. Alison
1948	Miss Q.M. Allen/Mrs H.S. Uber
1949	Miss Q.M. Allen/Mrs H.S. Uber
1950	Miss Q.M. Allen/Mrs H.S. Uber
1951	Mrs Q.M. Allen-Webber/Mrs H.S. Uber
1952	Miss I.E. O'Beirne/Miss E.F. Andrews
1953	Mrs Q.M. Allen-Webber/Mrs A.M. Horner
1954	Miss I.L. Cooley/Miss J.R. White
1955	Miss I.L. Cooley/Miss J.R. White
1956	Miss I.L. Cooley/Mrs E.J. Timperley
1957	Mrs T. Ahm/Miss T. Peterson
1958	Mrs W.C.E. Rogers/Mrs E.J. Timperley
1959	Miss W. Tyre/Miss M.A. McIntosh
1960	Mrs T. Holst-Christensen/Miss I. Hasselsteen
1961	Mrs F.W. Peard/Mrs G.C.K. Hashman
1962	Miss U.H. Smith/Mrs G.W. Barrand
1963	Miss M.U. O'Sullivan/Miss Y.W. Kelly
1964	Miss A.M. Bairstow/Miss H.J. Pritchard
1965	Miss C.E. Dunglison/Mrs A. Reid
1966	Miss A.M. Bairstow/Mrs G.W. Barrand
1967	Mrs D.O. Horton/Miss G.M. Perrin
1968	Mrs D.O. Horton/Miss U.H. Smith
1969	Miss M.B. Boxall/Mrs P.E. Whetnall
1970	Miss M.B. Boxall/Mrs P.E. Whetnall

1971	Mrs M.A. Gilks/Miss M. Beck
1972	Mrs M.A. Gilks/Mrs B. Cooper
1973	Miss N. Gardner/Miss B. Giles
1974	Miss M.B. Boxall/Mrs P.E. Whetnall
1975	Miss M. Leusken/Miss N. Gardner
1976	Mrs M.A. Gilks/Mrs P.E. Whetnall
1977	Mrs M. Ridder/Miss H. de Kort
1978	Miss J. Webster/Mrs S. Whittaker
1979	Miss J. Webster/Miss K. Puttick
1980	Miss K. Bridge/Miss P. Kilvington
1981	Mrs G. Gilks/Miss P. Kilvington
1982	Mrs G. Gilks/Miss G. Clark
1983	Mrs K. Beckman/Mrs B. Sutton
1984	Miss B. Beckett/Mrs A. Fulton
1985	Mrs K. Chapman/Miss J. Webster
1986	Miss D. Kjaer/Miss N. Nielsen

Mixed Doubles

1907	G.A. Thomas/Miss G.L. Murray
1908	F. Chesterton/Miss M. Lucas
1909	G.A. Thomas/Miss G.L. Murray
1910	G.A. Thomas/Miss G.L. Murray
1911	G.A. Thomas/Mrs W.S. Gill
1912	G.A. Sautter/Miss D.B. Drinkwater
1913	G.A. Thomas/Miss L.C. Radeglia
1914	G.A. Thomas/Miss L.C. Radeglia
1915-20	No Competition
1921	Sir G.A. Thomas, Bt./Miss L.C. Radeglia
1922	Sir G.A. Thomas, Bt./Mrs R.C. Tragett
1923	Sir G.A. Thomas, Bt./Mrs R.C. Tragett
1924	Sir G.A. Thomas, Bt./Mrs R.C. Tragett
1925	H.S. Uber/Mrs R.J. Horsley
1926	Sir G.A. Thomas, Bt./Mrs R.C. Tragett
1927	I. Maconachie/Miss M. Armstrong
1928	I. Maconachie/Miss M. Armstrong
1929	J. Barr/Miss C.T. Duncan
1930	A. Hamilton/Miss M. Hamilton
1931	T.P. Dick/Mrs R.J. Horsley
1932	W. Hamilton/Miss M. Story
1933	D.C. Hume/Mrs R.J. Horsley
1934	I. Maconachie/Mrs R.J. Horsley
1935	D.C. Hume/Mrs H.S. Uber
1936	I. Maconachie/Miss T. Kingsbury
1937	I. Maconachie/Miss T. Kingsbury
1938	I. Maconachie/Mrs H.S. Uber
1939	R.M. White/Mrs H.S. Uber
1940-6	No Competition
1947	R.C.F. Nichols/Mrs J.B. Shearlaw
1948	J.L. Rankin/Mrs H.S. Uber
1949	J.L. Rankin/Mrs H.S. Uber
1950	J.L. Rankin/Mrs H.S. Uber
1951	H.J. Wingfield/Mrs H.S. Uber
1952	H.A. Heah/Mrs G.F. Saunders
1953	E.L. Choong/Mrs A.M. Horner
1954	A.D. Jordan/Miss J.R. White
1955	J.R. Best/Miss I.L. Cooley
1956	A. D. Jordan/Mrs E.J. Timperley
1957	A.I. McIntyre/Miss E. McKenzie
1958	J.R. Best/Mrs W.C.E. Rogers
1959	R.S. McCoig/Miss W. Tyre
1960	A.D. Jordan/Mrs E.J. Timperley

1961	R.S. McCoig/Miss W. Tyre
1962	R.S. McCoig/Miss W. Tyre
1963	M. Henderson/Miss C.E. Dunglison
1964	A.D. Jordan/Mrs P. Page
1965	R.S. McCoig/Mrs A. Reid
1966	A.D. Jordan/Mrs D.O. Horton
1967	D.O. Horton/Mrs D.O. Horton
1968	A.D. Jordan/Miss S.D. Pound
1969	R.J. Mills/Mrs P.E. Whetnall
1970	R.J. Mills/Miss G.M. Perrin
1971	R.J. Mills/Mrs M.A. Gilks
1972	D. Talbot/Mrs M.A. Gilks
1973	F.D. Gow/Mrs C. Stewart
1974	P.E. Whetnall/Miss N. Gardner
1975	E.C. Stuart/Miss N. Gardner
1976	D. Talbot/Mrs M.A. Gilks
1977	W.A. Gilliland/Mrs J.D. Flockhart
1978	W.A. Gilliland/Mrs J.D. Flockhart
1979	W.A. Gilliland/Mrs J.D. Flockhart
1980	M.G. Tredgett/ Mrs K. Chapman
1981	W.A. Gilliland/Mrs G. Gilks
1982	W.A. Gilliland/Mrs G. Gilks
1983	M. Frost/Miss N. Nielsen
1984	W.A. Gilliland/Miss G. Gowers
1985	W.A. Gilliland/Mrs K. Chapman
1986	W.A. Gilliland/Miss G. Gowers

SCRATCH

A term in handicap events meaning that a player or pair are neither given (+6) nor owed points (−4) but start at 0.

Scratched: a tournament term to indicate that a player or pair have cancelled their entry, or that an entry has been cancelled by the referee for late or non-appearance.

SEARLE, Caroline
Born 1958

A freelance editor and journalist on racket games, having graduated from Bath University (European Studies) in 1980, she was appointed the BAE's Public Relations Officer in 1984, and in 1985 editor of *Badminton Now*. She hopes to capitalize on England's successes to gain greater media coverage.

SEBORG, Preben
Born 21 April 1943,
Copenhagen

Denmark's answer to Louis Ross. A bearded six-foot-plus Viking who never played badminton but threw the hammer considerable distances for Denmark (1977). Starting his career as a graphic designer, he turned to freelance writing and sports photography, including striking action photos for the Danish BF *Badminton*.

He illustrated Morten Frost's *Badminton My Way* and annually produces his own general *Sport* photographic annual. He complains that lighting gets more difficult and that photographers are pushed ever further back from the action.

SEEDS

Those entrants in a tournament considered by the committee most likely to reach the quarter-final, semi-final or final round. In events with fewer than sixteen entries, two seeds only are allowed; with between sixteen and thirty-two, four seeds; with over thirty-two, eight seeds.

Where two are seeded, No. 1 is placed at the top, No. 2 at the bottom. With four seeds, No. 1 and No. 2 are as above; No. 3 and No. 4, drawn by lot, are placed in the top of the second quarter and bottom of the third. With eight seeds, Nos. 1, 2, 3 and 4 as above; the remainder, all known, without specific ranking, as Nos. 5-8 seeds, drawn by lot: in the upper half at the top of the remaining unoccupied eighths, and in the lower half in the bottom of the unoccupied eighths.

SENAYAN STADIUM

Indonesia's famous badminton centre in the capital city of Jakarta. Although it seems, to Europeans, intolerably hot and humid, many famous Thomas Cup and Championship games have been played before packed houses (sometimes 14,000 in a hall built for 10,000) of wildly excited, enthusiastic and knowledgeable fans. It is also often used as a training centre for Indonesian squads.

SERVICE

The opening stroke of a rally. Its etymology is interesting. It is probably derived from 'real' or 'royal' tennis, played largely by the aristocracy who considered this first stroke demeaning and left a liveried *servant* to put the ball into play.

Various types of serve are employed. In singles the high serve was, until the last couple of decades almost invariably used. By hitting the shuttle high and with a dropping vertical trajectory, timing and clean hitting are made difficult for the opponent. By hitting it deep to the base-line, the opponent's attack is blunted and the forecourt left wide open.

More recently, the low serve has been much more used. The high serve gives the opponent the opportunity to hit down, to attack. The accurate low serve forces him to lift, to give the chance of attack to the server. With the advent of quicker movement and stronger backhands, the lift to the server's deep backhand corner is no longer a danger. The occasional use of the low serve at carefully chosen moments can be unsettling for the receiver and lead to nervous error in net-returns or lobs especially if the server, staying in, is quick to move in and attack slightly inaccurate net returns.

In doubles, when the shuttle can be hit only to the doubles back service-line ($2\frac{1}{2}$ feet (0.75 metres) nearer the net), the high serve is very vulnerable to a strong smasher. The low service is therefore the basic serve. In this, ideally, the shuttle rises on a flattish trajectory to within a foot (0.3 metres) of the tape, then drops to skim it and, generally, fall within a foot (0.3 metres) of the centre-line and front service-line T-junction. If it is falling as it crosses the net, it cannot be hit down.

The **high serve** is played with a sideways stance and the weight on the rear foot. The shuttle is held at shoulder height to drop about a foot (0.3 metres) in front of the leading foot. With arm bent and wrist cocked back, the racket is held upraised just to the rear of the body. The heel of the racket hand leads a downward, underhand throwing action. This steadily accelerates, like a golf swing, until, within 18 inches (0.45 metres) of impact, the arm is straight, and the wrist is uncocked to give height. The racket is swept forward, on line with the target, to give length and accuracy of placement, to above the left shoulder. At the same time the body turns square to the net and the weight sways onto the front foot.

The **low serve**, demanding delicacy of touch, is more compact. The shuttle, held less high, drops just beside the toe of the leading foot; the racket, head downwards, is generally held just beside the rear leg. The arm is bent as much as possible so that the shuttle is struck when it is just below the waist. The racket is then *pushed* forward *with the wrist cocked back throughout* to give the flattest possible, tape-skimming trajectory. As with the high serve, the body turns, weight sways forward and the follow-through (to waist height) is on target line. The shuttle is stroked or caressed rather than hit.

Two other variants, used occasionally and tactically, are the flick serve and the drive serve. Both, for the sake of deception, must be played, until the last fraction of a second before impact, exactly like the low serve.

Then, in the **flick**, the cocked wrist is crisply uncocked to flick the shuttle *just* above the receiver's reach to the back doubles service-line to gain an outright winner (rarely) or a weak clear (more usually). If it is hit along the longer line of flight to the *side*-line, it can be struck more crisply without so much fear of overshooting the back service-line.

In the **drive**, the racket (wrist still cocked) is stabbed forward to drive the shuttle fast and flat generally from the right court, down the centre-line and onto the opponents' possibly weakish backhand, direct into the face, or a gap. The angle of attack may be considerably increased by serving from the side-line.

All serving should be thoughtful, unhurried, relaxed (especially the grip) and confident after the eye has carefully observed the two targets: the height of the tape, and the actual target area and the distance to it.

Low and flick serves may be played equally well backhanded. This type of serve has two main advantages: (a) the shuttle is held 18 inches (0.45 metres) in front of, rather than behind, the front service line thus giving the receiver less time to move forward to attack it; (b) the short, push action is very simple. And two minor ones: (1) the white shuttle, held directly in front of the white-clothed body, is not so easily or quickly observed; (2) in some clubs, the stroke is still something of a rarity and thus imbued with some menace or mystery.

For the backhand low serve, the server stands with his right foot up to the front service-line. The racket, in a backhand grip, is held vertically downwards, elbow high, arm bent, well in front of the right foot. The shuttle is placed immediately in front of the racket-face. The racket is then drawn back (6 to 15 inches (15 to 38 centimetres) according to choice) and, with the wrist cocked, pushed forward, without pause, to impact.

The backhand flick serve is played similarly but with a last-second tightening of the grip and uncocking of the wrist.

Accurate serving is an essential for point winning.

SERVICE FAULTS

To avoid unfairness or bad feeling, all players should clearly understand the following points outlined in Law 14(a), (c) and (d) and Law 16.

1. The server's feet must be within his service court i.e. *not* on a line; they or a part of them must be stationary and in contact with the floor throughout the service. (A serve begins with the first forward movement of the racket.)
2. No part of the shuttle must be above the waist at impact.
3. The whole of the racket-head must be *clearly* below the whole of the racket-holding hand.
4. Initial impact must be on the base (not the feathers) of the shuttle.
5. The stroke must be one continuous movement without pause, or feinting (though speeding up or slowing down the racket is legal).
6. The stroke must not be unduly delayed.

The IBF Rules and Laws Committee in an endeavour to iron out inconsistent ideas of what is and what is not a fault put out the following re-drafting of the relevant Laws for comment before presentation to the 1987 AGM:

Principles

In a correct service the flight of the shuttle shall be upwards from the server's racket to cross the net so that, if not intercepted, it falls in the receiver's service court. The service should be regarded only as a means of putting the shuttle in play.

To Serve

1. The server and receiver shall take up their positions in diagonally opposite service courts.
2. In doubles, a partner may take up any position as long as the opponents are not unsighted or obstructed.
3. The server shall not serve before the receiver is ready, but neither shall cause the service to be unnecessarily delayed once they both are ready.
4. The receiver shall be considered to be ready if a return of service is attempted.
5. The server shall strike the shuttle with a continuous forward underarm

motion of the racket to strike initially the base of the shuttle at a point below the server's waist.

6. The first forward movement of the server's racket constitutes the start of the service and the movement must be continuous thereafter.

7. Throughout the delivery of the service neither the server nor receiver shall change their relative positions on the court by walking, sliding or running. However, it is not a breach of this Law should either player lift a foot from the court surface.

SERVICE JUDGE

A service judge is generally appointed only for major tournaments and international matches, but one may be called for in club or county matches if a player thinks one (or both) of the opponents is fault serving.

They are unfortunately becoming more of a necessity at all levels. In clubs, many players fault and so gain an unfair advantage simply because they do not know the rules, or 'know' them incorrectly; at higher levels, some players serve to the very limit of the rules and even beyond if the service judge is not decisive. If the latter is the case, the tournament referee may request the manager of umpires to replace him.

The service judge's task is difficult. The Laws relating to serving need discernment in fractions of seconds (the service must be continuous) as well as inches or centimetres (the whole of the racket-head must be discernibly below the racket-hand). In order to make his decision clear to players and umpires (perhaps not speaking his language) as well as to an actual or a TV audience, the service judge uses the following signs to indicate his reason for faulting the server. (See also *Service Faults*.)

Law 14(a)(i) – It is a FAULT if, in serving, the initial point of contact with the shuttle is not on the base of the shuttle.

Law 14(a)(ii) – It is a FAULT if, in serving, any part of the shuttle at the instant of being struck be higher than the server's waist. The top of the waist is an imaginary line round the body, level with the bottom of the lowest rib.

Law 14(d) – It is a FAULT if, once the service has started, any player makes preliminary feints or otherwise intentionally baulks his opponent, or if any player deliberately delays serving the shuttle or in getting ready to receive it so as to obtain advantage. When the server and receiver have taken up their respective positions to serve and to receive, the first forward movement of the server's hand constitutes the start of the service and must be continuous thereafter.

Law 14(a)(iii) – It is a FAULT if, in serving, at the instant of the shuttle being struck, the shaft of the racket be not pointing in a downward direction to such an extent that the whole of the head of the racket is discernibly below the whole of the server's hand holding the racket.

Law 14(c) – It is a FAULT if the server's feet are not in the service court from which service is at the time being in order ... until the service is delivered.

SETTING

A change of scoring system at thirteen all and/or fourteen all. The player first to reach either of these scores is given two options: to play straight through normally to fifteen or to play a further five points at thirteen all or a further three at fourteen all, i.e. eighteen and seventeen respectively. The called score, however, reverts to 'love all', 0-1, 0-2, 1-2 etc but is recorded as 18-16 or 17-14.

In ladies' singles these figures are changed to a further three points at nine, or two at ten, i.e. to twelve.

In twenty-one-up games, setting is at nineteen and twenty, to five and three.

A player choosing not to set at thirteen or nine may, however, do so at fourteen or ten. There is no setting in handicap events as these are based on the scoring of fifteen (or eleven) points only.

SHENGRONG, Lu

Better known perhaps as Da Lu (Big Lu) or 'the Iron Lady', Lu Shengrong, working for All-China Sports Federation, deals with many sports but prefers badminton. As team manager and interpreter ('aunt and teacher'), she has taken Chinese teams world-wide. She had a hand in reconciling WBF and IBF, was elected an IBF Council member in 1982 and became its first woman Vice-President in 1984.

She explains Chinese women's world domination: 'They are totally dedicated to excellence – and therefore not interested in early "dating".'

SHOES

With the ever-increasing speed of movement of the game, changes in shoe design have been numerous.

In badminton's infancy, simple, thin-soled, black or brown plimsolls or sandshoes were sufficient, but by 1910 the pendulum had swung to the other extreme when an English international, S.M. Massey, advocated three-quarter-inch rubber or chrome soles. Ladies frequently wore boots, presumably as support for frail ankles. Indeed, they were still being advertised by Lillywhite's in the 1937 AEC programme – at 7s. 6d. per pair.

If in 1912 Dr Hoggyes' Air Spring Asbestos socks may have suggested that movement was now faster and frictional, the 'Pioneers of Crepe Soled Footwear' were more practical in eulogizing not merely their 'extended wear' but, even more to the point, their all-important better grip.

In the 1930s, Scotia offered a more flexible sole; Garagard heel-shock absorbers, toe to instep lacing – and a six-month guarantee; and Dunlop, toe-cap reinforcement for foot-draggers. The 1950s saw the innovation of non-marking soles on the better floors of the period, nylon ventilation panels and a ribbed strip round the front of the shoe.

Still more innovations came in the 1970s. 'Spring Court' brought out side-strengthening; Adidas, a long, padded tongue and light nylon mesh uppers; Rucanor, an extended heel for better grip; and Inter, a padded collar round the heel to prevent Achilles tendon damage. Even decorative colour and logos were added.

The 1980s saw new materials: polyurethane in different densities for lightness and durability respectively in the soles; breathable, ladder-resistant nylon mesh and hard-wearing suede in the uppers. Sole patterns, aiming for still better grip,

were deep herring-bone.

Shoes are the springboard of speed. They should be chosen with great care for grip, insole cushioning, toe-to-instep lacing, toe reinforcements, lightness and flexibility. And they should be kept white!

SHUTE, Warwick (Kent and England)

One of England's most capped players (thirty-nine caps; 1948-57) in the days when international matches were 'rarities' rather than 'regularities'. After his starting badminton, not unfittingly, with the Hong Kong Fire Brigade Club, war-time Russian convoy duty halted his rapid advance. After the war, he toured South Africa, played in Denmark and the Thomas Cup, helped Kent to two ICC victories and became a leading National Coach.

Extrovert to a degree, he personified the fun of the game, with a lusty smash, complementary deceptive trick shots at the net and an unfailing sense of humour.

A fine tennis-player (with his twin brother), he won the Public Schools' Championships in two 'love' sets and reached the final of the British Junior Championships. Warwick played for Kent and the Navy and reached the third round at Wimbledon.

SHUTTLE, Keep Your Eye on the

An old but still effective maxim, it cuts down mis-hits and misses, and it aids early movement to the shuttle.

SHUTTLES, Consumption of

No fewer than 182 shuttles were used in the two game Singles final of the 1986 Indian National Championships, in which Syed Modi defeated Vimal Kumar 15-12, 15-12.

SHUTTLECOCKS, Care of

Shuttlecocks are extremely fragile (only 73 grains (4.74 gm), ephemeral (a single mis-hit can break a feather) and expensive (up to £1 each). It is therefore essential to treat them with great care:
Feathered Shuttles
1. If they are stuck together in the tube, part them very carefully.
2. Do not crush a tube or bang it on the ground to open it.

3. Store in a cool (below 50°F (10°C)), slightly damp atmosphere as heat dries out the feathers' ten per cent natural oil, so making them brittle. If this has not been done, wrapping the tube in a damp towel for twenty-four hours will help rectify the omission.
4. *Never* hit a shuttle on the half-volley.
5. From time to time smooth ruffled feather plumes.
6. Always use the correct speed; this prevents the need for overhitting and consequent frame-shots.

Synthetic Shuttles
1. Nos. 2, 4 and 6 above apply.
2. Use 'gold' colouring for better sighting – and fewer mis-hits.
3. Store in gentle warmth as this keeps the synthetic skirt from getting brittle in cold weather.
4. Or, use 'cold' type shuttles made of special material less susceptible to cold, and so less brittle.

SHUTTLECOCKS, History of

Shuttlecocks have probably been in use for over two thousand years but there are surprisingly few records of them.

Early fifteenth-century woodcuts show peasant lads hitting a 'missile' that might have been bark with a few feathers stuck in it. In the seventeenth century, Sweden's Queen Christina enjoyed 'featherball', and rather later prints show elegant aristocrats playing *jeu de volant* with a feathered 'missile' not unlike today's. Chardin's famous painting '*Le Volant*' shows a little girl holding a large shuttle with, seven different-colour feathers stuck into a big, domed base. The utilization of discarded quill pens may have started the use of stiff goose feathers rather than the much softer chicken feathers first commonly used.

Some of the earliest shuttles extant are on show at badminton's birthplace, Badminton House. Much larger and heavier than today's shuttles, they had velvet bases and often had binding ribbons running both round *and* over the cork base (1850s).

About this time badminton was also much played in India. Balls of wool were sometimes used but J.H.E. Hart, an early enthusiast, recalls that at his club in Poona shuttles were made from chicken feathers and champagne corks by a native servant – who refused to continue this work while in prison for stealing club funds. Although Laws were drawn up in Poona, no specifications for shuttles were included – and indeed this was not done until 1911.

As a result, shuttles, like courts, continued to vary in size – and also weight and flight. One monster, still preserved, had thirty-six chicken feathers, 4 inches (10 centimetres) long, a $5\frac{1}{2}$ inches (13.5 centimetres) spread, no encircling stitching, and weighed over 1 oz (28 gm) compared with today's 1/5 oz (6 gm). It was only the inception of the All-England Championships in 1899, when in early years the choice of the often sole shuttle used was between a 'whizzer' and a 'wobbler', that made players think of standardization. Strangely the shuttles first used were made in France, where badminton had – and has – only a miniscule following.

This was known as the 'barrel' because the chicken feathers used were inserted with the flat of the quill on the *outside*. They had the first-ever strengthening stitching halfway up the quills and a second one round their base, where its strengthening effect was negligible. Goose feathers, plentiful in *pâté-de-fois-gras* regions, and rich in natural oil from force-feeding, gradually ousted chicken feathers.

Despite these improvements, flight was still inconsistent. One tested recently flew 55 feet (16.7 metres) compared with today's forty-two feet 12.7 metres.

The *Guinness Book of Records* lists the longest ever hit as one of 79 feet $8\frac{1}{4}$ ins. by Frank Rugani at San José, California, on 19 February 1964. This however was almost certainly with a heavy, rubber-based outdoor shuttle so made to minimize the effects of breezes. Accordingly in 1910 they were replaced by the AEC by the 'straight' made by F.H. Ayres (manufacturers also of 'Hydera' and 'Gem' bats). Entirely hand-made, of No. 1 wine-quality cork (domed on a lathe and covered in Yeovil gloving leather) and goose feathers, they were the automatic choice for twenty-five years, until the war.

Although Law 4 clearly laid down speed, the tester 'of average strength' was still a nebulous figure. Even the invention of a compressed-air shuttle-gun in the late 1930s did not solve the problem, as it could not fire the shuttle the full court-length.

In 1930 RSL (q.v.) began building machinery which, based on American war-time improvements, at last achieved the vital uniformity of spread and exact weighting that resulted in a tube of a dozen shuttles, all of which, if similarly hit, would have dropped on a large serving-plate. Playing its part too was the use of feathers all from the *same* wing (right or left) of geese reared in the *same* locality; and the interweaving of a second stitching halfway between the existing stitching and the base; and its spraying with a lacquer adhesive.

As a result, thirteen speeds of shuttles (73-85 grains 4.74-5.52 gm), each differing in length of flight by as little as 6-8 inches (15.20 centimetres) were evolved so that a player in a large, cold English hall using an 83 would get the same length of flight as would a player in the heat and thin air of the Tropics with, say, a 74.

With the game booming and the goose birthrate remaining static, necessity pointed to a synthetic shuttle (q.v.). Top players still demanded the feel and perfect flight of feathered shuttles. But by the 1980s, in Britain, imported feathers were becoming so scarce, so expensive and of such poor quality that the main manufacture, RSL, was forced to transfer its machinery to the Far East (China). There, shuttles are being made in increasing numbers to satisfy the growing world-wide army of enthusiasts.

SHUTTLECOCK KICKING (Ti jian zi)

This is a traditional Chinese game dating back to the fifth century. A twelve-year-old boy was then recorded as making 500 consecutive kicks. In the Tang dynasty (618-907) *wushu* experts used it as a way of strengthening legs, stamina and determination.

It is still played today with small, unconventional 'shuttlecocks' made of metal wrapped in cloth bedecked with bright feathers. Basic kicks are made with the inner or outer side of the feet or the toes or jerked up on the knee. Only when 300 or 400 consecutive kicks can be made are more difficult techniques attempted, or three or more a-side games played.

SHUTTLECOCKS, Manufacture of

Among other data, Law 4 (a)(i) decrees precisely: 'A shuttle shall have 14-16 feather fixed in a cork base which is 25 mm to 28 mm (1-1⅛ inches) in diameter. The feather shall be from 64 mm to 70 mm (2½-2¾ inches) in length from the tip to the top of the cork base. The tips of the feathers shall form a circle with a diameter within the range of 58 mm to 68 mm (2⅛-2½ inches).'

Shuttles are manufactured just as meticulously to ensure perfect, consistent flight. Until the late 1970s the vast majority of top-quality shuttles were made in Britain; today most are made in the Far East.

Huge 8-foot (2.4 metres) sacks of goose feathers (formerly from central Europe or China) have first to be sorted, then washed and dried. This done, an automatic guillotine tops, tails and shapes them to 3 inches (7.6 centimetres) in length. For top quality, two geese, each providing only eight suitable feathers, are needed to provide the feathers for a single shuttle.

Meantime, the corks, from equally huge sacks, have been machined absolutely round to a thousandth of an inch (0.00254 centimetres), and domed. Onto this a 2-inch (5 centimetres) circle of white English kid leather is firmly secured without the smallest wrinkle. Sixteen holes are swiftly drilled round the circumference and also, in the centre, one for the weight.

In seconds, an ingenious machine slots sixteen pre-cut feathers into the sixteen drilled holes – at exactly the correct angle and height to ensure the spin needed for consistent flight. Equally ingeniously, two circlets of a strong thread are interwoven round the quills, partly to strengthen the shuttle and partly to ensure the correct and all-important spread. Fingers are defter than machines for tying the final knot. For extra strength, the threads are glued with a special adhesive lacquer.

A narrow, coloured ribbon, or lute, is securely glued round the circular edge of the cork to secure it and the leather circlet enduringly together. It also improves the appearance and visibility of the shuttle. Into the central hole is placed a tiny lead slug which is distorted so that it securely grips the cork; it is sealed in by a circular gummed label.

If the lead slug works free, the shuttle is too light to fly more than a few feet. In almost a billion-to-one chance, slugs have become detached and caused serious eye injury. Top-flight Australian Darren MacDonald is an example of a determined player who overcame such a handicap.

Slug weights vary to give different shuttle speeds (q.v.) to suit different temperatures, heights above sea-level, hall size, and humidity. Shuttles are normally made in thirteen different speeds from 73 to 85; the figure indicates the weight in grains (the metric equivalent is the milligram) and therefore speed, ranging from slow to fast. Some synthetic shuttles have a less exact colour-code system.

All that remains is to insert the shuttles in stout cardboard or polystyrene containers together with a humidifier: feathers with their natural oils dried become brittle, snap easily and render the shuttle useless.

Their life is ephemeral. Normally they last about one hour but, if mis-hit by beginners or used by top players who demand absolute consistency of flight, this time may be reduced to mere minutes or even seconds!

Considering the force with which they are struck, however, shuttles are modern miracles of aerodynamics.

SHUTTLECOCKS, SPEED OF

All games demand uniform speed, flight or bounce of its missile so that players do not have to break a grooved rhythm or action from one game to the next.

In this, the badminton shuttle has unusual difficulties to contend with in that its speed and length of flight are affected not only by mis-hits but also by temperature, humidity and air-pressure changes. In the heat of the Tropics the shuttle will fly much faster through the resultant thinner, less-resistant air than in the colder, heavier air of the north. Similarly, it will fly much further in the thin air of 6,000-foot (1,828 metres) altitude Johannesburg than in the denser sea-level air of, say, Cape Town.

Even in a single English town speed will vary according to the size of a hall (one-court, low village hall, or lofty eight-court sports centre) and its lack or super-abundance of central heating.

Shuttle-manufacturers have solved the problem by making shuttles in no fewer than thirteen different speeds ranging from 73 (slow) to 85 (fast). These figures stand for weight in *grains* (the metric equivalent of the milligram); the heavier a shuttle is (within limits), the farther and faster it will fly.

Just how far it will fly is clearly laid down internationally in Law 4(d). Unfortunately many players do not know this Law or how to apply it, or deliberately play with a slower shuttle that suits their style of play. This is just as much a breach of the Law as deciding to play over a 4-foot (1.2 metres) (not 5-foot) (1.5 metres) net.

The Law clearly states how such a speed test should be made. The player, holding the shuttle exactly over the baseline, hits it with *full underhand stroke* at an upward angle and parallel to the sidelines. A shuttle thus correctly struck should fall not less than a foot (0.3 metres) and not more than 2½ feet (0.75 metres) short of the base-line (amended in 1985 to 1 foot 9 inches (0.53 metres) and 3 feet 3 inches (1 metre).

Despite this clear instruction, there is still one great difficulty. The power of 'a full underhand stroke' varies, naturally or even deliberately, from one player to another. Pneumatic shuttle-guns exerting exactly the same force each time have been invented but they are too expensive to be purchased by every club.

The manufacturers stringently test their shuttles for the speed affecting factors of weight and feather-speed but even in a tube of a dozen first grade shuttles there may be a variation of an inch (2.54 centimetres) or two; in cheaper shuttles, of a foot (0.3 metres) or more.

SHUTTLEMASTER

Coaching device consisting of a metal post with adjustable arm from which a shuttle is suspended. It is so designed that the shuttle does not 'snare' itself when hit. It encourages use of the correct straight arm at impact.

SHUTTLER

Far Eastern term for a badminton player.

SIDE BY SIDE (OR 'SIDES')

Term used in describing men's or ladies' doubles positional tactics.

When one player of a pair has 'lifted' a shuttle, he has given the attack to his opponents and put his own side on the defensive. The best defensive formation they can then adopt is 'side by side', i.e. each player positions himself in roughly the centre of his half-court. From here, with two or three steps forwards or backwards, the length of the court can be covered, and by stretching out a racket, or making one step out to left or right, so can the width. These positions are maintained as long as their opponents are attacking and forcing them to lift.

When a pair is first in the 'back and front' attacking position, it is generally the player who has lifted the shuttle, and is therefore under some pressure, who moves into the *nearest* half-court. When the net player lifts, the back player can *see* to which side he moves and position himself accordingly. When the back player clears, the front player can *hear* where he is without looking round. When the former is centrally placed, he will call 'Go right' or 'Go left.'

Mutual understanding soon develops and the change becomes automatic.

SIDEK, Misbun (Malaysia)
Age: 26

After the brilliance of Wong Peng Soon and Ong Poh Lim, of Ng Boon Bee and Paddy Gunalan, and of the brothers Tan, the seemingly inexhaustible stream of Malaysian talent dried up. Not until the 1980s did the brothers Sidek appear on the scene – all five of them!

The most talented – and temperamental – was the eldest, Misbun, the inventor of the now banned cut-serve (q.v.) who boasted: 'I'll soon come up with another', the wearer in quick succession of Mohican, crew-cut and blonde-streak hair-styles!

His talent is underlined by his being Malaysian National Champion 1981-4; by his leading Swie King 10-1 in the third game of the 1982 Alba Quartz final; by being only narrowly forced into third place in the 1983 Pro-Kennex Grand Prix; and by scoring victories over Frost, Prakash, Nierhoff, Chen Changjie, Sugiarto and Nick Yates at various times. But he was trounced four and two by a rampant Sugarto in the 1985 Alba Quartz semis.

There is no doubt of his mobility and stamina, of a rocklike defence, of a deceptively crisp half-smash. There is doubt on occasion as to his wholeheartedness. Failure to play in the SEAP Games and a subsequent BAM ban led to his threatened retirement. His inexplicably lackadaisical 6-15, 0-15 loss to Steve Baddeley may have cost Malaysia a place in the 1982 Thomas Cup semi-final. And his 1986 AEC 2 and 8 finals defeat by Frost was similarly uninspired.

SILVER SHUTTLE

This fine piece of silvercraft was presented by the IBF to Herbert Scheele (q.v.), in recognition of his long service to that body.

In 1986 his widow, Betty Scheele (q.v.) handed it back to the IBF 'for presentation to a person who has given outstandingly exceptional services to badminton'.

The first recipient was Indonesia's Rudy Hartono, impeccably modest and sporting, who won the World Championship, and also, a record eight times, the AEC Singles title.

SINGAPORE BADMINTON ASSOCIATION

SBA, in 1929 only a State organization within the BA of Malaya, later produced such legendary world-class players as Wong Peng Soon, Ong Poh Lim and Ismail Bin Marjan, who played in its famous Guillemard Road Hall. Today, an ambitious U.18 training scheme produces talented players such as Wong Shoon Keat, Lee Ah Ngo and Tan Eng Han. A new $5,000,000 ($2,000,000 from one anonymous donor) six-court training hall and secretariat is an added incentive to regain lost glory.

SINGLES

A game, on a slightly narrower court (3 feet, 0.9 metres), between two players that demands great mobility and stamina.

With such a court where a centrally placed player can almost cover the width with a sideways step and outstretched racket, the basic strategy is to hit deep to the back-corners (especially the often weaker backhand one) with clears, and short to the forecourt corners with drop shots. This will force the opponent to do the running, to tire him and to elicit short clears or lobs that can be smashed into the body or down the narrow side-line gap for a winner.

Until the 1970s, the high serve was largely used. As it can be hit to the singles long service line (i.e. the base-line) it forces the opponent far back, blunting the power of his smash and creating an opening in the forecourt. It does, however, give the opponent the opportunity to hit down with drop-shot, smash or half-smash, to attack.

Modern players therefore intersperse the low serve quite often. This has several advantages. (1) It curbs a player with a strong rear-court smash. (2) It is difficult to 'rush' when the receiver must now stand a couple of feet further back than in doubles to cover the possible deeper high serve. (3) It breaks the receiver's rhythm and touch, forcing him sometimes to net or hit out a return. (4) It makes him hit up, so yielding the attack.

It is returned when possible by an early take and a very tight net return which may regain the attack, or a fast, low attacking lob to the backhand corner. The latter can be countered only by anticipation, quick footwork, supple round-the-head strokes or a strong backhand.

Other features of the singles game are (1) early, tape-high take of net-shots which are tumbled back with cut net-shots or neatly nipped off with a crisp dab; (2) attacking lobs and clears hit with a flat, fast trajectory to hurry an opponent and place the shuttle behind him; (3) deceptive, especially the reverse cut cross-court, drop shots (4) half and cut smashes to maintain the attack when an attempted outright winner may leave the striker stranded; (5) strong, wristy backhand clears or supple round-the-head shots.

Twenty years ago singles was largely a war of attrition at a slow, defensive tempo of high clears and lobs as each player angled for the weak return that alone could safely be put away. Today the whole pace of the game is speeded up, with fast attacking clears and lobs, powerful jump smashing from the back of the court and lightning following-in for a net kill.

The whole makes for a fascinating game of power, touch and chess-like tactics that are allied with nimble footwork, suppleness and great stamina.

SKOVSHOVED IDRAETS FORENING

SIF, as it is popularly known, is Denmark's oldest club. It was formed in 1923 when the football and tennis sections built a gymnasium hall in which badminton could be played. Among its members the following were early AEC title-winners: the brothers Poul Erik and Knud-Aage Nielsen, Tage Madsen (first-ever foreign AEC title-winner), Conny Jepsen, Ruth Dalsgaard and Marie Ussing. (AEC champions all.)

SLING

A 'fault' shot that must, where there is no umpire, be called by the perpetrator himself. A single clean hit off frame or shaft is a valid shot but when the shuttle is caught and 'held', even fleetingly, between frame and strings and 'slung' (rather as in a lacrosse throw) it is a fault (Law 14 (h)). The player himself can generally *feel* and hear that it is not a clean, crisp, single impact stroke and must call 'Sling' accordingly.

SMALLEST ASSOCIATIONS

The IBF has sixty-two affiliated full members (500 members minimum). Among the smallest of these are Zambia (550), Bahrain (530), Kenya (500), Malta (500) and Mauritius (500).

Associate members maintain enthusiasm despite still smaller memberships: St Helena (22), Antigua/Barbuda (50), Fiji (50), Gibraltar (50), Kuwait (70), Maldive Islands (300) and Falkland Islands (300).

SMASH

The exciting, rally-ending, power stroke of the game.

Generally it is used to hit down any lifted reply falling short of the doubles long service line. Very strong players will smash from the base-line but weaker ones will find that their stroke lacks sting, because of the swift deceleration of a shuttle, and they may be caught out of position by a quick, well-placed return.

It is played, like the clear, with the basic throwing action (q.v.), but the point of impact is 18 inches (0.45 metres) in front of the head; a powerful wrist action brings the racket-head over the shuttle, and a strong downward follow-through maintains that trajectory and power.

The smash has several variants: (1) The *half-smash*, hit with less power, is used to maintain the attack when the striker is off balance. (2) The *cut-smash* (q.v.) is used as in (1) and for added deception. (3) In the *jump-smash* (a favourite of agile but not-so-tall Far Eastern players) the player jumps up 2 to 3 feet (0.6 to 0.9 metres) vertically, thus taking the shuttle earlier and gaining a steeper angle. (4) The *round-the-head* smash (q.v.) is used to maintain a strong attack when the shuttle has been lifted to the backhand. (5) An *angled smash* is used, with pronounced wrist action, to hit steeply just behind the front service line when defenders have dropped back or against a back and front mixed formation.

The power smash is an amalgam of body-weight corkscrewing upwards, shoulder turn, arm speed, pronation of forearm, wrist action – and not a little psychological 'hate'. Together, they steadily accelerate the racket-head to maximum velocity in the 'zip' area (q.v.) 18 inches (0.45 metres) before and after impact.

The qualities of an effective smash are fourfold: (1) *Pace*: it has been estimated, probably optimistically, that a powerfully hit smash leaves the racket at 160 miles (258 km) per hour. (2) *Steepness*: aimed at the knees. (3) *Placement*: within 6 inches (15 centimetres) of a side line; between a defending pair; into a gap; into the right side of the body. (4) *Consistency*: a large percentage of consecutively hit smashes played on the run that maintain the attack and finally clinch the rally.

SMILLIE, Anne

Winning the Highland Open ladies' doubles and playing for Glasgow Churches hardly qualify Anne Smillie for mention in these pages. Her tireless work and patience as SBU's Executive Administrator, in a period of high growth and increased need for sponsorship, most certainly do.

SMYTHE, Don (Canada)

Smythe won the Canadian Open singles 1952-5 and doubles 1952-4 and 1957-8. Epitomized by the great Betty Uber: 'a stocky figure who was never beaten until the shuttle was on the floor'.

He shed 25 lb (11.3 kg) in special training for a comeback in the first World Masters Games!

SONNEVILLE, Ferry (Indonesia)

One of the finest players never to win the coveted AEC title – but one who has done much for world badminton. He was losing finalist to Tan Joe Hok (1959) and with him doubles runner-up to Kobbero and Hansen (1963).

His first major success was winning the Malaysian Open (1955) against the pick of the TC Singapore Inter-Zone finalists. Moving for business reasons to the Netherlands, he won many European and American titles. He played in the four TC series (1958-67), captaining Indonesia to victory on three occasions.

A brilliant linguist, he was the first – and only – Asian to become IBF President (1972-4). He generously founded an international coaching award.

SONNEVILLE, Ferry, International Coaching Award

In 1974 the immediate Past President of the IBF, Ferry Sonneville, a former Indonesian Thomas Cup player, gave $5,000 US to establish a coaching fund to help younger national organizations by either paying the travelling expenses of a coach or supplying coaching books that might later be translated into that country's language.

SOOK, Cho Young (Korea)
Born 1970

She was just fourteen when she made her début against England in 1984, losing only 9-12, 11-7, 5-11. Laddawan Mulasartsathorn of Thailand probably just edges her out of being the youngest-ever international.

SOUTH AFRICAN BADMINTON UNION

Formed in 1938, SABU held its first National Championships in 1948 to coincide with the first-ever visit by an England team that included Tom Wingfield, a youthful Warwick Shute, Betty Uber and Queenie Allen.

Distances hampered development but in 1950 the Melvill Cup, originally disputed only by Transvaal and Western Province, was opened to all nineteen affiliated provinces. In 1954 this and the SA Championships were brought together in an enormous week-long festival, followed by a similar junior event.

Politics have hampered development, but since 1948 twenty-one overseas teams have visited S. Africa, and four Springbok teams have toured Europe or Australasia. Danish and British players found very stiff competition from Ken Brann, Gordon Byram, Colin Bartlett, Alan and Kenny Parsons, Wilma Prade, Deirdre Algie (née Tighe), Barbara Lord and Ann Smith (Parsons).

Able administrators and unfailingly hospitable tour managers include A.S. Cornelius, H. Hadfield, W. Kerr, Roy Smith and Harry Stavridis.

Efforts by SA whites to encourage coloured and black participation have met with lukewarm response. To avoid political dissension, SABU refrains from entering for the Uber and Thomas Cups and World Championships.

STAMPS

Postage stamps have on a number of occasions featured badminton players.

Among them was a 1958 Japanese 5 yen. In 1975 Thailand issued a 1.25 baht for the 8th SEAP Games in Bangkok. Indonesia have issued some five sets, each to commemorate a Thomas Cup victory. Sweden issued a first-day cover for the 1st World Championships: the stamp showed play on court; the cover, an elegant, early-nineteenth-century lady playing battledore-and-shuttlecock by herself. A modernistic 13p English stamp in 1977 was one of a set of four racket games. And Lene Köppen was featured on the Danish 2.70 Dk stamp for the 1983 Copenhagen World Championships.

The leading badminton philatelic expert is Stig Axelsson of Sweden.

STEVENS, Ray (Essex and England)
Born 23 June 1951, Walthamstow

England's legend of the 1970s. Despite a National Table Tennis Champion for an uncle, he won early recognition as Essex's most promising U.12 badminton player – and obtained his first brand new racket. Thanks to encouragement by international John Havers and coach Frank New, he graduated to the prestigious Wimbledon Squash & Badminton Club – a twenty-two-mile motor-cycle trip across London.

International success soon followed. With Keith Arthur he won the 1969 European Junior doubles title. Thereafter, his successes were with Mike Tredgett: 1972 (and again 1980) saw them in the final for the AEC title they coveted but which they were each time denied by Indonesians. But they won the European Championships in 1976, and again in 1978 when they also took Commonwealth Games gold. And in 1977 it was bronze in the World Championships.

Just to keep the home pot boiling, between 1972/3 and 1980/81, Stevens won the English National singles five times and the men's doubles seven times including a 1976-81 run of six in succession with Mike Tredgett. Add to that 111 caps for England, for which he always gave 100 per cent.

Dedicated to fitness and training, he was England's 'hard man'. Not a natural mover, he won through on a powerful smash, a determined and aggressive defence, subtlety at the net and a rooted dislike of being beaten.

His high sense of sportsmanship was evidenced in the 1977 World Championships. He successfully pleaded with the referee not to disqualify his opponent Flemming Delfs when the latter overstepped the five-minute interval. For this Lord Killanin added a UNESCO citation for the highest sportsmanship to Ray's other awards.

Sadly a split knee cartilage in December 1982 ended his career on-court. Off-court, however, the game goes on as coach to Wales, his highly promising nephew Darren Hall and a squad of Redbridge youngsters – and as export manager for ISI sports equipment.

STRAIGHT GAMES

'Won in straight games' means a player or pair won two successive games, thereby obviating the need for a third.

STRATEGY

General overall plan of action for a game or match – e.g. to attack or defend, to go for quick winners or a war of attrition, to attack the backhand or, in mixed, the woman. (See also *Tactics*.)

STRINGING, History of

In 1911 S.M. Massey wrote that the commonly used Indian rackets 'suffered from Eastern lassitude'. Doubtless this was due to poor-quality cow gut from poor-quality animals being inexpertly strung. (See also *Gut*.)

The first major change in English rackets was, in 1912, closer centre-strings, across and down, in the FHA [yres], 'an excellent driver'. Strangely enough, this practice has been specifically forbidden in the first-ever definition of a racket written into the Laws as recently as 1984. The MRT [ragget] was the first to boast of 'higher tension stringing'.

1928 saw the first tentative introduction, by Eltra, of synthetic gut 'interlaced *diagonally* to prevent slipping'. Queens came back with extra trebling in both directions. Dimid broke new ground with 'the scientific principle' of diagonal stringing 'for extra devil' as well as a six-month guarantee.

Post-war, Silver Fox countered the problem of eyelet abrasion in the frame with rubber cushions that also prevented court-contact. Carlton sprayed the eyelets with nylon.

In the 1950s, ICI brought back nylon strings. These were welcomed by Carlton because they could be more tightly strung, did not fray and were damp-resistant.

Bow Brand, more orthodox, maintained that quality gut, from sheep and lambs (not cows or pigs), retained its tension better than did synthetic, was more responsive and had greater impact strength. Pacific backed this latter point with a guarantee against premature breakage, whilst Black Wedge, pessimistically perhaps, attached a packet of gut to each racket.

Despite synthetic gut improvements (see *Gut*), top and affluent club players have always demanded natural (but more expensive) gut just as they demand feathered rather than synthetic shuttles.

Synthetic gut, however, does a good job in the vast majority of rackets sold. And in 1985 Cresta claimed their Tecnifibre not merely equalled natural gut in both performance and durability but excelled it!

STROLLERS

A group of leading players who, under the aegis of Major McCallum (q.v.), introduced badminton to districts, in Ireland as well as on the Continent, where badminton was little known. The visit of six players to Denmark in 1927/8 was the first by foreigners and did much to set the game in Denmark on its splendid way.

STUART WYATT TROPHY

An inscribed silver salver presented in memory of twenty-year long BAE President Stuart Wyatt by his wife 'Mims' Wyatt, herself a distinguished county player. It is awarded for 'the best performance by an English player (or pair)' in the All-England Championships.

The first winner, in March 1986, was Martin Dew who reached the semi-finals of both the men's and mixed doubles.

SUGIARTO, Icuk (Indonesia)
Born 4 October 1962

He may go down in badminton history as the man who, after a meteoric rise to become a national idol showered with gifts, was within a few months booed off the court by his own fans.

An unusually strong wrist and smash had shown him to be a junior with a future. 1982 confirmed it when the nineteen-year-old, employing speed, powerful smashing and deceptive cut drops, demolished Pongoh to win the Indonesian Open; and with acrobatic retrieving and counter-smashing to beat Luan Jin in the Asian Games team event; he went on to win the men's doubles with Christian and lose narrowly to him in the mixed final.

Even so, few would have predicted that he would scale the World Championships ladder, treading down rungs such as Morten Frost, Padukone again – and finally Swie King in one of the greatest, longest ($1\frac{1}{2}$ hours), most suspense-filled (three Championship points saved!) games ever (15-8, 12-15, 17-16).

Like Icarus, Sugiarto had perhaps flown too high too early. Within months he had lost – though admittedly unwell – to comparative unknown Wong Shoon Keat from Singapore in the SE Asia Games; to Han Jian in the Alba Quartz semis for a mere 6 and 5, and to teenager Yang Yang in the Indonesian Open, when his fair-weather supporters booed him off court and he sullenly responded by crashing the shuttle into the net or out of court for the last 7 points.

Not surprisingly, worse followed: defeats by Europe's Nierhoff and Baddeley, and by Padukone, his recent 'bunny', and finally, in the 1984 AEC, after a first game 15-1 win, at the hands of almost unknown Michael Kjeldsen. In less than a year he tumbled from Indonesian No. 1 to a fortunate No. 3.

It was a Lucifer fall that showed little sign of reversal in 1984 when in the Thomas Cup he lost to England's youthful Steve Butler; in the 1985 AEC 5 and 9 to Padukone, who lost equally easily to Frost; and a World Championship loss of his title in the 'quarters' 6 and 8 to Yang Yang.

But, urged on by his fickle Jakarta crowd, he beat Morten Frost 15-11, 8-15 (a few boos), 15-4 to win the long-coveted Alba Quartz World Cup (1985).

Won the S.E. Asian 9 and 6 against Kurmiawan only to be demolished to a storm of Indonesian boos in the vital Thomas Cup Final game 7 and 1 after beating Sidek 5 and 1 in the semis.

In 1986 had convincing wins in Chinese and Indonesian Opens.

SUTTON, née Webster, Jane
(Suffolk and England)
Born 2 August 1956,
Peterborough

Quiet girl of the England team whose successes *were* something to shout about. She turned her back on tennis at thirteen but is a current Suffolk county player. Transported by ever-willing parents and coached by Peter Roper, she won the first of eight-five caps in 1974. Formerly a bank clerk, she married Phil Sutton of Wales in 1984.

She achieved her greatest successes with Nora Perry: the 1980 European title, and then an out-of-the-blue World gold in the heat of Jakarta, and a silver in 1983 when, after a brilliant semi-final win over AEC champions Xu Rong and Wu Jianqiu, they frittered away a 9-0 lead against Lin Ying and Wu Dixi.

1981 brought the AEC doubles title and English National singles and doubles titles (also in 1978, with Gilks, and 1982). Jane helped England to a 1984 Uber Cup silver but was bitterly disappointed to be replaced by Gillian Gilks as Perry's 1985 World Championship partner. Ranked No. 3.

Her swingeing, angled, left-handed smashes and her deceptive drops made her the ideal foil for Perry's aggressive net-play. A yen for absolute accuracy sometimes led to inconsistency.

SUTTON, Philip (Wales)
Born 4 May 1960, Ebbw Vale

Potential golf champion with an eye for a shuttle and an ear for classical music, Phil Sutton is the Principality's 'best ever' and modestly boasts forty-four caps. Coached initially by Alan Tudgay, he won the Welsh National singles 1978-85. Then in 1983, in the hands of father-figure Gordon Richards, he reached quarters of AEC after 9-14 down to Sompol, and last sixteen of World Championships. He also won Peruvian Open men's singles and doubles. 1984 saw him in the Indonesian Open semis with Jane Webster, whom he married a year later. Falling downstairs in 1985 not surprisingly sadly curtailed his progress.

Very fit, he delights in a war of attrition.

SVENINGSEN, Bent

He and Jan Paulsen reached the final of the 1984 Polish International Championships singles in Warsaw. A power-cut halted play, and the final had to be played later – in Copenhagen. In time and distance a unique occurrence.

SWEDEN – Svenska Badminton Forbundet

In 1932 badminton tentatively stepped across the narrow Sound from Denmark, first to Malmö and Stockholm and later to Gothenburg. Thirty years later there were still only 5,000 players, yet today badminton is a leading Swedish sport with some 42,000 devotees playing in specially built halls – some north of the Arctic Circle.

Sweden hosted the 1972 European Championships at Karlskrona and inaugurated the first World Championships in 1977 at Malmö. In ex-international Stellan Mohlin, the IBF had one of its greatest Presidents.

Sweden has produced such fine stroke players as Conny Jepsen (AEC men's singles 1947), Sture Johnsson (European men's singles 1968, 1970, 1974); Stefan Karlsson, Claes Nordin and Bengt Froman (all AEC men's doubles winners); and Thomas Kihlström (AEC European and World Champion in both men's and mixed doubles) (q.v.).

Sweden's only woman major championship winner was Eva Twedberg (1968 AEC ladies' singles) though Maria Bengtsson (European and World Championship mixed doubles runner-up) and

Christine Magnusson show great promise.

In both senior and junior European Team Championships Sweden almost invariably ranks third only to England and Denmark. Between 1970 and 1982 it was each time (five) runner-up to Denmark in the Thomas Cup European Zone but it has not achieved this position once in the Uber Cup. In forty-six encounters Sweden has beaten Nordic rival Denmark only three times.

SWEDISH RANKING LIST 1986

Men's Singles:
1 Ulf Johansson
2 Jan-Erik Antonsson
3 Pär-Gunnar Jönsson
   Jonas Herrgaardh
5 Stellan Osterberg
6 Peter Axelsson
7 Manfred Mellquist
8 Kläs-Gunnar Jönsson
9 Peter Skole
10 Torbjörn Petersson
   Jens Olsson
   Patrick Andreasson
Ladies' Singles:
1 Christine Magnusson
2 Lotta Wihlborg
3 Catharina Andersson
4 Maria Bengtsson
   Maria Henning
6 Lillian Johansson
7 Carina Andersson
   Ann Sandersson
9 Karin Eriksson
10 Jeanette Kuhl

SWEDISH OPEN CHAMPIONSHIPS

Men's Singles
1956 L. Ekedahl
1957 F. Kobberø
1958 F. Kobberø
1959 B. Dahlberg
1960 B. Dahlberg
1961 L. Ekedahl
1962 E. Kops
1963 E. Kops
1964 E. Kops
1965 E. Kops
1966 S. Andersen
1967 S. Andersen
1968 S. Andersen
1969 S. Andersen
1970 S. Pri
1971 E. Hansen

1972	S. Pri
1973	S. Pri
1974	S. Johnsson
1975	S. Pri
1976	S. Johnsson
1977	L.S. King
1978	S. Pri
1979	F. Delfs
1980	P. Padukone
1981	L. Pongoh
1982	M. Sidek
1983	M. Sidek
1984	J. Nierhoff
1985	Han Jian

Ladies' Singles

1956	A. Schiött-Jacobsen
1957	I. Kjaergaard
1958	I. Kjaergaard
1959	H. Jensen
1960	E. Pettersson
1961	T. Holst-Christensen
1962	U. Rasmussen
1963	U.H. Smith
1964	J. Hashman
1965	E. Twedberg
1966	J. Hashman
1967	U. Strand
1968	E. Twedberg
1969	G. Perrin
1970	E. Twedberg
1971	E. Twedberg
1972	E. Twedberg
1973	E. Twedberg
1974	L. Køppen
1975	L. Køppen
1976	G. Gilks
1977	L. Køppen
1978	L. Køppen
1979	L. Køppen
1980	Y. Yonekura
1981	S.A. Hwang
1982	D. Wu
1983	H. Troke
1984	F. Tokhairin
1985	Han Aiping

Men's Doubles

1956	B. Dahlberg/B. Glans
1957	J. Hammergaard-Hansen/F. Kobberø
1958	O. Mertz/P.-E. Nielsen
1959	B. Dahlberg/B. Glans
1960	F. Kobberø/P.-E. Nielsen
1961	A.D. Jordan/P.J. Waddell
1962	J. Hammergaard-Hansen/F. Kobberø
1963	H. Borch/K.-A. Nielsen
1964	J. Hammergaard-Hansen/F. Kobberø
1965	E. Kops/K.-A. Nielsen
1966	H. Borch/J. Herlevsen
1967	S. Andersen/P. Walsöe
1968	H. Borch/E. Kops
1969	S. Andersen/E. Kops
1970	S. Pri/P. Walsöe
1971	S. Pri/P. Walsöe
1972	S. Pri/E. Kops
1973	S. Pri/P. Petersen

1974	K. Garbers/G. Kucki
1975	R. Stevens/M. Tredgett
1976	F. Delfs/E. Hansen
1977	A. Chandra/Tjun Tjun
1978	F. Delfs/S. Skovgaard
1979	F. Delfs/S. Skovgaard
1980	A. Chandra/C. Hadinata
1981	S. Karlsson/R. Kihlström
1982	C. Hadinata/L. Pongoh
1983	S. Fladberg/J. Helledie
1984	J.B. Park/M.S. Kim
1985	Li Yongbo/Ding Qiqing

Ladies' Doubles

1956	A. Jörgensen/K. Thorndahl
1957	I.E. Rogers/L.J. Timperley
1958	K. Grandlund/A. Hammergaard-Hansen
1959	H. Jensen/I. Kjaergaard
1960	I. Dahlberg/B. Olsson
1961	H. Andersen/T. Holst-Christensen
1962	B. Kristiansen/A. Winther
1963	K. Jörgensen/U. Rasmussen
1964	J. Hashman/M.U. O'Sullivan
1965	K. Jörgensen/U. Rasmussen
1966	J. Hashman/E. Twedberg
1967	L. Funch/U. Strand
1968	L. Funch/U. Strand
1969	M. Boxall/S. Whetnall
1970	M. Boxall/G. Perrin
1971	M. Beck/G. Gilks
1972	M. Beck/G. Gilks
1973	M. Beck/G. Gilks
1974	H. Nielsen/G. Giles
1975	S. Whetnall/G. Giles
1976	G. Gilks/M. Lockwood
1977	G. Gilks/B. Giles
1978	N. Perry/A.E. Statt
1979	J. van Beusekom/L. Køppen
1980	Y. Yonekura/A. Tokuda
1981	N. Perry/S. Leadbeater
1982	R. Xu/J. Wu
1983	N. Perry/J. Webster
1984	Y.J. Kim/H.S. Yoo
1985	Li Lingwei/Han Aiping

Mixed Doubles

1956	J. Hammergaard-Hansen/A. Jörgensen
1957	A.D. Jordan/L.J. Timperley
1958	J. Hammergaard-Hansen/A. Hammergaard-Hansen
1959	B. Glans/B. Olsson
1960	P.-E. Nielsen/B. Sterner
1961	B. Holst-Christensen/T. Holst-Christensen
1962	F. Kobberø/A. Hammergaard-Hansen
1963	P.-E. Nielsen/U. Rasmussen
1964	F. Kobberø/A. Flindt
1965	H. Borch/U. Rasmussen
1966	P. Walsöe/P. Mölgaard-Hansen
1967	P. Walsöe/P. Mölgaard-Hansen
1968	S. Andersen/U. Strand
1969	R. Mills/G. Perrin
1970	P. Walsöe/P. Mölgaard-Hansen
1971	D. Talbot/G. Gilks

1972	D. Eddy/G. Gilks
1973	D. Talbot/G. Gilks
1974	R. Maywald/B. Steden
1975	M. Tredgett/N. Gardner
1976	S. Skovgaard/K. Køppen
1977	D. Talbot/G. Gilks
1978	M. Tredgett/N. Perry
1979	M. Tredgett/N. Perry
1980	L. Wengberg/A. Borjesson
1981	W. Gilliland/N. Perry
1982	D. Bridge/G. Clark
1983	T. Kihlström/N. Perry
1984	T. Kihlström/M. Bengtsson
1985	S. Karlsson/M. Bengtsson

1986 Swedish and Danish Opens will be replaced in alternate years by Scandinavian Cup.

SCANDINAVIAN CUP

Championship
November 1981
26/30 October 1983
25/28 October 1984
March 1986

Men's Singles
1981	M. Frost
1983	M. Frost
1984	M. Frost
1986	M. Frost

Ladies' Singles
1981	L. Køppen
1983	C. Ruizhen
1984	Han Aiping
1986	Qian Ping

Men's Doubles
1981	Luan Jin/Lin Jiang Li
1983	Kartono/Heryanto
1984	Zhang Qiang/Zhoo Jincan
1986	S. Fladberg/J. Helledie

Ladies' Doubles
1981	N. Perry/J. Webster

1983	Y. Yonekura/A. Tokuda
1984	Lin Ying/Wu Dixi
1986	Kim Yun Ja/Sang Hee Yoo

Mixed Doubles
1981	M. Tredgett/N. Perry
1983	M. Dew/G. Gilks
1984	M. Dew/G. Gilks
1986	M. Dew/G. Gilks

SWEDISH SWISH

Alternative name for the Danish Wipe (q.v.), emphasizing that wrist as well as arm and body must be used.

SWISS BADMINTON FEDERATION

Founded in 1954 after an international tournament had been held in Lausanne in 1952. Visits by Malaysian (1956) and Chinese (1976) teams may have helped build up its total of 4,000 enthusiastic players. Switzerland produced an AEC champion, Guy Sautter (q.v.) 1913 and 1914, and a European Champion, Liselotte Blumer, 1980, founded the Helvetia Cup competition (originally 'Coupe des Nations') for the middle-of-the-badminton-road countries (1962) and built a fine sixteen-court hall in Lausanne.

T

T-JUNCTION

The joining point of the centre-line and the short service-line. This important forward position is an excellent base for the average net-player who, centrally placed, will have to move only 10 feet (3 metres) to left or right, and 18 inches (0.45 metres) backwards or forwards, to deal with most pushes or net-shots.

Ideally, the server and the receiver (when in the right hand court) often position themselves close to it. And, within an 18-inch (0.45 metres); arc, it is often the server's target area for the low serve, so placed to narrow the angle of return (q.v.).

TACTICS

Application of particular strokes to achieve overall strategy: e.g. service rushes and net shots to test the woman in mixed; attacking clears to the backhand after a shot wide to the forehand; alternating attacking clears and cut drop shots in singles to elicit a short, 'smashable' return. (See also *Strategy*.)

TAILOR, Dipak Prabhudaj (Middlesex and England) Born 6 June 1964

Shades of cricket's Ranji and Duleep are evidenced in his steely wrists that give deception *and* flashing power. He started play in Kenya at the age of five, long before his family moved to England.

With hard training and help from his older, talented brother Dilip, he won a hatful of National junior titles that included a rare run of three successive U.18 mixed victories and being Triple Champion in 1980/81 when still only sixteen.

Since then he has won thirty-two English caps, the Hungarian Triple Crown (1981), the Welsh Open mixed with Nora Perry (1982) and a place in the 1984 Thomas Cup team.

Having won the 1985 Danish Open with Nora Perry, he was seeded No. 2 in the 1985 World Championships but lost in the quarters to runners-up Karlsson/- Bengtsson, 16-17, 6-15.

TAIWAN – Chinese Taipei Badminton Association

The small Association which became the political bone of contention that led to the IBF-WBF split, and a case in the English Law Courts which upheld blameless CTBA's appeal against IBF expulsion.

Founded in 1956, CTBA had two indoor courts and some 200 members. Today there are 200 clubs, a steadily rising 62,000 registered players, and almost 100 per cent school and college involvement. Among these are several hundreds of all ages who start play at 6 a.m. on Tapei's famous 'Hill' with its 200 open-air courts!

CTBA's activities have been widespread: two championships, an enormous

Taiwan team tournament, competition in ABC tournaments, Thomas and Uber Cup competitions, Asian Games and friendly overseas matches. Much of this is owed to dynamic Secretary C.Y. Wong (q.v.).

TALBOT, Derek
(Northumberland and
England)
Age: 38

A gutsy Geordie all-rounder, he won eighty-three caps (1969-81), more than a hundred-plus Open and twenty international titles, eleven English National titles including two Triple Crowns (1971/2, the first since their inception, and 1973/4); three Commonwealth gold; and three European gold and three AEC titles (1973, 1976 and 1977), all with Gillian Gilks.

Talbot was one of the fastest-moving players of his day, aggressive, remarkably consistent and a shrewd tactician, especially in mixed doubles.

A man of many parts too: farsighted, he was a first instigator of player representation in Open badminton, promoter of Vicort rackets, Promotions Manager of the grandiose Coventry Rackets Club, author of *Badminton to the Top*; designer of the 'Gripshaft' (q.v.), England selector, and BBC commentator.

TAN, Yee Kahn

With thirty-five caps each, he and Boon Bee were Malaya's 'greats' of the 1970s. With speed and power, they won the All-Malayan Open six times in 7 years the AEC men's doubles twice and the Asian Games twice, all between 1962 and 1968. Tan Yee Khan had an unusually powerful wristy smash which might account for his also being Malayan Golf Champion.

TAPE

The top edge of the net is bound with 3-inch (75 mm) wide strip of white material doubled over. Through it runs the net-cord by which the net is tensioned and secured to the posts.

A 'tape-shot' is one in which the shuttle hits the tape, then, still in play, topples or bounces over into the opponent's court. A 'let' cannot be claimed for this either during a rally or in service.

TEAM CHALLENGE CIRCUIT

A team competition instituted in 1984/5 partly to bring England's top players to centres otherwise seldom visited, partly to meet the criticism that such players were so often abroad that they all too seldom played against each other so that ranking became rather meaningless. It helped replace the Laing Grand Prix of the late 1970s.

Sponsored by the Norwich Building Society in 1985/6.

THAILAND BADMINTON
FEDERATION

Badminton started in 1913 as a back-garden game. King Rama VI, playing outdoors, gave the game such a fillip that, with players far outnumbering courts, 'triples', a fast game of long rallies and accurate placement, became the main tournament event.

In 1950, with the formation of the BA of Thailand, indoor courts were used in Bangkok and the game spread, outdoors, throughout Thailand. The game received great support from King Bhumipol Adulyadej and the royal family, who built palace courts and sponsored top players. Luang Thamnoon Vudhikorn, President of the Supreme Court, instituted scientific training which produced world-class players such as Miss Pratang Pattabongs, first Thai ABC participant, Miss T. Kingmanee, T. Khajadbhye, C. Wattanasin (q.v.), S. Rattanusorn, B. Jaiyen, and R. Kanchanaraphie and C. Ratanasaengsuang, who became leading Canadian coaches.

Eagle Sports, long-established shuttle and racket manufacturers, subsidized Thailand's first Thomas Cup entry in 1951/2. Thailand reached the Inter-Zone finals five times. Unfortunately there was dissension on two occasions. in 1960/1 they lost to Indonesia 3-6 in the Challenge Round, owing – to quote a Thailander – to 'incredible Indonesian umpiring', which was not commented on in a *Gazette* report. Positions were reversed in 1969/70, when Indonesia at 3-2, 12-all in the 6th match, protested 'at the spirit in which the tie was conducted'. It was a charge vehemently debated before the IBF in London but never publicly elaborated. BAT refused to replay the last three games previously awarded to them, and Indonesia were adjudged 6-3 winners.

In 1979, the Thailand Badminton Federation was formed. Since then TBF and BAT have been in conflict, with a regrettable split in Thailand's playing strength. A dispute happily resolved in Spring, 1986.

Today's leading singles players are Miss Darunee Lertvoralak, Panwadee Jinasuyanond and Miss Juthathip Banchongsilp; and Sompol Kukasemkij, Sakrapee Thongsari and Wichit Assawanapakas.

THOMAS CUP

The Men's World Team Badminton Championship. It was first proposed by England's Sir George Thomas, Bart (q.v.), in 1939. Owing to the war, the first championship was not played until 1948/9. Formerly played triennially, now biennially.

The silver gilt trophy, 28 inches (0.65 metres) in height and with a 16-inch (0.4 metres) span consists of plinth, cup and lid, the latter surmounted by the figure of a static player.

Nations were divided into four regional zones (Asian, East and West, European, American and Australasian) for preliminary knock-out matches. Zone winners then came together to play for the right to challenge the holders, with the following championship to be played in the winner's country.

Over the year, changes were made: choice of venue was decided by the IBF; the Challenge Round was abolished after 1966/7; holders and host nation became exempt until the inter-zone ties.

For 1984, the format was completely changed to encourage entries by more smaller nations. Preliminary rounds of Thomas and Uber Cup competitions were played (weekend 26 February) at the same time and venue, on a round-robin basis, in one-to-four groups of three or four teams with a seeded team in each. The four different venues were New Delhi (one), Hong Kong (one), Toronto (one) and Ostend (three). From these, six qualifiers emerged to join the holders (the People's Republic of China) and the hosts (Malaysia) in the final rounds at Kuala Lumpur (weekend 7-8 May). These were again put into two groups (with a seeded team in each) who played on a round-robin basis, with the winners playing in the final.

Match format, originally five singles and four doubles, was changed to three singles and two doubles. Overall sponsorship, to the tune of £350,000, was given by Marlboro, equally divided between men and women, five per cent (£17,500) going to the winners, three to losing finalists, and two to the winner of a three-four play-off.

1986 saw the biggest-ever entry: thirty-nine Thomas Cup, thirty-four Uber Cup. Qualifying centres were Mulheim (nineteen and nineteen), Bangkok (eleven and nine), Vancouver (nine and six). The finals were held in Jakarta and, despite their great prestige and importance, were characterized by genuine friendliness and impeccable sportsmanship. Even amid Senayan's bedlam, China regained the trophy by a gamble, successfully substituting youthful Yang Yang for their heat-sapped No. 1, World Champion Han Jian, against Indonesia's No. 1, Sugiarto. Heat also forced Denmark's Frost to retire so helping Malaysia to 'bronze'.

THOMAS CUP

Year	Venue	Competing Nations	Winner	Runner-up	Score
1948-9	Preston (England)	10	Malaya	Denmark	8-1
1951-2	Singapore	12	Malaya	USA	7-2
1954-5	Singapore	21	Malaya	Denmark	8-1
1957-8	Singapore	19	Indonesia	Malaya	6-3
1960-1	Djakarta	19	Indonesia	Thailand	6-3
1963-4	Tokyo	26	Indonesia	Denmark	5-4
1966-7	Djakarta	23	Malaysia*	Indonesia	6-3
1969-70	Kuala Lumpur	25	Indonesia‡	Malaysia	7-2
1972-3	Jakarta	23	Indonesia	Denmark	8-1
1975-6	Bangkok	26	Indonesia	Thailand	8-1
1978-9	Jakarta	21	Indonesia	Denmark	9-0
1981-2	London	26	China	Indonesia	5-4
1983-4	Kuala Lumpur	33	Indonesia‡	China	3-2
1985-6	Jakarta	41	China	Indonesia	3-2

* 2 ties conceded by Indonesia
† No Challenge round
‡ New format

THOMAS, Sir George Alan, Bart (Hampshire and England)
Born 14 June 1881 (Istanbul); died 23 July 1972

Player, administrator and gentleman – for many years the games' Grand Old Man.

In 1901, with the help of a small entry and a bye, he reached the semi-final of the AEC men's doubles. In 1903 he won the mixed, the first of eight victories which included four consecutive wins (1914-22) with Hazel Hogarth. Surprisingly the singles title eluded him until 1920, the first of four successive wins, the last of which, at forty-one, made him the oldest-ever winner. The trophy he thus won outright was the original one competed for in 1900. Nine men's doubles titles gave him a still standing record of twenty-one titles; the last of these, twenty-seven years after his first appearance, was won at the age of forty-seven. He missed the first-ever tournament (1899) but thereafter never missed an AEC finals day up to 1948!

Deception, accuracy, a wristy smash, fizzing drives and astute chess-like tactics (befitting a Grand Master and British Champion of that game) were the keynotes of his play. To those, in these McEnroe days, should be added consideration, courtesy and unquestioning sportsmanship. His *bête noire* was the player who bustled his elegantly flowing strokes.

Between 1902 and 1929 he played in all but one of thirty international matches – winning fifty of his games. He also won sixty-nine UK national titles and took touring teams to Canada and France. He was also a tennis international who reached the 1911 Wimbledon men's doubles semi-final, a county hockey player and an 'invincible ping-pong player'.

In World War I, spurning a horse, he trekked 240 miles (385 km) on foot with his men across the unmapped Mesopotamian desert. In peace, despite a natural shyness, he visited boys' clubs and prisons.

He gave much too as an administrator. For many years he was a selector, until, with his own place in doubt, he insisted on stepping down. BAE Vice-President for twenty years (1930-50), President for two (1950-52), IBF Founder President for twenty-one years, attending every meeting. He helped in the revision of the Laws, edited the *Badminton Gazette* and wrote the best book of its time, *The Art of Badminton* (1923).

It was his vision that saw the Badminton Association must yield its powers to a truly international body, the IBF. He also saw the need for the international competition that keeps his name alive today – the Thomas Cup.

In his old age his trophies were stolen and he became blind. He died aged ninety-one, in the words of Major

McCallum *'un chevalier sans peur et sans reproche'*.

THROWING ACTION

With a 5-foot (1.524 metres) high net to be cleared, a large number of badminton strokes are necessarily overhead ones: clear, drop-shot and smash. These are all played with the same basic action as that used in throwing a ball or stone a long distance.

In a sideways-on stance, the hand is brought straight back over the right shoulder, and the racket-head, thanks to a cocked wrist, is dropped down between the shoulder blades. Simultaneously, the body is turned and arched backwards, so bringing the weight onto the right, back foot (*preparation*).

As the bent arm snaps upwards and straight, with the heel of the hand leading, and the wrist uncocks, the body corkscrews upwards and turns square to the net at impact, and body weight thrusts forward (*execution*).

Impact (q.v.) is made at varying points along the arc of the swing according to the desired trajectory.

The racket-head continues down to waist or knee level along the desired line of flight to the target area in the *follow-through*.

With body weight on the right foot, now in front of the left, instant *recovery* to base and the position of readiness must be made.

Many beginners, especially women, not as accustomed to throwing balls as are men, find difficulty with this action. Instead of thrusting the hand upwards, they *dab* it forwards, with an almost dart-throwing action. As a result, they lose elevation, or steepness, and power.

A flat throwing action, akin to that used in cricket to throw from cover-point, or to throw a frisbee, or skim a stone along water, is employed in drives or pushes. It is basically the overhead action but executed in a horizontal, not vertical plane.

So too the lob, like a strong underarm throw, inversely mirrors the clear.

TIMING

The ability to produce a stroke in which the racket-head is moving at the desired maximum speed in the split second of correct impact. This ensures that the full force of the racket-head is applied neither too early nor too late, when it is not actually in contact with the base of the shuttle.

An arc extending 18 inches (0.45 metres) either side of the point of impact is often called the 'zip' or 'zing' area as it is there the racket-head should be travelling at its fastest.

Timing is also vital in the preparation (see *Throwing action*) of the stroke. Beginners, unable to judge the flight of the shuttle accurately, invariably start drawing the racket back much too late – as the shuttle is actually descending. As a result, the stroke is rushed, and as the arm does not have time to straighten fully, power, control and steepness are all lost.

TIMPERLEY, née White, June (Surrey and England)

England's joint leading lady of the 1950s. She and Iris Cooley (q.v.) broke the winning sequences of the Devlin sisters and the all-conquering Danes by winning the AEC in 1953, 1955 and 1959.

She achieved equal success in the AEC mixed: winning in 1953 with Malaysian tactician David Choong, and in 1956 and 1958 with his English counterpart Tony Jordan. A grooved low serve and a velvet touch made her the best net-player for a decade.

She is unique as an All-England champion in all three championships, junior (1950), senior (1953) and veteran (1978), and won forty-four caps (1952-63).

She is still active on and off-court at Wimbledon S & BC.

TJUN TJUN (Indonesia) Born 1 December 1952, Cirebon, W. Java

He had a name that sounded like a labouring steam engine but he was one of the most explosive movers in the history of the game. At fourteen, a late starter, he more than made up for this by fifteen years of brilliance, until 1981 when back trouble forced his retirement.

His first National doubles title came in 1971. In 1973 he and Johann Wahjudi lost badly in the AEC to compatriots Chandra and Christian. Tjun Tjun found singles consolation in beating Sweden's Sture Johnsson 15-13, 15-7 in the quarters but was very much on the receiving end in the semi-final against a rampant Hartono (7 and 1).

In 1974 he and Wahjudi won the AEC title that was to be theirs until 1981 with only a single defeat – that in 1976 by Sweden's Froman and Kihlstrom. Unshaken, they re-established themselves head and shoulders above any other pairs by crushing Christian and Chandra 15-3, 15-4, in the 1977 World Championships.

Their closest call thereafter – in two ways – was in the 1979 AEC against Japan's Tsuchida and Iino. Seconds after the five-minute break (at 15-6, 14-17), they returned to the arena just in time to hear umpire Alan Jones announce their disqualification. They – but not the crowd – made no protest, and referee Herbert Scheele unconventionally over-ruled the umpire and restored them. Shaken, they were soon 4-12 down but fought back magnificently to win 18-17 and rob Japan of a first-ever men's doubles final place to counterbalance its women's many victories.

Tjun Tjun more than played his part in his three Thomas Cup finals appearances (1973-9). In thirteen games, he and Wahjudi lapsed only once (13-15), suffered only one double-figures score (11), and for the rest romped home against Denmark's and Malaysia's best, 7 and 6; 5; 7 and 6; 6 and 2; 2 and 3; 9 and 5. He also won a third single, 1 and 7!

He was the complete men's doubles player. A tight backhand serve and a leap net-return kill; wolfish reflex net-interceptions; serves low and flick constantly attacked; steep and powerful jump smashes; flat, fast defence followed by lightning net incursions. With speed, severity and non-stop attack, he scourged his opponents – thanks to perfect understanding with his talented but less flamboyant partner Wahjudi.

TOUCH SHOTS

Those where absolute accuracy of trajectory and distance rather than power are of prime importance. Upward net-shots are the best example: a perfect one is played so delicately that the shuttle travels only an inch (2.54 centimetres) or two upwards, caresses the tape and drops vertically down the other side of the net.

The low serve is another example, though the shuttle travels much further. Ideally it literally skims the tape (to avoid being 'rushed') and falls on or 9 inches (22 centimetres) beyond the short service line.

The slow drop-shot played from the back of the court is another example. The shuttle, although hit half the length of the court should again skim the tape and drop within 12 or 18 inches (0.3 to 0.45 metres) of the net.

For all touch shots the grip is slightly relaxed to give greater 'feel' of the stroke. Great care and delicacy must be employed.

TOURNAMENTS, Largest

Among the largest ever held must be a Northern Tasmanian BA (900 members) tournament. It ran three championships, five handicap and various junior and veteran grades. With, in all, fifty events and 600 entries, it was played on eight courts over nine nights.

The Leinster (Ireland) Closed Tournament played 846 matches over twenty-two days on four courts, including forty-five pairs in the married couples event!

The Scottish Junior tournament is held on Edinburgh's Meadowbank Centre's eighteen courts.

TRAGETT, née Larminie, Margaret (Middlesex and England)

She started her badminton on an hour-glass court in Heidelberg and for nearly thirty years was one of England's greats – Sir George Thomas's counterpart. A wide range of adventurous strokes, including trick-shots, sturdy defence and unusual mobility won her eleven AEC titles (three ladies' singles – her last win seventeens years after her first; five ladies' doubles, three mixed doubles) and fifteen caps (1909-29). Her first AEC was in 1902, yet in 1933 she reached the fourth round of the ladies' doubles *and* played in the singles. She made her final bow only in 1935.

She endorsed the MRT racket, was a regular contributor to, and editor of, the *Badminton Gazette* (1921-2 and 1926-7) and was author of *Badminton for Beginners* as well as many novels

TRAMLINES

A court term generally referring to the parallel singles and doubles side-lines. In doubles, mixed especially, a shot hit within their eighteen inch (0.46 metres) span is considered effectively placed as it is often out of the opponent's direct reach.

It may also, as 'back tramlines', refer to the doubles and singles long service lines – a rough target area ($2\frac{1}{2}$ feet – 0.76 metres wide) for all clears and lobs, and singles high serves.

TRAVERS, Dan (Scotland)
Born 16 June 1956, Glasgow

A travelling grocer who has travelled far in the badminton world. Has won over fifty Scottish caps and many major championships (including six Scottish National and two Open titles) in a long-lasting partnership with Billy Gilliland in which his dogged rocklike defence complements the latter's speed. Highlights: runner-up in 1982 AEC final; quarters of 1985 World Championships (where he celebrated his birthday by kissing twenty-four girls – each of different nationality), and the 1986 CG.

An outspoken correspondent for Scottish Badminton and a real on-court entertainer.

TREBLING

The top and bottom three horizontal strings in a racket. They are generally not of the usual white gut but of a thinner, coloured one. Their purpose is to prevent movement and consequent bunching or separation of vertical strings.

They also provide a fortuitous method of tossing-up, by spinning the racket in the hand, as one side of the trebling feels 'rough' to the touch and the other 'smooth': a 'heads' or 'tails' equivalent.

Trebling is, however, fast disappearing from modern rackets, where more efficient stringing make it unnecessary.

TREDGETT, Mike, MBE
(Gloucestershire and
England)
Born 5 April 1949

Arguably England's finest-ever doubles all-rounder; its most capped player (137); and a deserving MBE. His early games were across a neighbour's privet hedge, and on a 4-foot (1.2 metres) short village hall court, with a gas fire in close proximity to the base-line.

Despite that, he has won sixteen English National (ten men's and six mixed doubles), two Commonwealth Games and five European titles. Better still he won the AEC mixed three times with Nora Perry but, despite two men's doubles finals appearances, could not achieve his other ambition.

Nor could he in the 2nd World Championships, where he and Nora Perry surprisingly lost to Asians Hadinata and I Wigoeno. In the 3rd, Nora, now playing with Kihlström, forced Karen Chapman and him into third place. And in the 1981 World Games he and Nora Perry lost in the final to Kihlström and Gillian Gilks.

His partnerships with Ray Stevens and Nora Perry made him the backbone of English doubles for a decade. When Stevens' injury forced his retirement, Tredgett struck up an all left-handed partnership with Martin Dew. With him he won the 1981 Friends Provident English Masters when the latter came in as a last second substitute; they were runners-up in both the 1983 AEC and WC, and the 1984 AEC.

Mobile, aggressive round the net and with an armour-plated defence, concentration and coolness are the keynotes of his game: 'He wouldn't know if there was a gorilla on the other side of the net.'

Still playing well, he restricts his tournament play to Europe. He works as a building executive – MIB and FFB qualified.

TRIPLES

A form of badminton peculiar to Thailand where players far outnumber courts.

When serving, there are two players in the forecourt and one in rear-court. Thereafter tactics generally dictate two at the back and one at the net.

Scoring is as for doubles except that in the first innings each side has only one server; in the second, two; and in the third and thereafter, three. There are two receivers, one at the front and one at the back. The front receiver may not step forward over the front service line to 'rush' (q.v.) a serve; nor may he move until the opponents have hit the shuttle twice.

Games are 21 points up with setting to 2 or 5 at 19 all, and to 1 to 3 a twenty all.

TROKE, Helen (Hampshire and England)
Born 7 November 1964, Southampton

'Trokie' to friends but 'Tiger' to her opponents. At $16\frac{1}{2}$ one of the youngest girls to represent her country, 1980/1 (with a début against Zhang Ailing) and at $17\frac{1}{2}$ to win gold at the 1982 Commonwealth Games.

She is England's best singles prospect since Gillian Gilks' heyday and ranks as No. 1 in Europe also.

Even as a twelve-year-old, her aggression, hard-hitting and determination were so clearly evident that they caught the eye of Hampshire coach, Brian Hooper. They have 'gelled' together ever since. 'His dedication rubs off,' avers Helen.

She won the English National junior singles U.15 (1979/80), the U.18 (1981/2) and the U.21 (1980 and 1981). Senior National titles have eluded her, losing to Jane Webster (1981/2) and Karen Beckman, often her doubles partner, (1982/3).

But Helen had greater and wider triumphs. In 1981 and 1983 she comfortably won the European Junior. 1982 was Commonwealth gold. In 1983 she reached the World Championship semis, losing 10-12, 6-11 to the ultimate winner, Li Lingwei.

1984 was a red-letter year. She pressed Lingwei, still closer to 10-12, 8-11 in the AEC quarters and to three games in the Pro-Kennex Grand Prix round-robin, finally taking bronze when the injured Lingwei scratched. She won the European title but lost tearfully in the British Masters to her arch rival Kirsten

Larsen in front of her home Portsmouth crowd. But as a member of the Uber Cup team it was silver – winning all her singles except one – against Lingwei. Seeded 5/8 in the 1985 World Championships, she lost in the quarters to runner-up Wu Jianqui, 10-11, 4-11.

She beat Larsen to win the Indian Open and with her lost in the semis 4 and 1 to Sun Ai Hwang/Hang Suk Kang. She failed to reach semis in both Malaysian Masters and Alba Quartz.

She started 1986 with a flourish, for after 7-11, 7-11 4th round AEC defeat by Gu Jiaming, she beat Larsen, her conqueror over the previous six months, to retain her European title 9-12, 11-3, 11-2, and then, in the Senayan Uber Cup sweat-box, outlasted AEC winner Yun Ja Kim 6-11, 11-5, 11-4. Won 1986 CG LS title, and lost only narrowly in Indonesian Open final to China's dark horse Shi Wen, after winning a three-game semi in which she took the last nineteen points without reply.

Troke comes from a badminton family. Her parents spent three years savings to be in her corner at the Brisbane Commonwealth Games. Her elder sister, Catherine, led the way until, by unkind chance, Helen met her in the 1982 AEC and beat her 11-3, 11-4. She thrives on hard work. Currently England's No. 1 (already with fifty-two caps), she has her sights set on the World No. 1 spot, Chinese or no – and is fast becoming an excellent doubles player. She has unusual power and mobility, but is developing a more varied game and re-modelling her backhand to that end. 62 caps.

TROPHIES

Challenge trophies become the property of the player who wins them three times in succession or four times in all, *provided it is the same trophy* and with the same partner.

U

UBER, Betty (Surrey and England)
Died 30 April 1983

England's 1930s counterpart to Sir George Thomas. Fate perhaps played a part in her badminton career. A Junior Wimbledon winner she turned to badminton because of poor local tennis facilities. And she caught the eye – and the heart – of H.S. (Bertie) Uber (twenty-two England caps, 1920-32).

He won the AEC men's doubles in 1925 and coached his wife so well that she quickly graduated from the Crystal Palace 'Shy Ladies' Court'. Together they won the mixed trophy outright (1930-32), a feat she repeated in almost unbeatable combination with D.C. Hume (1933-6) and with Bill White in 1938 – a still unbeaten record.

Singles she 'never quite got the hang of' though she won the AEC singles in 1935 and the doubles four times in a nineteen-year span, 1931-49.

Her international record was even more impressive: thirty-seven appearances between 1926 and 1951, winning every one of the first fifty-one matches.

She moved well, hit accurately and strongly, had an armour-plated defence, analysed opponents shrewdly and served with almost unassailable accuracy. More, she showed unvarying modesty, charm and sportsmanship.

In 1949 she wrote *That Badminton Racket*. In 1956 she gave the cup that fittingly bears her name, for what is known as the Ladies' World Team Badminton Championship, having first mooted the idea in 1950.

UBER CUP

The Ladies' World Team Badminton Championship was proposed in 1950 by England's Betty Uber (q.v.) and strongly supported by New Zealand's Nancy Fleming. It was not played for until 1956/7 because of financial difficulties.

The trophy itself, donated by Mrs Uber, consists of a swivelling globe mounted on a plinth and surmounted by an active female player standing on a shuttle.

Until 1983/4 matches consisted of three singles and four doubles; thereafter of three singles and two doubles. General organization was similar to that for the Thomas Cup (q.v.), though the two competitions were not played together until 1983/4.

The new format proved so popular that thirty-six countries, a record entry, played in the preliminary, zoned rounds held at Mulheim, Vancouver and Bangkok. England, Denmark, Sweden, Canada, Korea and Japan all played and qualified; holders, China, and host nation, Indonesia, were automatically added for the May 1986 Jakarta finals.

New look England, 1984 runners-up, sadly disappointed, and second favourites S. Korea mysteriously lost to a youth and vintage Indonesian team. In Group A, China dropped only one game in thirty, and 167 points on 552! In the final, they clinched the issue in the singles, dropping only thirty-four points but surprisingly lost both doubles. A typical Chinese face-saver for host Indonesia, it was suggested.

faults'. Thereafter probationary membership is generally granted for a year during which the candidate works with experienced umpires and attendS a one-day refresher course. If satisfactory, the candidate becomes one of the BUAE's 200-plus full members.

These are divided into three grades.

Grade III: must show a higher standard of control and an ability to recover from errors.

Grade II: must, in the first two years,

UBER CUP

Year	Venue	Competing Nations	Winner	Runner-up	Score
1956-7	Lytham St Annes	11	USA	Denmark	6-1
1959-60	Philadelphia	14	USA	Denmark	5-2
1962-3	Wilmington (USA)	11	USA	England	4-3
1965-6	Wellington (New Zealand)	17	Japan	USA	5-2
1968-9	Tokyo	19	Japan	Indonesia	6-1
1971-2	Tokyo	17	Japan*	Indonesia	5-2
1974-5	Jakarta	14	Indonesia	Japan	5-2
1977-8	Auckland	16	Japan	Indonesia	5-2
1980-1	Tokyo	15	Japan†	Indonesia	6-3
1983-4	Kuala Lumpur	21	China‡	England	5-0
1985-6	Jakarta	36	China	Indonesia	3-2

* No Challenge Round
† Thomas Cup format
‡ New format

UMPIRES, Manager of

When the BUAE is requested by a tournament committee to supply umpires and service judges, the referee generally decides *which* matches shall be umpired. It is, however, the manager of umpires, appointed by the BUAE, who alone decides exactly which officials are appointed to a particular match.

The referee's request for the removal of an unsatisfactory court official however cannot be refused.

UMPIRES, Training of,

With ever more events appearing on the badminton calendar, new umpires are at a premium. The independent, thirty-year-old BUAE (q.v.) trains and supplies umpires at the request of the BAE.

An initial weekend training course for six to eighteen applicants covers Laws, use of the score-pad, and on-court practice, identifying 'faults' and 'service

be able to handle the first two rounds of international open tournaments and work abroad under supervision; in the third year must be able to handle quarter and semi-finals and work abroad unsupervised.

Grade I: must be able to officiate world-wide and to act as 'umpire in charge'.

The IBF has its own International Badminton Umpires Organization (IBUO). Their highest award, Certificated Umpire Status, is awarded after practical evaluation and a written test. England, with Len Bowsher, Mike Gilks, Stewart Hague and Mrs Sue Smallwood, has more such umpires than any other country. There is also a list of Accredited Umpires.

After the 1985 World Championship furore, when a player was faulted at championship match point, it is likely a signal to indicate 'official warning' will have to be evolved for benefit of non-English-speaking players and coaches.

The Scottish BU have used the signal below to show that, after a breach of Law 22(e), the umpire is about to (a) issue a warning (b) fault the offender (c) summon the Referee who has power to disqualify.

UMPIRING DIFFICULTIES

Good umpiring is unobtrusive but far from easy. In a fast-moving game of four players, the umpire has much to observe:

1. Forms of obstruction: (a) shouting; (b) sliding (or even a toe) under the net: (c) throwing racket over the net; (d) baulking with racket; (e) unsighting an opponent during service.
2. Coaching from off court.
3. Serving or receiving out of turn or from wrong court, or receiver moving before the service is hit.
4. Hitting or touching net; hitting shuttle before it crosses the net.
5. Shuttle touching partner's racket, clothing or hair during a rally.
6. Undue delay in serving or receiving.

7. Interfering with the speed of a shuttle.
8. Intimidating official or opponent.
9. Correct application of setting; ends change; and five-minute interval.
10. Play not being continuous.
11. Indiscriminate changing of shuttles.
12. Delay caused by injury or sickness.
   And, if there is no service judge, all the Laws pertaining to service!

UNFORCED ERRORS

Errors made by a player not because of his opponent's good play but because of his own bad play. These may result basically from lack of care, concentration, technique or tactical awareness. Top-class players, because they have practised forty or fifty consecutive shot routines, make very few such errors.

They thus *give* away virtually no points unless under the relentless and continuous pressure of an equal or better player. Their opponents have therefore to play to even finer limits to gain points – and, in doing so, are themselves possibly forced into error.

At club level, the underlying cause is often lack of essential 100-per-cent concentration. This may lead to:

1. Lifting the head just before impact so not seeing the shuttle onto the racket, and missing or mis-hitting it.
2. Late backswing cause by failure to appreciate shuttle-flight, resulting in a hurried or cramped stroke.
3. Turning the racket-head at an angle to the desired line of flight with the result that the shuttle is missed by the sharply-angled racket-face or hit over the side-line.
4. Sluggish or uncontrolled footwork which leaves a player off-balance, or not behind the shuttle, and so unable to control it.
5. Aiming at no specific target area – and therefore often hitting 'out'.
6. Tension or over excitement resulting in a 'snatched' or wild shot.
7. Lack of control of racket-head at impact.
8. Lack of stamina which brings concentration and stroke failure in its train.
9. LACK OF CARE

UNITED STATES BADMINTON ASSOCIATION

Today giant of the tennis world, pigmy of the badminton world. And yet the USA was three times Uber Cup winner (1956/7, 1959/60 and 1962/3); producer of the incomparable Dave Freeman and Judy Hashman; claimant to the oldest club (New York BC formed in 1878); one-time lessee of huge twenty-plus court Armouries; and employer of great professionals such as Jess Willard, Hugh Forgie, Jack Purcell, Ken Davidson and Frank Devlin.

Such is the contradiction of American badminton, where hundreds of thousands idly hit a shuttle on beach and lawn but only 2,500 take it seriously enough to affiliate.

Six times US singles champion, Chris Kinard equated US lack of interest with badminton's lack of prize money, and so its reputation as an amateur 'nothing' game. He cited that in 1982/3 twenty-seven licensed badminton players between them won £77,583, at which rate they would have needed some forty-three years to equal Martina Navratilova's career earnings of £3,485,161. He also claimed that a basketball 'rookie' could earn $100,000 a year simply from wearing one firm's shoes; in badminton, a mere handful of dollars.

Even from so small a number of players, there have also emerged such greats as glamorous Margaret Varner, FBI man Joe Alston and his wife, Lois, stetsoned Wynn Rogers, almost undefeatable Ethel Marshall and Bea Massman, Sue Devlin and Tyna Barrinaga, and Don Paup and Jim Poole.

From the academic background of Boston University (1926), USBA finally emerged in 1936 when nine Regional Associations joined forces. Within a year the first National Championships were held.

USSR BADMINTON FEDERATION

Founded in 1961, USSRBF now has 5,500 registered clubs with some 150,000 affiliated players in its fifteen republics. Doubtless the overall total is much greater as badminton is encouraged in junior schools and widely played in parks and even on frozen lakes. Hundreds of paid coaches work in these clubs, and there are some twenty major internal championships, including Moscow's Cosmonauts Cup.

Surprisingly, knowing the USSR's wide-ranging sports skills, its players have not made world impact, and little interest has been shown in Uber or Thomas Cup competitions, though both junior and senior European Championships are entered. National and Team Championships were inaugurated in 1963, and International Championships in 1973. It hosted, and won, the Helvetia Cup in 1977 in Leningrad, and won again in 1979 in Klagenfurt.

Leading players today are A. Skripko, V. Shmakov, A Antropov, V. Sevrukov, Svetlana Beliasova, Tatjana Litvinenko and E. Rybkina. Unfortunately they were not entered for 1985 World Championships.

To increase keenness, they, uniquely, publish a ranking list of the top 200 men, 150 women and 200 juniors. The top ten men (eight women) and USSR Championships doubles winners are designated 'Masters of Sport'.

Marked improvement was shown in the 1986 European Championships with Beliasova reaching the LS semis.

V

VARNER, Margaret (USA)

Triple sport international and American legend, her meteoric badminton career, like that of Dave Freeman, was all too brief. 'The Texan Bronze' (reputed to carry a pistol in her handbag) slugged it out with 'Little Red Dev' (Judy Hashman) for world superiority. She won the AEC singles in 1955 and 1956 by beating the holder, Judy Devlin, but lost to her in the 1957, 1958 and 1960 finals. In 1958 she won the AEC doubles with England's young Heather Ward, who was to beat Judy Devlin the following year.

Thereafter, unfortunately for badminton, she turned more to tennis (1958, with Margaret Dupont, lost in the Wimbledon final 3-6, 5-7 to Althea Gibson and Maria Bueno) and squash (USA Champion in 1960). She ran race-horses 'Wembley Blue', 'Half Smash' and 'Service Over'.

VELLA, Sue

One of only two IBUO Certificated Women Umpires, she achieved notoriety at the 1985 World Championships when, after two previous warnings, she faulted Wu Jianqiu at her fifth championship match point for 'time-wasting between rallies'. Miss Vella firmly declined to alter her decision when asked by the referee if she wished to do so. Han Aiping recovered from 6-11, 11-11 to beat a tearful Wu 6-11, 12-11, 11-2.

Controversy raged and some felt that, despite her certification, the twenty-four-year-old Canadian law student had had insufficient top-class experience to be put in charge of so important a match.

VERSTOEP, A.A. (Ton)

A Dutchman who first helped the IBF as Belgian delegate in 1968. As Chairman of the finance committee, he used his business and linguistic skills to good effect, especially in his pet interest, the development of the game in newly interested nations. Lilleshall trained and formerly a keen tournament player, he has recently refereed the Dutch Open and the Europe Cup.

VICTOR CUP

One of Germany's major open tournaments sponsored by Victor Rackets, Taiwan. Prize money in October 1984 was £5,300. In 1985 it was added to the Grand Prix circuit.

An unusual feature is the presentation of Victor Cups to the most successful man and woman overall. Nigel Tier won in 1983 and 1984; a 1985 victory could have gained him a free trip to the Victor factory in Taiwan, but the event was cancelled, owing to a sponsorship dispute at the last minute.

VISION

Amongst less skilled players points are often lost because of poor sports vision: lack of acuity, poor binocular vision, slow perception or weak hand-eye co-ordination.

WARD, Roy (Australia)

A big man, a human dynamo and a multi-sport enthusiast who made badminton his priority, he recently won an award as Best Sportswriter on the Women's World Bowls Championship! He was elected President of Victoria BA after eighteen years as Hon. Secretary and has been technical adviser at Brisbane Commonwealth Games and assistant referee at the 1980 World Championships. An IBF Vice-President particularly involved in Rules and Laws (he also helps to make them in Victoria State Parliament) and Chairman of the International Badminton Umpires' Organization.

WATTANASIN, Charoen (Thailand)
Born 4 April 1937, Chiang Mai

Thailand's greatest-ever player – who coached a king, Bhumibol Adulvadej – he might well have gone one better than being born with a silver spoon in his mouth as his father was a goldsmith. The boxing-ring rather than the badminton court could have known him had not a badly cut eye convinced him that opponents are best separated from him by a net.

His dominance of North Thailand events forced him to seek sterner competition in Bangkok when – silver spoon again? – he was given great help by international Pravat Pattabongs and Luang Thamnoon Vudhikorn.

In 1957/8 he made his Thomas Cup début only for Thailand to fall to newcomer Indonesia, 8-1 in the inter-zone final. In 1960 he went to Liverpool University on a business management scholarship given by King Bhumibol.

Here the thinking 'Human Machine' allied stamina to a well-placed smash. He twice won the Glasgow World Invitation – first in 1959, then in 1962, completely dominating Ferry Sonneville 15-5, 15-3. But he was less successful at the AEC final hurdle in 1960, losing to Erland Kops – with whom he had just trained and whom he had beaten in the Far East – and again in 1962. He won fifteen caps (1957-66) and was also All-Malaya champion in 1958, 1959 and 1962 (including the defeat of Finn Kobbero).

Now Managing Director of a big multi-national (Flowers & Fragrances Ltd), he lives in Bangkok. Next door is the Hall of Fame court; financed by HH Princess Sudasiri Sobha, a great enthusiast, it houses the rackets and photos of 'greats' from Kops to Han Jian. His *Let's Play Badminton* (in Thai) went into two editions.

He was appointed Secretary-General of the reformed TBF in 1980 and is both IBF Council member and on the Development sub-committee with responsibility for all Asia and Oceania.

For his services to the game he was awarded the Most Noble Order of the Crown of Thailand.

4   Sarah Doody
5   Claire Hybart
6   Cathy Vigar
7   Rachel McIntosh
8   Alison Hayes
9   Lisa Rees
10 Julie Gardiner
    Gail Davies

WELSH BADMINTON UNION

With badminton centred largely in N. Wales, around Llandudno, local Trevor Williams became its driving force for twenty-five years. In 1927 he founded the WBU and the widely popular Welsh Open, played on Craigside Hydro's indoor tennis courts. Trevor and his Welsh Rarebits were among the first to tour – and defeat – Denmark (1935). In 1938/9 the much improved Tage Madsen became the first foreigner to win the Welsh Open men's singles. (The cup was buried in his garden throughout the war and returned in perfect condition after it.)

Though a founder member of the IBF, lack of halls and transport difficulties between north and south rendered WBU development difficult. Today with sixty sports centres available and 280 clubs affiliated overall, playing strength has switched to the south, which has won the annual Inter-Branch Competition on the last twenty-three occasions. Angela Dickson (née Davies) won the Welsh National ladies' singles sixteen times and ladies' and mixed doubles nine times each between 1961 and 1979. Today Chris Rees and Lyndon Williams, who won the European junior men's doubles in 1983, and Angela Nelson, Sarah Doody and Sian Williams, have great potential.

WELSH RANKING LIST 1986

Men's Singles:
1   Philip Sutton
2   Chris Rees
3   Y.C. Lim
4   Andrew Spencer
5   Barrie Burns
6   John Murtagh
7   Andrew Carlotti
8   Jeff Davies
9   Steven Yates
10 Peter Hybart
Ladies' Singles:
1   Lesley Roberts
2   Denise Lewis
3   Jane Banham

WELSH NATIONAL CHAMPIONSHIPS

Men's Singles

1960-1	G.E. Rowlands
1961-2	G.E. Rowlands
1962-3	M. Anis
1963-4	P.A. Seaman
1964-5	G.E. Rowlands
1965-6	G.E. Rowlands
1966-7	P.A. Seaman
1967-8	G.S.R. Tan
1968-9	H.R. Jennings
1969-70	H.R. Jennings
1970-1	H.R. Jennings
1971-2	H.R. Jennings
1972-3	Not Held
1973-4	H.R. Jennings
1974-5	H.R. Jennings
1975-6	S. Gully
1976-7	H.R. Jennings
1977-8	Y.C. Lim
1978-9	Y.C. Lim
1979-80	P. Sutton
1980-1	P. Sutton
1981-2	P. Sutton
1982-3	P. Sutton
1983-4	P. Sutton
1984-5	P. Sutton
1985-6	C. Rees

Ladies' Singles

1960-1	Mrs J. Warwick
1961-2	Mrs A. Davies[1]
1962-3	Mrs A. Davies[1]
1963-4	Mrs A. Davies[1]
1964-5	Mrs A. Davies[1]
1965-6	Mrs A. Dickson
1966-7	Mrs A. Dickson
1967-8	Mrs A. Dickson
1968-9	Mrs A. Dickson
1969-70	Mrs A. Dickson
1970-1	Mrs A. Dickson
1971-2	Mrs A. Dickson
1972-3	Not Held
1973-4	Mrs A. Dickson
1974-5	Mrs A. Dickson
1975-6	Mrs A. Dickson
1976-7	Mrs S. Brimble
1977-8	Mrs A. Dickson
1978-9	Mrs A. Dickson
1979-80	Miss S. Williams
1980-1	Miss S. Williams
1981-2	Miss A. Nelson
1982-3	Miss S. Williams
1983-4	Miss A. Nelson

1984-5   Miss S. Williams
1985-6   Miss L. Roberts

Men's Doubles
1959-60   J.C. Morgan/G.E. Rowlands
1960-1   J.C. Morgan/G.E. Rowlands
1961-2   S. Dickson/G.E. Rowlands
1962-3   P.A. Seaman/H. Jennings
1963-4   P.A. Seaman/H. Jennings
1964-5   P.A. Seaman/H. Jennings
1965-6   P.A. Seaman/H. Jennings
1966-7   J. Hartstill/D. Colmer
1967-8   P.A. Seaman/H. Jennings
1968-9   P.A. Seaman/H. Jennings
1969-70   H.R. Jennings/A. Fisher
1970-1   H.R. Jennings/A. Fisher
1971-2   H.R. Jennings/A. Fisher
1972-3   Not Held
1973-4   H.R. Jennings/A. Fisher
1974-5   B. Jones/D. Colmer
1975-6   B. Jones/D. Colmer
1976-7   B. Jones/D. Colmer
1977-8   B. Jones/D. Colmer
1978-9   B. Jones/D. Colmer
1979-80   B. Jones/D. Colmer
1980-1   P. Sutton/R. Eastwood
1981-2   C. Rees/L. Williams
1982-3   C. Rees/L. Williams
1983-4   C. Rees/L. Williams
1984-5   C. Rees/L. Williams
1985-6   C. Rees/L. Williams

Ladies' Doubles
1959-60   Mrs C. Davies/Miss E.G. Davies
1960-1   Mrs K. Samuel/Miss E.G. Davies
1961-2   Mrs A. Davies([1])/Mrs H.H.
              Anderson
1962-3   Mrs A. Davies([1])/Mrs H.H.
              Anderson
1963-4   Mrs J. Stewart/Miss B. Fisher
1964-5   Mrs A. Davies([1])/Mrs A. Roberts
1965-6   Mrs M. Withers/Miss B. Fisher
1966-7   Mrs M. Withers/Miss B. Fisher
1967-8   Mrs M. Withers/Miss B. Fisher
1968-9   Mrs M. Withers/Miss B. Fisher
1969-70   Mrs A. Dickson/Miss P. Jeremiah([2])
1970-1   Mrs A. Dickson/Miss P. Jeremiah([2])
1971-2   Mrs A. Dickson/Miss P. Jeremiah([2])
1972-3   Not Held
1973-4   Mrs A. Dickson/Mrs S. Brimble
1974-5   Mrs A. Dickson/Miss B. Fisher
1975-6   Mrs A. Dickson/Mrs S. Brimble
1976-7   Mrs S. Brimble/Mrs L. Blake
1977-8   Mrs S. Brimble/Mrs L. Blake
1978-9   Mrs S. Brimble/Mrs L. Blake
1979-80   Mrs S. Brimble/Mrs L. Blake
1980-1   Miss S. Williams/Miss A. Nelson
1981-2   Miss S. Williams/Miss A. Nelson
1982-3   Miss S. Williams/Miss A. Nelson
1983-4   Miss S. Williams/Miss A. Nelson
1984-5   Miss L. Roberts/Mrs L. Blake
1985-6   Miss L. Roberts/Miss S. Doody

Mixed Doubles
1937-8   F.P. Griffiths/Mrs W. Griffiths
1938-9   F.P. Griffiths/Mrs W. Griffiths

1939-52   No Competition
1952-3   J.C. Morgan/Mrs H. Tomlin
1953-4   J.H. Evans/Mrs N. Anderson
1954-5   No Competition
1955-6   B.E. Fletcher/Miss E.A. Whitehead
1956-7   J.C. Morgan/Mrs H.H. Anderson
1957-8   J.R.C. Weber/Mrs P. Saunders
1958-9   J.C. Morgan/Miss M. Perkins
1959-60   J.C. Morgan/Mrs C. Davies
1960-1   G.E. Rowlands/Miss E.G. Davies
1961-2   S. Dickson/Mrs A. Davies([1])
1962-3   P.A. Seaman/Mrs M. Withers
1963-4   P.A. Seaman/Mrs M. Withers
1964-5   P.A. Seaman/Mrs M. Withers
1965-6   H. Jennings/Mrs A. Dickson
1966-7   H. Jennings/Mrs A. Dickson
1967-8   P.A. Seaman/Miss B. Fisher
1968-9   H.R. Jennings/Mrs A. Dickson
1969-70   H.R. Jennings/Mrs A. Dickson
1970-1   W.D. Colmer/Miss P. Jeremiah([2])
1971-2   A. Fisher/Miss B. Fisher
1972-3   Not Held
1973-4   B. Jones/Mrs S. Alfieri
1974-5   B. Jones/Mrs S. Alfieri
1975-6   H.R. Jennings/Mrs A. Dickson
1976-7   B. Jones/Mrs S. Alfieri
1977-8   B. Jones/Mrs A. Dickson
1978-9   B. Jones/Mrs A. Dickson
1979-80   B. Jones/Mrs A. Dickson
1980-1   Y.C. Lim/Mrs L. Blake
1981-2   Y.C. Lim/Mrs L. Blake
1982-3   Y.C. Lim/Mrs L. Blake
1983-4   L. Williams/S. Doody
1984-5   L. Williams/S. Doody
1985-6   A. Spencer/Miss L. Roberts

([1]) Now Mrs A. Dickson
([2]) Now Mrs P. Wooding

WELSH OPEN
CHAMPIONSHIPS

Men's Singles
1927-8   A. Titherley
1928-9   T.P. Dick
1929-30   D.C. Hume
1930-1   T.P. Dick
1931-2   W. Hamilton
1932-3   W. Hamilton
1933-4   W. Hamilton
1934-5   R.M. White
1935-6   R.M. White
1936-7   T.P. Dick
1937-8   R.M. White
1938-9   Tage Madsen
1939-55   No Competition
1955-6   J.P. Doyle
1956-7   Oon Chong Teik
1957-8   Oon Chong Jin
1958-9   H.T. Findlay
1959-66   No Competition
1966-7   R.J. Mills
1967-8   R.J. Mills
1968-9   H.R. Jennings
1969-70   H.R. Jennings
1970-1   Not Held

England's world class '70s pair, with some 250 caps and innumerable titles between them; Mike Tredgett (*left*) and Ray Stevens

Fashions of 1913! Modelled by Miss M.K. Bateman (*left*) and Miss H. Hogarth, winners of the All-England Ladies' Doubles

Doyen of badminton, Sir George Thomas, Bart. At 48, he is ready to play his 29th and last international — and win both his matches — each in three hard games! (1929)

Much less encumbered are the Men's Doubles runners-up, Dr Crombie (*left*) and H.J.H. Inglis

The Scheeles! Betty and Herbert specially 'snapped' by all-action photographer
Louis Ross just after H.A.E.S. had received the OBE at Buckingham Palace

With seemingly effortless ease, England's Nora Perry plays an elegant backhand
during the Friends Provident Masters in London's huge Albert Hall

Sweden's brilliant all-rounder Thomas Kihlström defends aggressively against a body-smash whilst England's Gillian Clark waits alertly

Side-by-side, Jesper Helledie and Steen Fladberg, Denmark's 1983 Copenhagen World Champions, alertly parry fierce attack

Male chauvinists once hurriedly sought the bar when ladies' doubles were played. Not now, when exciting and superbly fit players such as China's Wu Dixi and Lin Ying are 'on court'

Two of China's early 'greats' (1970): 'Miss Chen' (Yu Niang) (*above*) and Hou Chia Chang (*below*)

England's great '70s Singles rivals. Margaret Beck (now Lockwood) draws long-legged Gillian Gilks to the net with a perfect, tape-hugging net shot

A fitting end-piece! Tjun Tjun (*right*) and Wahjudi (World Champions and six times AEC winners) of Indonesia, which dominated world badminton from 1968–81

1971-2	M.G. Tredgett
1972-3	J. Gardner
1973-4	M.J. Wilkes
1974-5	M.J. Wilkes
1975-6	K. Jolly
1976-7	D. Eddy
1977-8	M. Tredgett
1978-9	K.R. Jolly
1979-80	T. Kilhström
1980-1	R. Stevens
1981-2	S. Baddeley
1982-3	S. Butler
1983-4	S. Butler
1984-5	M. Frost
1985-6	D. Hall

Ladies' Singles

1927-8	Miss R. Finch
1928-9	Mrs R.C. Tragett
1929-30	Miss D.J. Colpoys
1930-1	Miss D.J. Colpoys
1931-2	Miss T. Kingsbury([3])
1932-3	Miss A. Woodroffe([1])
1933-4	Mrs H.S. Uber
1934-5	Miss T. Kingsbury([3])
1935-6	Miss T. Kingsbury([3])
1936-7	Miss G. Graham
1937-8	Miss D.M.C. Young([4])
1938-9	Mrs H.S. Uber
1939-55	No Competition
1955-6	Mrs H.B. Mercer
1956-7	Miss M.A. McIntosh
1957-8	Miss M. O'Sullivan
1958-9	Miss H.M. Ward([5])
1959-66	No Competition
1966-7	Miss D.M. Thompson
1967-8	Miss J.E. Charles([8])
1968-9	Mrs A. Dickson
1969-70	Mrs A. Dickson
1970-1	Not Held
1971-2	Miss B. Fisher
1972-3	Miss B. Beckett
1973-4	Miss B. Beckett
1974-5	Mrs A.E. Statt
1975-6	Miss P. Davies
1976-7	Miss P. Kilvington
1977-8	Mrs G. Gilks
1978-9	Mrs J.P. Perry
1979-80	Miss J. Webster
1980-1	Mrs G. Gilks
1981-2	Miss K. Bridge
1982-3	Mrs S. Podger
1983-4	Mrs K. Beckman
1984-5	Miss C. Hattens
1985-6	Miss F. Elliott

Men's Doubles

1927-8	J.D.M. McCallum/A. Titherley
1928-9	F.L. Treasure/F.B. Malthouse
1929-30	D.C. Hume/L. Nichols
1930-1	T.P. Dick/W. Basil Jones
1931-2	A. Hamilton/W. Hamilton
1932-3	D.C. Hume/R.M. White
1933-4	D.C. Hume/R.M. White
1934-5	W. Hamilton/I. Maconachie
1935-6	I. Maconachie/K.L. Wilson
1936-7	H. Morland/K. Wilson
1937-8	T.P. Dick/H.E. Baldwin
1938-9	T.H. Boyle/J.L. Rankin
1939-55	No Competition
1955-6	J.K.D. Lacey/J.P. Doyle
1956-7	K.R. Derrick/A.R.V. Dolman
1957-8	K.R. Derrick/A.R.V. Dolman
1958-9	A.D. Jordan/H.T. Findlay
1959-66	No Competiton
1966-7	R.J. Mills/R.S. McCoig
1967-8	R.J. Mills/J.G. Pearson
1968-9	M.G. Tredgett/A. Finch
1969-70	H.R. Jennings/A. Fisher
1970-1	No Competition
1971-2	P. Smith/W. Kidd
1972-3	J. McLoy/P. Moore
1973-4	M. Wilkes/A. Connor
1974-5	M. Wilkes/A. Connor
1975-6	T. Stokes/K. Jolly
1976-7	J. Eddy/E. Sutton
1977-8	J. Eddy/E. Sutton
1978-9	R.P. Stevens/M. Tredgett
1979-80	T. Kihlström/B. Froman
1980-1	R. Stevens/M. Tredgett
1981-2	D. Eddy/E. Sutton
1982-3	M. Tredgett/D. Tailor
1983-4	M. Tredgett/M. Dew
1984-5	W. Gilliland/D. Travers
1985-6	M. Dew/D. Tailor

Ladies' Doubles

1927-8	Mrs Thompson-Smith/Miss Reid
1928-9	Mrs R.J. Horsley/Mrs L.W. Myers
1929-30	Mrs R.J. Horsley/Mrs L.W. Myers
1930-1	Mrs R.J. Horsley/Mrs L.W. Myers
1931-2	Mrs H. Hogarth/Miss T. Kingsbury([3])
1932-3	Mrs L.W. Myers/Miss A. Woodroffe([1])
1933-4	Mrs H.S. Uber/Miss T. Kingsbury([3])
1934-5	Mrs H.S. Uber/Miss T. Kingsbury([3])
1935-6	Mrs H.S. Uber/Miss T. Kingsbury([3])
1936-7	Miss D. Graham/Miss G. Graham
1937-8	Mrs L.W. Myers/Miss D.J. Colpoys
1938-9	Mrs H.S. Uber/Miss D. Doveton
1939-55	No Competition
1955-6	Mrs H.B. Mercer/Mrs R. Smyth
1956-7	Mrs J.A. Russell/Miss M.A. McIntosh
1957-8	Mrs E.J. Timperley/Miss P.K. Dolan([6])
1958-9	Miss H.M. Ward([5])/Mrs P.E. Broad
1959-66	No Competition
1966-7	Mrs M. Withers/Miss B. Fisher
1967-8	Miss J.E. Charles([8])/Mrs A. Dickson
1968-9	No Competition
1969-70	Mrs A. Dickson/Miss B. Fisher
1970-1	No Competition
1971-2	Mrs A. Dickson/Miss B. Fisher
1972-3	Miss A. Forrest/Miss K. Whiting
1973-4	Mrs S. Alfieri/Miss B. Beckett
1974-5	Mrs A. Statt/Miss M. Winter
1975-6	Mrs S. Brimble/Mrs A. Dickson
1976-7	Mrs A. Statt/Miss J. Webster
1977-8	Mrs B. Sutton/Mrs R. Ridder
1978-9	Mrs B. Sutton/Mrs J.P. Perry

1979-80	Miss J. Webster/Miss K. Puttick
1980-1	Mrs G. Gilks/Miss P. Kilvington
1981-2	Mrs K. Chapman/Mrs S. Podger
1982-3	Mrs J.P. Perry/Miss J. Webster
1983-4	Miss H. Troke/Mrs K. Chapman
1984-5	Miss H. Troke/Mrs G. Gilks
1985-6	Mrs K. Beckman/Miss S. Halsall

Mixed Doubles

1927-8	F.L. Treasure/Mrs Meredith
1928-9	T.P. Dick/Miss H. Hogarth
1929-30	T.P. Dick/Miss H. Hogarth
1930-1	T.P. Dick/Miss H. Hogarth
1931-2	R.C.F. Nichols/Miss N. Coop([2])
1932-3	T.P. Dick/Miss H. Hogarth
1933-4	D.C. Hume/Mrs H.S. Uber
1934-5	B.P. Cook/Mrs H.S. Uber
1935-6	I. Maconachie/Mrs R.J. Horsley
1936-7	R.M. White/Miss T. Kingsbury([3])
1937-8	T.H. Boyle/Miss O. Wilson
1938-9	T.H. Boyle/Miss O. Wilson
1939-55	No Competition
1955-6	K. Carlisle/Mrs R. Smyth
1956-7	K.R. Derrick/Mrs B. Maxwell
1957-8	Oon Chong Jin/Mrs E.J. Timperley
1958-9	H.T. Findlay/Miss H.M. Ward([5])
1959-66	No Competition
1966-7	R.S. McCoig/Mrs McCoig
1967-8	R.J. Mills/Miss J.E. Charles([8])
1968-9	H.R. Jennings/Mrs A. Dickson
1969-70	H.R. Jennings/Mrs A. Dickson
1970-1	No Competition
1971-2	M.E. Tredgett/Miss K. Whiting
1972-3	C. McIlwaine/Miss B. Beckett
1973-4	M. Wilkes/Miss A. Forrest
1974-5	S.A. Connor/Miss M. Winter
1975-6	H.R. Jennings/Mrs A. Dickson
1976-7	D. Eddy/Miss B. Giles
1977-8	E.C. Stuart/Mrs G. Gilks
1978-9	M. Tredgett/Mrs J.P. Perry
1979-80	W. Gilliland/Miss K. Puttick([9])
1980-1	M. Tredgett/Mrs J.P. Perry
1981-2	W. Gilliland/Mrs K. Chapman
1982-3	D. Tailor/Mrs J.P. Perry
1983-4	M. Tredgett/Mrs K. Chapman
1984-5	M. Dew/Mrs G. Gilks
1985-6	J. Knudsen/Miss N. Nielsen

([1]) Now Mrs R.J. Teague
([2]) Now Mrs D.E.F. Canney
([3]) Now Mrs C.W. Welcome
([4]) Now Mrs J. Warrington
([5]) Now Mrs E.B. Neilsen
([6]) Now Mrs H.T. Findlay
([7]) Now Mrs E.T. Bryan
([8]) Now Mrs W.R. Rickard
([9]) Now Mrs K. Chapman

WEMBLEY ARENA

An 8,000-seater hall, a quarter of a mile from soccer's famous FA Cup Final stadium, it was originally built as a swimming pool for the 1948 Olympics – and filled in in 1977. As the home of the All-England Championships since 1957, it has become badminton's Wimbledon.

WHETNALL, Paul and Sue (Kent and England) 19 February 1947, Birmingham and 11 December 1942, Swanley

Probably the badminton world's most distinguished married couple. Paul won four National titles (three men's singles and one mixed doubles) and thirty-six caps (1969-80); Sue won six National ladies' doubles titles (five with Margaret Boxall), one Commonwealth Games (ladies' doubles), five European Championships (three ladies and two mixed doubles) and four AEC (two ladies' and two mixed doubles) titles as well as forty-one caps (1966-76). Despite all this they loyally supported their county, Kent. Paul was noted for his consistency and footwork, Sue for studied calm and lightning if nonchalant reflex.

In 1970, ahead of their time, they, Ray Sharp, Margaret Boxall (also Kent) and Tyna Barrinaga (USA) turned professional. Unsuccessful, they were reinstated in 1973. Paul became National Coach for the Canadian BA and is now, as a senior and staff coach, in charge of BAE national teams and ESBA and youth squads – and still playing for Kent. Together they wrote *Badminton* (1975).

WHIP

1. The ability of a racket shaft to flex slightly.

Early wooden shafts had much less whip than steel, and steel less than carbon-fibre. Manufacturers have long concentrated on producing, and advertising, more and more whip to give added power and speed to shots. In the early 1980s it was realized that too much whip could lead to difficulty in control and exact placement except by very skilled players.

In the mid-1980s a research scientist, after exhaustive tests, turned the long-held concept upside down by declaring that a rigid shaft (and not too tight stringing) gave greater power, a hypothesis not yet fully accepted.

Shuttle-manufacturers maintained that with too much whip the racket head arced slightly over the feather tips, so damaging them.

2. To strike a shuttle hard, with little backswing by fully utilizing the wrist.

WHITE, Brian (Wiltshire)
Born 3 October 1944,
Salisbury

Unfortunate never to have made the England team, he was recompensed perhaps by being probably the most prolific restricted titles winner with nineteen consecutive Wiltshire men's singles titles, and twelve men's and twenty mixed doubles, the latter with his sister Gillian. He made 169 county appearances and toured Malaysia as BAE team manager 1981. He was no mean cricketer either, still playing for Wiltshire after twenty-two years – 124 top score.

His father, E.H., Wiltshire current BA Chairman, since 1952 inception, was also a long-serving BAE Vice-President.

His mother, Morva, played for Wiltshire 118 consecutive times – all after the age of forty! Now over seventy she still plays a sound game and is, not surprisingly, President of the County Association.

WHITE, Gillian (now Scott)
(Wiltshire)
Born 9 December 1939,
Salisbury

With 204 *consecutive* appearances for Wiltshire before retiring in favour of marriage in 1985, she won nine Wiltshire restricted ladies' singles titles, thirteen ladies' and twenty mixed doubles, the latter with brother Brian.

WHITE, R.M. (Bill) (England)

A 1930s zestful, twenty-four-times capped international who won four consecutive AEC men's titles with D.C. Hume (1932-35) and one mixed with Betty Uber (1938). Heaviest smasher of his day, he could also, machine-gun like, test four or five shuttles so that all were in flight simultaneously. He played also for Middlesex, Gloucestershire and Lancashire.

White was the first top player to wear shorts – and to fly (seventy miles) to a tournament. He was the only one ever to report to the referee still in his dinner-jacket. His father was tragically killed by a Cornish cliff fall the day after Bill won an AEC title.

He joined Liverpool Fire Service in the Blitz and became Chief Fire Officer. After the war he won county archery colours – feathers again.

WILLIAMS, Lyndon
(Glamorgan and Wales)
Born 24 October 1964, Cardiff

'Will' first played when he was six. He won the Glamorgan U.14 Triple Crown for three years in succession, and the first of his thirty-two caps in 1981 v. Ireland. With Chris Rees, with whom he seldom practised, he won the National title 1981/2-1984/5 and the European Junior Championships title in 1983. A year later they reached the quarters of the 1984 European Championships (senior) as the first-ever seeded Welsh pair.

Also, with Sara Doody, he won the National mixed in 1983/4 and 1984/5.

Sociable off-court but fast and hard-hitting on, he has a racket-snapping backhand modelled on that of Flemming Delfs. He prefers doubles to singles: 'Less running; more thinking.'

WILSON, Frank
Born 1 July 1934, Helprington,
Lincs

England's leading referee. Having served a six-year apprenticeship running the Warwickshire Open, he was ready to take over the English National Championships when they were centred at Coventry (1977), near his Leamington Spa home. He served as Herbert Scheele's deputy in the 1980 AEC and has been in charge since 1981. He refereed the 1982 Thomas Cup final at the Albert Hall and was appointed referee for the 1986 European Games in Sweden. Secretary and Chairman of the BUAE, he is a firm believer in 'Get it right on paper: then it's right on the day.' Quiet and unflappable.

WILTSHIRE SCHOLARSHIP

Bill Wiltshire, a Wimbledon S & BC and Surrey BA enthusiast, made a bequest to the BAE in his Will. The interest from it is used to provide 'special coaching for a promising junior who would benefit from it'.

Recent Winners
1983/4 Tracy Salmon (Essex)
1984/5 Richard Harmsworth (Essex)
1985/6 Tracey Allwright (Essex)

WIMBLEDON SQUASH AND BADMINTON CLUB

Its four courts, homely lounge and bar, and tiny 'goldfish bowl' spectator area (from which players can be seen but not heard), situated within sound of thundering main line Southern expresses, has long been regarded as England's premier club. From the 1950s, top players in the South, including the Choongs, joined it to be sure of the essential competitive play engendered by its strict sectioning.

It was the home of the Surrey Championships, the All-England Junior, the AEC qualifying rounds, and the 'Wizards' and 'Witches' for many years, as well as, more recently, of the Slazenger Junior Invitation Tournament.

The club won the Europe Cup in 1980 and in 1984 built three more courts.

Noel Goddard was the first Director, followed after the war by Secretary Tony Hunt, who held that position for some thirty-seven years. Building was started in 1936, and a Surrey v. Middlesex match played in a half-completed club.

WING

General term referring either to the forehand or to the backhand side.

WINNER

Shot that wins a rally outright.

WITCHES BC

Veteran ladies' club founded at Wimbledon BC in 1962 by Esmé Andrews, Nancy Horner, Betty Grace, Evelyn Windsor-Aubrey, Audrey Stone and Sylvia Ripley, when their county and international days were over. Later they were joined by Surrey's great England foursome Iris Rogers, June Timperley, Jennie Horton and Barbara Carpenter.

A formidable coven!

WIZARDS BC

Male veterans (some over seventy) of former county and international standard who still take weekly exercise at Wimbledon BC. On occasion they mingle with their female counterparts, the Witches BC (q.v.).

WOBBLER

A shuttle that wobbles erratically in flight and has therefore to be discarded. Such a defect is generally caused by the lead weight not being centrally positioned in the cork base, more rarely by feathers being inserted at an incorrect angle or the stitching losing tension and so the feathers, their circular shape.

C.Y. WONG

Badminton breeds enthusiasts: of them C.Y. is surely one of the most high-powered. It was only his steadfast resolve, even when badly outnumbered, that kept unoffending Taiwan in the IBF when other members sought her expulsion to allow, politically, China's entry.

Between flights across the infamous India-China 'Hump' during the war, he played badminton eight hours a day with local Chinese on jungle-clearing courts – and even organized championships! Since his return in 1949, he has ceaselessly played and organized Taiwan badminton.

Now aged seventy-four, retired from his job of Director of Communications for Air America, he still trains himself *and* top Taiwanese players.

WONG, Peng Soon, MBE (Malaya)

One of the all-time greats, he won the Malaysian Open singles eight times (five in succession) and the mixed three times, twice with his sister, between 1940 and 1953, and the Singapore National singles seven times and the doubles three times between 1938 and 1951.

His greatest triumphs were undoubtedly in losing only one match (to Dave Freeman) in the first three Thomas Cup series and winning the AEC title four times (three in succession) between 1950 and 1955. His last victory, against a very fit Eddy Choong, lasted nearly seventy minutes (15-7, 14-17, 15-10). Thirty-seven years of age, he was the oldest man to win the title since Sir George Thomas.

Wong never appeared to run. He had a steely backhand, clears and drops of impeccable length, very accurate placement – and patience. He always wore trousers and had a mannerism of twiddling his racket round before serving.

On retirement he turned professional, coached in Malaysia, Singapore and Thailand and was awarded the MBE. In 1982 he suffered a stroke after playing

Korea's woman champion, Sun Ai Hwang. ('I said I'd take on the best men when young; best women when old.') He was exercising his right side within six months. An indomitable player!

Favourite maxim: 'Don't talk big. Think big – and play with big heart.'

WOOD SHOTS

Shots mistimed so that the shuttle is hit by the frame of the racket-head, not the strings. With the advent of the metal racket-head, they are beginning to be known as 'frame-shots' – though custom dies hard. It has long been a moot (and often changed) point of law as to whether a shot so mis-hit should gain advantage or be faulted. Currently legal.

WORLD BADMINTON

The official publication of the IBF. Edited by and the brainchild of its Secretary, Herbert Scheele, it first appeared in January 1972. On his retirement in April 1978, after thirty-three issues, it was produced in Canada under the wing of former Canadian BA President Lorne Wortman.

March 1980 saw the production transferred to Scotland under an editorial board of Craig Reedie (IBF), Willie Kemp (a professional journalist) and Scottish BU's Judy Budge (replaced in 1982 by IBF's Wendy Bennett). There it flourished until March 1984 when, with Willie Kemp replaced by Ronnie Rowan (q.v.), it was taken over by IBF HQ in Cheltenham. In September 1984 P.E. Nielsen, the new President, replaced Craig Reedie, and in 1985 Julie Hutchings replaced Wendy Bennett.

It has steadily grown with the world-wide spread of the game to cover full and interestingly all its facets with articles (and photographs) by leading administrators, players and reporters. Available on subscription from the IBF for all who wish to know the full, fascinating story of badminton.

WORLD BADMINTON FEDERATION

A breakaway body from the forty-four-year-old IBF formed on 24 February 1978 by thirteen Asian and six African Associations convened in Hong Kong by Teh Gin Sooi (Malaysia). Indonesia and Japan did not take part.

WBF's dissatisfaction was based on (1) refusal to expel Taiwan to allow the People's Republic of China to join IBF; (2) desire for a 'one nation, one vote' voting system (large numbers of affiliated players, and Thomas and Uber Cup entry gave some nations one or two additional votes); (3) disapproval of England, Wales, Scotland and Ireland's being treated as separate associations; (4) disapproval of S. Africa's membership.

WBF immediately promoted a World Invitation Championship. As it was not IBF sanctioned, participants knowingly rendered themselves liable to ineligibility for IBF events. WBF members responded with a partial boycott of the All-England Championships and Thomas Cup withdrawals. Talks were, however, soon entered into but it was not until 26 May 1981 that differences were settled when a Deed of Unification was signed in Tokyo by Stellan Mohlin (IBF) and Air Marshal Dawee Chullaspya (WBF).

As a result, (1) Taiwan BA became known as Chinese-Taipei BA; (2) associations with more than 50,000 members had one extra vote only; (3) three rules, dealing only with membership, were to be applied on 'one nation, one vote' basis; (4) S. Africa agreed not to take part in Thomas or Uber Cup competitions or World Championships; (5) all five continents were to be represented on a Council enlarged to twelve.

WORLD CHAMPIONSHIPS

The All-England Championships were long regarded as the world's most prestigious tournament. In the early 1970s it was felt that there should be an official World Championships. Finance, or lack of it, seemed likely to be the only possible impediment.

Wisely a trial run was made on 12-15 November 1972, with a World Invitation Tournament held in Jakarta. Although only men's events (twenty-four players from twelve countries in each) were held. It was a resounding success with 10-12,000 crowds each session.

In the singles, Hartono beat Pri 5 and 2; in the all-Indonesian doubles final, J. Wahjudi and Tjun Tjun beat A. Chandra and C. Hadinata, 10 and 10, to gain probably the world's biggest trophy, a silver-gilt model court with players, surmounted by a globe (presented by S.R. Ruia of the ABC).

Accordingly in 1975 an IBF vote of 64-0 decided the first World Championships should be held at Malmö, Sweden in 1977. These were followed by Jakarta 1980, Copenhagen 1983 and Calgary 1985. (See *Championship Results*.) 1987 will be in Beijing.

As Thomas and Uber Cup competitions were held simultaneously in 1984, it was decided that World Championships could be held biennially instead of triennially.

Date/Venue
1977   Malmo
1980   Jakarta
1983   Copenhagen
1985   Calgary

Men's Singles
1977   F. Delfs
1980   R. Hartono
1983   I. Sugiarto
1985   Han Jian

Ladies' Singles
1977   L. Køppen
1980   V. Wiharjo
1983   Li Lingwei
1985   H. Aiping

Men's Doubles
1977   Tjun Tjun/Wahjudi
1980   A. Chandra/C. Hadinata
1983   S. Fladberg/J. Helledie
1985   Joo Bong Park/Moon Soo Kim

Ladies' Doubles
1977   E. Toganoo/E. Ueno
1980   N. Perry/J. Webster
1983   Lin Ying/Wu Dixi
1985   H. Aiping/Li Lingwei

Mixed Doubles
1977   S. Skovgaard/L. Køppen
1980   C. Hadinata/I. Wigoeno
1983   T. Kihlström/N. Perry
1985   Joo Bong Park/Yoo Sang Hee

WORLD GAMES

A one-off gathering of sports that could not gain Olympic status, held in Santa Clara, California, July 1981. Although poorly publicized and organized, it served badminton well as it early showed the strength of the IBF's new member, China, which took four of the five titles.

MS   Chen Changjie
LS   Zhang Ailing
MD   Sun Zhian and Yao Ximing
LD   Zhang Ailing and Liu Xia
Mxd D   T. Kihlstrom and G. Gilks

WORLD INVITATION TOURNAMENT

Several tournaments so named have been held but the most famous and long-lasting was the first of a series held in Glasgow's 3,000-seater Kelvin Hall in 1954. It was backed by the Scottish BU, run largely by David Bloomer and John McCarry, and held two years in three (to avoid a clash with the Thomas Cup) in a week proximate to the All-England. With a carefully selected invitation list, good play, manners and fun were in evidence.

Craig Reedie, apprentice since 1960, shouldered Bloomer's mantle in 1969. After twelve tournaments, in 1977 it did not take place because of foreign players' ever-growing world-wide commitments.

The first WIT in Asia was played in 1972 as an experimental forerunner for the 1977 World Championships. Others gave useful organizational data and magnificent play.

WRIGHT, L.D. ('Les')

Cheerful London East Ender who was appointed Assistant Chief Coach to Roger Mills and, on the latter's retirement, Staff Coach. Now one of the four BAE Senior Coaches, he has lectured at European and world seminars and is author of *Successful Badminton*.

WRIGHT, Len D.

A schoolmaster who in 1965 launched the English Schools' Badminton Association (q.v.) from Whitehaven, a Cumbrian backwater.

WRIST

In contrast to tennis, badminton, with its very light racket ($3\frac{1}{2}$ oz, 99 gm) and much ligher shuttle (73-85 grains, 4.74-5.52 gm) employs the wrist to greater or lesser degree in all strokes except low and drive serves. Giving last-second deception *and* extra power, it is of prime importance.

Like the universal joint of a car, the wrist (and forearm) can rotate virtually through 180 degrees. This enables the racket to be turned left or right fractionally before impact to change (deceptively) the shuttle's apparent direction of flight, or to cut it.

The wrist also moves strongly backwards (cocks) and forwards (uncocks) as well as side to side. In all power strokes, the wrist is cocked in preparation and, in execution, strongly uncocked just before impact. This adds wrist speed to arm speed: it is *audibly* illustrated by the very much louder 'swish' resulting when wrist and arm are used rather than only the arm.

Uncocking the wrist also affects trajectory. In the smash, it helps in hitting steeply downwards; in lob or high serve, in hitting high upwards. If the uncocking of the wrist is delayed to the last possible fraction of a second ('holding the shot') in an attacking lob, clear or flick service, an over-eager opponent may be 'wrong-footed' as the shuttle is flicked over his head.

WRONG FOOT, To

To deceive an opponent, by delayed wrist action, into moving in the direction opposite to that in which the shuttle is actually hit. Thus the opponent (a) fails to reach the shuttle at all; or (b) off balance, is forced into making a weak or uncontrolled shot; or (c) is rendered hesitant to move early to attack other shots.

See *Deception.*

WU, Dixi (China)
Born 1963

Perhaps the only player by her skill ever to force the IBF to abrogate a rule.

With regular partner Lin Ying, she made an impressive début at the 1981 Indian Masters as 14-17, 15-13, 15-17 runners-up to World Champions Perry and Webster.

In the 1982 AEC (with Lin) her veering, erratically flighted reverse cut serve (q.v.) almost as unplayable as a McEnroe blockbuster, made Indonesia's experienced Verawaty and Damayanti look like hesitant novices – 8 and 5 – and the game almost a farce.

In 1983 the title was lost to compatriots Wu Jianqiu and Xu Rong (16-18, 15-11, 6-15), but two months later in Copenhagen they snatched the World Championship crown from Perry and Webster (15-4, 15-12).

In 1984 they regained the coveted AEC title in one of the most exciting ladies' doubles' ever seen at Wembley against the almost fanatical resistance of Korea's Yun Ja Kim and San Hee Yoo (15-8, 8-15, 17-14). Still more triumphs followed: the Alba Quartz, British Airways Masters and a team Uber Cup gold. In the latter event they had only one double-figure score against them (by Gilks and Beckman) and trounced Denmark's best, Kjaer and Larsen, 15-0, 15-1.

Wu injured her ankle in the 1985 AEC quarters but after a controversial delay narrowly beat Gilks and Perry – only to scratch from the semis. Lost 9-15, 18-14, 9-15 to Aiping and Lingwei in the World Championships, but on the Alba Quartz beat Kim and Yoo (4 and 5) who had beaten Aiping and Lingwei 15-11, 11-15, 15-3 in the semis.

She is endowed with typical Chinese speed, power, tireless stamina and rock-like defence – as well as a lively sense of fun and a liking for Western 'pop' and clothes.

A pity perhaps that her name is pronounced 'Dicee' – not 'Dixi'.

After losing in the Uber Cup final 10-15, 13-15 to Indonesia's Amazon Fajrin and tiny Kusmiate (a completely untried pair) in a possible diplomatic throw-away to avoid an Indonesian whitewash, announced her retirement.

WYATT, Stuart, OBE, BEM
1904 (Fareham) –
5 September 1985

The BEM was awarded for twenty-five years as Divisional Commander of Special Constables, the OBE for equally meritorious service to badminton (1972). Wyatt played against fellow Hampshireman Sir George Thomas and represented his county seventy-two times – as compared with his wife 'Mims" hundred-plus appearances.

With his playing days behind him, he has given great service as an administrator: President of the BUAE (1963-6), Chairman of the BAE Council (1961-70), Vice-President (1961-5) and President (1965-1985).

On a still wider front: IBF Council member (1955-69), Vice-President (1969-74), Chairman of the Council (1974-6) and President (1974-6).

Six feet two inches (1.87 metres) of genial charm and diplomacy, who never overlooked the smaller cogs in the badminton machine.

Y

YANG YANG (China)

A brilliant left-hander of touch, and accuracy to the side lines, rather than power, he won all his 1984 Thomas Cup matches with only three double-figure scores against him.

He became China's National Champion by beating Zhao Jinhua but lost soon after in the 1985 AEC to veteran Swie King whom Zhao demolished. He has beaten Frost on several occasions but seeded 3/4, lost 8 and 5 to him in the World Championships. After winning all his team games, he was only runner-up to Zhao in the 1985 ABC championships.

Won the 1986 Japanese Open and in the Thomas Cup final justified his promotion over Han Jian as No. 1 by beating Sugiarto 7 and 1 to ensure a Chinese victory.

YAO, Ximing (China)
Born 15 August 1956

Born in Zhanjiang, 1,400 miles from badminton's hub, Peking, he did not start playing until thirteen in its steamy upper 80°s. After he was adopted as a teacher of physical culture, full-time badminton training produced a grooved backhand serve, a terrifying jump smash and aggression as controlled as his temperament.

He won the World Games men's doubles and was undefeated against England's best in China's 1981 tour. He won four of his 1982 Thomas Cup matches, including a 15-6, 15-1 defeat of Fladberg and Helledie (World Champions a year later). It was he and partner Sun Zhian who won the incredible turnabout match which gained China the trophy, 4-3. Pulverized 3-15 in the second

game by a whirlwind Kartono and Heryanto (1981 AEC Champions), they turned the tables 15-1 in under five minutes. An unforgettable display! But they lost in the quarters of the 1983 World Championship to Indonesians Hadinata and Ertanto.

YATES, Nick (Kent and England)
Born 1962, Lee Green, Kent

After winning the English National U.18 title in 1978/9, he was quickly pushed to the top, together with the other 'likely lad', S. Baddeley, with whom he vied for No. 1 ranking. Injury and illness have hampered his chances of a major title but he has beaten both Sugiarto (booed off court) and Arbi, under their own humid conditions.

His greatest victory was the defeat in 1984 of the AEC holder Luan Jin. Had he won the next round against Kjeldsen, he would have been the first English AEC semi-finalist since 1939.

He lost unexpectedly to India's Modi in the 1982 Commonwealth Games final, beat Nierhoff for the fourth successive time to give England the 1984 European team title, and was unbeaten in Korea's 1984 England tour.

He won the 1985 German Open, beating T. Carlsen 18-16 after a seventy-stroke rally at 16-16, and then 15-0!

With his own specially devised training programme, he has stamina and a wide range of consistent and often cut strokes. Thrives on a war of attrition. He already has eighty-four caps.

Hit a new high in 1986 Chinese Open by defeating Han Jian.

A computer enthusiast.

YOO, Sang Hee (S. Korea)
Age: 22

One of Korea's fast-developing batch of superbly fit girls, Yoo first hit the headlines by winning the AEC singles (1983). With Yun Ja Kim she narrowly lost the 1984 AEC final to Lin Ying and Wu Dixi (having beaten Xu Rong and Wu Jianqiu in the semis) in one of the most exciting finals. They then won all but one of their Uber Cup matches (including a 15-0, 15-0 defeat of Malaysia's Poon and Hoon) to help S. Korea to Bronze.

In the 1985 AEC, as No. 2 seeds, they lost tamely in the semis' 5 and 9 to ultimate winners Li Lingwei and Han Aiping. They regained form in the World Championships and lost to them again only by the narrowest of margins, 10-15, 15-9, 17-18. Then Yoo, unseeded with Park, shattered Denmark, Sweden and England's best to win the mixed.

1986 started inauspiciously. She and Kim lost to S. Korea's unseeded second string 5-15, 15-6, 8-15 in the AEC Final and 1 and 6 to China's Li and Han in the Uber Cup semis.

A very talented all-rounder.

YUKI, Hiroe (Japan)
Age: 37

Japan's most successful singles player, she won the AEC trophy outright with victories in 1969, 1974, 1975 and 1977, beating such 'greats' as N. Takagi, G. Gilks (twice), L. Køppen. A robust competitor with a powerful backhand and finely balanced movement.

Z

ZAN, Moe Thida (Burma)
Born 1970

A fifteen-year-old high school student who defeated experienced Kyaw Kyaw to win the 1985 national title. Of a badminton family, she started playing at nine years old. In 1980 she won the U.11, U.13, U.15 and U.17 age-group titles! She has played for her country in the Nepal-Burma and Soviet-Burma Goodwill Matches and the King Mahendra Memorial Tournament (Nepal).

ZHANG, AILING (China)
Born 17 December 1958

Picked for China while still in her teens, Zhang, a Shanghai PE instructor, could not prove her ability internationally for five years whilst China protractedly negotiated admission to the IBF.

In July 1981, at the World Games (q.v.) at Santa Clara, California, then little known, she made a great impact in both singles and doubles. Her brilliance was underlined by the fact that she beat Lene Koppen (AE Champion in 1979 and 1980) 11-4, 11-1, and, in the final, the very powerful Sun Ai Hwang who had demolished Lene in the 1981 AEC final. She also won the doubles with Liu Xia, beating then World Champions Nora Perry and Jane Webster. She beat Lene Koppen again in September in the English Masters, as well as winning the doubles with Xia.

Her motto became 'I fear no player' and she proved it with brilliant results including All-England singles victories in 1982 and 1983. But she lost to her twenty-year-old compatriot Han Aiping on the ultimate quest for the World Championships.

In 1984 she won all her three singles, though as third string to Aiping and Lingwei (against Indonesia, Japan and England), in the Uber Cup to help her country win that coveted trophy by an unprecedented five 5-0 victories against the world's premier nations. Marriage rumour links her name with that of equally talented Chen Changjie, and she herself has said, 'I am getting too old for the game. It is time I retired to make way for younger players' – of whom there are a formidable number. She did not appear at the 1985 AEC or World Championships.

Zhang's singles skills were the complementary ones of power from back-court and deftness of touch at the net linked by speed of foot.

ZHAO, Jianhua (China)
Born 21 April 1965

A left-handed, 6-foot-plus (1.82 metres), nineteen-year-old bolt from the blue. Not picked for the 1984 Thomas Cup, in October, unheralded, he lost in the Scandinavian Cup semis' 8-15, 7-15 to Han Jian, who in turn lost 10-15, 9-15 to Frost.

And yet Zhao shortly beat Frost in both the Scottish and Japanese Opens – and finally 6-15, 15-10, 18-15 on his first appearance in the all-important 1985 AEC, having beaten Swie King, 15-10, 15-5 *en route*. He beat his China National conqueror, Yang Yang, in the 1985 ABC championships. High hopes of winning the 1985 World Championships were sadly dashed when he had to be flown home from Calgary with pneumonia without a shuttle struck. After a twelve month lay-off, showed all his old venom in defeating Chinese Open winner Sugiarto, and then Misbun Sidek, to win the 1986 Malaysian Open.

Tall, almost gangling, he moves fast, is 'incredibly deceptive' and hits his jump smashes tirelessly, angled, cut and steep, with all the ferocity of the horror films he loves. Add to this strong defence and varied strokes. A great prospect; despite disliking training, he learns fast.

ZHU, Ze

'Unity is strength' is his watchword, and as Vice-President of the Asian BC (1978) he did much to bring together IBF and WBF. Vice-President IBF from 1981 and President of BA of People's Republic of China. Given IBF Distinguished Service Award, 1985.

ZING (or ZIP) AREA

The 18 inches (0.45 metres) or so on either side of the point of impact of power strokes in which the racket-head by perfect timing should be moving at its fastest to give maximum impetus to the shuttle.

Appendix

The Laws of Badminton

as revised in the year 1939 and adopted by THE INTERNATIONAL BADMINTON FEDERATION subsequently revised up to date
Note: Imperial measurements, some of which vary from the metric measurements, are quoted in brackets and comply with the Laws.

COURT
1. (a) The Court shall be laid out as in the following Diagram 'A' (except in the case provided for in paragraph (b) of this Law) and to the measurements there shown, and shall be defined preferably by white or yellow lines or, if this is not possible, by other easily distinguishable lines, 40mm (1½ inches) wide.
       In marking the court the width 40mm (1½ inches) of the centre lines shall be equally divided between the right and left service courts; the width 40mm (1½ inches) of the short service line and long service line shall fall within the 3.96 metres (13 feet) measurement given as the length of the service court; and the width 40mm (1½ inches) of all other boundary lines shall fall within the measurements given.
   (b) Where space does not permit of the marking out of a court for doubles, a court may be marked out for singles only as shown in Diagram 'B'. The back boundary lines become also the long service lines, and the posts, or the strips of material representing them as referred to in Law 2, shall be placed on the side lines.

POSTS
2. The posts shall be 1.55 metres (5 feet 1 inch) in height from the surface of the court. They shall be sufficiently firm to keep the net strained as provided in Law 3, and shall be placed on the side boundary lines of the court. Where this is not practicable, some method must be employed for indicating the position of the side boundary line where it passes under the net, e.g. by the use of a thin post or strip of material, not less than 40 mm (1½ inches) in width, fixed to the side boundary line and rising vertically to the net cord. Where this is in use on a court marked for doubles it shall be placed on the boundary line of the doubles court irrespective of whether singles or doubles are being played.

NET
3. The net shall be made of fine natural cord or artificial fibre of a dark colour and even thickness not less than 15 mm (⅝ inch) and not more than 20 mm (¾ inch) mesh. It shall be firmly stretched from post to post, and shall be 760 mm (2 feet 6 inches) in depth. The top of the net shall be 1.524 metres (5 feet) in height from the floor at the centre, and 1.55 metres (5 feet 1 inch) at the posts, and shall be edged with a 75 mm (3

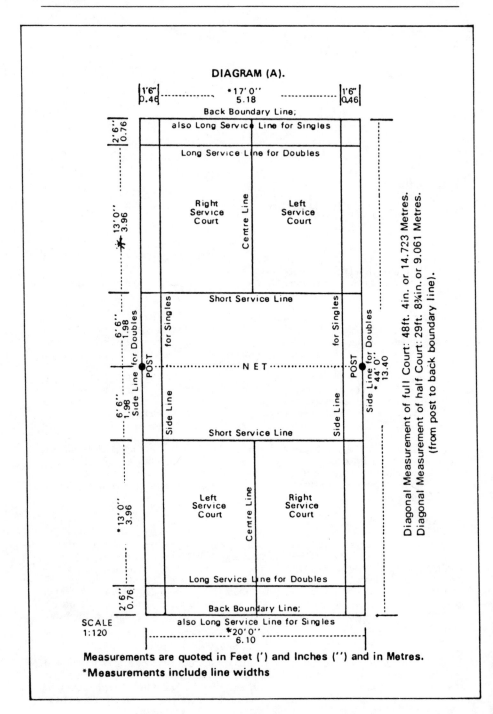

DIAGRAM (A).

Measurements are quoted in Feet (') and Inches ('') and in Metres.
*Measurements include line widths

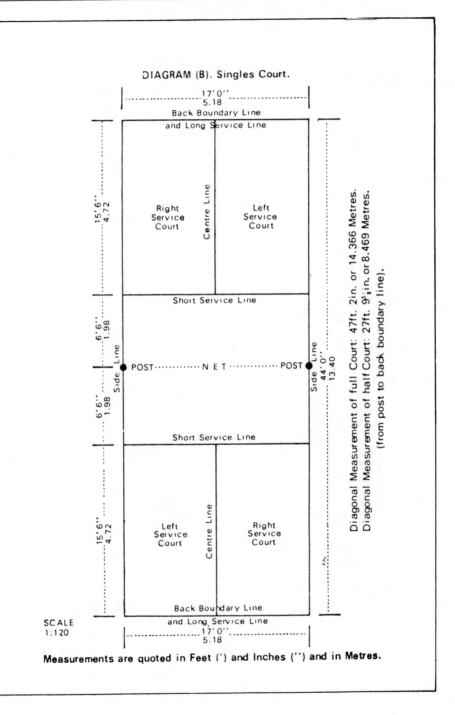

DIAGRAM (B). Singles Court.

Measurements are quoted in Feet (') and Inches ('') and in Metres.

inches) white tape doubled and supported by a cord or cable run through the tape and strained over and flush with the top of the posts.

SHUTTLE AND RACKET
THE SHUTTLE
Principles

4. The shuttle may be made from natural, synthetic or other manufactured product or any of those combinations.

The feel on the racket and the flight characteristics, generally, should be similar to those produced by the natural feathered shuttle, which has a cork base covered by a thin layer of leather.

Having Regard to the Principles:

(a) **General Design:**
    (i) The shuttle shall have 14 to 16 feathers fixed in the base.
    (ii) The feathers can have a variable length from 64 mm to 70 mm. (2½ to 2¾ inches), but in each shuttle they shall be the same length when measured from the tip to the top of the base.
    (iii) The tips of the feathers shall form a circle with a diameter within the range of 58 mm to 68 mm (2¼ to 2⅜ inches).
    (iv) The feathers shall be fastened firmly with thread or other suitable material.
    (v) The base shall be
      — 25 mm to 28 mm (1 inch to 1⅛ inches) in diameter.
      — rounded on the bottom.

(b) **Weight:**
The shuttle shall weigh from 4.74 to 5.50 grammes (73 to 85 grains).

(c) **Non-feathered Shuttles:**
    (i) The skirt, or simulation of feathers in synthetic or other manufactured materials, replaces natural feathers.
    (ii) The base is described in paragraph 4(a)(v).
    (iii) Measurements shall be the same as in paragraph 4(a)(i)-(iv). However, because of the difference in the specific gravity and behaviour of synthetic and manufactured materials in comparison with feathers, a variation of up to ten per cent in the stated measurements is acceptable.

(d) **Pace and Flight:**
A shuttle shall be deemed to be of correct pace when it is hit by a player with a full underhand stroke from a spot immediately above one back boundary line in a direction parallel to the sidelines and at an upward angle, to fall not less than 530 mm (1 foot 9 inches) and not more than 990 mm (3 feet 3 inches) short of the other back boundary line.

(e) **Modifications:**
Subject to there being no variation in the general design, pace and flight of the shuttle, modifications in the above specifications may be made, with the approval of the national organization concerned:
    (i) in places where atmospheric conditions due either to altitude or climate make the standard shuttle unsuitable; or
    (ii) if special circumstances exist which make it otherwise necessary in the interests of the game.

RACKET
(f) (i) The hitting surface of the racket shall be flat and consist of a pattern of crossed strings connected to a frame and alternatively interlaced or bonded where they cross − and the stringing pattern shall be generally uniform and, in particular, not less dense in the centre than in any other area.
    (ii) The frame of the racket, including the handle, shall not exceed 680 mm in overall length and 230 mm in overall width.
    (iii) The overall length of the head shall not exceed 290 mm.
    (iv) The strung surface shall not exceed 280 mm. in overall length and 220 mm. in overall width.

(v) The frame, including the handle, and the strings
   — shall be free of attached objects and protrusions, other than those utilized solely and specifically to limit or prevent wear and tear, or vibration, or to distribute weight, or to secure the handle by cord to the player's hand, and which are reasonable in size and placement for such purposes; and
   — shall be free of any device which makes it possible for a player to change materially the shape of the racket.

The International Badminton Federation shall rule on the question of whether any racket or prototype complies with the above specifications or is otherwise approved or not approved for play. Such ruling may be undertaken on its own initiative or upon application by any party with a bona fide interest therein, including any player, equipment manufacturer or National Association or member thereof.

PLAYERS

5. (a) The word 'Player' applies to all those taking part in a game.
   (b) The game shall be played, in the case of the doubles game, by two players a side, and in the case of the singles game, by one player a side.
   (c) The side for the time being having the right to serve shall be called the 'In' side, and the opposing side shall be called the 'Out' side.

THE TOSS

6. Before commencing play the opposing sides shall toss, and the side winning the toss shall have the option of:
   (a) Serving first; or
   (b) Not serving first; or
   (c) Choosing ends.

The side losing the toss shall then have choice of any alternative remaining.

SCORING

7. (a) The doubles and the men's singles game consists of 15 points provided that, when the score is 13-all, the side which first reached 13 has the option of 'setting' the game to 5, and that when the score is 14-all, the side which first reached 14 has the option of 'setting' the game to 3. After a game has been 'set' the score is called 'love all', and the side which first scores 5 or 3 points, according as the game has been 'set' at 13-all or 14-all, wins the game. In either case the claim to 'set' the game must be made before the next service is delivered after the score has reached 13-all or 14-all.
   (b) The ladies' singles game consists of 11 points. Provided that when the score is '9-all' the player who first reached 9 has the option of 'setting' the game to 3, and when the score is '10-all' the player who first reached 10 has the option of 'setting' the game to 2.
   (c) A side rejecting the option of 'setting' at the first opportunity shall not thereby be debarred from 'setting' if a second opportunity arises.
   (d) Notwithstanding paragraph (a) above, it is permissible by prior arrangement for only one game to be played and also for this to consist of 21 points, in which case 'setting' shall be as for the game of 15 points with scores of 19 and 20 being substituted for 13 and 14 respectively.
   (e) In handicap games 'setting' is not permitted.

8. The opposing sides shall contest the best of three games, unless otherwise agreed. The players shall change ends at the commencement of the second game and also of the third game (if any). In the third game the players shall change ends when the leading score reaches:
   (a) 8 in a game of 15 points;
   (b) 6 in a game of 11 points;
or, in handicap events, when one of the sides has scored half the total number of points required to win the game (the next highest number being taken in case of fractions). When it has been agreed to play only one game the players shall change ends as

provided above for the third game.

In a game of 21 points, the players shall change ends when the leading score reaches 11 or in handicap games as indicated above.

If, inadvertently, the players omit to change ends as provided in this Law at the score indicated, the ends shall be changed immediately the mistake is discovered, and the existing score shall stand.

DOUBLES PLAY

9. (a) It having been decided which side is to have the first service, the player in the right-hand service court of that side commences the game by serving to the player in the service court diagonally opposite. If the latter player returns the shuttle before it touches the ground, it is to be returned by one of the 'In' side, and then returned by one of the 'Out' side, and so on, until a fault is made or the shuttle ceases to be 'in play'. (*Vide* paragraph (b).) If a fault is made by the 'In' side, its right to continue serving is lost, as only one player on the side beginning a game is entitled to do so (*Vide* Law 11), and the opponent in the right-hand service court then becomes the server; but if the service is not returned, or the fault is made by the 'Out' side, the 'In' side scores a point. The 'In' side players then change from one service court to the other, the service now being from the left-hand service court to the player in the service court diagonally opposite. So long as a side remains 'in', service is delivered alternately from each service court into the one diagonally opposite, the change being made by the 'In' side when, and only when, a point is added to its score.

   (b) The first service of a side in each innings shall be made from the right-hand service court. A 'service' is delivered as soon as the shuttle is struck by the server's racket. The shuttle is thereafter 'in play' until it touches the ground, or until a fault or 'let' occurs, or except as provided in Law 19. After the service is delivered, the server and the player served to may take up any positions they choose on their side of the net, irrespective of any boundary lines.

10. The player served to may alone receive the service, but should the shuttle touch, or be struck by, his partner the 'In' side scores a point. No player may receive two consecutive services in the same game, except as provided in Law 12.

11. Only one player of the side beginning a game shall be entitled to serve in its first innings. In all subsequent innings each partner shall have the right, and they shall serve consecutively. The side winning a game shall always serve first in the next game, but either of the winners may serve and either of the losers may receive the service.

12. If a player serves out of turn, or from the wrong service court (owing to a mistake as to the service court from which service is at the time being in order), *and his side wins the rally*, it shall be a 'Let', provided that such 'Let' be claimed and allowed, or ordered by the umpire, before the next succeeding service is delivered.

If a player of the 'Out' side standing in the wrong service court is prepared to receive the service when it is delivered, *and his side wins the rally*, it shall be a 'Let', provided that such 'Let' be claimed and allowed, or ordered by the umpire, before the next succeeding service is delivered.

If in either of the above cases the side at fault *loses the rally*, the mistake shall stand and the players' positions shall not be corrected.

Should a player inadvertently change sides when he should not do so, and the mistake not be discovered until after the next succeeding service has been delivered, the mistake shall stand, and a 'Let' cannot be claimed or allowed, and the players' positions shall not be corrected.

SINGLES PLAY

13. In singles Laws 9 and 12 hold good, except that:

   (a) The players shall serve from and receive service in their respective right-hand service courts only when the server's score is 0 or an even number of points in the game, the service being delivered from and received in their respective left-hand service courts when the server's score is an odd number of points. Setting does not affect this sequence.

(b) Both players shall change service courts after each point has been scored.

FAULTS

14. A fault made by a player of the side which is 'In' puts the server out; if made by a player whose side is 'Out', it counts a point to the 'In' side.
It is a fault:

(a) If in serving, (i) the initial point of contact with the shuttle is not on the base of the shuttle, or (ii) any part of the shuttle at the instant of being struck be higher than the server's waist, or (iii) if at the instant of the shuttle being struck the shaft of the racket be not pointing in a downward direction to such an extent that the whole of the head of the racket is discernibly below the whole of the server's hand holding the racket.

(b) If, in serving, the shuttle does not pass over the net, or falls into the wrong service court (i.e., into the one not diagonally opposite to the server), or falls short of the short service line, or beyond the long service line, or outside the side boundary lines of the service court into which service is in order.

(c) If the server's feet are not in the service court from which service is at the time being in order, or if the feet of the player receiving the service are not in the service court diagonally opposite until the service is delivered. (*Vide* Law 16.)

(d) If, once the service has started, any player makes preliminary feints or otherwise intentionally baulks his opponent, or if any player deliberately delays serving the shuttle or in getting ready to receive it so as to obtain an unfair advantage. (When the server and receiver have taken up their respective positions to serve and receive, the first forward movement of the server's racket constitutes the start of the service and such must be continuous thereafter.)

(e) If, either in service or play, the shuttle falls outside the boundaries of the court, or passes through or under the net, or fails to pass the net, or touches the roof or side walls, or the person or dress of a player. (A shuttle falling on a line shall be deemed to have fallen in the court or service court of which such line is a boundary.)

(f) If, when in play, the initial point of contact with the shuttle is not on the striker's side of the net. (The striker may, however, follow the shuttle over the net with his racket in the course of his stroke.)

(g) If, when the shuttle is 'in play', a player touches the net or its supports with racket, person or dress.

(h) If the shuttle be caught and held on the racket and then slung during the execution of a stroke; or if the shuttle be hit twice in succession by the same player with two strokes; or if the shuttle be hit by a player and his partner successively.

(i) If, in play, a player strikes the shuttle (unless he thereby makes a good return) or is struck by it, whether he is standing within or outside the boundaries of the court.

(j) If a player obstructs an opponent.

(k) If Law 16 be transgressed.

(l) If a player is guilty of flagrant, repeated or persistent offences under Law 22.

GENERAL

15. The server may not serve till his opponent is ready, but the opponent shall be deemed to be ready if a return of the service be attempted.

16. The server and the player served to must stand within the limits of their respective service courts (as bounded by the short and long service, the centre, and side lines), and some part of both feet of these players must remain in contact with the surface of the court in a stationary position until the service is delivered. A foot on or touching a line in the case of either the server or the receiver shall be held to be outside his service court. (*Vide* Law 14(c).) The respective partners may take up any position, provided they do not unsight or otherwise obstruct an opponent.

17. (a) If, in the course of service or rally, the shuttle touches and passes over the net,

the stroke is not invalidated thereby. It is a good return if the shuttle having passed outside either post drops on or within the boundary lines of the opposite court. A 'Let' may be given by the umpire for any unforeseen or accidental hindrance.

(b) If, in service, or during a rally, a shuttle, *after passing over the net*, is caught in or on the net, it is a 'Let'.

(c) If the receiver is faulted for moving before the service is delivered, or for not being within the correct service court, in accordance with Laws 14(c) or 16, and at the same time the server is also faulted for a service infringement, it shall be a let.

(d) When a 'Let' occurs, the play since the last service shall not count, and the player who served shall serve again, except when Law 12 is applicable.

18. If the server, in attempting to serve, misses the shuttle, it is not a fault; but if the shuttle be touched by the racket, a service is thereby delivered.

19. If, when in play, the shuttle strikes the net and remains suspended there, or strikes the net and falls towards the surface of the court on the striker's side of the net, or hits the surface outside the court and an opponent then touches the net or shuttle with his racket or person, there is no penalty, as the shuttle is not *then* in play.

20. If a player has a chance of striking the shuttle in a downward direction when quite near the net, his opponent must not put up his racket near the net on the chance of the shuttle rebounding from it. This is obstruction within the meaning of Law 14(j).

A player may, however, hold up his racket to protect his face from being hit if he does not thereby baulk his opponent.

21. It shall be the duty of the umpire to call 'fault' or 'let' should either occur, without appeal being made by the players, and to give his decision on any appeal regarding a point in dispute, if made before the next service; and also to appoint linesmen and a service judge at his discretion. The umpire's decision shall be final, but he shall uphold the decision of a linesman or service judge. This shall not preclude the umpire also from faulting the server or receiver. Where, however, a referee is appointed, an appeal shall lie to him from the decision of an umpire on questions of law only.

CONTINUOUS PLAY, MISCONDUCT, PENALTIES

22. (a) Play shall be continuous from the first service until the match be concluded except that:
   (i) in international competitive events there shall be allowed an interval not exceeding five minutes between the second and third games of a match;
   (ii) in countries where conditions render it desirable, there shall be allowed, subject to the previously published approval of the national organization concerned, an interval not exceeding five minutes between the second and third games of a match, either singles or doubles or both;
   (iii) when necessitated by circumstances not within the control of the players, the umpire may suspend play for such a period as he may consider necessary. If play be suspended, the existing score shall stand and play be resumed from that point.

(b) Under no circumstances shall play be suspended to enable a player to recover his strength or wind, or to receive instruction or advice.

(c) Except in an interval provided above, no player shall be permitted to receive advice during a match or, without the umpire's consent, to leave the court until the match be concluded.

(d) The umpire shall be the sole judge of any suspension of play.

(e) A player shall not:
   (i) deliberately cause suspension of play, or
   (ii) deliberately interfere with the speed of the shuttle, or
   (iii) behave in an offensive manner, or
   (iv) be guilty of misconduct not otherwise covered by the Laws of Badminton.

(f) The umpire shall administer any breach of (e) by:
   (i) issuing a warning to the offending side;
   (ii) faulting the offending side, if previously warned;
   (iii) in cases of a flagrant offence or persistent offences, faulting the offending

side and reporting the offending side immediately to the Referee, who shall have the power to disqualify.

(g) Where a Referee has not been appointed, the responsible tournament official shall have the power to disqualify.

Note. The international competitive events referred to in (a) (i) above are:

1. The Men's Team World Badminton Championship (Thomas Cup);

2. The Ladies' Team World Badminton Championship (Uber Cup);

3. The World Championships;

4. All official international matches;

5. International Open Championships and other international events of a higher status as sanctioned by the International Badminton Federation.

INTERPRETATIONS

1. Any movement or conduct by the server that has the effect of breaking the continuity of service after the server and receiver have taken their positions to serve and to receive the service is a preliminary feint. For example, a server who, after having taken up his position to serve, delays hitting the shuttle for so long as to be unfair to the receiver, is guilty of such conduct. (*Vide* Law 14(d).)

2. It is obstruction if a player invades an opponent's court with racket or person in any degree except as permitted in Law 14(f). (*Vide* Law 14(j).)

3. Where necessary on account of the structure of a building, the local badminton authority may, subject to the right of veto of its national organization, make bye-laws dealing with cases in which a shuttle touches an obstruction.

Annex to the Laws of Badminton

BADMINTON FOR DISABLED PEOPLE

The following amended Laws of Badminton are applicable to the various categories of disabled people as listed:

(a) AMBULANT (No change in the laws)
Persons requiring no mechanical aid to perambulation.

(b) SEMI-AMBULANT
Persons capable of erect perambulation but only with mechanical aid such as:
Crutch(es), stick(s), support frame, leg brace(s), artificial leg(s)

(c) NON-AMBULANT
Persons whose disabilities dictate that they adopt a sedentary posture using such support as:
chair, wheel-chair, stool.

The table below shows the changes to laws

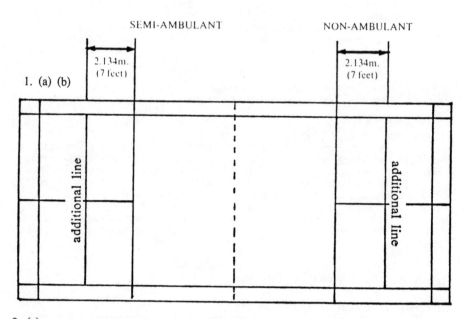

SEMI-AMBULANT   NON-AMBULANT

2.134m.
(7 feet)

2.134m.
(7 feet)

1. (a) (b)

additional line

additional line

9. (a)
(Doubles Play)   shaded area indicates extent of court

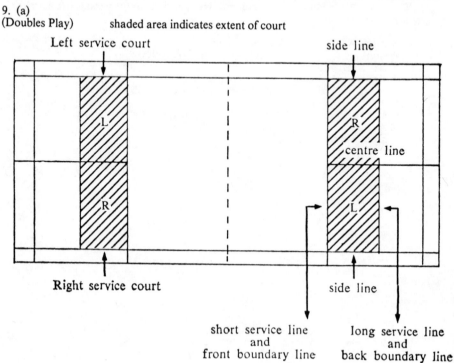

Left service court   side line

L   R

centre line

R   L

Right service court   side line

short service line
and
front boundary line

long service line
and
back boundary line

Players must serve from and receive within the same service courts as adopted at the beginning of a game, throughout that game.

When the service is not returned or a fault is made by the 'Out' side and the 'In' side thereby scores a point:

the service passes to the other player of the 'In' side and is delivered by him from the other side court and continues to alternate thus as long as the 'In' side continues to score.

13. (a) and (b)
Singles Play   shaded area indicates extent of court.

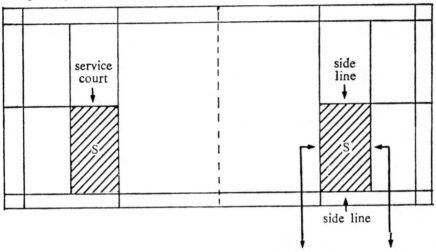

short service line   long service line
and   and
long boundary line back boundary line

As only ONE service court exists at each end, references to 'LEFT' and 'RIGHT' and 'change service courts' do not apply.

Law (b) – '(i.e. into the one not diagonally opposite to the server)' shall not apply.

LAW   SEMI-AMBULANT   NON-AMBULANT
14. (a) No Change   As some medical conditions which render a player 'Non-Ambulant' may also positively preclude compliance, this Law to be deleted in its entirety.

14. (c) The wording of this Law to be extended so as to require the servers and receivers 'mechanical aid' or 'support' also to be within the appropriate service court. The word 'diagonally' to be deleted.

14. (i) The wording of this Law to be extended so as to make it a fault if the player or his 'mechanical aid' or 'support' is struck by the shuttle.

16.   Every part of the player's person and 'mechanical aid' and 'support' **that is in contact** with the surface of the court shall be within the appropriate service court and in a stationary position until the service is delivered.

All other
Laws   To remain unchanged for all classifications. (This includes Law 4 with the pace of the shuttle being measured against the length of a **standard** court by an able-bodied or ambulant player of average strength. A shuttle passing this test is suitable for play by all.)